NET
HAMBURG WORK
BREMEN
FOR DANCE
TANZ FOERDERUNG.DE
BIENNALE DANCE BERLIN
POTSDAM
DANCE EDUCATION EDUCATION
ESSEN CONFERENCE
TANZNETZ.DE DANCE TECHNIQUES 2010
DÜSSELDORF TANZPLAN
TRANSITION
ZENTRUM
PUBLICATIONS CO-PRODUCTION
FOR DANCE LOCAL FUNDING / NPN
FRANKFURT DRESDEN DANCE / CURATING
TANZPLAN BETWEEN
THEORY
EDUCATIONAL AND
PROGRAM PRACTICE
GERMAN DANCE DANCE-
PLATFORM GERMANY.ORG
PROGRAM DANCE
CULTURAL IN SCHOOLS
MÜNCHEN
LEGACY OF DANCE
TANZARCHIVE.DE

tanzplan deutschland

Ingo Diehl, Friederike Lampert (Eds.)
DANCE TECHNIQUES 2010 TANZPLAN GERMANY

www.henschel-verlag.de
www.seemann-henschel.de
www.tanzplan-deutschland.de

tanzplan deutschland

 This publication is a project by Tanzplan Deutschland, an initiative of the German Federal Cultural Foundation.

> **Dance Techniques 2010 — Tanzplan Germany**
> Edited by Ingo Diehl/Friederike Lampert for Tanzplan Deutschland, Berlin
> Published by Henschel Verlag in der Seemann Henschel GmbH & Co. KG, Leipzig
>
> © 2011 Tanzplan Deutschland e.V. and Henschel Verlag in der Seemann Henschel GmbH & Co. KG, Leipzig
>
> ISBN 978-3-89487-689-0

For detailed information about this publication in the catalogue of the Deutsche Nationalbibliothek, please visit http://dnb.d-nb.de.

This book is also being published in German under the title *Tanztechniken 2010 — Tanzplan Deutschland*, ISBN 978-3-89487-412-4.

Cover Design Nicole Schwarz
Cover Illustration Photo of one of the training sessions at the Rotterdam Dance Academy/Codarts—University for the Arts;
Photographer: Andrea Keiz; © 2011 Tanzplan Deutschland e.V.

Translation into English Anthony B. Heric (pp. 8–9, 98–124, 126–135, 238–263, 272–295, DVD subtitles, class plan Passow),
Nickolas Woods (pp. 10–27, 36–57, 94–96, 136–146, 147–157, 158–163, 174–195)
English Language Editor Jacalyn Carley
German Language Editor Wibke Hartewig
Photographs Andrea Keiz, Katja Mustonen
Layout and Typesetting Nicole Schwarz
DVD Camera/Editing/Photographs Andrea Keiz
DVD Authoring Yoann Trellu
DVD Production OK-Medien Service

Printed by Druckhaus Köthen
Bound by Leipziger Kunst- und Verlagsbuchbinderei
Printed in Germany

Ingo Diehl, Friederike Lampert (Eds.)

DANCE TECHNIQUES 2010
TANZPLAN GERMANY

HENSCHEL

TABLE OF CONTENTS

Hortensia Völckers

FOREWORD

What do we know when we dance? When we asked this question at the first Dance Congress Germany *(Tanzkongress Deutschland)* in 2006, 1700 people came to Berlin in search of answers. The next time we ran the conference (concurrently with the *Tanzplan Deutschland* initiative), the number of participating dancers, choreographers, teachers, critics, scholars, producers, and cultural politicians doubled. The Dance Congress Germany was established as an international platform for professional exchange.

When launching Tanzplan Deutschland in 2005, our goals at the German Federal Cultural Foundation (*Kulturstiftung des Bundes*) were to make dance more visible to the public and to increase its cultural–political recognition. With a 12.5 million Euro budget, this five–year funding program provided a national platform for dance practitioners to network; it gave them space and ensured that (cultural) politicians would listen to them.

Tanzplan local offered nine cities an opportunity to access equal shares of funding based upon plans submitted for improving dance in their region. Since then, more than four-hundred artists have taken advantage of a residency in Potsdam where they conduct research prior to staging a production; over the past years, several thousand young people and children were introduced to the aesthetics and various contemporary dance techniques in cooperation with partners from education and culture in Düsseldorf; and, there is now a dance center in Hamburg where up–and–coming choreographers can test themselves in a residency program. The city of Hamburg's budget for independent dance projects has finally been decoupled from the theater sector, and increased. Pioneering structures have been created everywhere—in Essen, Munich, Frankfurt, Berlin, Bremen, and Dresden.

Another main thrust of the initiative was *Tanzplan Deutschland's Educational Program*, which aimed to integrate the next generation of dancers, choreographers, and scholars. Ideas came, again, from various cities and thus the original plan for a mobile academy took a different direction: universities founded study programs that innovatively coupled artistic–scholarly research with professional vocational training. In cooperation with the independent dance scene (*Freie Tanzszene*), which started the Inter–University Center for Dance (*Hochschulübergreifendes Zentrum Tanz*), Berlin's University of the Arts and Ernst Busch Academy for the Dramatic Arts established three choreography–oriented study programs. Frankfurt University of Music and Performing Arts created Germany's first masters program for contemporary dance teaching. The nearby University of Giessen created a master's program for choreography and performance. Colleges and universities offering dance programs in Germany have taken up Tanzplan Deutschland's invitation to roundtable discussions, and now act jointly, as the Dance Educational Conference, to further their interests. In 2012, students, teachers, and directors will be able to attend what will be the Third Dance Education Biennale, presenting the public with dance of the future.

What knowledge do contemporary dancers harbor? How do they teach it? And where are their actions positioned within society and history? By establishing the teaching practices of contemporary dance as new areas of scholarly study, this book fills a gap. It presents the results of a multi-year research project that has been developed in close cooperation with national and international universities that have provision for dance.

I would like to take this opportunity to thank those people on location who have helped make dance more visible in this part of the world over the past five years. Thanks go to the team at Tanzplan Deutschland, who coordinated this plan with vigor and farsightedness—especially Ingo Diehl, who tirelessly and knowledgeably coordinated a variety of educational initiatives. Through longstanding and close contact with the various universities, he not only developed the vision for the research project and helped achieve its results—which we have in front of us in this book—but he also ensured, together with Dr. Friederike Lampert and a team of advisors, that the project was realized despite numerous complex stages.

Where will our movements take us? Answering this question, dear readers, is now up to you. I hope reading brings you much joy and inspiration.

Hortensia Völckers, Artistic Director of the German Federal Cultural Foundation, Halle, October 2010

Ingo Diehl, Friederike Lampert

INTRODUCTION

"Thinking about dance technique has been almost taboo in recent years. That is something that needs to change."
Anouk van Dijk

Contemporary dance is characterized by many styles and ways of working, and the different types of training each have a unique role to play. Dance teachers can source a hybrid network of dance forms and body–work techniques, along with presentation methods and teaching forms. Yet, at the same time, the method of training contributes to the style: the way of working informs any individual artistic practice. How do these factors relate to one another?

What exactly do contemporary and modern dance teachers teach? What influences factor into a teacher's fusion of material? What is the relationship between artistic production/process and technique? Might we be even more general and ask: How do we define dance technique today? And, moreover, what constitutes good teaching?

Until now there has been no comparative study examining practices employed by contemporary and modern dance educators, a fact that became clear during our initial research in 2007. This publication intends to close this gap—and can be seen as the beginning, not the end, of practice–based research into dance. For three years we worked and researched with approximately one-hundred-and-eighty participants in dance departments at seven universities. Our aim was to look at both artists' and educators' practice, as well as theoretical approaches taken by dance scholars. Our goal was to learn more about the histories and contexts of contemporary dance techniques, about approaches taken toward the body and movement, and about the principles behind the teaching methods. Our ultimate goal was to make this knowledge available.

1 Practice here refers to the knowledge of dancers, choreographers, and dance educators in relation to physical and mental processes, as well as dancing itself.

2 Theory here refers to the contextualization, written documentation, and analysis carried out in the field of dance studies.
3 Edith Boxberger, Pirkko Husemann, Claudia Jeschke, and Antje Klinge.

4 Scott deLahunta, Nik Haffner, Andrea Keiz, Yoann Trellu.
5 Alan Danielson, Anouk van Dijk, Barbara Passow, Daniel Roberts, Gill Clarke, Jennifer Muller, Lance Gries.

BACKGROUND AND STARTING POINT

The connection between practice[1] and theory[2] was discussed in various ways—in working groups as well as during training sessions that were held in conjunction with various German institutions as part of Tanzplan Deutschland's Educational Program. In the last several years, dance scholarship has been institutionalized in German–speaking regions—driven by both historical and theoretical knowledge—and has influenced university dance curricula. It is time to envision new structures in which dance practitioners' knowledge will become more accessible and available. This publication is the result of a joint effort by dance practitioners and scholars; it proves the quality and relevance of practice–based research at dance departments housed in the various universities. Practice and scholarship are given equal value.

The foundations for this project were laid by Ingo Diehl, and Friederike Lampert joined him two years later. They embarked on a three–year project that would involve cooperation with various consultants,[3] a DVD team,[4] dance educators,[5] dance scholars, sports' scholars, and dance students at the seven universities in Germany, Austria, the Netherlands, England, and Belgium.[6] Tanzplan Deutschland's close cooperation with the public–sector training institutions was integral to its success.

The results published in this book include the work of seven research teams; it offers models—structured presentations—about method and craft, theories, and artistic working processes that reflect current practices of selected dance educators. These structured research projects are designed to provide certain insights into the contemporary and modern dance world and, above all, to be employed as prompts and tools (materials and methods) in both practical and theoretical contexts. The aim is to make knowledge available to dancers, educators, dance academics, students, and other interested parties.

6 Participating authors: Edith Boxberger, Gill Clarke, Franz Anton Cramer, Anouk van Dijk, Henner Drewes, Wiebke Dröge, Claudia Fleischle–Braun, Yvonne Hardt, Wibke Hartewig, Sabine Huschka, Irmela Kästner, Gisela Müller, Vera Sander, Sylvia Scheidl, Irene Sieben, Gerald Siegmund, Patricia Stöckemann, Maren Witte, Gabriele Wittmann.

THE COMPLEX RELATIONSHIP BETWEEN DANCE EDUCATORS, CLASS CONTENT, AND TEACHING STRATEGIES

Educators draw upon many experiences and skills, and integrate them into their teaching approaches. A dance educator's role cannot be reduced to the simple passing–on of a 'pure' technique, and this applies equally to formal dance styles, for example classical ballet, as well as to training programs in modern, postmodern, or contemporary dance that have been personalized and constantly reworked and remodeled. Any given teacher's personal preferences, experiences, or encounters with other techniques and teaching methods inevitably influences and even transforms that teacher's body of information.

An example: A dance educator teaches Limón Technique. This teacher was originally a ballet dancer, also trained in Pilates and yoga, and goes to contact jams in her free time. Her teaching of Limón Technique is influenced by all of these—as a result of Pilates training, a greater focus might be placed on the body center, or perhaps contact improvisation has stimulated a more playful approach to movement exploration. Through multiple experiences, the educator has assumed new textures and made connections that expand or refine her Limón teaching. The individualized and resulting shifts of focus on the educator's part will inform the original technical and aesthetic goals, as well as the contexts in which the Limón class is offered.

The way in which a dance technique is taught, and passed on, is influenced by personal background, evolving cultural situations, as well as by the crossover and fusion of material and methods. This book pays particular attention to this: using case studies from today's dance scene, we can define hybrid elements and qualities, make them clear and comprehensible. In this way, the book attempts to provide a pluralistic dance history of the twentieth and twenty-first centuries. It also wants to define the features and specifics of the materials and ideas presented. This hopefully enables us, for the first

7 Revealing the experts' personal approaches provides additional information that can be discovered in comments made during the training sessions (on the DVD) and in the interviews carried out by Edith Boxberger.

time, to go beyond the (potentially) codified nature of dance styles, to discover and understand them as being dynamic in both the teaching and communication processes.

The concept and resulting framework that was developed for this project demands a precise appraisal of the individual approaches taken by the invited dance educators (hereafter referred to as 'experts'). This research perspective presents a shift in how dance techniques are understood: no longer perceived as codified systems, we discover, describe, and discuss any given technique's potential to change and develop. Details and correlations became apparent as the work progressed. And, although personality is always an aspect in teaching art and dance, this project has succeeded in presenting the experts' work in a structured way—almost objectifying their knowledge—so we understand the validity of their work for the dance scene. The relevance of this material for future studies becomes apparent.[7]

These considerations are also reflected in the sorting and working–out of the individual project titles. The experts' names are listed with their 'technique', all are accorded equal status, regardless of whether the technique has been developed by the experts (as is the case with Anouk van Dijk and Jennifer Muller, for example), or if the expert worked with a known technique (i.e., Cunningham Technique as taught by Daniel Roberts, Barbara Passow's development of the Jooss–Leeder Technique, or Alan Danielson's Humphrey/Limón tradition). The project's course was dynamic; it was interesting how the titles of the research projects changed during the process, and emerged with a more descriptive character, for example Gill Clarke's 'Minding Motion', or Lance Gries's 'Release and Alignment Oriented Techniques'.

The underlying pretext was that—alongside the linear historiographies—personal and biographical contexts have, in fact, influenced new dance forms and training methods to a greater extent than has previously been appreciated. This approach to dance history is also reflected in the book title. *Dance Techniques 2010* is meant to define the research project as a contemporary document. The book becomes a historical document the moment it is published, providing evidence of how dance techniques, and the idea of technique itself, are being dealt with at a particular point in time.

DANCE TECHNIQUES AND THEIR HYBRID CONTENT

As already mentioned, contemporary dance techniques and training methods are in a state of constant change. Given the myriad of approaches to the work, any attempt to codify them would seem doomed to fail. The experts' teaching styles and methods are also hybrid in nature, fusions of various approaches. It is ultimately a matter of interpretation as to whether these experts are teaching a 'technique', a 'technology', a 'knowledge system', or a 'working method'. All these approaches, however, have one thing in common: They link enhanced physical performance with aesthetic and/or philosophical principles and guidelines.

Thus one of the questions posed is concerned with the ideologies, ideals, and guiding principles a technique subscribes to. The history of stage dance shows that different concepts and approaches have shaped the development of different dance genres: Classical ballet is primarily characterized by a physical–aesthetical approach to performance in which the body learns disciplined movement coordination in order to perform specific shapes that are presented on a predetermined temporal–spatial axis. The aim is virtuosity, but also expressiveness. In this respect, ballet training focuses particularly on muscle development, and the external (as well as) internal shaping of the body in accordance with a system whose rules are, in the widest sense, based on controlling the body and the world.[8]

Historical and generalized approaches to technique are often used in the dance world without question. Differing ideas about training methods surveyed for this publication appear as variations, updated and individualized versions, of dance techniques. Selected aspects and particular working methods represent the approaches. Gill Clarke, for example, sees contemporary dance technique as something implying constant change and conscious decisions:

/ "Today's dance training consists of a combination of different methods, some of which are concerned with a better understanding of the ways in which the body generates movement and how this movement generation can be

8 See: Rudolf zur Lippe: *Vom Leib zum Körper. Naturbeherrschung am Menschen in der Renaissance.* Reinbek bei Hamburg: Rowohlt, 1988.
9 Quoted from a discussion between Gisela Müller and Gill Clarke in April 2010.

10 Quoted from a discussion between Edith Boxberger and Anouk van Dijk on 20 April 2009.
11 The German term *Ereignishaftigkeit* is used in theater studies to mean experiencing the here–and–now. It paraphrases, and gives equal weighting to, characteristics of discovering and experiencing.

12 Insights into the experts' processes and goals can be found in the chapters Teaching: Principles and Methodology and in the Class Plans on DVD 1.

individual, sensed, and efficient. The various ways of offering kinesthetic/proprioceptive tools and developing skills of students in the field of contemporary dance and movement practice differ widely and are not easily subsumed under one umbrella term, such as 'technique'."[9]/

Anouk van Dijk describes the problem as being with the term 'technique'. It is unsatisfactory, to her, for the following reason:

/"What is release? How do we release? And what is the difference between release and relax? These are all skills to be learned. A wide range of possibilities will emerge from more knowledge of oneself and one's body, and the decisions one makes...A musician would probably talk about technique from a different perspective—I think of phrasing, timing, musicality, decision–making, or improvisation skills."[10]/

These reflections inform our discussion about the term 'technique', as all of the thoughts quoted explicitly point to the importance of the method chosen to pursue particular teaching goals. As such, both the teaching process and *Ereignishaftigkeit*[11] are included in the discussion.[12]

During the first Dance Education Biennale—Tanzplan Deutschland in 2008, William Forsythe encouraged students to learn as many techniques and body languages as well as possible, regardless of personal preferences, in order to expand their decision–making scope. In other words, he motivated them to free themselves through the acquisition of skills—free in the sense that they might decide for or against things, free to take on something new, free to be able to realize something. Against this background, taking responsibility for one's self, and even for one's own dance training, could be considered a learnable skill and, consequently, a technique in and of itself.

During the project's realization, it became clear that the experts were guided by multiple demands—skills and teaching methods—that they integrate into their work differently according to the technique's concept, philosophy, and goals. The primary challenge of traditional dance techniques—that of improving physical performance—plays a subordinate role here. Of course, improving physical performance is part of dance training, but there is more to it than that: it is about optimizing diverse skills. Perception, performance skills, timing, personal awareness, sensing, use of energy—methods used to improve those skills are as individual as they are manifold.

THE RESEARCH SITES

All university dance departments in Germany, as well as a few foreign dance departments, were invited to take part. In an open dialog with interested institutions in 2007, we discussed participation and a respective thematic direction. Once Tanzplan Deutschland assigned the universities a fixed budget, the first task (of phase one) was to choose the experts and assemble research teams. Individual institutions were able to work with a renowned contemporary or modern dance educator who was interesting for them. Decisions were made in consultation with Tanzplan and the university, taking the artistic profile of the respective training location into account. The aim of the entire project was to examine a diversity of approaches to dance technique while, at the same time, stimulating an exchange among practitioners, theoreticians, teachers, and students. It was never intended that this project provide a comprehensive survey of dance techniques or teaching models and include taste or history in its scope, nor was it intended to be conclusive. However, when choosing our experts, we ensured that the projects were related to modern dance, the emergence of postmodern dance, as well as to the hybrid dance forms that exist in both the U.S. and Europe. Individual projects are categorized by experts' first names so as to avoid any form of hierarchy or historical classification.

The texts have been developed either by teams of authors or by a single author, but in all cases students, teachers, and experts were involved. At the Institute of Dance Arts Anton Bruckner Privatuniversität in Linz and at the Frankfurt University of Music and Performing Arts, students contributed to the research not only as observers of the process but also as participants; they were also encouraged to provide reflections and written analyses as part of a theory–based framing for their project. The invited experts were also involved in the writing process, for example at the Inter–University Center for Dance—Pilot Project Tanzplan Berlin. University scholars (like the newly appointed dance studies professor at the University for Music and Dance

13 See pp. 24–27.
14 The questions for the chapter Understanding the Body / Movement are based on, among others, Rudolf von Laban's movement analysis theories and on Claudia Jeschke's *"Inventarisierung von Bewegung"* (Inventory of Movement). Regarding these methods, see Wibke Hartewig's contribution *Observation Techniques.*

in Cologne), as well as outside guests, were responsible for the writing. At the Palucca Schule Dresden, this partnership and approach to the work has resulted in continued cooperation with a dance scholar who has since been offered teaching assignments.

Rotterdam Dance Academy is currently testing how Countertechnique, developed by Anouk van Dijk, can be integrated into the standard curriculum: The existing partnership between the academy and an independent dance company thus offered a solid basis for carrying out this particular research project. At LABAN in London, Barbara Passow's workshop was integrated into the institution's annual reconstruction project during which performances of different styles of modern and postmodern dance are developed alongside technique classes. Reinhild Hoffmann and the entire research team used the opportunity to travel to London and investigate the Jooss–Leeder Technique, thus establishing an historical connection between Barbara Passow's training and one of Hoffman's choreographies.

PROCEDURE AND MATERIALS

What questions did we want to ask? And more importantly, how did we want to ask them? Designing a pragmatic, analytical form and observational structure was a great challenge. Different methods were considered that would enable us to look specifically at the historical context and, at the same time, highlight the physical, ideological, as well as the invited experts' methodical-didactic approaches. The catalogue of questions[13] that emerged from this discussion became our navigation system. Each research team had to deal with eighty-four qualitative research questions, although each question's relevance to the respective dance technique varied. Alongside the ongoing dialogue with consultants and university teams about content and the practical side of the project, the working structure was determined by theater and dance studies' observational methods as well as sport and movement analysis methods.[14]

The research teams were composed of members from different fields, which meant that questions were tackled differently. All the teams took a journey through the 'eye of the needle'—namely the eighty-four questions—and this journey served to highlight both the diversity of the techniques as

Consultants *Edith Boxberger, Pirkko Husemann, Claudia Jeschke, Antje Klinge*

INGO DIEHL, FRIEDERIKE LAMPERT

TANZPLAN DEUTSCHLAND'S EDUCATIONAL PROGRAM

Conception, coordination of overall project, team–building, communication, work-shops, guidelines/interviews, research model, compilation of materials

ALAN DANIELSON
Maren Witte, José Biondi

PALUCCA SCHULE DRESDEN— HOCHSCHULE FÜR TANZ

ANOUK VAN DIJK *Gerald Siegmund, Nina Wollny, Jerry Remkes*

ROTTERDAM DANCE ACADEMY CODARTS—UNIVERSITY FOR THE ARTS

BARBARA PASSOW *Claudia Fleischle–Braun, Wiebke Dröge, Patricia Stöckemann, Reinhild Hoffmann, Anna Markard*

LABAN, LONDON

DANIEL ROBERTS *Sabine Huschka, Rose Breuss, Henner Drewes*

IDA—INSTITUTE OF DANCE ARTS ANTON BRUCKNER PRIVATUNIVERSITÄT LINZ

Development

DVD Team *Nik Haffner, Andrea Keiz, Scott deLahunta, Yoann Trellu*

DVD Filming

Specials Class Plans

DVD Production

Supplementary Contributions *Wibke Hartewig, Irmela Kästner, Irene Sieben, Patricia Stöckemann*

Research Contributions

Literary Research

Dance Genealogy Interviews with Students

Interviews with Experts *Edith Boxberger*

Henschel Verlag

Language Editors *Wibke Hartewig (german) Jacalyn Carley (english)*

Translation *Anthony B. Heric, Nadine Püschel, Nickolas Woods*

Graphics *Nicole Schwarz*

GILL CLARKE *Franz Anton Cramer, Gisela Müller*

INTER–UNIVERSITY CENTER FOR DANCE— PILOT PROJECT TANZPLAN BERLIN (HZT)

JENNIFER MULLER *Vera Sander, Yvonne Hardt, Susanne Dickhaut, Martin Stern*

CENTRE FOR CONTEMPORARY DANCE UNIVERSITY FOR MUSIC AND DANCE COLOGNE

LANCE GRIES *Gabriele Wittmann, Sylvia Scheidl, Gerald Siegmund*

FRANKFURT UNIVERSITY OF MUSIC AND PERFORMING ARTS

DANCE TECHNIQUES 2010 TANZPLAN GERMANY

TANZTECHNIKEN 2010 TANZPLAN DEUTSCHLAND

well as reflect the varying interests and characters of those doing the investigating. Even though the catalogue of questions provokes specific results, the results nonetheless revealed a wide spectrum for interpretation.

Along with the results from each set of research questions, biographical information is presented graphically in the form of a dance genealogy that includes other influences.[15] Structured interviews with experts along with student questionnaires explore personal teaching and learning experiences. The literature and links compendium provides sources of inspiration for further research.[16]

BOOK–INSIDE–THE–BOOK

Four contributions seek to broaden the discussion about dance techniques: Irene Sieben's essay provides basic insights into somatic working methods, highlighting characteristics and its growing significance for dance technique nowadays. She establishes a direct link between materials found in various research projects. In contrast, Wibke Hartewig explores movement analysis methods that can be used for contemporary and modern dance technique. Her contribution underscores the notion that the method of observation will influence or even direct specific results. The analytical systems she presents inspired research questions for the chapter "Understanding the Body/Movement." Patricia Stöckemann's interviews with contemporary witnesses of German Expressionist dance and German dance–theater[17] offer personal experiences and assessments about dance techniques and their development after World War II. Irmela Kästner, along with dance teachers at P.A.R.T.S.[18], discussed the structure and focus of various dance techniques as found in current training programs.

15 Biographies as well as the dance genealogies have been created by the experts and others involved.

16 The research process at the institutions has been documented in many ways and goes beyond the material presented in this publication. Additional interviews, texts, sketches, photos, and / or video documentation can be viewed for further research purposes at the dance universities.

17 Ann Hutchinson Guest, Anna Markard (1931–2010), Reinhild Hoffmann, Katharine Sehnert.
18 Performing Arts Research and Training Studios (P.A.R.T.S.) is one of the leading contemporary dance training centers in Europe. The school was founded in 1995 under the

DIGITAL DOCUMENTATION

Discussion with the research teams also informed the DVD team's concept for digital and technological documentation. By presenting a visual documentation of classes, the accompanying DVDs provide practice–based insights into the work with students. Class excerpts are supported and contextualized by commentaries, interviews, extracts from choreographies, and photos. For copyright reasons, improvised music is used in all classes; the improvised musical accompaniment attempts to reflect the experts' preferences.[19]

Class plans on the first DVD provide detailed insight into the methodical–didactic goals as well as into the progression of individual exercise sequences. Each lesson was recorded on one–to–two days. The classes are spread over both DVDs, and the experts' commentaries on their classes offer insight into background material that has not been readily available before. The language of instruction, English, was kept; there has been no dubbing. Barbara Passow's German–language class commentaries are subtitled in English.[20]

CONCLUSION

Considering the layers of text and material, this publication is a practical handbook that can be used interactively. As an essential contribution to contemporary dance education, it provides insight into the precision and diversity that characterizes the day–to–day work of artists, educators, and scholars in the field of contemporary and modern dance. The book and accompanying DVDs encourage reflection and research, and hopefully provide inspiration for new approaches to teaching dance for educators planning their own lessons. Direct replication is not the intention; rather, we wanted to provide detailed suggestions as to how broad the perspective on one's own teaching content might be.

direction of Anne Teresa De Keersmaeker. The interview was carried out with Steven de Belder, David Hernandez, Mia Lawrence, Janet Panetta, Chrysa Parkinson, Salva Sanchis, and Theo van Rompay.

19 We were unable to use specific pop songs, like those Jennifer Muller uses in her classes. We have also not been able to show Trisha Brown's *Set and Reset* choreography on the DVD (in relation to Lance Gries's workshop), due to rights-issues.

20 Detailed information on how to use both DVDs is provided at the end of the book. The DVDs are NTSC.

At this point, we would like to thank all those who worked on this project—who committed themselves tirelessly for a long period of time. We would particularly like to thank the authors—Edith Boxberger, Gill Clarke, Franz Anton Cramer, Henner Drewes, Wiebke Dröge, Claudia Fleischle-Braun, Yvonne Hardt, Wibke Hartewig, Sabine Huschka, Irmela Kästner, Gisela Müller, Vera Sander, Sylvia Scheidl, Irene Sieben, Gerald Siegmund, Patricia Stöckemann, Anouk van Dijk, Maren Witte, and Gabriele Wittmann—for their continued willingness to communicate. We are grateful that the participating universities incorporated this project into their training programs: Palucca Schule Dresden—Hochschule für Tanz; Rotterdam Dance Academy, Codarts—University for the Arts; LABAN, London; IDA—Institute of Dance Arts, Anton Bruckner Privatuniversität Linz; Inter-University Center for Dance—Pilot Project Tanzplan Berlin; University for Music and Dance Cologne; and Frankfurt University of Music and Performing Arts. This would not have been possible without the experts who shared their knowledge and experience patiently and analytically: Alan Danielson, Anouk van Dijk, Barbara Passow, Daniel Roberts, Gill Clarke, Jennifer Muller, and Lance Gries. We would also like to thank our consultants, Edith Boxberger, Pirkko Husemann, Claudia Jeschke, and Antje Klinge for their impartial support. And the DVD Team—Scott deLahunta, Nik Haffner, Andrea Keiz, and Yoann Trellu—for the productive working relationship. And, last but not least, we thank all the participating students for their enthusiasm.

We would like to thank Ann Hutchinson Guest, Anna Markard, Reinhild Hoffmann, Katharine Sehnert, and the teachers at P.A.R.T.S.—Steven de Belder, David Hernandez, Mia Lawrence, Janet Panetta, Chrysa Parkinson, Salva Sanchis, and Theo van Rompay—for illuminating discussions. Henschel Verlag, particularly the language editors Wibke Hartewig and Jacalyn Carley, and the translators Anthony B. Heric, Nadine Püschel, and Nickolas Woods for their tireless dedication—and especially Nicole Schwarz for the graphic realization, as well as Christiane Berger for her historical research. Also the Tanzplan team—Marguerite Joly, Frank Ottersbach, Madeline Ritter, Barbara Schindler, and Katja Tewes—for their patient and generous support. And, finally, we would like to thank the German Federal Cultural Foundation—without whose Tanzplan Deutschland-initiative the realization of such a comprehensive research project would have been impossible.

The years to come will reveal the extent to which Tanzplan Deutschland's Educational Program has stimulated content questions in a changing dance education field. This publication is also intended to support further questioning. We hope the book inspires and excites you—whether it be in the hand, in front of the screen, or in the studio!

Ingo Diehl and Friederike Lampert, Berlin, November 2010

Ingo Diehl, Friederike Lampert

RESEARCH QUESTIONS — GUIDELINES FOR ANALYSIS AND DISCUSSION

HISTORICAL CONTEXT

TIME, PLACE, AND SOCIO-POLITICAL CONTEXT
When, where, and in what socio-political context was the dance technique developed?

BACKGROUND: BIOGRAPHIES AND ENVIRONMENT
Who developed the dance technique, and in what environmental/biographical context?

RELATION TO OTHER ART FORMS
Was there a relationship between the technique and other art forms during the formative stages?

RELEVANT THEORETICAL DISCOURSES
Which theoretical and aesthetic discourses are relevant?

CURRENT PRACTICE/CURRENT UTILIZATION
How and where is the dance technique currently applied in pedagogical and artistic processes?

INDIVIDUAL APPROACH
How is the dance technique used by teachers, companies, and choreographers?

RELATION TO OTHER DANCE AND MOVEMENT TECHNIQUES
Is there a relation between the technique and other body and/or dance techniques? What is it?

CONCEPT AND IDEOLOGY

IMAGINING THE BODY / UNDERSTANDING THE BODY
How does this technique understand and see the body?
Which body image (or body model) is conveyed?
What is the relation between physical appearance and the body as an instrument?

Gender
What role does gender play for the movement and training?

Space
How is space used/conceived?

Music
Is there a special relationship to music?
What influence does music have on phrasing movement sequences?
What kind of music is preferred?

INTENT
Is an aesthetic evident? If so, what aesthettic, and how is it evident?
Which concept/understanding of 'dance culture' is produced?
Which concept/understanding of 'dance culture' should be furthered?
Which notion/understanding of art is taught?
Is the technique connected to a performance practice?
What is the relevance of the technique if taught independently of performance practice?

Quality/Attributes
What is the notion/understanding of 'quality'?
Is it possible to say at what point a movement sequence 'works'?
How do technical ideals relate to the physical potential/physique of the dancer?

Presence
Is presence trained? If so, how?

UNDERSTANDING THE BODY/MOVEMENT

PREREQUISITES
What educational background is helpful?
Are there certain physical requirements that can influence learning in a positive way?
Which motor capabilities (i.e., strength, endurance, speed, coordination) are particularly relevant?
If some abilities and/or skills are missing, how can deficiencies be compensated?
What kind of secondary/support training is helpful?
Wherein lies potential for injury?

MOVEMENT CHARACTERISTICS AND PHYSICALITY
Which body parts are physically active?
Do these body parts trigger movement?
Is there a special approach to body–part coordination? What is it?
Is the body addressed as a whole or as isolated parts?
How are joints, bones, and muscles viewed and engaged?

Strength
How much strength and muscle tonus is preferred?
Should muscles be 'built–up'?

Center
Which notion of center is used?
Where is the center of the body located?
Is it a physical or imagined center?
Are different centers used?
Is balance/off–center work involved? If so, what work?

Body Weight/Gravity
How is gravity being used/countered?
How is energy spent/distributed?
Are there special qualities and attributes when shifting weight?

Space
How is the periphery/space used?
Is there a sense of big/little, opening/closing, and body volume?
How are directions used?
How are dimensions used?
How are spatial levels used?

Rhythm
How do inner and outer rhythms influence movement execution?
How does the breath influence movement execution?
Does rhythm and music influence movement execution? If so, how?
What role does tempo and phrasing play in movement execution?
How does reaction time and/or other factors influence rhythmic phrasing?

Movement Principles/Types of Movement
What are the basic movement principles?
What are the basic movement forms/elements?
How are these applied?

TEACHING: PRINCIPLES AND METHODOLOGY

CONCEPTUAL BASIS
What are the goals?
Who is the target group?
Is it important to differentiate between individual or group classes?
In which timeframe can the technique's basic principles be learned?
Is previous knowledge helpful? If yes, what?
What results can be produced/expected inside of which timeframe?

Approach to the Work
What approach to the work is taken?
Is the work more result–oriented or more experiential?

PEDAGOGICAL METHODS
Lesson Structure
How is a lesson constructed?
Which spatial levels does the training use, during which phases of class, and why?
What methods are used to train movement acquisition?
Which learning pathways are embarked upon?

Skills/Abilities
What abilities and skills are relevant for teaching this technique?

Rhythm and Motor Learning
What influence does rhythm have on motor learning?
How is time structured (i.e., by music, by sound/noise, by breath, etc.)?

Artistic Process
Which artistic processes are relevant in teaching or sharing the technique?

Preparation for Teaching
Which overarching themes and learning goals are used to prepare lessons/classes?
How are movement phrases and exercises developed?
How are phrases/exercises organized in relation to each other?
What role does music/rhythm play in preparation for teaching?

Self–assessment/Feedback
Are there different formats for evaluating a class?
If so, what are they?

Communication
What role does the teacher play in communicating content?
What is transmitted through language, visual input, and through physical contact? How much is each emphasized?
What is the relation between dancer and movement realization (i.e., is the body considered to be an instrument, or is individual interpretation preferred)?
How relevant is imagination/visualization in the technique? How is the imagination used?

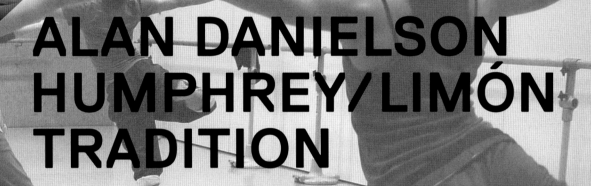

ALAN DANIELSON
HUMPHREY/LIMÓN
TRADITION

PALUCCA SCHULE
DRESDEN
HOCHSCHULE FÜR TANZ

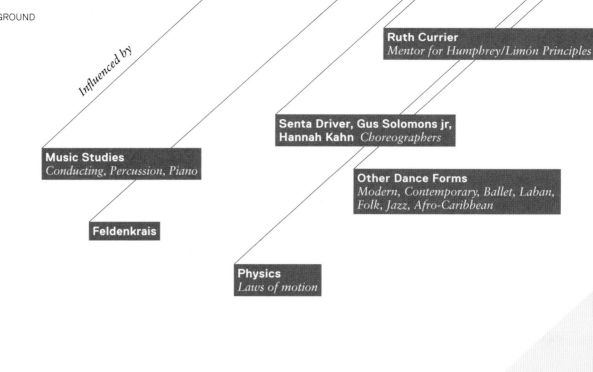

Influenced by

Ruth Currier *Mentor for Humphrey/Limón Principles*

Senta Driver, Gus Solomons jr, Hannah Kahn *Choreographers*

Music Studies *Conducting, Percussion, Piano*

Other Dance Forms *Modern, Contemporary, Ballet, Laban, Folk, Jazz, Afro-Caribbean*

Feldenkrais

Physics *Laws of motion*

Ruth Currier, Clay Taliaferro, Betty Jones *Limón*

His teachers

Dr. Nancy Fichter *Professor of Dance, Florida State University*

Zena Rommett *Floor Barre*

Jocelyn Lorenz *Ballet*

Ann Vachon *Director, Limón Institute*

Renee D'Aoust *Writer*

Dr. Harry Langsford *Professor of Music, Wayne State University*

Geraldine Cardiel *Dancer, Choreographer*

Norton Owen *Cofounder Limón School*

Collaborations with

Andy Monroe, Melinda Haas, Toby Twining, Holgar Naust *Musicians, Composers*

ALAN DANIELSON —

HUMPHREY/LIMÓN TRADITION

Research team at the Palucca Schule Dresden—Hochschule für Tanz:
Alan Danielson, Dr. Maren Witte, Prof. José Biondi

AUTHOR
Maren Witte

INTERVIEW
Edith Boxberger

STUDENTS AND GRADUATES
of the dance and teacher–training degree programs (years three and four): Anna Fingerhuth, Cindy Hammer,
Maria Nitsche, Dagmar Ottmann, Camilla Schmidt, Eila Schwedland, and Zongwei Xu

ALAN DANIELSON (*1954)
creates and teaches contemporary dance in the Humphrey/Limón tradition. His company, Dance by Alan Danielson,
is based in New York City and has performed throughout the United States, South America, Europe, and Asia. His
choreography has been commissioned by Danspace Project (NYC), Gala Arte (Mexico), Institut del Teatre (Spain),
and F.E.D.E Danza Laboratorio (Italy) among others. Danielson is the school director of the Limón Institute in
New York City. He is an internationally acclaimed master teacher of dance, music, and the methodology for teaching
Contemporary Limón Technique. He has taught professional classes in New York City since 1984 and has been on
the faculty at New York University, Florida State University, and the Alvin Ailey School. Danielson was a professional
musician before he began dancing, and worked as a conductor and music director in a variety of venues—from
orchestra to rock band. He holds a Bachelor of Music in Choral Conducting and an MFA in dance from Florida
State University.

Alan Danielson Interviewed by Edith Boxberger

FINDING YOUR OWN VOICE

/ **When did you first learn about the Limón Technique?** I didn't discover dance until I was twenty-two years old. I'd played music since I was very young—drums, flute and saxophone, guitar, piano. I went to a university to study conducting and that's where I took my first dance class. It was wonderful! I loved the feeling of moving, especially because we had a great pianist. I studied many dance forms, like Cunningham and Graham, ballet, and Afro-Caribbean. After several years I realized if I wanted to really excel, I needed to concentrate on either music or dance. I thought, 'I'll dance while I'm young, and then go back to music.' So I went to Florida State University and earned a master's degree in dance. As I was finishing, we had a residency with Clay Taliaferro, an incredible Limón dancer. Right away I thought, 'This feels like me, this is how I want to dance.'

/ **When was this?** This was 1981. So I went to New York and studied with Ruth Currier. She was in the Limón Company for many years and became the company director after his death. She was also Doris Humphrey's assistant for many years. When we say Limón technique, we're actually referring to the Humphrey/Limón tradition of dance. Ruth was my direct link to both Humphrey and Limón.

/ **And what made you immediately relate to it?** Well, I loved moving! Limón Technique is really based in movement, and not only shapes. I especially loved falling and being off–balance, using weight and dynamics. But definitely the most important aspect was the musicality. I was amazed at how much emphasis was placed on timing, not just rhythm, but on the conscious use of time to define quality and dynamics.

/ **Which teachers influenced you?** Ruth Currier had the most influence on me, she was my mentor for many years. And I studied with Betty Jones, Carla Maxwell... actually, all of the Limón teachers. I was also influenced by teachers of other techniques: Gus Solomons Jr. in Cunningham, Jocelyn Lorenz in ballet, Senta Driver in choreography. And I was very influenced by Dr. Harry Lansford, a choral conductor. He taught me about phrasing, which I have used both in music and dance.

/ **Can you tell me more about studying with Ruth Currier in New York?** Ruth Currier had her own studio and school. I thought, 'This is exactly the information I want.' She was an amazing dancer, and she also had an analytic mind. She was able to translate what we were doing and feeling into specific principles and ideas, which is how I learned the essence of Humphrey/Limón dancing. I became her assistant and also played piano for her classes. And as I started choreographing and teaching, she became my mentor.

/ **There was no Limón school at that time?** No, they sponsored classes and workshops but there wasn't an organized program to train dancers. In 1991 the Limón Institute asked me if I would help them organize a school—the Limón School. So Norton Owen, the institute director, and I started to bring some order to the training.

/ **How did you build the school?** We began having open technique classes at different levels, from beginning to advanced. We added repertory workshops and encouraged choreographers working in the tradition to show and teach their work. After a few years we started an intensive nine–month program. Up until then, students came and went as they wanted. With the intensive program, we could work in-depth with a smaller group over a longer time.

For the intensive course, we needed to make a curriculum. We started with technique and repertory classes, and music classes so the dancers could understand the use of rhythm and phrasing. We included sessions so the company members could coach the students individually, and we added seminars to teach the history and analyze the choreography. Gradually we started to define and enunciate the main principles of the tradition. Because beyond teaching what Humphrey and Limón did, we wanted the dancers to understand the concepts and ideas. Humphrey and Limón always said, 'Don't do what I am doing, find your voice in this.' So we wanted to articulate those ideas and teach a technique training based on them.

/ **After you identified those principles, was there a discussion about what is original and what had changed over time?** Yes, there was. We identified the main concepts that began with Humphrey, and the additions to those concepts by Limón. And we continue to discuss how these principles have developed with each generation. You see, there were some who believed that Limón Technique was limited to the things that Limón did but, actually, the tradition started before him and it continues after him. Today the Limón Dance Company performs classic works by Limón and Humphrey, but they also perform works by contemporary choreographers. This idea is reflected in the school: We teach exactly what José taught, and we also teach in a contemporary way based on the same principles he worked with. That is really my passion—how these basic principles are alive today.

/ **What does that mean, 'alive today'?** It means the principles are just as relevant for dancers and chore-ographers today as in 1950. We work with the same ideas now, but the result is different. Yes, the world has changed; technology, society, our consciousness has changed, so, of course, our art has changed. But even if we're different, we're still human. We breathe, we laugh, and love and die. We will always be affected by gravity, our lives will always be defined by time. Even if we say different things, we will always be trying to communicate. Limón Technique is still alive today because it's based on things that define our humanity.

/ **What are the personal aspects that you bring to the work?** My music background shapes my views of dance. Rhythm and phrasing are very important to the way I choreograph and teach. There are painters that come into dance and their priority is shape— I just naturally define movement in terms of time. I also love the analytic approach—not just how something feels, but knowing how and why. I love understanding the movement principles and the physiological process of making those ideas come alive.

But in class my focus is usually on rhythm and phras-ing. I also use music as a teaching tool, and sometimes I play piano for classes. When I travel and I don't speak the language, I sit down and play and the dancers under-stand what I want. Yesterday I had a drummer and when I played piano with him, the dancers understood in a different way. It's another way of communicating these ideas.

/ **Is that what you did today with your voice?** Yes, I use my voice a lot in class, it's a great way to signify movement. I use sounds and words to help the dancers understand. If I say, 'Eeeeee,' they get a sense of the energy as well as the acceleration and the decelera-tion of time. I could also use the image of waves, and they can imagine waves, but the voice can be much more articulate about movement qualities.

/ **What is difficult in this technique?** Well, the com-plexity. The idea of limitless possibilities is artistically lib-erating, but that means dancers have limitless demands! It means you don't practice one shape or movement over and over until you perfect it, rather that you learn how to articulate and control the body without prefer-ence or prejudice. You study to consciously use and defy gravity, which changes the weight and dynamics of movement. You strive to become articulate in rhythm and timing, in defining shapes, in manipulating energy—

and all of these to the extreme. Limitless possibilities means there is no right and wrong. It's not black and white, so it's not easy to pass on.

/ **What consequences does this have for teaching?** It gives you freedom and responsibility, the same as with the dancers. Teachers have to be aware of the stu-dents' needs and abilities, and vary the material to suit them. When I teach ballet dancers, I emphasize the use of weight and the body yielding to gravity; they're used to holding their weight up, so to them this feels heavy and floppy. When I teach dancers only trained in Contact Improvisation, I can teach the same class but I emphasize the resistance to gravity, or the shapes in the movement.

/ **What do you think is useful in training?** Training gives the dancer articulation of body, mind, and psyche. It widens their ability to meet the artistic demands of choreography and performance. If you train dancers to be articulate, without preferences or prejudices, you give them the potential and freedom to express themselves and grow as an artist.

/ **Is there something you like in training, and something you don't like in training?** I love training because I learn about my body and myself. I always get metaphors for my life through dance, and I also get metaphors for dance in my life. To me, they are the same.

/ **What kind of abilities and skills do you need in order to pass on this technique?** Well, there are certain things that apply to all dance teachers: expertise in what you're teaching, the ability to impart this knowledge to your students, a good understanding of anatomy, communication skills, imagination, compassion for your students.

Musicality is important in all dance techniques, but in Limón Technique it's vital. Defining time is an intrinsic part of the technique since it defines the movement dynamics. And it helps a lot to have choreographic abilities; since Limón is not codified, we are always creating phrases and exercises.

/ **Considering these principles, is there one particularly important quality for a teacher to have?** You have to be human! Seriously, it helps to understand the philosophy behind the principles. We believe we are people first, and dancers second. We dance as a way to express our humanity, all of our principles come from there. Everything we do is a reflection of that core idea, from the physical movements to how we relate to each other. For example, the energy in the room: I have to create an atmosphere where the dancers feel safe enough to release and fall. If I wanted them to contract all their muscles I could yell at them, which makes them contract. But what I want them to do is trust and feel themselves in gravity. In that way, the atmosphere in the room is very important. I need to create an atmosphere where they feel safe to fall, where they are encouraged but also challenged to go further.

/ **What is your role as a teacher?** My role is to guide dancers as they discover and develop the potential of their body—their instrument. I try to train them in the core principles of weight, space, breath, and rhythm so they can use these things in all situations. I try to prepare them for all the challenges of dance and choreography, not just the movement in my choreography. I don't want to teach my aesthetic—I want to give them a concept of moving and a wide range of experiences. For example, I don't always give the same shapes; I give different shapes so they learn to be articulate in what they see and do.

/ **And how do you relate to the dancers?** I relate to them as people, as fellow artists. Actually, you can't teach anything—students have to learn. So I try to give them a safe and supportive environment to grow in. Occasionally I have to be the authority figure, I have to lead them and sometimes say, 'That's not enough,' or, 'Try this instead.' Above all, there has to be a mutual respect.

/ **Has your teaching changed? And what has changed?** Well, it's been twenty-five years and I still learn as I teach. Things have become clearer and clearer for me—what I believe, what I want to give, what the students need. I feel like I am able to give a more distilled version of the principles and concepts without the 'Alan Danielson' things that are personal to me. I've learned to separate my work as a choreographer from the material I teach in a technique class.

/ **And where did you pick up other information?** I pick up information everywhere—from Alexander Technique, from yoga to walking a dog—really, anything physical. I learn about movement and get ideas from physics, from astronomy, from watching sports. I think it all relates. Also from cartoons! Because of the extreme sense of motion and the sound that goes with it to explain that motion. I love the very old ones! They could express emotions and define situations just by motion and sound. Each shape and action has many different possibilities.

/ **How do you prepare for class?** I consider the dancers I'm teaching—their level, their previous training, and how much time I will work with them. Then I can decide on my goals and what the material will be. For an advanced class I have to have more material. Beginning classes have less material; they can be the hardest to teach, but also the most fun.

/ **Has the preparation changed?** The preparation is essentially the same, but the dancers have changed so the material and goals have changed. Today many dancers believe a daily training in ballet or yoga is sufficient to keep them prepared to dance. Well, perhaps if the choreography is ballet or minimal movement, but not for all choreography. It's not possible to dance with an articulated use of weight unless it's in your training. It's not something you add in rehearsal—it's an integral part of this technique. How you train is how you dance. I see a lot of dancers that train in ballet and yoga.

/ **What do you see when dancers only study ballet and yoga?** It gives them certain strengths, and deficiencies. It gives them strength and flexibility, and a tendency to fixate on certain shapes—but rhythmic articulation is lacking and there is a narrow range of movement dynamics. Overall there is a lack of movement specificity and difficulty in learning new material.

/ **What does 'accomplishment of a movement' mean for you?** For me, it's achieving the fullest range of motion and dynamics with efficiency. Jaques–Dalcroze said each musical gesture has a unique and specific preparation. The same pertains to dance. Each movement has a unique preparation that defines it. To accomplish the movement you use a hundred-percent of the energy required—no more, no less. Whether it is a battement or arabesque, or a release of the weight into the floor, it has a particular energy and timing.

/ **What characteristics have you found in teachers for whom you have the greatest respect?** I guess there are a lot of things that go into being a good teacher. Part of it is having the knowledge, but one must also really have a desire to pass the knowledge on. And to remember it's not about themselves: it's about the students, so the ego is not involved. One of the best things Ruth Currier told me about teaching was, 'Don't get in the way of the movement.' I think she meant that, in the end, the dancer has to learn by doing. We give them the best situation, the best possibility to learn, and then we have to let them discover for themselves.

/ **What role will this technique have in the future?** There seems to be two general approaches today— the somatic approach based on how movement feels and the physical approach based on how it looks. This technique can be a bridge between them. It uses a wide range of energies to produce highly defined shapes and movements. It challenges the physical limitations of the body while developing awareness of body sensation, use of breath, gravity, and natural body movement.

Because of this humanistic approach to moving, it's useful for a wide variety of choreographers. For instance, it's valuable for dance companies as a way to maintain and recalibrate the body. After a rehearsal where you beat yourself up experimenting and pushing limits, the next day in training it's important to clean all of that out and come back to a neutral place.

/ **In which context and in which way should it be taught?** It can be used in many ways. At the Limón School we have teachers teaching 'Classic Limón', and others teaching 'Contemporary Limón'. The vocabulary is different but it all derives from the same source material. There are also countless teachers around the world giving Limón–based classes. In our teacher–training courses we have many participants who are teaching other styles, some have eclectic back-grounds, some teach ballet or children's classes. They're looking for ideas that will enhance their teach-ing. They often find clarity about what they are teaching because all of these principles can be used in other styles and techniques.

/ **Does it have broader implications than it did in the 1970s?** Over the years people have learned these ideas and adapted them in very broad range. You can see the influences in contemporary and modern classes as well as in classes for children, other adults, actors, etc. There is even a book on applying Limón principles to ballet. The wonderful part of this technique is its ability to develop with each generation. As years go by, the human experience changes, therefore our art changes. Likewise, our understanding of technique develops. The continuity of the principles is most important because these principles allow us to express our existence, even as our existence changes.

/ **Are there new influences on this technique?** Anything that happens today is an influence on this technique—developments in other arts and culture, other dance styles, politics. Students of mine who are now teaching, each has a different way than I do. The beautiful part is that I see where it comes from, and the clarity of the tradition continues. They are from different gen-erations and they have experienced life differently than I have, especially those from other cultures. They all influence the development of this technique.

/ **What is 'training' now compared to what it was when you grew up?** In modern/contemporary classes, there was more emphasis on movement definition. I think choreographers were more interested in movement invention, so dancers had to be able to learn a wide range of movement quickly. In class, we usually didn't hear, 'Feel the movement your way,' or, 'Do your own timing.' This experimentation was done in rehearsal or workshops. We didn't only do things that felt good—it seems there was more struggle to do the impossible.

/ **What would you like to offer young dancers today?** I would like to share my love for movement—what it feels like and what it projects to those who are watching. I would like to share my joy in working with music and creating with other dancers. I'd like to show them how dance is life, and how it communicates our existence as human beings.

Maren Witte

INTRODUCTION

"Start standing. One–two–three, let the head drop, release your neck." Training has begun. Alan Danielson goes through the exercise once to establish rhythm and tempo. He brings in the piano accompaniment as students repeat the movement. Music and dance come together and fill the space with a soft, flexible dynamic. "Melt and curve. We are allowing gravity to affect our body."

Focusing on Doris Humphrey's ideas and principles, Danielson teaches a movement–oriented technique that works with breath, weight, tension and relaxation, opposition and succession, dynamics and rhythm, movement initiation, and space.[1] Of note in Danielson's interpretation of the work is his strong focus on the pelvis as the center of the body and initiator of movement.

Professor Alan Danielson, director of the Limón School in New York, was invited to teach a group of students at the Palucca Schule on fifteen mornings from 23 November 2009–16 January 2010. The Humphrey/Limón Technique is named after its two founders, Doris Humphrey and José Limón. Alan Danielson's teaching transfers this knowledge, and its innovative quality, to the next generation of dancers, while, at the same time, he continues to investigate these principles in his own work. The Palucca group consisted of students in the final years of the dance degree program (BA), former students, graduates of the teacher–training degree program, an MA student, and an external dance professor and former dancer. Since the 1980s, experts in the Humphrey/Limón Technique have regularly been invited to teach at the Palucca Schule, ensuring good conditions for analyzing this technique inside an educational system.

1 For a full description of basic principles, see
Understanding of the Body/Movement.

I was at Palucca as an observer and author for two of the three weeks. I gathered research material primarily from my notes, daily talks with Alan Danielson, and by actively participating in classes. These impressions and information form the body of my research material. I also interviewed two musicians and spoke with the master's degree candidate, Maria Nitsche, and the graduate Anna Fingerhuth. At the end of my research phase, José Biondi (another expert in the Humphrey/Limón Technique and professor at the Palucca Schule), Alan Danielson, Ingo Diehl, and myself came together to discuss key terms and issues in both the Humphrey/Limón Technique and the research project in general.

Maren Witte

HISTORICAL CONTEXT

The movement technique in which the choreographer Alan Danielson specializes, and which he taught as a guest professor[1] at the Palucca Schule as part of the research project, has a double-barreled name: Humphrey/Limón. Danielson attaches great importance to this and, for several reasons, always mentions both names when talking about origins and content. On one hand, he is indicating the genealogy: The technique was founded by Doris Humphrey and further developed by José Limón. Many of these ideas and principles would later inform the beginnings of several Release Techniques. Secondly, he uses the double-barreled name because of his own background: Danielson was never a student of José Limón personally, but was mentored by Ruth Currier who had been a student of both Humphrey and Limón as well as their assistant. As she had trained with both Doris Humphrey and Jose Limón, Currier was able to develop their movement principles in her own teaching. Alan Danielson continues to develop the legacy on his own terms, in his own way.

TIME, PLACE, AND SOCIO-POLITICAL CONTEXT

A timeline helps us understand the context in which the Humphrey/Limón Technique emerged around 1950: Doris Humphrey, an American dancer and choreographer, belongs to the second generation of American modern dance founders along with Charles Weidman and Martha Graham. Humphrey lived from 1895–1958 and trained at the Denishawn School[2] in Los Angeles. In 1928, with Charles Weidman, she founded the Humphrey Weidman Group. Their student, José Limón (1908–1972), was born in Mexico and immigrated with his parents to the U.S. at the age of seven. Thirteen years later, he began dancing with Doris Humphrey and Charles Weidman in New York.[3]

At the time, the issues and themes that concerned dancers were closely linked to social and political events. The first generation of American modern dancers—represented by Ruth St. Denis, Ted Shawn, and Isadora Duncan—had already established itself by around 1930 (as Limón was completing his training with Humphrey and Weidman). For American modern dancers, 'modern dance' in any

serious context was essentially American-made. With the exception of German Expressionist dance, whose representatives (such as Hanya Holm and Harald Kreutzberg) had traveled and toured the U.S. extensively, one generally associated Europe with classical ballet. American modern dancers considered it necessary to revolt and establish a serious and meaningful American alternative to ballet. Thus modern dance—from the viewpoint of (U.S.) Americans—is often considered to be uniquely American.[4]

The second generation of modern dancers, including Doris Humphrey, wanted to distinguish themselves by developing their own, new ideas about movement. This young generation had one common 'enemy' with the first generation, i.e., classical ballet, yet they also strongly opposed the older generation's exotic Denishawn style and the ancient Greek influences in Isadora Duncan's work. While searching for an alternative, Doris Humphrey developed a movement repertoire that, in Alan Danielson's words, was aimed at the common man. In people and their movement potential, Humphrey saw immeasurable value and inexhaustible potential to create art, or, more precisely, dance art. José Limón, Humphrey's student and the future founder of the Limón Dance Company, also incorporated this approach—implicating an inclusivity of all humankind. Humphrey choreographed the first works for Limón and his company. She became artistic director of his newly formed company in 1947 and worked for him and the company until her death in 1958.

In a departure from ballet (which strives for decoration and lightness), from the Denishawn choreographies with their exotic and folkloric components, as well as from Martha Graham's powerful, expressive, and forthright dances, Doris Humphrey and José Limón sought to develop an aesthetic and a movement system in which each person, regardless of age or technical ability, could find a voice.

BACKGROUND: BIOGRAPHIES AND ENVIRONMENT

Alan Danielson discovered dance while studying for his Bachelor of Music in Choral Conducting. He took his first dance class at the age of twenty-two, was impressed by it, and soon afterward faced the decision whether he should continue studying music or transfer to dance. He decided upon a Master of Fine Arts in Dance at Florida State University where, toward the end of his studies, he attended a workshop given by a dancer from the Limón Dance Company. Here, he discovered the Humphrey/Limón

---

1 Other Humphrey/Limón guest teachers who have been invited to teach at the Palucca Schule include, for example Risa Steinberg and Clay Taliaferro. Among the professors and lecturers employed at the school, both José Biondi and Jenny Coogan teach a train-

ing program based on the Humphrey/Limón tradition.
2 The Denishawn School was founded by Ruth St. Denis and Ted Shawn in Los Angeles (with a branch in New York) in 1915 and trained dancers in various styles and techniques,

i.e., classical ballet, pantomime, ethnic, and folk dance from different countries and cultures (the Middle East, Asia, Spain, and Africa). Doris Humphrey, Charles Weidman, and Martha Graham were all students at the school, which existed until 1931.

Technique, which prompted him to move to New York after completion of his MFA where he could focus on training in the Humphrey/Limón tradition.[5]

RELATION TO OTHER ART FORMS

As she searched for her own style and her own technique, Doris Humphrey was influenced by other artists and art forms: these included contemporary composers, folk dances, and Baroque music. Music played a central role in both Humphrey and Limón's work; both engendered a close relationship between musicians and dancers in their classes and choreographies. Dancers were taught and encouraged to improve their sense of rhythm and to articulate music accurately. In his later years, Limón, in addition to maintaining his musical focus, depended more and more upon language that evoked highly expressive, dramatic images—possibly inspired by his love for the Renaissance painters El Greco and Michelangelo—and he also included more sophisticated anatomical and physical information.[6]

The emphasis on music in Alan Danielson's work is the result of both his own Bachelor of Music in Choral Conducting and the influence of his dance mentor, Ruth Currier, who came from a musical background. Danielson's all–embracing approach to teaching is a direct link to Humphrey's doctrines and ideals. Although he is aware of the fact that we live in a different era and that he is teaching under very different circumstances to Humphrey's, he quotes her regularly and bases his movement ideas and theories closely upon her teaching. There have always been people who have danced, in Danielson's view, and he adopts a humanistic approach similar to Humphrey's in believing that people who dance should develop and train to the fullest, discover themselves, and blossom in accordance with their own unique character.

"Alan works a great deal with dynamics and rhythm because of his musical background. This supports the various ways the body works."
Maria Nitsche, student

RELEVANT THEORETICAL DISCOURSES

The Humphrey/Limón tradition focused on other areas that remain relevant, even if people today view them differently. Three key aspects include interacting with gravity, timing, and the use of space. Commenting on this, Danielson says, "These three are the basic principles, then as now, although today we have a different notion of timing and gravity. Those of us who teach in the Humphrey/Limón tradition therefore take the principles and use them with our understanding of time and gravity *today*." The same applies to what he calls 'neutral body alignment':

⁄ "Humphrey/Limón teachers work with a neutral body alignment. Neutral alignment for Limón was something different than it is for dancers today. Today, we use another term and talk of 'efficiency' rather then 'neutrality'. We speak of energy efficiency—for our cars as well as our bodies. We apply the same principles, but we do it from a different perspective—a perspective provided by living today." ⁄

CURRENT PRACTICE

Where is Humphrey/Limón movement material being taught today, in what form, and for which target group?

Danielson says it is taught in its purest form at the Limón Institute in New York, where traditional Humphrey/Limón classes are on the roster along with classes given by Alan Danielson and others who utilize the principles in a more contemporary context. The Limón School offers training directly related to the Humphrey/Limón style, i.e., a style expressing an unconditional interest in human movement and a clear focus on the human being's potential to communicate through movement. The teaching approach, as well as the material that Humphrey and Limón taught in their respective lifetimes, have changed over time.

In addition to classes and the Limon Institute's commitment to Humphrey/Limón principles, the tradition is preserved by the Limón Dance Company (which has been in existence since 1947). Company dancers study and perform both repertory works—original choreographies by Humphrey and/or Limón—and pieces by contemporary choreographers.

3 The following myth is found in literature about José Limón's epiphany regarding the moment he knew he wanted to become a professional dancer: Limón saw a guest performance by the German Expressionist dancer Harald Kreutzberg in New York in 1928 and was so fascinated by the expressiveness and virtuosity that he decided on the spot to become a dancer. (Cf. Daniel Lewis: *The Illustrated Dance Technique of José Limón.* New York: Harper & Row Publishers, 1984, p. 17.)

4 Cf. Don MacDonagh in Lewis, loc. cit., p. 16.
5 Edith Boxberger's interview with Alan Danielson contains more biographical information.
6 See Lewis, loc. cit., p. 24.

INDIVIDUAL APPROACH

Alan Danielson sees a great scope for utilizing the Humphrey/Limón Technique. Choreographers like Mark Morris, Jennifer Muller, and Doug Varone use Limón's material as a basis for their training, as Limón's principles serve as a jumping-off point for exploring and differentiating their own potential and styles—Mark Morris, for example, has been inspired by many techniques of which the Humphrey/Limón technique is only one. Danielson says that Limón classes in New York are an ideal preparation for dancers before they begin rehearsing. In a Limón class, dancers train and maximize their movement potential—articulation and extension of the body—and thereby extend the range of movement they will later command on stage.

A systematic exploration of the body's articulation is at the forefront of Danielson's teaching. He maintains that he and his colleagues are interested primarily in movement, as it makes communication on stage—as in life—possible. Movement talks. Movement can be read. Drama is inherent in every moment, whether intended or not.

RELATION TO OTHER DANCE AND MOVEMENT TECHNIQUES

When Danielson does reference other techniques or somatic principles in his teaching—like Contact Improvisation, the Feldenkrais Method, or Tai Chi—these references merely help illustrate a desired movement quality and in no way imply that the dancer must actually practice the technique mentioned.

Maren Witte

CONCEPT AND IDEOLOGY

IMAGINING THE BODY

In Alan Danielson's classes, the body is considered to be the instrument that allows a human being to practice the art form of dance. The body, and everything this term encompasses, is, for Danielson, the sum of who we are as humans: creatures, energy, spirit, thinking, and consciousness. The body, here, is the physical manifestation of consciousness and spirit. Body and mind are the same; both are human forms of expression—simply on a different plane. And according to Danielson, such a holistic approach to the body is apparent in all historical stages of development in the Humphrey/Limón Technique: from the beginnings with Humphrey, in the further development by Limón, in Danielson's own style, and in the work of younger generations. The principles remain the same; only the experiences made by our consciousness and our physical bodies have changed over time. Danielson says that we have become increasingly interested in the self and that we now concentrate more intently on exploring what this 'self' can be. Doris Humphrey and José Limón were both members of an artistic community that Danielson claims defined an individual's identity based upon their relationship to the environment—i.e., by their peers and the surroundings in which they lived and worked. Danielson believes that this way of thinking, this fundamental approach to life and work, was more common then than today. He also notes that the world moved more slowly at that time and that our sense of speed is different.

Danielson believes that the body image manifested in the Humphrey/Limón teachings is the "unique, aware body" (Humphrey's words). This implies that each body is unique in the sense that every person is different—everyone breathes differently, everyone has a different body weight, and everyone takes up a different amount of space. The training also aims for dancers to become as articulated and precise as possible; the ideal approach is therefore to strive for precision and awareness, or, as Danielson puts it, to work on maximizing one's individual, physical intelligence.

Danielson explains the relationship between the body's appearance and the body as an instrument as follows: The body's physicality and shape derive from a specific energy. For him, shape evolves from a particular use of energy. The body is therefore a physical manifestation of this energy—a physical instrument that expresses energy and psyche (our conscious and unconscious selves).

There is little difference in the training for men and women in Humphrey/Limón Technique, at least as far as Danielson is concerned. Both genders learn all movements equally. Women can dance as powerfully and vigorously as men, and men can move as cleanly and poetically as women. Despite this, Danielson stresses that his training is not gender–neutral, as all bodies are different. Size, strength, and weight are some factors that influence the gender issue. Some solos in the Limón repertoire, for example in *Chaconne*,[7] are physically quite demanding and in Limón's lifetime were only danced by men. Nowadays, the Limón Dance Company is made up of an equal number of men and women and these roles are danced by both sexes—even though the dancers often claim, as before, that these choreographies are particularly manly.

Danielson creates a relationship to the space in his classes, as he sees this relationship as one of the fundamental parameters of personhood: People are always in a space, and they are always in contact with their environment. Danielson is happy to paraphrase Limón in this respect: "You never dance alone. Even in a solo, it is always in a relationship with the space, with gravity, with the space around you."

Alongside the relationship to the space, there is another, possibly more fundamental, relationship in Danielson's technique training—namely, the one to music. The importance of music may stem from the fact that Danielson is himself, as mentioned above, a trained musician. Music and musicality were dominant features in Danielson's classes in Dresden. Every now and then, he would sit at the piano and demonstrate to both the pianist and students how a melody or a rhythm should sound, thus emphasizing and illustrating the exact quality desired from the movement. The musicians who accompanied the classes mostly did so on piano, although some of them also played percussion instruments every now and again.

Danielson says that music's role in class is to support the movement tasks. From time to time the music presents a certain quality, for example something desired in the movement, and, by hearing this quality in the music, dancers can get a perception, an idea, a picture of how the

---

7 Choreography by José Limón, 1942.
8 This emphasis on 'everydayness' and 'normality' came up at other times as we discussed the external characteristics that distinguish his Limón students in New York: "They look like I do: casually dressed, everyday, just normal." One has to understand Danielson's perspective in order to consider what is meant by 'normal' and 'everyday'. One observer, like myself, socialized in a different cultural, professional, and dance environment, found the movement aesthetic in his training anything but 'everyday', and his way of dressing not at all 'careless', and cannot imagine a valid definition of 'normal'. As a spectator, the underlying muscle tonus in the Humphrey/Limón Technique appears to be very high: In comparison to the Release Technique, for example, the movements seem to be linked and controlled, and the overall impression is less 'neutral' than in the Release Technique or Contact Improvisation.

movement should be, feel, and finally look. But it is important that dancers and the teacher do not merely follow the music—to the same extent that the music should not slavishly follow the dancers' movements.

The two musicians working with Danielson saw themselves in different roles. Antje Ladstätter saw her task as a comprehensive one: to react in a creative, compositional way and work, together with the dancers, on theme and expression. She created music based upon her own repertoire and played what she instinctively believed was appropriate for the situation and exercises. Jens Baermann, on the other hand, considered it his task to respond—to be an accompanist who endeavored to understand Danielson's verbal and acoustic stimuli as best he could and transform these into dynamics and rhythm. When absorbing and transforming Danielson's information, Baermann felt he should also watch for students' reactions to his music and that he should sense physically (kinesthetically) if and how they respond to his music. For Baermann, this double interplay—with Danielson and the students—guided his work.

Danielson gives a two–pronged answer to the question about music's influence on phrasing and movement order. On one hand, he says that music itself has no influence on the movement sequences in a class, and yet, on the other hand, dancers are influenced by everything they hear and movement characteristics change when influenced by music or noises. In Danielson's class, music helps students move in a way that is more attentive to the image used for any particular exercise or situation.

To an observer, it appears that Danielson prefers music to be primarily harmonious and dynamic. This can also be seen in Danielson's and his students' dancing: holistic, swinging, lyrical, powerful, and precise movements work from the center of the body outward. This means there is a direct correlation between the ideological aspects of this technique (its humanistic core, as Danielson would say), the physical realization of the technique, and the music that enables this realization, i.e., between the movement and its musical accompaniment. Danielson used his voice, his piano music, or live musical accompaniment for the classes in Dresden—it remains open to speculation how or if the students' dancing would have changed if, for example, street and traffic noise were used as a dominant soundscape. One suspects that antagonistic acoustic information could influence the movement execution in such a way that phrases and combinations might be interpreted in a less rounded and harmonious way, and that there could be accents on non-binding and incompatible aspects, thereby jeopardizing flow.

Asked about his favorite instrument to accompany his classes, Danielson answers piano. Because of the different possibilities when using the left and right hands, piano provides both melodic and rhythmic stimuli, both of which are fundamental in his teaching.

INTENT

The relationship between music and movement is closely linked to the following question: What purpose does Danielson's interpretation of the Humphrey/Limón Technique serve?

Danielson does not consider it his role to teach an aesthetic: his task is not to say that something is good or bad. He wants to offer choices. Curve or straight—both are good. Plié is not better than relevé—one needs to be able to do both, and do both well. It is about training the body. This, if nothing else, makes it clear why Danielson prefers that students wear clothing that reveals body contours and lines. Taken as a whole, Danielson says that it is not necessarily about doing 'less', rather about dancing in a more articulated way—determining what is really needed and exerting the effort, or input, that a particular movement requires.

Another element that might be considered a goal of this technique, namely the 'purging effect', emerged in various discussions with Barbara Passow, José Biondi, Annette Lopez Leal, and the students Maria Nitsche and Anna Fingerhuth. They responded to the training in the same way: i.e., afterward they felt a purging, neutralizing, restoring, and 'balancing' effect.

This beneficial effect indicates a large analytical field: the question of where and how Danielson sees himself and his work fitting into society and the dance world of today. Danielson understands the term 'dance culture' as a social method, a cultural 'technique', i.e., a means humans have developed in order to discover each other by doing, to communicate with each other, to feel life, and to celebrate life. Dance is the physical expression of "I am alive, ecstatic, communicative—that is all I am, all we are." And he adds a quote from José Limón, "We are never more truly and profoundly human than when we dance." The type of dance is irrelevant to Danielson, the important thing is that humans move and express themselves in movement. In other words, in the Humphrey/Limón tradition, humans are taught, cared for, and celebrated as modern individuals who can use dance to find themselves (again), sense themselves and their environment, experience themselves, and who are willing to lose control.

This basic tenet goes back to Doris Humphrey. For Humphrey, art represented an essentially positive, hopeful, and whole human being—one whose nobility was shown through expressivity and virtuosity. According to Danielson, the construction of the anti-hero over the past fifty years has expanded the meaning of art in the Humphrey/Limón Technique to the extent that nowadays both virtuoso as well as everyday movements are trained and appreciated. "In training Limón dance students, we train them to do all of that: both the natural *and* the virtuoso movements. So coming back to the aesthetics, we try our best not to achieve one defined look."[8]

In the Humphrey/Limón Technique, quality is defined by *how* a movement is performed rather than by the movement itself. Danielson explains that the Humphrey/Limón Technique differentiates between various movement attributes and categorizes them according to tension ratios; for example active–passive, strong–weak, etc. What happens on stage or in the studio is also determined (for example) by what the dancer actively engages in, as well as by the influence of momentum, gravity, and the like. This scope for articulation and differentiation gives rise to an infinite range of movements that dancers should be aware of and play with, as a Limón dancer—like any dancer—essentially only articulates, combines, and varies what Danielson sees as the core elements of movement: energy, time, and shape.

So if the number of combinations is endless, how can we determine if a movement sequence is successful? Danielson says:

⁄ "A dancer succeeds just by doing. The moment class starts, we are dancing. In this sense, there is no preparation for the dance proper, but rather class begins and ends with dance. We train to articulate the body more and more so that the movements become more and more precise and refined. And when I see that this 'refining process' is taking place, then I talk of students 'succeeding'. Of course, nothing is ever perfect. We work towards a movement phrase that every dancer can integrate fully into his or her own body. This means that all students can 'succeed' in the phrase—regardless of their training level." ⁄

Moreover, there is a difference between the working and learning goal, i.e., the technical ideal students should strive for and an individual's physicality. Danielson sees the relationship between the two as follows: the better the dancer's physical condition, the more possibilities for movement he or she has.

Another learning and working goal is presence. What notion of presence is created, communicated, and taught, both in and through his teaching? Which part of the body is particularly important? The eyes? The back? Is it the head's placement, or the alignment of the entire body? Danielson gives a precise definition: it is found in an ever–present body consciousness in space and time. In short: awareness.

Maren Witte

UNDERSTANDING

THE BODY/MOVEMENT

PREREQUISITES

No particular dance education is a prerequisite for training in the Humphrey/Limón tradition. It makes no difference if students have learned ballet as youngsters or practice it in their leisure time, do capoeira or yoga, or go to contact jams. According to Danielson, Humphrey/Limón class materials can be oriented toward any type of dance or movement. By varying the energy and timing (i.e., rhythm and tempo), the material can be adapted to ballet students, for example, or to a group of release dancers.

Danielson stresses that all motor skills should be finely honed. The goal of Limón training is to make the body as capable of articulation as possible, thus class work not only focuses on basic motor skills but also on the ability to isolate and separate different shapes and energies. And no physical skill should be given more relevance than another. "It is not just about speed, for example, but also how to move as slowly as possible; not just about power, but also allowing the body to let go and be passive and allow gravity to take over." The technique aims to provide general physical knowledge that enables dancers to discover their own strengths and weaknesses in a relaxed and realistic way, and to help them to focus on what they are lacking—on weakness or uncertainties. Important in a training method like this, one that requires students to take responsibility for their own bodies, is that each dancer accepts his or her own strengths and weaknesses. As soon as dancers start to compensate, they are ignoring their physical realities and thus cannot recognize nor improve weaknesses.

> "Falling is also very important for Alan— simply because you then move out of your comfort zone." *Anna Fingerhuth, student*

Other physical activities are recommended and considered complementary to training in the Humphrey/Limón tradition—because a) humans can learn something about their bodies and environments from every movement they make, and b) because performing the most diverse range of activities as possible strengthens bodies and thus reduces the risk of injury. The Humphrey/Limón Technique

9 See: DVD 1, Phase 1, "Opening."

is well known for being very user–friendly for students, which means, for example, that teachers will insist on a turn–out that corresponds with a dancer's individual anatomy. Danielson adds that the motto in the Limón method, as in art generally, is: "Push your limits!" Students can learn to take risks by practicing falls or testing extreme situations. There are risks of injury, of course, but these risks are minimal because no one is forced to do anything, and no one should force him- or herself to do anything. The goal is to produce emancipated dancers who handle themselves sensibly, who know how to play and take risks.

MOVEMENT CHARACTERISTICS AND PHYSICALITY

A Humphrey/Limón class attempts to move every part of the body in as many variations as possible, and to explore and exploit the potential of every moveable joint. Every part of the body should remain or become flexible—a dancer must ensure that no excess tension emerges in any body part and that existing tension is addressed. This may be why many students who have trained with Danielson emphasize how healthy this training method is, and that it has a purifying, centering effect.

Any body part should be able to initiate a movement. The goal is to isolate each joint and thus help dancers gain awareness of its potential. There is much leg–work in the Humphrey/Limón Technique, as well as work with the pelvis as the center and initiator of movement. But it is also about finding movement initiation not only in a particular region of the body, but in external, physical factors, such as gravity. The body is always in a dual relationship with gravity: If it engages with gravity and gives in to it, a movement is triggered by a passive, release initiation, i.e., the movement is initiated by releasing. The dancer would collapse and sink to the floor were it not for the oppositional force that holds the body upright and resists gravity's pull. An example of a movement sequence based on this dual principle of giving in and opposition is found in sequential or successive movement wherein a movement is initiated in the head and then 'travels' down the vertebrae, one at a time, toward the pelvis.[9] This happens step–by–step as follows: When the head gives in and drops, the uppermost cervical vertebrae become the highest point and thereby have the task of keeping the remaining vertebrae vertical against gravity. If the dancer also lets the cervical vertebrae drop, the next vertebrae takes over and responds accordingly, and so on, until the entire upper body is bent over forward. During this sequence, the point of resistance to gravity moves from the head, down the length of the spine, to the tailbone.[10]

Individual body parts are coordinated with the notion that there can be infinite variations, maximum isolation, and conscious interplay. Danielson often refers to José Limón, who saw the body as an orchestra in which every member begins by practicing alone to discover the instrument's potential. The orchestra then assembles and plays together, hence creating a complete work of art. This metaphor also works for isolating individual body parts as consciously as possible, combining these parts with each other, and coordinating movement.

But what can be trained in isolation? One can isolate individual body parts, and one can isolate energies. One can, for example, utilize a particular energy in the left leg (i.e., swing), while utilizing a different energy in the right leg or torso (i.e., hold firm).[11] Each leg is utilizing an individual and specific energy. If the left leg is swinging, then it is reacting in an almost passive manner to momentum and gravity. The other leg, the standing leg, is meanwhile stretching and staying firmly planted on the floor and is thus extremely active, just as the dancer's center is active. All the while, the upper body remains calm and upright in this exercise; it is soft and pliable.

Joints, bones, and muscles are utilized to facilitate movement and energy. The joints should be available, i.e., without tension (unless a particular movement requires it). Practitioners of Humphrey/Limón Technique want to be able to move their bones and rely on their muscles so that both function as natural roles and ranges allow. A Limón teacher does not necessarily make an anatomical analysis when thinking about the muscular system, nor does a teacher break a muscle group down into individual components. In contrast to other movement practices in which a great deal is said about fascias, fluids, or organs, Humphrey/Limón Technique focuses on the bones' articulation potential. This was confirmed in student observations: Clear shapes resulted from the specific energy when attention and focus was placed on the bones. Utilized energy, not the dancer's will, leads to shape.

In the Humphrey/Limón Technique, the term strength is defined primarily through the concept of energy, which applies to all quantities and nuances of strength. Dancers either confront strength/energy or consent to it. As outlined above, gravity triggers movement whenever possible. Gravity is allowed to work with, and influence, all downward movements. This requires that muscles be strengthened and trained more actively and clearly. Much time is spent in plié, i.e., a demanding position for the leg muscles, because many movements lead here, take place here, or are initiated here. By contrast, many movement sequences in Danielson's classes end in relevé. He does not say that muscles should be built–up, as this has a negative connotation (it evokes, for him, an approach found in gyms and workout studios), although his training does impact muscles in a way that can be described as strengthening and stretching.

For Danielson, the center is

╱ "…a neutral place. And it is the place that you can move from at any time with any body part imaginable in any direction we want. By contrast, when there is unnecessary tension in a particular region of the body and I want to move sideways, then I need to first release this tension and establish neutrality before I can actually move sideways. I adjust this with the center. The center would therefore be a neutral orientation for the body: you are active when you stand and resist gravity, when there is no excessive use of energy." ╱

And where is this center? Danielson describes it as a region between the rib cage and pelvis. A Limón dancer should be long and active here. The term is being used both in a physical context but also in reference to ideas and feelings of what it means to find a center and to locate it in this region of the body.

According to Danielson, there are different ways of thinking about the center and locating it. Various movements can also have different centers. It can be observed among classically trained students, for example those at the Palucca Schule, that movement initiation comes from a very high center (rib cage level). When working in such a group, Danielson understands his task as helping these students find a center that is located between the rib cage and pelvis, i.e., to lower it.

Is more work performed in Danielson's classes balanced or off–center? Danielson says:

╱ "We want to work first and foremost with movement. Find your balance and take your center with you as you move between on/off balance. There is never a standstill, a fixed position. I always want to keep my body and mind open to multiple directions in movement. I never think and move in only one direction. For me, it is important to learn how I transition from one movement to another and how the shift of weight feels when doing it." ╱

Another important aspect in the relationship between on/off–center is called the *arc*. This is an essential image

10 See Maria Nitsche's master's thesis entitled *The Constant Play with Gravity*, Palucca Schule Dresden, February 2010, p. 9 (unpublished manuscript) for description of the opposition principle. Maria's lengthy

research–stay at the Limón Institute in New York enabled her to study Danielson's teaching in detail and to summarize his principles.

11 See DVD 2, Phase 2, "Leg drop/swing."
12 See DVD 2, Phase 6, "Traveling through space."
13 See DVD 2, Phase 8, "Elevation."

for Limón dancers, one that places the body at a particular point on an arc at any given moment while dancing. This image has movement being performed along an arc. If referring to an energy arc, it moves from lack–of–energy to full–of–energy and then back to lack–of–energy. Or, referring to the arc of balance, the body moves from centered to off–balance, then back to centered.[12] The arc image is also key to Doris Humphrey's principle of fall and recovery—an interplay between tension and balance, between relaxation and loss of balance. The human body will always find itself at some place on this dynamic arc, and is kept balanced by the arc's opposing poles.

The principles of body weight and gravity are ever–present in Danielson's teaching and he references them repeatedly. for example in connection with movement initiation, strength, and balance (as described above). In regards to the quantity of energy, an economical expenditure should be maintained—which means using as much energy as is needed yet as little as possible, i.e., precisely the right amount. This can be a lot of energy, depending on the movement, but, according to Danielson, in com-

Regarding space in the Humphrey/Limón Technique, Danielson says that the dancers' sense of space should be as big and wide as possible, adding that dancers send energy into space through their movements, i.e., they send movement beyond the body's extremities and, in doing so, actively use the entire space. His combinations include frequent changes of direction for the sole purpose of helping students avoid choosing habitual directions, to help them remember changes of direction in movement combinations, and to enable students to feel more secure and able to move with awareness in any direction. One effective exercise that Danielson uses for teaching spatial awareness is having two students face each other while dancing a movement combination.

Alongside directions through space, Danielson's teaching also focuses on levels in space. He attempts to use as many levels as possible in each class, although there are situations, such as the guest training sessions at the Palucca Schule, wherein some levels are not used as often as at the Limón School in New York. The Dresden group did little floorwork, for example, and jumps at the end happened rarely and very briefly.[13] Jumping technique and flowing,

parison to other styles and techniques, Humphrey/Limón Technique aims for a nuanced expenditure of energy. This means that a dancer always appears to be expending maximum energy but is, in fact, using well–measured energy and strength.

Another theme in connection with gravity is a conscious and well–measured shifting of weight. With Danielson, weight shifts often begin with the pelvis, meaning that conscious and well–controlled falling initiates a weight shift. Falling, in this case, means that gravity and resistance to gravity are used in equal measure in order to achieve an articulated shift of weight.

powerful movements are key elements found throughout Danielson's teaching, but, that said, he will concentrate on Humphrey/Limón elements that have not been duly practiced with a particular group of students, and which might need special attention. Jumping is something the Palucca Schule students could already do well. By contrast, Danielson's New York classes end with about ten minutes of jumping. Floorwork is done more often during the New York classes and integrated into every part of class. When speaking about floorwork, Danielson adds that the body is never looking for rest and relaxation on the floor, rather the floor is seen as a station through which the body passes on a movement arc, on its way back to standing.

Danielson says that rhythm changes have a big impact, in all respects, simply because changing the rhythm means changing the energy of the movement. To help us understand, Danielson outlines different types of rhythms. First and foremost, there is the inner rhythm, namely the breath. In Humphrey/Limón Technique, one tries to separate this inner rhythm from the outer rhythm. The exterior rhythm, a fixed beat, can be present, but it is not essential. Regardless of whether there is an outer rhythm (beat/meter) for a movement phrase or not, the inner rhythm (breathing) is the key as it launches and shapes a dancer's movements. By interacting sensitively with the breath, dancers can perform movement in the required time and quality, and using the appropriate energy and speed. Only when a dancer has learned to work with the inner rhythm will she or he move in time (the final link in this complex chain, so to speak), and simultaneously be full of energy and able to express and articulate time with awareness and precision.

In a discussion with Annette Lopez Leal and Alan Danielson, we attempted to work out the meaning of the term 'breath' in the Humphrey/Limón tradition. We agreed that the term is used in three different ways. First, 'breath' means simply in- and exhaling. Second, he uses the breath every now and again as an image when he says, for example, "breathe into your arms," or, "let the breath flow under your armpits." Danielson hopes this image will focus awareness on relevant body parts and help achieve volume, presence, and flow. A third meaning emerges when Danielson uses a breath sequence as a rhythmic unit for execution of a particular movement: "With the next inhale, lift your heads and straighten yourselves up."

Rhythm—understood as a musical component—helps Danielson structure movement in respect to time. Time, energy, and space are, for him, three key elements that play an equal role in defining movement; they are intertwined and mutually define each other. In his classes, Danielson articulates the rhythm for a particular movement sequence either through melodic or percussive music, through vocal sounds, clapping or snapping the fingers, or using the breath.

Danielson's goal is to move the body through a full rhythmic spectrum during a single technique class—although most important for him is not speed but phrasing, as it is phrasing that truly defines movement. Thus Humphrey/Limón Technique is not only about exact movements and positions to a specified beat—an overriding arc exists for individual movement sequences, a sense of something longer and whole. Dancers are trained to understand the dynamic arc, which is highly demanding.

14 See DVD 1, Phase 5, "Feet / Leg gestures 2."
15 See Nitsche 2010, pp. 11 / 12. Nitsche learned Humphrey / Limón principles at the teacher–training program at the Limón Institute, and learned the anatomical and dynamic elements from Limón personally.

Danielson highlights the foot–work he used in the sessions with Palucca Schule students to provide an example:[14] "This foot articulation work is not just a sequence of five actions, but I see the arc of one, single overriding phrase."

Finally, a look at the principles and types of movement found and used in Alan Danielson's interpretation of the Humphrey/Limón Technique. In her study of the Humphrey/Limón Technique, the dancer and dance educator Maria Nitsche separates the movement *principles* from the

Anatomical Movement Elements

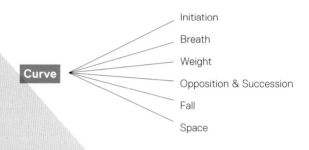

Curve — Initiation / Breath / Weight / Opposition & Succession / Fall / Space

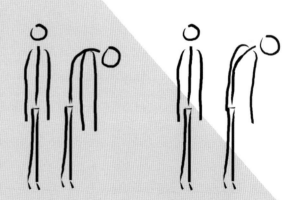

Curve from a neutral position to the front.

Curve from a neutral position to the side.

Sketches © Maria Nitsche

movement *elements*, and, in my opinion, both stood out clearly during Danielson's classes at the Palucca Schule. According to Nitsche, the fundamental principles in Humphrey/Limón Technique are breath, weight, fall/recovery, opposition and succession, rhythm, gesture and initiation, and space.[15] Movement elements are divided into a) anatomical, and b) dynamic. Anatomical movement elements are curve, tilt, tilt and curve, lunge, arch, spiral, and flat–back. Dynamic movement elements are suspension, rebound, off–balance, swing, and momentum. For an explanation of this system, see the illustrations of curve and suspension in Nitsche's work.

Danielson references the principles listed above because they essentially cover everything that directly affect people: gravity, time, the relationship between humans and their environment, as well as the ability to communicate. As human beings, we are always trying to achieve and create something, and we drive and push our bodies to this end. We do this with the intention of communicating something. Even when performing an abstract dance, a human being is performing. Danielson adds another component to this—namely, drama—which, in his opinion, is inherent in every human movement:

/ "Because we are humans, and because humans move, there is potentially something dramatic behind every movement—because another human sees the movement and interprets it. We don't need to add any drama to it. Even Doris Humphrey choreographed abstract dances, for example. But her dances are nonetheless characterized by the intrinsic communication of gestures—and this is where the entire human drama plays out." /

As mentioned, all movement variations are important and used—adjusted to the respective situation and learning group—in the Humphrey/Limón Technique. According to Danielson, this means there are fewer codified steps and movements, as in ballet or Graham Technique. The idea is more to teach the elements and principles (for example, exhalation as the initiator of a swing and as a measure of its duration) so that students acquire, assume, and integrate concepts into their own actions and bodies. This allows for the creation of individualized Limón material that will have different accents depending on whether the dancer is Swiss or Japanese, or born in either 1920 or 2000. Danielson is referencing an idea often stated at the Limón Institute: Everything is possible, but not everything is free and undefined. In fact, everything is quite clearly defined, but nonetheless all dancers are free to remodel the principles and elements, making adjustments for their own bodies, which allows for the technique to grow, develop, and stay enlivened.

Dynamic Movement Elements

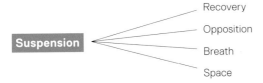

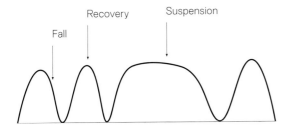

Maren Witte

TEACHING: PRINCIPLES AND METHODOLOGY

CONCEPTUAL BASIS

Alan Danielson pursues another goal that he explains by referencing Limón's notion that dance training exists to show dancers the body's infinite possibilities for movement. Danielson is not looking for a particular aesthetic; rather, he hopes the concepts will enable dancers to explore their potential as well as to help them optimize their skills in realizing limitless movement possibilities. Whether it be a focus on articulation, strength, sense of timing and rhythm, and mental and/or physical elements, or when it comes to taking risks, daring to move slowly, to alternate between being still and going fast, and to articulate, control, release, and also do the opposite—the goal, according to Danielson, is to train the entire body, the human dancer who has a body, mind, and soul.

There is no clearly defined target group; this technique is for anyone with a genuine interest in the body and movement. Amateurs particularly enjoy Danielson's training because of its holistic approach, while, at the same time, it is challenging and demanding. In ballet–oriented schools, students sometimes see Humphrey/Limón training as sloppy and write it off as avant–garde. In schools focusing on somatic training procedures, his technique conversely could be seen as bound and rigid. In other words, how dancers respond to Danielson's teaching and the way in which they can benefit from it will depend a great deal on the individual's experience and the respective training context.

Class material at the Limón School in New York is the same in individual and group classes. Most teaching takes place in groups. One–to–one teaching occurs in repertoire rehearsals.

Danielson estimates that the basic principles can be learned in a two–week fundamental course that familiarizes students with the technique, regardless of previous training. Students subsequently acquire an in–depth knowledge of the principles during the nine–month program at the institute. In most cases, it takes years to really integrate the technique, to master it, and 'dig deeper'. A clear learning curve was observed in some students during

Danielson's three weeks at the Palucca Schule, in particular regarding the ability to articulate and initiate movement, timing, and a certain, quite precise, 'softness' and 'roundedness' to the quality of movement.

Previous knowledge can be both helpful and a hindrance. Ballet, for example, can be a hindrance because of its focus on shapes, yet, on the other hand, it can be a good pre-training for Humphrey/Limón students as it gives them strength, flexibility, and coordination.

In addition to learning and perfecting movement principles, teaching the Humphrey/Limón Technique also involves a particular approach to the work. The learning process is always at the forefront of Danielson's teaching; he encourages students to go inside themselves and be aware of how they are feeling. He also wants them to find a voice for what they have experienced, and to articulate subtle experiences and feelings. Finally, an essential part of the learning program involves investigating one's own potential and taking responsibility for oneself. In this learning and working phase, training is therefore targeted both toward results and a dancer finding his or her own voice in the material.

PEDAGOGICAL METHODS

Lesson structure is goal–oriented in that material is organized and presented so that it contributes to the combination danced at the end of class. This combination will make many demands on the body, for example regarding use and apportioning of energy, timing, changes of direction, or accentuating small and large details with precision. Class prepares the body for this combination, which means working on strength, stretch, and maximum range of motion. During initial phases of class, specific movements and concepts are introduced that will appear in the final combination.

It must be emphasized that, overall, the class is based upon strength, coordination, and stretch work, and is less dependent upon somatic work. Danielson appreciates his students grounding themselves or 'getting themselves together' with somatic work on their own before class starts—indeed, he expects it of them—so that they are ready for class.

Danielson trains four different 'regions' of the body systematically during a class. With regard to physiology, he wants to teach centeredness; the students should develop a sense of center that can then be abandoned when working off–center. He also demands they use their brains—i.e., thinking and reaction skills—so they are able to quickly

16 See DVD 1, Phase 1, "Opening."
17 See DVD 1, Phase 2, "Leg drop/Swing."
18 See DVD 1, Phase 3, "Feet/Leg gestures."
19 See DVD 1, Phase 4, "Pelvis/Spine articulations."
20 See DVD 2, Phase 6, "Traveling through space."
21 See Class Plan on DVD 1.

and easily change direction and timing. Alongside physical and mental training, a third element comes into play, namely the mind–set, or the 'spirit', as Danielson calls it. This means getting students to feel and enjoy moving the body in space. Finally, there are psychological aspects to his teaching, namely the development of concentration skills and a willingness to go into positions wherein the dancer risks losing balance. Danielson offers dancers a learning environment wherein they not only feel secure and protected, but also where they are challenged and encouraged to move out of comfort zones.

A detailed and structured plan steers Alan Danielson's technique classes. Dancers begin by standing center floor. Spinal exercises are used to warm up, stimulate circulation, and enable the dancer to yield to weight. This takes place very simply with dancers standing on both feet and arms hanging, using as little effort as possible, in order to establish a basic relation to the floor and the space above the head. He tells them to let the pelvis drop, then, slowly, let the head drop. From there, things get more complicated. The head drops to the chest while the dancers stand with straight legs or go into plié, or all the way down to sitting on the floor. This is not just about lowering the head and letting it hang—the *drop*—but simultaneously about the opposite movement—the *rebound*—when the head swings back. This exercise is varied with weight shifts and articulations of the spine.[16]

Then comes work on the spine, as straight and curved alignment are explored in the same way as the relationship between stretch and release. Danielson develops these exercises first with the feet in parallel, in a neutral stance—an alignment that is as efficient and active as possible and promises the largest movement potential—and afterward in first and second positions.

After the spine, Danielson works on balance by having students stand on one leg.[17] He adds upper body movements then weight shifts. Movement that follows is concerned with articulating the feet and legs in a controlled and *legato* (connected) fashion.[18] For Danielson, this is when students 'organize their bodies'. These exercises include more falling and shifting weight, and work involving the hips and pelvis in which the biggest, deepest and widest movements are initiated from the pelvis in second position.[19] These movements grow larger and more complex.

Work continues on a diagonal through the room.[20] There is a clear change of rhythm here: instead of the previous 2/4- and 3/4-meter, a 5/4-meter comes into play. Here again it is obvious why Danielson prefers to work with his voice with piano as the accompanying instrument: unlike other percussion instruments, with the piano he can indicate phrasing. Drums create beats and rhythm with little or no melodic component; piano and voice lend themselves to melodic phrasing. Music therefore provides the dancer with the timing, as both a quantity and quality.

After moving through space, class ends with the lengthier movement combination for which the students have been prepared.[21]

Training takes place on different spatial levels, depending on the phase of the class. Four spatial levels are used as much as possible: (1) floor, (2) middle, (3) standing, and (4) elevation. Use of these four levels occurs throughout the class and there is a separate phase for each one. The class begins with loosening–up and swinging exercises in standing. These are followed by sequences using the floor; students stretch their legs and torso while sitting or on all fours. (In the floor section in Dresden, no movement brought the entire body into contact with the floor apart from a quick sideways roll over the back before returning to sitting.) The next part of class took the students through standing exercises and incorporated leg– and foot–work, followed by work in relevé. After that, combinations through space were given. During these sequences, as taught in Dresden, the feet were usually the only body parts in contact with the floor, though the hands, knees, or back touched the floor briefly.

Danielson's division of a class into the abovementioned sections or phases is a fundamental structure. Each section of class focuses on a particular aspect of the overall training goal: stretching the spine, more precise foot–work, instruction in timing and rhythm, etc. The principle of repetition is applied throughout: First Danielson shows the movement combination or exercise, then students mark it with him; the musician plays and everyone dances the combination at least once, together, in order to internalize the movement and become more precise. This is often followed by work with individuals or corrections for some or all of the dancers. The movement sequence or exercise is then danced again providing dancers an opportunity to apply corrections before moving on to the next part of class.

Another pedagogical method he employs is an increase in dynamics and complexity. This requires that students use both body and mind, and thereby train concentration skills and stamina.

Only one brief rest–phase is offered, about three minutes long, so that students can drink something. In New York, where the classes generally run two hours, Danielson does a collective cool–down at the end. At the Palucca Schule, where classes are shorter (ninety minutes), he passed this responsibility along to the students.

Danielson describes his teaching style and the resultant 'learning path' as 'inductive', by which he means that while the content of a class starts off easy and becomes increasingly more challenging, he also expects that, in every exercise, the dancers should follow and comprehend what they are doing in the moment. He asks them to observe how it *feels* when the head is dropped, for example. In the next exercise, he asks them to drop the head while performing a plié and again notice how it feels. Danielson also uses imagery to stimulate learning through feeling and experiencing. One example of this would be "Reach back as if the sun was shining on the chest" versus "Reach back as if it was raining on the chest. How does that feel?" The dancers thus bring life–knowledge into the studio and integrate it into their dancing.

Here Danielson adds that there are times when he proceeds in a deductive fashion, for example, when demonstrating movement. He is convinced that visual information can help students learn how a movement should be. More precisely, he adds that this is not about everyone performing and looking the same in the end, rather it is about each dancer learning how to sense movement personally.

I would like to expand at this point on Danielson's "looking the same" remark. Interestingly, I was able to observe Danielson's lessons and methods, and I know from my own experience that he attaches great significance to understanding one's own body. On the other hand, during the three weeks at the Palucca Schule, the core group of students performed precise and homogenous movements in which individual nuances had been reduced to a minimum. So I might summarize the relationship between induction and deduction as follows: In a technique class, Alan Danielson clearly expects that certain, specific movement material be performed to a certain, specific rhythm and/or timing, and that a particular, predetermined quality is thus achieved. He works on this with the students. An additional learning goal is teaching his students to sense how a set, normative quality feels.

Danielson also works with improvisation: Students work alone or with partners in order to find an arc or to experiment with phrasing. This way of working also takes place in other teaching contexts, not only in technique classes. Danielson only gives students the option to make choices and decide for themselves when he says, for example, that they are free to add a particular movement, or turn, or whatever—or not.

Regarding mirrors, Danielson has no standpoint. He says that the mirror is *sometimes* useful. He uses it so students can see how something—of which they have an internal image and which they have felt—'looks from the outside'. However, Danielson says it is always important to turn away from the mirror afterward, as it is important to feel what you are doing. Other Limón teachers never use a mirror precisely for this reason.

The **skills and abilities** that a Humphrey/Limón teacher should have are dependent upon her or his pedagogical concentration, teaching expectations, and the target group.

As broad an educational background as possible is a great advantage for anyone teaching Humphrey/Limón Technique. Anatomy, physiology, physics, philosophy, music, and visual arts inform Alan Danielson's teaching. References from architecture and psychology are also useful. Danielson explains that by drawing upon a wide spectrum of sources, his dance technique understands movement and dance from a human perspective. Everything that humans do belongs to the Limón teacher's area of interest, even the most seemingly everyday of human activities—like, for example, having children and watching them grow up.

A Limón teacher should also, ideally, bring certain physical characteristics to the classroom. These include a well–developed memory, body awareness, good physical coordination and combination skills, strength and stamina, and good alignment. Finally, for Danielson, it is also

22 See also Understanding of the Body/Movement, keyword 'Movement Principles and Types of Movement'.

useful if a teacher is, or has been, physically active in another art or sport, for example leisure sports, relaxation techniques, music, or in the performing or visual arts.

Danielson believes certain skills and abilities are essential for teaching the technique. In particular, a teacher must have an expert understanding and command of Limón principles both physically and analytically. Knowledge of kinesiology and anatomy certainly help in this context. The teacher should also be able to communicate specific movement principles—and the ability to create an open learning environment in which the students are encouraged and enabled to experience the *spirit* of a movement is part of these communication skills. Choreographic experience is also extremely helpful. A good sense of rhythm is an advantage as well—one need not be a musician (like Danielson), but the ability to communicate rhythm and timing is important. Finally, the teacher should be able to adjust and model movement material to the students' level and situation. Danielson says some Limón teachers believe a class should never be planned; he, however, believes the opposite.

As already mentioned, rhythm plays a major role in Danielson's understanding of the Humphrey/Limón Technique, both in individual movements, exercise sequences, and throughout the entire class. The class is strongly characterized by use of music—melody, rhythm, timing, phrasing, and arcs. In contrast to more shape–oriented techniques, Danielson sees the Humphrey/Limón Technique as a school of thought in which time, space, energy, breath, and gravity are central principles. Only by using these will shapes emerge.

Alan Danielson's ideas about timing became clear in the following teaching situation. The professor and former dancer Barbara Passow, who, on occasion, trained with Danielson during the Palucca workshop, asked the following question during a swinging exercise: "What is your priority, the timing or the quality? I have trouble achieving the quality inside your rhythm and timing—it's so quick." Danielson replied that the goal was to learn how to relax either in ten counts or in three counts, i.e., both quality *and* timing are important. He added:

/ "We are here in a dance class, and the special quality about a dance class is that we're doing something together—you feed on each other's energy and you become a group. In order to exploit this special quality, I would say that the priority would be on timing—for now." /

Two visual examples can help explain the relationship between timing and quality: the image of innumerable pixels in a digital picture, and the image of an analog clock with hands that either turn either smoothly or intermittently across the clock face. What does Danielson imply with these images? That time consists of innumerable tiny parts, or sections, that each person must discover and fulfill by engaging the body's fullest volume and entire potential.

Danielson works with a multilayered model when structuring a class—large or small—and strives to make a particular movement clear in terms of its duration within this structure. First, the overall time structure for a combination or exercise is determined by using physiological and emotional factors. He then works on fine–tuning the structure. To achieve this, Danielson provides rhythm and marks—using his voice, vocal noises, or by clicking his fingers and clapping—to denote the timing and tempo he has in mind. One should imagine these rhythms and marks as a metronome ticking away mechanically, reliably, and uninterrupted. There is another layer on top of this fine, metric structure that Danielson calls 'phrasing', i.e., the energetic, qualitative level. A subjective, creative structure should encourage and ultimately shape a sound or movement in time and space.

Students have the opportunity in every exercise (but especially in combinations through the space during the second section of class) to watch Danielson perform movement and to copy. They thus appropriate the material, gradually develop a personal attitude towards it, and can perform the combination for themselves. This individual and creative interpretation or 'formulation' of the material by the dancers sometimes corresponds with Danielson's working methods in artistic processes outside of the classroom, like when he is developing choreography.

In preparation for teaching, Danielson references the major themes of the Humphrey/Limón Technique: physical and physiological work, as in going from off–balance to balance, swinging, *undercurve* patterns (shifting the body weight from one leg to the other by simultaneously moving the weight deeper into the center of the curve), suspension, rebound, opposition, isolation of shapes, isolation of energy, isolation of time, ways and variations on falling, traveling through space, focusing on meter and rhythm, as well as going from tilt to curve.[22] He works with students on this wide range of themes. As he proceeds, the focus is on matters relating to the individual dancer's experience: feeling the love of movement, experiencing physical energy, and experiencing something that is bigger than oneself. It is about moving, about the movement itself, in these intense moments of class. Danielson does not plan his classes around the value of individual exercises; rather, he works systematically on the above-mentioned technical themes and learning goals.

Danielson smiles and admits that individual combinations and exercises designed to warm up and prepare the body physiologically are developed in his apartment or in a corridor. The phrases must be coherent, which means, for example, that one does not begin with jumping. Danielson introduces movements and ideas throughout class that will be incorporated into the combination at the end, the culmination of the class.

Regarding the importance of music in preparing classes, Danielson says that rhythm in particular is of enormous importance as it defines the energy that later develops in the class—which explains why he is so precise about musical accompaniment.

Students have the opportunity to ask questions during class, although he likes to postpone answering those that require a complex answer until afterward. He does not offer any other means of feedback. At the Limón School, there is a separate opportunity for reflection and exchange; in Dresden, it was possible to talk and discuss inside the workshop situation.

When asked about the role communication plays in the Humphrey/Limón Technique, he quotes the following advice from his teacher, Ruth Currier: "When you are teaching, don't get in the way of the movement!" By this he means that he aims to let the dancers feel the movement for themselves. He sees himself, at that moment, as the initiator and generator of a particular research task that each student can and should work out and experience for her- or himself.

Danielson uses the following teaching methods (in order of quantitative and qualitative relevance):

→ Vocal–phonetic description: "Da–da–ti! Ha–ha!"

→ Verbal–descriptive description of a movement: "Go down, put your hands on the floor," (using as little ballet vocabulary as possible);

→ Visual–physical information: showing a movement;

→ Verbal–functional information: "Release this muscle here so that this part can do that!"

→ Verbal–metaphoric information: "Imagine rain dripping down onto your spine. How does that feel?"

→ Direct body contact: touching individual body parts in order to direct awareness into these regions.

Looking more closely at these six items, it becomes clear that learning takes place by setting explicit and specific structures and principles, although Danielson places great value on the notion that the acquisition process remain personal and individual. A student should, for example, launch a movement from the pelvis as much as possible, or swing the leg backward and forward using its real, physical weight. The reach of a forward movement or radius of a swing are not fixed in advance; students should understand the principle, reproduce it, and learn how to integrate it into their bodies. Danielson is convinced that training such concrete movement principles also touches upon Limón's great themes of 'formation' and 'education'—namely Limón's humanistic values about the development of an individual's identity or the "nobility and inestimable value of the common man."

When asked about the role imagination plays in physical learning and the way he works with imagination, Alan Danielson responds: "I find imagery very important and I hope that the students use my metaphors in an inductive way and, in doing so, enhance their movements." He explains what he means with a musical example. He once gave the dancer Anna Fingerhuth a correction by referring to the sound of a note on the piano, played *marcato*: "Anna, make your hip look like the sound of this note." He told me later: "I could have said 'release your hip,' which would be physical information, or 'keep your leg moving,' which would be a time correction. But Anna understood the movement by the musical image. When she heard the note being struck on the piano, her hip released and she smiled!"

"I think it's great how Alan works with his voice. He is able to express the dynamics of the exercise one hundred percent using his voice. That helped me a lot. He asks, for example: 'Did you just hear how the pianist hit the keys? That is how it should feel in the leg.' This approach establishes a concrete relationship with the idea of how the movement feels in the body." *Anna Fingerhuth, student*

Maren Witte

CONCLUSION

In conclusion, I would like to return to a word in Danielson's vocabulary, a core concept and reflection upon his positive and artistic approach toward Doris Humphrey and José Limón's work. This word—namely, humanism—is interpreted and assessed quite differently in the field of human sciences. What are Danielson's—and what were Humphrey's and Limón's—humanistic values?

╱ "I can't speak for Humphrey and Limón, but for me personally, humanism means looking at everything through the lens of a human being. It is the lens of human experience, not a lens that takes scientific measurements or shows how high the leg goes. First of all, it is about defining what movements are, what breath is, what momentum is…and then being conscious of the human experience. For example, 'Why do we jump?'—because one thing is certain, that we are going to come right back down! It is that thing about the human being—striving and desiring to try out new things, and to explore, and to search, and to live…" ╱

LITERATURE

Benbow–Pfalzgraf, Taryn | Benbow–Niemier, Glynis (Ed.)
International Dictionary of Modern Dance
Detroit: St. James Press, 1998

Burt, Ramsay
The Male Dancer
London: Routledge Verlag, 1995

Cohen, Selma Jeanne | Dance Perspectives Foundation (Ed.)
International Encyclopedia of Dance
New York: Oxford University Press, 1998, Vol. 4

Cohen, Selma Jeanne
The Modern Dance. Seven Statements of Belief
Middletown (CT): Wesleyan University Press, 1977

Fischer, Dagmar
"Tanzende Präsidenten und andere Häuptlinge"
In: Ballett Intern, 2/2008, pp. 10/11

Fischer, Dagmar
"Vom Einwandererkind zum Künstler mit Weltruf"
In: Ballett Intern, 1/2008, pp. 20/21

Fischer, Dagmar
"Folkwang tanzt Limón"
In: Tanzdrama 38, 9/1997, p. 39

Garafola, Lynn (Ed.)
José Limón: An Unfinished Memoir
Middletown (CT): Wesleyan University Press, 1998

Gradinger, Malve
"Die Musik in der Bewegung: Carla Maxwell im Gespräch über Technik und Stil von José Limón."
In: Ballett Intern, 02/1989, pp. 23–25

Jeschke, Claudia
Tanz als BewegungsText: Analysen zum Verhältnis von Tanztheater und Gesellschaftstanz (1910–1965)
Tübingen: Niemeyer Verlag, 1999

Jowitt, Deborah
"Heroes and Visions"
In: Dance Now, 4/2008, pp. 23–28

Lewis, Daniel
Illustrierte Tanztechnik von José Limón
Wilhelmshaven: Florian Noetzel, 1990 (1984)

Nitsche, Maria
"The Constant Play with Gravity. Studienergebnisse 2008–2010"
Unpublished dissertation for the masterclass,
Palucca Schule Dresden— Hochschule für Tanz, 2010

Postuwka, Gabriele
Moderner Tanz und Tanzerziehung: Analyse historischer und gegenwärtiger Entwicklungstendenzen
Schorndorf: Verlag Karl Hofmann, 1999

Reynolds, Nancy
Dance Classics: A Viewer's Guide to the Best-Loved Ballets and Modern Dances
Chicago: A Cappella Books, 1991

Reynolds, Nancy
No Fixed Points: Dance in the Twentieth Century
London: Yale University Press, 2003

Schmidt, Jochen
"José Limón"
In: Schmidt, Jochen (Ed.): Tanzgeschichte des 20. Jahrhunderts
Berlin: Henschel Verlag, 2002, pp. 104–107

Seed, Patricia
José Limón and La Malinche: The Dancer and the Dance
Austin (TX): University of Texas Press, 2008

Tracy, Robert
"Silver. Limón lives through Carla's passionate preservation"
In: Dance Magazine, 7/2003, pp. 24–27

Vachon, Ann
"Honing in on Limón"
In: Dance Magazine, 5/2007, pp. 64–66

Wolf Perez, Edith M.
"Eine prekäre und unvorhersehbare Angelegenheit"
In: Tanz Affiche, 11/1999, pp. 14–17

LINKS

www.dorishumphrey.org
www.limon.org

ANOUK VAN DIJK
COUNTERTECHNIQUE

ROTTERDAM DANCE ACADEMY CODARTS—UNIVERSITY FOR THE ARTS

Influenced by

Alexander Technique
Tom Koch

**Improvisation Technologies/
9-point-technique of William Forsythe**
*Michael Schumacher, Richard Fein,
Elisabeth Corbett*

Nina Wiener Approach *Nina Wiener,
Jacqueline Knoops, Diane Elshout*

Amanda Miller
Use of space and fragility

Stephen Petronio *Moving in sequence
and introduction to Alexander Technique*

David Hutuely
Introducing her to the soul

Charles Czarny
Methodology and inspiration

Louise Frank
Limón Technique—for the guts

Her teachers

Tom Koch, Ariejan Hoorweg
Alexander Technique

Daniela Graça, Vitor Garcia *Common sense and
Alexander Technique in ballet training*

**Daniela Graça, Jack Gallagher,
Nina Wollny** *First development CT/dancers*

Jerry Remkes *Dramaturg*

Collaborations with

Falk Richter *Director/playwright*

This is only a partial list.

ANOUK VAN DIJK — COUNTERTECHNIQUE*

Research team at the Rotterdam Dance Academy, Codarts—University for the Arts in cooperation with anoukvandijk dc Amsterdam: Anouk van Dijk, Prof. Dr. Gerald Siegmund, Nina Wollny, Jerry Remkes

AUTHORS
Gerald Siegmund, Anouk van Dijk

INTERVIEW
Edith Boxberger

STUDENTS AND GUESTS
participating in the class and workshops in Countertechnique as seen on the DVD: Valeria d'Amico, Matt Bade, Sven Bahat, Yorrith de Bakker, Joris Bergmans, Antonio Borriello, Alex Deijmann, Patscharaporn Distakul, Sonia Egner, Sabine Groendijk, Fem Has, Audie Jansen, Sandra Klimek, Eline Koeman, Asja Lorencic, Lisa Meijer, Catia Oliveira Nicolau, Xanthe Opstal, Vincent Plas, Christopher Renfurm, Federica Rizzo, Chanel Selleslach, Ewa Sikorska, Naima Sommacal, Cosimo Walter Spalluto, Karl Staaf, Roisin Verheul, Thijs Vlak, Zoe Wijnsnouw; dancers of anoukvandijk dc: Philipp Fricke, Yichun Liu, and Nina Wollny

ANOUK VAN DIJK (*1965)
is choreographer, dancer, teacher, and artistic director of her own company anoukvandijk dc. Her choreographies are characterized by a virtuosic, unpredictable dance vocabulary and thematically revolve around people managing to stand their ground despite the uncertainties and opposing forces in today's world. Since 1989 she has created more than forty choreographies, works that have been presented around the world. Not only does her company produce new work, she also initiates co-productions with theaters, festivals, dance academies, and other dance companies both nationally and internationally. In 2009, Anouk van Dijk renewed her collaboration with playwright/director Falk Richter, associate director at the Schaubühne Berlin. In their recent work, she has also resumed dancing. During her career Anouk van Dijk has developed her own movement system: Countertechnique. She applies this technique in her own choreographies and teaches the technique to students and professional dancers all over the world.

Anouk van Dijk Interviewed by Edith Boxberger

PRACTICAL TOOLS

FOR A DEMANDING PROFESSION

/ **What techniques have you studied, and what has influenced you?** I studied at the Rotterdam Dance Academy, a contemporary dance school where Graham, Cunningham, and Limón were the main techniques taught, where we also had ballet six days a week. I had several important teachers, but one really inspired me to find my own method: Charles Czarny, a man with the sunshine on his face. He would go to the mirror and kiss his own reflection. I found it very peculiar, being seventeen, eighteen, but I also understood that this man is very happy. He taught me, as I now teach my students, that as a dancer you have to come to terms with yourself, love yourself—and do so rather sooner than later because dancing is such a demanding profession.

A lot of my fellow students found Czarny's classes extremely boring because he would teach the same class for weeks in a row, but for me it was an eye–opener. Every day he chose a distinct topic that we worked on exclusively—like breath, tension in the neck, parallel position, musicality, weight, phrasing in the music. It was endless. In Countertechnique, this conscious shift of focus has become a very important facet.

/ **What happened after you graduated?** After my graduation in 1985 I went to New York and studied downtown, midtown, uptown. Downtown was Movement Research, where I took classes in Release Technique and Contact Improvisation. Uptown, I studied tap and midtown I took ballet classes. I just felt I needed more knowledge.

Then, after contracts at Werkcentrum Dans and De Nieuwe Dansgroep in 1988, I joined the Rotterdamse Dans Groep. This company was going through a golden era at the time: Stephen Petronio, Randy Warshaw, Tere O'Connor, and Amanda Miller all did their first commissioned works there, so I was really lucky. I was in every piece, doing a lot of dancing. But I didn't know how to deal with it, stamina–wise. The mentality of the company was: Do it all by will power. And since I am physically a very strong person, I would get injured because of over–powering, putting too much strain and power on my muscles when I was tired. I got really skinny, I didn't know how to keep up eating enough because I was so exhausted the whole time. So then, it became like, 'I have to find ways how on earth to survive this career.'

/ **Which 'ways to survive' did you discover?** In that difficult time, I first heard about Alexander Technique. I was intimidated at first, I really came from the 'doing' side, not from 'contemplating what I was doing.' And since Alexander Technique is not a dance technique, I found it a bit scary when I heard dancers say, 'I am truly transformed, I dance so much better this way.' But since it was clear I needed to find some other way to survive in this career, I was determined to find new information. In 1991 I started Alexander Technique lessons with Tom Koch and I can say from the heart that without him, I would not be dancing still—I would have destroyed my body. And I think a lot of dancers who have to stop by the time they are thirty-three or thirty-four have to do so because they never learned to dose the power and flexibility they have in their bodies.

/ **What changed in your dancing?** It took me much longer to find out what was helpful from Alexander Technique than I had anticipated. Only when I gave up trying did it suddenly click for me. I even remember standing in the room with Tom's hands on me, desperately thinking, 'Okay, I've tried it all, I understand what the technique is about—but I just don't get it.' So I was standing there and decided to do nothing more than repeat, in my head, after Tom: 'Now let go of this and this, Anouk, and widen that and that—with no expectations whatsoever. And suddenly it worked. And I remember thinking—very Dutch–like—'Did I spend all this money to find out it's that simple, not expecting, not doing anything?'

Of course it took me another year before I started to find out how to use it in dancing. I remember the piece I was in, the section, the music, the movement, when I realized that what I was thinking was really working. While I continued moving, I doubted I could still have this Alexander–directing going on in my head while I was moving full–out. I was afraid I would start to mark. But I found that I could actually move with less energy. By the end of the piece I was not nearly as exhausted as I usually was. I realized, 'This is really important, I'm learning to apply the Alexander principles in movement!' That was really a turning point.

/ **Why did you develop your own technique?** I started choreographing almost the same time I started to dance professionally. In the beginning I choreographed on my fellow dancers. Soon my work became too specific for them and I realized that if I wanted this specific quality, I would have to help them to find it.

In my early classes I made my first attempts to analyze what I was doing and how to teach this. In 1993, when I joined Amanda Miller's Pretty Ugly Dance Company, I really went deeper into research on my own body. The other dancers were always taking ballet in the morning, but that was not very helpful for my body. So one day I started to develop my own class, to find a format that would keep me in shape while I was on tour. One other dancer joined me, so that's basically when Countertechnique as a teaching method started.

I started by thinking about which exercises, from all I had learned over the years, were good for my body. The next question was: Why is this exercise working so well for me? And then: Why is it working this way, but not when I approach it that way? I started to basically analyze everything I had learned until then and very soon I found I was doing something essentially different from other teachers.

/ **What did you find?** When I would teach movement phrases, dancers would try to copy them and then afterwards couldn't walk anymore! So I started to analyze: 'Why is it so different, what I'm doing? The movements I do seem to be very extreme on other bodies, but they don't feel extreme to me.' Since I could do the movement just as easily on the right side as on the left, it was not an intricate choreographic thing that only felt good on my body. They were simply dance steps, but with a different coordination and speed. One day Michael Schumacher and I were doing partnering work and he said to me, 'When you bring your arms towards me, send your pelvis away from me.' This created a nice stability. From his remark, I started to think about the concept that if the primary movement moves in one direction, it doesn't mean the whole body does—another body part can actually be moving the opposite direction so that the first part can move more in the primary direction. With that in mind, I started to reflect more consciously on my own classes. And I realized that whether I was thinking from my fingertips, my whole arm, or from a joint, the outcome was always the same: Two things are moving away from each other. Then I started to work with that principle.

/ **Why did you decide to call this a 'technique'?** Sometimes people say, 'this sounds like that special training for basketball players that I saw on tv,' or, 'it sounds like that method for actors that was developed in Brazil.' And probably it does! None of these thoughts, taken by themselves, are completely new. When I

explain about the kinetic logic of the weight going outside the central axis, and that by sending something else the other direction you can stabilize yourself, it is a physical law. This is nothing new. But to put these different elements together and use it in dancing is definitely a new approach. And because the process to accomplish this takes time, it has become a technique that you need to study in order to master it. That's why I decided to call it Counter*technique*.

/ **Isn't the term 'technique' in some ways contradictory to what you are trying to achieve?** The word technique seems to imply a dogmatic restriction, but it's actually the opposite. Technique is something that gives you tools, offers you possibilities. I hear a lot of choreographers say that they denounce technique or don't use technique, but what do they mean by that? The assumption seems to be that technique can only restrict. But technique is something different than kicking your leg up high or holding a shape, so people need to rethink what technique is. Technique encompasses different skills one can learn; these skills will add up to the knowledge of your body, of yourself, and the choices that you make—and will provide you with a range of physical and mental possibilities. So technique is much more than just the aesthetic outcome.

/ **What is your goal with Countertechnique?** Countertechnique stems from an interest in helping dancers to have a less strenuous daily practice. It is a really hard profession, and we have a lot of things that work against us. The aim in Countertechnique is to give dancers tools to make it lighter, to make standing on your legs, bending your legs, bending forwards, falling, jumping, and so on, easier. Equally important is to make dancers feel less negative about themselves, to trust themselves, and have them be less judgmental on how they are progressing.

/ **How do you communicate that as a teacher?** A Countertechnique teacher needs to be interested in the process of helping dancers and have compassion for the fact that when a dancer makes mistakes, it is rarely because of laziness or disinterest but mostly because of misunderstandings or fear. In Countertechnique we're gentle, yet demanding. The aim is to get a wider range in our movements, a bigger capacity in our bodies. But to go beyond our limits and to stretch our possibilities, we don't need to forcefully push ourselves. We can achieve this by thinking differently about our bodies and trust the fact it's actually possible that by using less power and energy, we can create a greater effect.

/ **Do you follow a strict concept in class?** Already in the early beginning—inspired by Charles Czarny—I decided that the first part of the class should always be the same, with exercises that you can dream. As professional dancers we need to train our bodies in order to rehearse and perform the work. And assuming the work you're doing is interesting enough by itself, you don't want to be busy in class with picking up someone's steps or choreography. Therefore I was determined, at a very early stage, to never develop a class based on my own choreographic material.

/ **So the first part of all classes is exactly the same?** We have, of course, more exercises than can fit into the approximately thirty minutes, but a teacher picks x amount of them so the progression within that timeframe remains the same. In the first part there are always elements that prepare for the rest of class, and where exercises change every two or three days. All the exercises have a clear purpose and a specific name, and there is an entire rule system in how to choose exercises for class. This one is for this, the other one for that, and if you do more of this one, you do less of that one. It might sound dogmatic, but the whole point is that the exercises actually serve as a framework for the dancers to free up their mindset.

/ **How much has the teaching changed over time?** First, there were teaching exercises and movement phrases, classes, and finding out that people could not do it. Then it went through the phase of helping dancers find out how to do it, figuring out why they could not do it. Now we are in the process of breaking it down even further. My main interest now is how we train communication between our minds to our bodies, in movement. And what effect does this have on understanding and applying the principles of the Countertechnique?

/ **What ideas or images do you use in your teaching?** Countertechnique is a task–oriented approach: it is not an imagery–based or sensory–input approach, which is really distinctly different from, for instance, the Muller Technique and Body–Mind Centering. We don't use imagery as a teaching tool because it doesn't work with our task–oriented approach. I am not going to teach the sensations of what I am experiencing while dancing to somebody else. I teach the process, the way into it, so the dancers will have their own, personal sensations.

/ **Are dancers able to relate to that?** Some dancers ask, in the beginning, whether they are allowed to feel anything because they come from a background that uses imagery as the source of inspiration to move. And I say to them, 'Of course you can feel, you are human beings!' If one wants to use Countertechnique principles, however, he or she should not start out with a fixed idea

of what the experience is going to be like. That is the big difference. When you use our task–oriented approach, you can go into a complicated multidirectional turn with a fall and then, while you are in it, you can experience the sensation. Of course.And the sensation can be totally trippy. But you cannot accomplish the same movement sequence by trying to predict beforehand how the experience is going to be; then you are not in the moment of the process.

/ **What is so crucial about this kind of presence?** My aim is for the dancer to establish a quality of movement that is so sincere that both the dancer and the viewer experience it as if it was really created in that moment and can never be repeated that way ever again—the dancer in dialogue with his body, the space, his audience, fellow dancers. It is a presence very closely related to improvisation, a presence where the craft of the performer can really stand out. Through Countertechnique the dancer can achieve that same state in a movement that's choreographed. The person is not busy with the audience's perception of him- or herself, the person is in the process of 'doing'. In the doing, all the layers of putting up appearances disappear. And if a dancer works from that, through that, towards that, then movement always becomes more interesting to watch. Always. And I think that's the key—the key to depart from and to aim for. It is both the pathway and the goal.

/ **How exactly do you accomplish that as a dancer?** In Countertechnique, only the process really counts. Certain things you can only do in process, things are all happening at the same time: You turn, and while you do this turn, body parts go in different directions (head makes a circle, right arm goes the opposite way, your working leg is slowly unfolding), *and* you are also in the process of falling horizontally from your central axis *and* you change direction in space as well. Moving this way, it is impossible to visualize or predict the outcome. The only way it can work is to go into the process of doing it. You cannot predict the end result; you cannot control movement from one center or the body parts are not able to operate independently of one another. One can only let go. That's why we say Countertechnique is a very task–oriented way of learning how to move. You are not judging yourself, or hiding that you are judging yourself. You are just there doing your thing: observing, making decisions, being in the flow of the moment—all at the same time.

/ **And how does that translate to your classes?**
People who see the class for the first time, especially the first half, might think it looks like Cunningham, Limón, Release, even like ballet. We work, for instance, on becoming aware of the space, aware of the people around you, and aware of the trajectory of your weight, your breath, and more—doing this *while* you do plié, while you turn, while you swing your head, while you détourné. We work on really seeing what is around you, really sensing the floor underneath you, on a very direct and immediate presence. This immediate presence will lead into *double presence*, which leads into scanning and working with directions and counter directions. The movements and steps simply accompany the dancers in this process–oriented way of observing what's happening, and in making decisions. That's why a format using the same exercise progression for the first part of every class is so important; the class serves as a skeleton. Within that skeleton, you can focus on what you want to be working on.

/ **How do you see the future of the Countertechnique?** We are, in a way, only at the beginning. The formats on how to use it and in which circumstances are in the process of development. We teach in different places. We have a four-year relationship with Codarts/Rotterdam Dance Academy to implement the Countertechnique into the curriculum of all first, second, third, and forth year students. In the beginning we only taught senior students, but our experience showed that a dancer has to unlearn so many things in order to be able to move in multiple directions—like having false assumptions about themselves, fear, or being over–judgmental—a lot of things that are basically in the way of just being here, so we thought why not start in the first year so they don't have to unlearn all this? I am really curious what will result in the next couple of years.

/ **What background do people need in order to teach this technique?** At the stage we're in now, the people who teach this need to have a dance *and* an Alexander Technique background. They don't need to be Alexander Technique teachers, but they need to have studied it thoroughly. One has to be very smart in analyzing what is happening in the body, and one needs to understand the refined differences. This you cannot learn in two years; it takes much longer.

/ **What do you think has changed in the last years in respect to technique in general?** The whole hierarchy has changed; dancers have become enormously emancipated over the last twenty years. A dancer has a different role in the creative process now, and bodies have different knowledge. I am sometimes shocked, however, to find wherever I teach in the world that people still have similar information in their bodies as twenty-five years ago—very often not helpful to help improve their dancing. That motivated me to really pursue the development of this technique and to try to present it in an accessible format. So I developed the Countertechnique toolbox that, in the end, enables dancers to work independently of a teacher. All this information will eventually become accessible in the format of a Countertechnique website, as well as a workbook for dancers.

/ **Are there new influences on the technique?**
I am teaching more into the details of specific Countertechnique skills, peeling back more of the layers, and thus discovering more about the essence of it all; this leads to interesting discussions with young and inexperienced dancers, and leads me to think further about what needs to be developed next. The other day I had a discussion with a young dancer on what 'thought' is. Is thought coming out of a feeling or an observation, a judgement? Is it coming as a response, or is it an initiation? If we are talking about directing your movement by thinking, for example, and I think, 'I release my arm joint and I take the weight from my fingers in space,' is that a thought or an image? Or is it the observation of what is *going* to happen? Those are things that I find are important to be able to clarify.

/ **Language seems to play an important role.** I found that the language we use when teaching is crucial. When something is being explained in dance, we all assume we hear the same, but in practice most dancers interpret what's being said differently. I think this is a problem we cannot completely solve in the dance world. What is different in Countertechnique is that we specifically address the communication problem so students and teachers are aware of it and communicate *about* it. I want all the teachers to really know why we do which exercise when, and how, and why it's there. And to share this gradually with the dancers so they, too, deepen their understanding. Therefore a Countertechnique class is extremely detailed. I want to use some sort of common sense language that is least likely to be misunderstood.

/ **What do you want to give to young dancers?**
A smile, first and for all. That they trust themselves. And that they feel confident to use their own mind. Not as something rational, not as something holy, not as something apart from the body. Your mind is your body! That's what I love about the Chinese character for mind: Mind is heart, and heart is mind. I wish we Westerners could express these two notions in one single word because it says everything about how we are, in essence, connected with ourselves.

Gerald Siegmund, Anouk van Dijk

INTRODUCTION

THE DIFFICULTY OF RUNNING

On the ninth floor of the Codarts building in Rotterdam, Netherlands, the first-year students at the Rotterdam Dance Academy prepared for their first morning class. Like the day before, they were working with Anouk van Dijk, Dutch choreographer and dancer, who, over the course of four weeks, would introduce them to Countertechnique. As if by instinct, every dancer positioned him- or herself to face the mirrored wall on one side of the studio, checking on their appearance. Anouk van Dijk began what she calls the 'Practical Tools Workshop' by breaking up the arrangement. She asked them to find a position in the room, facing any direction. "You are here as a person," she said, "so be aware of your environment." Although the frontal teaching arrangement was, in fact, used for almost all Countertechnique classes for practical reasons, the message to the students at this moment was clear: Countertechnique is not about the shape of the body. The technique is not concerned with how movement looks, nor does it deal with body part coordination for the sake of shape.

So what, then, is it about?

After a couple of awareness exercises, Anouk van Dijk asked the students to run through the room. Why not? None of them seemed to mind. On the contrary, they had fun running past each other, brushing arms, feeling the air, and spending energy. Indeed: Countertechnique is about the fun and joy of moving and, eventually, dancing. The carefree running exercise, however, raised some serious questions. What is it that one does when running? Learning how to run implies an understanding of weight distribution in space. Nobody thinks about this while running because it seems such a natural thing to do. Students ran as they would in the streets—relying on habits. Their bodies pushed weight into the floor to gain stability while sticking their necks out and propelling arms forwards. Their running made a heavy thudding and trampling sound, audible throughout the room. Their movement required much strength and energy, and they quickly became fatigued.

Van Dijk made suggestions: "Try being soft in the ankles." "Try sending your head above your spine." "Catch up with your legs." But this is easier said then done and not everyone managed to apply the instructions. Integrating the teacher's suggestions into the way one moves would mean changing a learned motor skill, and involve distributing weight differently in space. Few of the dancers were able to change their thinking about running. Old habits die hard. For those who caught a glimpse of what this could mean, the movement appeared lighter, much more alert and freer, ready to take on any direction. Countertechnique enables a dancer to use less energy for moving; it makes one 'available for movement'.

Without using the term Countertechnique or explaining its principles to the students, Anouk van Dijk was already working with Countertechnique principles in the running exercise. Running is a type of falling; the head falls forward and forces the body to actively use its weight. If the students followed the shift of weight from the head without allowing the legs to react, they would fall over. To prevent falling over, almost all of them tightened their muscles, i.e., gripped their bodies to maintain equilibrium, and ran. Gripping, however, blocks movement; in order to move on, they had to use more strength than necessary. Holding onto a center will also restrict the ability to change direction, i.e., to move. Anouk van Dijk's suggestions encourage students to give up gripping in order to gain a flexible stability. If the legs go downward, the trunk and head must go upward—if one actively directs the head and trunk upward, space opens up for the lower body and the legs. Following Anouk's instructions, falling forward while moving upward meant that running could be sustained for a longer amount of time; downward force was relieved and the dancers were open for more and different movement.

Anouk van Dijk: "For every direction, there is always a counter direction. Always." After the first exercise, students already understood why the use of a counter direction is effective. What this implies, and how one can work with this principle, will be the topic of this text.

Countertechnique, or the effective use of directions and counter directions in both the body and space, offers many possibilities for dancers. As exemplified in the falling/running exercise, the core assumption of Countertechnique is that when dancing, the weight—or the weight of a body part—falls out of the central axis. This weight becomes available for movement. In order to neither collapse nor grip, a counter direction is called upon that will enable freedom and help retain control while moving. The principles of Countertechnique are based upon the body's skeletal and muscular structure and the relation to space. Countertechnique is not oriented towards an end–result; it does not aim to help dancers develop a specific body image nor does it strive towards an idealized form, shape, or aesthetic.

Countertechnique offers dancers a way of thinking about the body and mind that supports training, rehearsing, and performing.

The core research team included Dr. Gerald Siegmund, professor of dance studies at the Justus Liebig University, Giessen, Germany; Anouk van Dijk, artistic director of anoukvandijk dc in Amsterdam; and Nina Wollny, artistic assistant to Anouk van Dijk and dancer in the company. Jerry Remkes, managing director and dramaturge of anoukvandijk dc, made valuable contributions. The first meeting of the core group took place on September 22–23, 2009 in Berlin. From December 18–20, 2009, one session of Countertechnique Teachers Training (CTTT) took place in Anouk van Dijk's studio in Amsterdam, Netherlands. During the three days, general concepts of Countertechnique and teaching strategies were discussed. Anouk van Dijk's workbooks for dancers and teachers were used as reference. The team met again from January 4–8, 2010 in Rotterdam, Netherlands, where Anouk

van Dijk and members of her company had a four-week teaching engagement at Codarts/Rotterdam Dance Academy. During these four weeks, first-, second- third- and fourth-year students were familiarized with Countertechnique principles.

Codarts/Rotterdam Dance Academy has asked Anouk van Dijk to be director of a test program from 2009 to 2012. During this time, she has, and will, continue to research how Countertechnique can be implemented into a four-year professional dance education curriculum. The second-year students served as the school's first test group and had begun Countertechnique the year before; it was evident that they had experience. Teaching formats included Countertechnique workshops as an introduction to the principles (Practical Tools Workshop), regular Countertechnique classes, and partnering workshops. Apart from Anouk van Dijk, the teaching team consisted of Nina Wollny, Philipp Fricke, Jack Gallagher, and Birgit Gunzl, and was assisted by Peter Cseri. The aim of this residency is to develop a way in which Countertechnique can be integrated into a dance education syllabus as well as to further develop the technique's teaching strategies.

Gerald Siegmund, Anouk van Dijk

HISTORICAL CONTEXT

TIME, PLACE, AND SOCIO-POLITICAL CONTEXT

Countertechnique emerged in the 1980s, in the context of the independent dance scene in Holland. It was developed by Anouk van Dijk, who was trained at the Rotterdam Dance Academy (from which she graduated in 1985). "Since the 1970s in Holland, cultural policy became an increasing part of the government's welfare policy. The benefit and relevance of culture to society as a whole became a priority, notably in terms of cultural participation. The social role of culture was perceived on both the levels of social class and geographical spread."[1] The Dutch national arts–funding system (which considers project–based grants for independent artists as well as supporting large institutions), allowed Anouk van Dijk to fully concentrate on her artistic and choreographic work when she started her company. In 1996, she received her first grant to create an evening–length piece. "The funding was enough so I could survive for a few months and hire a small group of dancers," she remembers. "In the mornings I would organize a dance training for my dancers and afterwards we would research and create." This way of working was different from how independent artists worked in the U.S. There, choreographers had to teach to support themselves and their artistic work, and used classes to generate movement vocabulary for choreographies. Because of the funding Anouk van Dijk was able to concentrate on class material as such, and began to develop it according to the dancers' needs. "I thought, what would be the best way to prepare our bodies and minds for rehearsal?" says Anouk van Dijk. She and elaborated by adding questions: "What did all other training methods teach me? What works? What's missing?" To understand Countertechnique, it is important to note that it is neither a movement style nor does it presuppose a certain aesthetic; it is a daily training method that helps the dancer prepare for his or her professional life, whatever style or aesthetic might be called for. It supports dancers by encouraging them to take more responsibility in their personal growth as an artist.

Countertechnique tools can also be applied in partnering work, in creating choreographic material, for improvisation, and in performance. The technique continues to evolve with Anouk van Dijk's ongoing analysis, and is based on her evaluations of over twenty years of experience as a professional dancer. Although she began teaching in 1987, it was only in 2002 that she began considering Countertechnique as a coherent system of interrelated physical and theoretical principles that could be integrated into a specific training method. From 2006 onwards, the implications of the practice were translated back into a theoretical framework, resulting into two workbooks: one is for dancers, one for teachers. Both are updated annually. Thus the knowledge is being transferred and continues to be tested and evaluated by a growing number of teachers. Countertechnique is a relatively new technique, and its scope is still developing.

BACKGROUND: BIOGRAPHIES AND ENVIRONMENT

As a student at Rotterdam Dance Academy, Anouk van Dijk, like most contemporary dancers of her generation, also trained in ballet for strength and coordination. At the time, ballet training served the needs of many choreographers working in Holland. In addition, the RDA curriculum included modern techniques like Cunningham, Graham, and Limón.

Before joining De Nieuwe Dansgroep in 1986, Anouk van Dijk went to New York to explore the booming dance scene in Manhattan. There she concerned herself with contemporary techniques such as Contact Improvisation and Release Technique (both developed in the 1970s), as well as with tap and jazz. Returning to the Netherlands, she met Nina Wiener, who taught classes and workshops and strongly influenced the work of De Nieuwe Dansgroep and its artistic director, Jacqueline Knoops. Whereas most Release work began on the floor in order to help discover natural alignment, Wiener worked on alignment while moving through space and by consciously shifting weight at the same time.

Several years later, Anouk van Dijk left De Nieuwe Dansgroep to join De Rotterdamse Dansgroep. In 1988, this Rotterdam–based company commissioned young choreographers unknown at the time in Europe, like Randy Warshaw and Stephen Petronio, both of whom had worked with the Trisha Brown Dance Company (until 1986 and 1987 respectively). Both used Release Technique fundamentals. Petronio was of particular importance to the Dutch dance scene at the time because he worked with

1 www.culturalpolicies.net/web/netherlands.php?aid=1 (access 20.01.2010)

2 See Christy Harris: "The Influence of the Alexander Technique on Modern Dance Aesthetics". *Movement* Research 19 (Fall/Winter 1999), 18/19.

3 See Gerald Siegmund: *William Forsythe – Denken in Bewegung*. Berlin: Henschel Verlag, 2004.

4 Cf. Alva Noë: *Action in Perception*. Cambridge (MA)/London: MIT Press, 2004.

movement isolation before it became popular in Hip Hop; he isolated individual limbs and sequenced their movement rhythmically. Anouk van Dijk began choreographing at this time and was also introduced to the Alexander Technique, which has served as an inspiration for various Release Techniques and subsequently became a major influence on Countertechnique.[2]

Amanda Miller was still a member of Ballet Frankfurt when she created her first piece, *Brief,* for the dance company De Rotterdamse Dansgroep in 1990. Amanda Miller's influence (whose Pretty Ugly Dance Company Van Dijk would join as a dancer in 1993) opened up a new and specific way of working with spatial references to Van Dijk. Since the mid-1980s William Forsythe had been experimenting with Rudolf von Laban's models for spatial orientation of the moving body. Laban, a German choreographer and dance theoretician, placed the upright body inside a cube, with nine points equally divided on each side. This allowed for twenty-seven points in space towards which movement can be directed. The forty-five degrees between each direction compose the *nine point cube,* a useful spatial matrix for dancers that facilitates clear and observable direction changes. Using Laban's cube, William Forsythe developed a way of destabilizing the body by multiplying the number of cubes the body can operate inside of.[3] Miller used this model for her own aesthetic purposes.

Triggered by Nina Wiener's work on shifting weight, by attention-directing ideas borrowed from the Alexander Technique, and by Forsythe's and Miller's Nine Point Technique, Anouk van Dijk explored the space between going to the floor and reaching higher levels until she succeeded in finding a state of balance in between. Going to the floor and up again was no longer the only possibility. On the contrary, by distributing weight in space, any direction in the body and its counterdirection could be used simultaneously to explore all twenty-six directions. Moreover, a multidirectional use of the body—i.e., not only up and down but also forwards and backwards, left and right, and rapidly changing between these directions—was now possible.

RELATION TO OTHER ART FORMS

Countertechnique works within the parameters of the dancing body. Anouk van Dijk did not consciously seek or use forms, concepts, or any related discourses from other art forms.

RELEVANT THEORETICAL DISCOURSES

The implications of Countertechnique go beyond physicality. Countertechnique increases dancers' awareness of both their bodies and the space they occupy; dancers examine the space around them and the details of the room as well as other dancers to promote awareness of what they are doing and how the actions of others influence their own actions. Countertechnique hones an individual's ability to relate to their own body as well as to other dancers in the space—which is always a social space. Dancers thus develop an openness towards situations; they learn to be prepared, to be ready, and to shift awareness quickly. Such awareness has implications for social life: It touches upon the relationship of individuals to groups and how societies cohere. Awareness always operates on those two levels: shifting rapidly between what is happening outside the body to what is happening inside the body, and vice-versa.

It is significant to note that Countertechnique follows a non-essentialist and pragmatic approach towards various dance styles and methodologies; it may be considered a post-essentialist method and, as such, it builds upon already existent techniques, uses knowledge provided, develops the ideas further, and applies them so different movement qualities can become available. It is a modular system that focuses on efficiency and individual learning skills. One may therefore make a connection between the developments of Western societies after the fall of communism and the ways these societies restructured their respective fields of knowledge in a non-hierarchical way. Countertechnique opens interesting routes for thinking about the relation between the physical constituents of human perception and movement. Cognitive philosophers like Alva Noë hold that perception is actually based upon acquired movement patterns, so one can say that there is no perception of meaningful forms without prior knowledge or experience of physical spatial orientation.[4]

CURRENT PRACTICE

Countertechnique is a registered trademark; both the classes and the system of principles can be taught only with Anouk van Dijk's approval. Current teachers are Anouk van Dijk, Nina Wollny (her artistic assistant), and the core members of her company: Birgit Gunzl, Angie Müller, Philipp Fricke, and Peter Cseri. The main place to study Countertechnique is at Rotterdam Dance Academy. There, over a four-year period, it is taught at all levels in four-week intensive blocks. Several other institutions, such as Henny Jurriëns Foundation and ArtEZ Dance Academy, offer Countertechnique classes on a less frequent but regular basis. Apart from this institutional affiliation, dancers of Anouk van Dijk's dance company use Countertechnique both when teaching and giving workshops, and when they perform in Van Dijk's or other choreographers' pieces. Also, several former company dancers and teachers in different countries have adopted many Countertechnique principles in their teaching, some of whom also have an official Level I (basics) certification, which was achieved by participation in the Countertechnique Teachers Training (CTTT).

INDIVIDUAL APPROACH

Many dancers and choreographers who have studied Countertechnique apply the principles to their regular training and rehearsal processes. This is possible because Countertechnique is not a style but, rather, consists of organized and pragmatic information that provides a means to work with the body efficiently. Ideally, every Countertechnique student should become his or her own teacher. In order to achieve this, Anouk van Dijk has developed what she calls a 'toolbox'. This toolbox contains the essential theoretical information needed to understand and apply Countertechnique. It is a virtual cabinet with six drawers, each of which contains a different aspect of the technique: Basic Principles of (Counter) Directing; Directions and Counter–Directions; Physical Parameters; Mental Parameters; Body in Space; Basic Facts of Anatomy.

The toolbox provides answers to the following three questions: 1) *Why* do I use (counter)directing? 2) *What* are the possibilities of (counter)directing? 3) *How* do I (counter)direct effectively? (For a more detailed description of its content, please refer to the end of chapter: Understanding the Body/Movement.) These topics provide dancers with an overview of available information; any information can be used at any given time, there is no hierarchy.

Countertechnique offers dancers a way of thinking about the body and mind in relation to movement that supports training, rehearsing, and performing. Be it in a ballet class, in a contemporary class, in rehearsal, or while performing—dancers can utilize the principles. By creating a frame of mind that allows movement to happen, Countertechnique helps dancers to lose anxieties and fear of failure; they will dance more freely. Dancers who have lost this fear prove, in practice, to be more open to movement and to have better access to their instincts. Their bodies are not working against them.

RELATION TO OTHER DANCE AND MOVEMENT TECHNIQUES

Countertechnique aims to change the way dancers perceive and think of themselves and what they do. This makes Countertechnique not only a physical technique but also one with a strong theoretical component. In the basic assumptions that physical and mental activities in humans are connected, Countertechnique is related to Alexander Technique and other somatic practices. It shares the belief that the way a person thinks about the body is directly reflected in the way the body moves and behaves; both Alexander Technique and Countertechnique assume that dancers often house many wrong assumptions about anatomy and physiology. Changing the way of thinking about the body and its movement potential will actually change the way a person moves. In this respect, Countertechnique also aims to undo habitual movement patterns a dancer has acquired in favor of a healthier, or better, way of moving. Countertechnique is also related to Release Techniques that work to actively remove obstructions in the body's organization. Countertechnique shares the goal of creating space inside the joints in order to realign limbs and the body's position in space. In contrast to other Release Techniques, however, Countertechnique does not refer to the floor and gravity as a main reference point for the body in space, nor does it refer to a core center in the body. Instead, Countertechnique works from the principle of directing and counter–directing while performing every movement, consequently, in relation to space, weight, joints, muscles, and the mind.

In summary, one can say that Countertechnique is a combination of alignment–work practices based on pragmatic anatomical knowledge and a strong outgoing sense of moving into space. Interior space in the joints is made available by emphasizing exterior trajectories that help redistribute the body's weight in space. Emphasizing spatial trajectories, it becomes easier to have more freedom in the joints. Using a counter–direction helps maintain freedom and balance in movement; it enables the distribution of weight without falling down, holding on to a center, or gripping. This principle is applied consistently and consequently in every movement, hence the name: Countertechnique.

Gerald Siegmund, Anouk van Dijk

CONCEPT AND IDEOLOGY

UNDERSTANDING THE BODY

Countertechnique has a holistic understanding of the body. Mind and matter, thinking and moving are intricately related and influence each other, as in Alexander Technique. Building on William Forsythe and Amanda Miller's work on spatial orientation, Countertechnique also systematizes how one thinks and directs energy in space. It looks carefully into the use of a dancer's energy, and the implications for daily training, rehearsal, and performance.

The Countertechnique 'body' can be described as a three–dimensional body that takes all spatial levels and planes into consideration. In Countertechnique the notion of space is therefore an extremely dynamic concept. Countertechnique views the body as essentially a multidirectional and traveling body that can move in several directions at the same time. It thinks of the body as a volume; this volume consists of space and occupies space, which it produces and transforms at the same time. Since there is no predetermined ideal image of the body, the way the body looks is unimportant. The engagement in a process of thinking multidirectionally, along with rethinking assumptions about appropriate movement execution, will eventually affect the dancer's use of shape.

Body weight is not considered to have an objective value, rather to be the result of varying individual energy relations in time and space. A dancer's body may objectively weigh sixty kilos, but if the dancer distributes this weight in space by counter–directing when doing partnering work, it will look, feel, and therefore be much lighter. If this principle is taken seriously, it can be concluded that our ability to direct energy transforms not only our body's physical shape and spatial orientation, but also its weight. The body is not primarily understood as consisting of fixed particles or of matter with a specific density, rather as one that is brought into being by the constant transformation of energy that, in turn, transforms the body's physical shape and spatial orientation. The Countertechnique body finds stability in vectorial trajectories of energy that counterbalance. In class, the body finds support within itself by standing center floor and not, as in ballet, by using a barre. The body is centered and de-centered at once, finding sta-

bility only if it is expanding in space and sending energy into two directions simultaneously.

As a result, the most important concept is that of a body without a center. Rather than thinking from a physical core, Countertechnique views the body as a bundle of energy lines that are constantly reconfiguring. These lines operate above, under, and across an absent core to find stability only in a momentary orientation and relation to each other, which means constantly acknowledging the weight of different body parts, countering that weight with other body parts, and thus creating a weight flow in which balance is ever–changing. This continual (re)alignment of body parts takes place even in minute movements, meaning the body is constantly in negotiation with itself and its environment.

Practical anatomical knowledge is crucial for an understanding of Countertechnique. Understanding how the joints work will greatly influence the effectiveness of the dancer's movement. By directing the constituent parts of the joints away from each other, the body's volume is increased, allowing for a different movement articulation. Because movement is articulated in the joints, opening the joints up allows for possibilities of *re-joining*, or reconnecting, the body in relation to itself and the space surrounding it. Countertechique makes it much easier to both isolate body parts and move them in sequence, which results in an increased range of motion as well as in more refined coordination. This opens up the potential for more creative ways of moving.

Although there are no gender–related exercises in Countertechnique training, women may find certain aspects—like widening the pelvis or lengthening the hamstrings—easier to do than men. This is due to different bone and muscular structure. This difference, however, does not reflect any value or judgment on the quality of movement or body. Movement in Countertechnique therefore has no gender specificity.

In class, music is used primarily to enhance the joy of dancing and to create an agreeable working atmosphere to help reduce the pressure of having to achieve something. This open and comfortable environment is an important starting point that enables the dancer to stay available and open to movement. Percussive music, when used, is preferred either with a live percussionist or a pianist using a distinctive percussive approach. Most of the time, however, contemporary pop and r'n'b music is used. This is music most dancers know, are familiar with, and like to dance to. Usually, music is not used for basic exercises. As a rhythm often helps dancers structure and memorize steps, different meters with different accents are used for chosen exercises or combinations.

Certain physical parameters such as *popping*, i.e., releasing unnecessary tension in the major joints, or working on *horizontal falling*, i.e., releasing the weight in space so that it is easier to direct body parts away from each other, are explored more easily with music. It is, however, important to note that learning movement combinations is not the aim of a Countertechnique class; combinations serve as a framework within which dancers work. Other key elements from the toolbox, including some of the mental parameters, can be worked on without music. This means that music is not intrinsically needed for and related to Countertechnique.

INTENT

The intention of Countertechnique is not to produce a specific aesthetic, nor does it strive for form. Instead, Countertechnique focuses on using an individual's movement potential to the maximum in a physically and mentally healthy way. The principles can be applied to almost any movement style, from ballet to Contact Improvisation. On a practical level, using it takes pressure off the dancing body. Since the principles of the Countertechnique movement system facilitate movement, this may be valuable foremost in performance.

During Anouk van Dijk's teaching period at Codarts, practicing Countertechnique was conducted in two phases. For students unfamiliar with Countertechnique, a Practical Tools Workshop was taught for up to two weeks. After this workshop and the introduction to basic elements of Countertechnique, the actual classes in Countertechnique were taught.

In class, exercises were developed for training purposes that, on first glance, seem to include much material from existing movement vocabularies: the basic bending, folding, reaching, and rotating are found in many forms of dance, be it ballet, Cunningham or Limón, or even Release Technique. What has been re-evaluated, however, is the order and approach to such basic movements. Anouk van Dijk analyzed their essence and added small, effective exercises to help find, as she says, the most efficient and yet safe way of rotating a leg or an arm. Apart from that, she developed specific traveling exercises wherein falling horizontally through space helps dancers use counter–direction in an organic way.

Using these movements and combinations as 'empty shells', the dancers can focus on applying the principles of Countertechnique. Continued training will change the initiation of movement from inside the body, how the dancer experiences the movement, and what the movements eventually look like (less inhibited and more personally engaged). The result might appear subtle, but for a dancer it can make the difference between hating and loving the same movement. To give an example: a dancer often executes a tendu with too much gripping. If he or she wants to move on, the applied muscle tension blocks further movement, meaning the dancer must activate a lot of energy in order to garner momentum. Alternatively, a dancer can execute a tendu by counter–directing. This implies that he or she moves the tendu leg forward and down while the trunk goes backwards and up in space, simultaneously maintaining width in the trunk. The body thus finds stability by extending beyond its sphere, using less force and energy and thereby making it easier for the dancer to continue moving. The tendu is, technically speaking, still a tendu that might be seen in any ballet performance, but the dancer will find it easier to execute it, with an increased range of rotation in the legs and a stronger, freer upper body that is ready to change direction at any given moment.

By finding a healthier way to execute movements, dancers can also enjoy a longer professional career. On a fundamental level, one could argue that Countertechnique champions a dance culture that is less exploitative of its dancers. It helps dancers cope with the daily stress of training, rehearsal, and performance without losing their scope of movement and, most importantly, as Anouk van Dijk insists, their joy of dancing. The quality of Countertechnique training does not lie in the successful execution of a movement phrase or the perfect imitation of an image; ideally it engages the dancer in a thought process that enables him or her to train on one's own.

As described by Anouk van Dijk, the physical body in Countertechnique is purely relational; the body has no core center. It has a dynamic system of vectors that creates energetic volumes. Within that system, even the most subtle movement of a body part (like lifting an arm), will take weight away from the central axis, thus redistributing body weight in space. Countertechnique enables the body to execute spacious dynamic movement. In other words: If you want to move big, Countertechnique helps you to do it.

Although Countertechnique, as Anouk van Dijk sees it, does not favor a specific understanding of art, it lends itself to a strong, energetic, and outgoing movement aesthetic. The preoccupation with space explains its association with ballet—a technique not averse to big lifts and dynamic diagonals. But whereas a ballet dancer's body is centered and derives its presence from posture, bodily presence in Countertechnique is determined by the absence of a fixed center.

The heightened alertness that is typical for dancers trained in Countertechnique stems from the need and ability to be in at least two places at the same time, both mentally and physically. Dancers have to think and focus on direction as well as counter–direction, thus dividing their attention. To that, the dancer must be attentive to other moving bodies and, of course, the space, and the room. Thus the dancer must operate simultaneously internally and externally. A body dealing with this *double presence* is always actively scanning and processing information, ready for interaction in the here and now, making choices and decisions.

An outside observer can actually see the dancers engaging in this interactive personal dialogue, which grants them a natural presence even when performing complex choreographic material. In Anouk van Dijk's opinion, the most important outcome of Countertechnique is that it provides tools to create a stronger stage presence, and more freedom to engage in the moment of performance, both physically and mentally.

"I have to admit that this is the first class in which I can actually connect the mental work and the physicality. It's not like you see your legs literally go through the floor, but it's so clear what you have to do. And when you're doing it, you feel it, you feel the stability you gain. I've never before been able to stand in first position and circle my head at the same time. It's just a really clear connection between the thoughts and the movements. And the best part of it is that the atmosphere is nice in the class. It's not about judging, but it's really about helping and giving the information in order to make you more free in your learning process."

Matt Bade, student

Gerald Siegmund, Anouk van Dijk

UNDERSTANDING

THE BODY/MOVEMENT

PREREQUISITES

Anouk van Dijk developed Countertechnique over time, on a day-to-day basis with contemporary and ballet trained professionals who needed a more balanced muscular training. The idea is to expand physical capacities by deepening the mental understanding of physical processes. Since Countertechnique helps dancers to think differently about their bodies and movement capacities, an educational background or some knowledge of body awareness techniques is helpful. Anouk van Dijk's study of Alexander Technique influenced the development of Countertechnique, thus experience in Alexander Technique is helpful. Dancers who have studied Alexander Technique understand the connection between mind and body; they are aware that thoughts can influence the body and the way it moves. They are already familiar with certain anatomical facts such as exact joint location. This information helps the informed dancer efficiently direct and counter–direct movement into space. Most importantly, however, experience in body awareness techniques changes the students' frame of mind; it shifts their attention away from an ideal or a goal that is to be achieved and allows them to focus on process. "It is not important how it looks. What is important is whether it makes more sense to you," says Anouk van Dijk.

In general, those students or dancers who are accustomed to working on their own projects, to making choices, and taking responsibility for their work are the quickest to pick up the principles of Countertechnique; their learning attitude is more conducive. Whether or not dancers have a strong technique or have already attained a certain level of strength is not of primary importance, the information gained by studying Countertechnique will help them build strength and coordination in a healthy way. That said, certain physical characteristics can influence the learning path in a positive way. Dancers who have deep hip flexors, supple shoulders, and a deep plié will find it easier to create and use the space in their joints for directing and counter–directing. Apart from that, it is helpful to have muscles that are both flexible and strong. Anatomical attributes, however, are only as good as what one does with them. Having an inquisitive mind and an analytical eye for picking up movement, as well as the ability to structure and process abstract information and actively access it, are helpful mental skills for dancers who work with Countertechnique.

Analytical thinking is utilized in a practical, down–to–earth context. Dancers should trust their instincts and their joy of risk–taking, and simply see what happens, i.e., go with the flow and see where the movement tasks lead. If the situation in class becomes too tense, Anouk van Dijk holds up the image of a bright yellow smiley. Her saying, "Fuck it. It's just dance," might sound like blasphemy to some, but it helps take pressure off dancers and reduces fear. The dancers shouldn't take themselves and what they do too seriously. If they are stuck on an exercise or a movement phrase, or even with the Countertechnique information, they should just smile, drop it, do something else, and come back to it later refreshed.

"She talks about 'distraction' a lot. She gave the example of opening her mail while walking up the stairs: Taking the stairs this way is a lot easier than when you concentrate on how many stairs you still have to go. You know? I mean you don't come up exhausted if you're thinking of something else. But if you think of walking the stairs, you get exhausted. So, in dancing you can apply the same idea. Okay, so when I try to widen my trunk and it is not working, I should not focus on widening my trunk, but do something else, like lowering the tension in my neck. So by doing another thing you distract yourself from the actual goal."

Yorrith de Bakker, student

Whereas the ability to structure and process information is helpful in the learning process, the most essential motor skill for Countertechnique is coordination. Coordination implies both the physical coordination of body parts as well as the coordination between mind and body that directs and counter–directs movement in space. If dancers have good coordination, other motor capabilities like endurance or speed will follow. Dancers are able to move faster when their directions are clear, they will utilize less strength if they learn how to use the space inside the joints instead of blocking them with too much tension. As a result, the dancer will have more endurance.

Initially dancers are apt to associate the extreme spatial range of movement in a Countertechnique class with hard work; in the first classes they often use far too much undirected strength, leading to exhaustion and muscle pain. As they learn more about the principles, they understand that extreme spatial range is achieved by coordination of weight in space through clearly directed thoughts, an efficient use of the body's anatomy, and by always providing a counter–direction to each movement. This way the movements are lighter and less exhausting. When applying Countertechnique principles in daily training, combined with rest between sessions for the body and mind to adapt to the new information, coordination will improve—and other motor skills will follow.

"It has a certain system that helps you to recollect certain movements. There is an echo in the body...she's constantly making you reflect on the way how you move from one point in the space to the other point in the space—with less tension, the most organic and logical way."

Sven Bahat, student

As Countertechnique's goal is improved functionality and efficiency, as opposed to an aesthetic that only people with specific anatomical dispositions can meet, studying it teaches students how to use natural capabilities to their fullest potential. Training can be individualized to meet a student's needs.

A core element in Countertechnique is called *scanning*. Scanning means that dancers actively observe their own physical and mental state, and consciously access 'drawers' from the Countertechnique toolbox that enable them to work on specific problems as well as on their dancing in general.[5] In the beginning, teachers introduce basic information from and about the toolbox. Next, they help students to make a simple choice between two components. Beginning thusly, students learn by actively applying only a limited amount of information. Once dancers are more advanced in the technique, they can begin to use the toolbox independently. By actively scanning one's own body and deciding which tools are needed, the toolbox provides orientation for an individual's learning process. Anouk van Dijk believes that dancers should ultimately become

5 See chapter "Historical Context". "Individual Approach".

their own teachers: Reaching one's own fullest potential means taking an active and personal role in the ongoing learning process that spans a dancer's entire career. Some dancers are naturally faster, others are naturally stronger, and still others are naturally more coordinated—but all this is beside the point. If dancers with a good understanding of the basic principles of Countertechnique need to become faster in a specific movement, they have the tools that will help them to actually become faster. This holds true for all motor skills. What one sees, in the end, are dancers who are 'in the moment', applying their whole self to technically challenging movement.

"This is really a new level I'm going through, going beyond my borders."

Fem Has, student

Countertechnique tries to create more space and freedom of movement inside the body, especially inside the joints. Very flexible dancers may hurt themselves when working on this if they are not yet strong enough to support a wider range of movement. Dancers who are hyper-flexible might need additional strengthening exercises to prevent joints from dislocating. Dancers who have built up much muscular strength, on the other hand, often find it helpful to take Alexander Technique lessons to soften. Alexander Technique is not concerned with working on movement but with the state of the body as such. As a body awareness technique, it focuses on how people are misusing the natural state of their body and aims to help the unlearning, inhibiting obstructive or harmful habits and patterns in order to regain freedom. In Alexander Technique, releasing movement inhibition and directing the body can be experienced in a pure way, which can help Countertechnique students in understanding what reducing unnecessary tension really means. Countertechnique incorporates principles from Alexander Technique, and propels them into action.

Especially during the first couple days spent practicing Countertechnique, students might feel sore. Since Countertechnique goes against acquired habits of initiating and controlling movement, the full range of exercises in class can cause pain in the lumbar area due to increased pressure and lack of use of a counter–direction (which would take away the increased pressure). In the third part of the class, extreme upper body and head movements are combined with refined leg–work so that with every movement, the true weight of the limbs is acknowledged. Apart from that, the movement combinations require a lot of bending and folding in the hip joint. Some dancers don't use the hip joint to its full potential; they perform the necessary movement by bending the lumbar spine instead. So, the reasons for pain in initial phase of practicing Countertechnique are twofold: First, the dancers are not yet strong enough, which creates pressure on the psoas muscles, the sides of the back, and the lower region of the spine and, second, some dancers do not use the joints' full movement potential and compensate by moving other body parts.

This was apparent during the second day of Anouk van Dijk's residency at Codarts in Rotterdam. The second–year students were sore from class the day before. Instead of pushing them through another set of exercises, Anouk van Dijk took the time to explain possible reasons for their pain and to review what she calls some 'basic facts of anatomy': Where is your hip joint? Where does your arm connect to the shoulder? Where is the head/neck joint located? This questioning helps students understand how movement happens in the joints. After that, a series of simple head rolls helped them experience and understand the principle that

the head goes forward and up in space and not backward and down. Anouk van Dijk chose to explain anatomical details of the head/neck joint to help students change their perceptions about how the head moves in space. "Allow that everything in your body can move. Widen between the shoulder blades and the back, be easy in the knee joints, soften your ankles. Allow the head to move into the space above you." In this way, pressure was taken off the neck and back area, and movement became lighter and less painful.

MOVEMENT CHARACTERISTICS AND PHYSICALITY

The principle of directing and counter–directing body parts away from each other enables dancers to achieve a more effective and overall control of their movement without gripping muscles and blocking further movement. As a result, alignment is achieved by continuously sending body parts away from each other and into the space outside the dancers' kinesphere. While moving, the body parts' relationship with each other changes constantly. It is therefore necessary for the dancers to continually direct and redirect body parts to keep the dynamic balance functioning. This means that all body parts are active most of the time.

Anouk van Dijk is very particular in designating body parts, which helps students to be clear about what they

should move. The body is divided into arms, legs, head, and trunk; the word 'torso' is not used because no clear anatomical definition of 'torso' exists.

Countertechnique teachers refer often to the sit bones (not to be mistaken for the tail bone). Working with the sit bones is functional for various reasons: The sit bones are the lowest part of the pelvis and there are two of them, implying dancers can move them away from each other, which helps to widen the pelvis. This designation already includes possibilities for movement, directing, and counter–directing. Furthermore, the hamstrings, which are attached to the sit bones, can support and initiate many leg movements—be it jumping or rotation. Knowing where the sit bones are—"Lower than you think they are," as Anouk van Dijk says with a smile—is a good start for finding a more efficient use of the hamstrings.

A dancer needs anatomical knowledge to understand one of the basic ways of directing and counter–directing, which Countertechnique terms *distance*. Distances always refer to the ends of two chosen body parts that move away from each other. There are longer or shorter distances in the body, for example the distance between the head and the sit bones (long), or the distance between the pubic bone and sit bones (short).

To move, dancers need to engage joints, bones, and muscles alike. As Nina Wollny puts it: "The movement happens between the two bones that together form a joint. The muscles make movement happen." Therefore, when seen from inside the joint, two bones are moving away from each other. Here, another technical term comes into play: *point of view (POV)*. In order to create more space in the joint (which enables more movement), dancers can temporarily adopt a joint's point of view. The point of view will determine in which direction the bones will be sent. Bones attached to the chosen POV joint always move away from the joint (i.e., away from each other). So, envision stretching up from the lowest moment in a first position plié: seen from the hip joints' POV, the pelvis moves upward, and the femurs move downward. From knee joints' POV, however, the lower legs move downward and the femurs are moving upward. Hence, the direction in which a bone is seen to be moving is always relative to the joint's POV. When solving a technical problem, shifting the attention to a different POV can be very helpful; often even a slight change of direction in the body can mean better alignment.

difference between heavy and light legs in dancing. This is an analytical way of thinking through movement, breaking it down into individual components. Every movement or impulse in the body has consequences, i.e., if you do this, that will follow.

Since Countertechnique aims at utilizing the body's movement potential to its fullest—and Countertechnique wants the dancer to be able to move in a big way—the use of muscles is indispensable. This, however, does not mean that dancers should use too much strength or that

Understanding that all body parts are active most of the time, and that two things always move away from each other, means there is a specific way of coordinating the direction and its counter–direction to achieve and access a dynamic balance. Anouk van Dijk calls it *sequential thinking*, meaning the counter–direction is engaged slightly prior to the obvious direction. The counter–direction is always the less manifest direction of the two. The logic behind sequential thinking is to achieve a connectedness in moving. Since gravity tends to pull the entire body down and thus limits the creation of space and mobility inside the body, sequential thinking helps the dancer trick gravity. Stretching up from a plié works better when the head moves upward *first*, granting space for the legs to unfold downward. Instead of thinking that the legs initiate the stretching action out of plié, one must first indicate an upward direction for the head. Or, in a different situation, this can be reversed. For example: if the upper body rolls upward (returning to upright) from a curved position during the plié at the same time the legs are stretching upward, then the legs should lengthen downward slightly prior to the upper body rolling up—thus providing stability, especially when the legs are rotated outward. Although hardly visible to the eye, sequential thinking can make the

a high tonus is desirable. The muscle tonus in a dancer's body should be efficient rather than high. As opposed to certain Release Techniques, students should not dispense with employing muscular strength, but rather learn how to employ it effectively.

Apart from general awareness exercises, students in Van Dijk's Practical Tools Workshop place much attention on reducing unnecessary tension. Reducing unnecessary tension is a prerequisite for directing and counter–directing because it takes pressure off the body parts thus freeing them to work in space. Anouk van Dijk has developed a set of what she calls *physical parameters* that promote kinetic understanding about how Countertechnique works. One of them is called *popping*. Popping is a fast way to describe the process of reducing unnecessary tension in the jaw and hip, shoulder, and ankle joints. So, every once and again in class, before doing a movement combination, students are asked to *pop*, i.e., release tension and to take pressure off major joints. This prepares students for dancing because it makes the actual weight of the body parts available without forcing the student to expend energy. Given the need for muscular strength in Countertechnique, it is important to remind students that muscle activity should not close off the joints and thus block movement.

As has been pointed out in the chapter Concept and Ideology, Countertechnique's understanding of the body is one without a fixed and localized center. The notion of center is replaced by a dynamic balance of directions and counter–directions, and is continually shifting. To create an alternative stability, the idea of directions in space, distances in the body, point of views (POV), and sequential thinking are used. Moving bones, therefore, is always relative to the perspective that is being used when directing and counter-directing. Strictly speaking, there is no center.

To move means having the weight of the body at one's disposal. If movement is triggered by a particular body part, this can lead to falling horizontally through space, which, as has been pointed out, is one of the main principles in Countertechnique. It appears as if dancers using Countertechnique are frequently off–center, but what is called off–center in other techniques is, in Countertechnique, only a moment of moving through space to get somewhere else. So falling horizontally is not considered to be moving off–balance, rather it strives towards a different notion of balance that is not dependent upon an upright body.

To consider horizontal falling as one of the basic activities while dancing automatically implies that gravity and the weight of the individual body parts are being acknowledged in every movement. When the body is directed downward, gravity augments the direction the body is taking. But with Countertechnique there is never one single direction of movement. If a body part is going downward with gravity, the dancer sends the weight of another body part upward and away from the floor. In this way, the body is held in limbo between two directions. In order to establish the *dynamic balance* that is characteristic of Countertechnique, the weight of the body is always being shared by various limbs and thereby directed outward into space. One might say that when weight is sent off into space, the burden of the full weight on the dancer's spine is relieved. To distribute weight in space, the dancer has to send energy away from his or her body in two directions; this minimizes the amount of effort and blocking in the joints. To begin, there are the basic directions up and down, side and side, front and back that can be further elaborated upon by adding different diagonals, circular, and other spatial trajectories. When various possibilities are combined, movements will become multidirectional. In class, Anouk van Dijk reminds students that when sending energy they should remember the periphery of their bodies. Energy going through the body has to be sent all the way out through the fingertips, top of the head, or toes to prevent it from being held inside the body. By increasing or decreasing the amount of energy, the dancer can maintain balance. Sending more energy in one direction implies moving in that direction.

The principle of sending weight off into space becomes important in the partnering workshops. Students who grip muscles and keep the energy inside the body become heavy for a partner to lift or move. Students who send their energy outward become lighter and therefore increase their possibilities for moving or being lifted; they share the weight with the space around them.

In general, a weight shift might initiate a movement. More specifically, shifting weight is crucial for directing and counter–directing. The weight of the head and the trunk—the trunk being the part of the body from the sit bones up to the neck—must be directed away from the energy direction used by the legs. Weight should be sent into opposite directions in space. If the trunk and the legs move away from each other, more space is created in the hip joints, enabling the dancer more freedom in a leg movement. Dancers who don't acknowledge the weight shift of the head and trunk in space, and who then try to achieve full range in leg movements, will have to use excessive energy because they have decreased the availability of the hip joint. Their lower backs will press down on the legs, thereby restricting the movement radius.

Space is a crucial component of Countertechnique. Space is an active partner for the dancer, supporting him or her. The space inside and the space outside the body are interconnected and are constantly engaged in a dialogue. The dancer directs energy into the space surrounding him or her in order to create more space inside the body. Vice versa, the more space the dancer creates inside the body, the more the dancer can direct movement into the space outside.

This concept of space has many implications physically and mentally, and also on a practical level. In order to explore the practical possibilities and give students an idea of how they can use space, Anouk van Dijk takes recourse to improvisation techniques developed by Forsythe in the early 1980s. This analytical introduction to spatial orientation is a practical tool; it provides an overview of the many possibilities that directing and counter–directing offers a dancer. In exercises from Van Dijk's Practical Tools Workshop, students are asked to begin standing, imagining a plane with Laban's nine points in front of them—three high in front of them, three on the middle level, and three on the floor. They may send any body part to any of the nine points. Gradually the exercise becomes more complicated as planes and levels are added until, ultimately, students have all twenty-seven points at their disposal. The exercise increases spatial awareness and three–dimensional thinking because the entire space is being used. Not only do students project to the front, they also experience their bodies as a volume connected to space. Making use of Laban's cube for directing and counter–directing implies that various spatial levels are always available, either at the same time or in sequence. If a dancer engages in a falling movement, for instance, he or she will neither fall straight down nor stop at the floor. They will either continue to move horizontally along the floor or pass through the floor to return to a higher level. This means the dancer actively passes through all spatial levels while falling. Developing awareness of all spatial possibilities will support the student later on in the Countertechnique class.

Directing and counter–directing should be an unforced activity. Students should not direct a body part by exerting tension and thereby forcing it in a direction. As everything is interconnected, this would only create tension. Popping can help reduce unnecessary tension and enable the weight of a specific body part to become available. A crucial concept in Countertechnique is that the thought of a direction will help to consciously direct a part of the body. This 'thought' anticipates the actual movement; the mental process will influence how the body is used. When teaching, Anouk van Dijk always gives clear tasks so students are busy with what is happening in the here–and–now. This prevents their thoughts from jumping ahead and anticipating a physical result or an imagined shape, so the mind is preoccupied with the task at hand. Leaving no room for expectations about the physical outcome, concentrating on the task and initiating the movements necessary to master it can influence the body in a practical and down–to–earth way. The pressure of expectations is reduced and the dancer can act in the moment, to what happens right here, right now.

Breath is unimportant in this context. Countertechnique only works on the breath when dancers breathe irregularly and thus generate unnecessary tension. On the other hand, using Countertechnique will help dancers to develop a regular breathing pattern. Popping can have a positive effect on the use of breath too. Reduced tension in the muscles and around the joints also affects the lungs in that breathing becomes easier. Instead of initiating movement with the breath, the breath will follow the movement, supporting and responding to the coordination of the body. There is literally more space to breathe, allowing the breath to follow a natural rhythm, again promoting movement efficiency.

The more dancers are trained to work with their minds, the easier it is for them to be attentive to the outer rhythm, i.e., situations that include other dancers, the teacher, and/or the music. They learn to consciously shift their attention. Anouk van Dijk claims that dancers trained in Countertechnique find it easier to stay connected with their environment. They should be able to communicate with each other on several levels at the same time, aware of each other's proximity, weight changes, rhythm, and sounds while constantly referring back to their own physical state—attuned to what the body and mind need in a specific context. This double presence, as described above, is put into practice all the time and creates the freedom to focus on the creative process or performing. As one of Anouk van Dijk's dancers, Angie Müller, says, "Countertechnique helps me to access my instincts on stage."

Countertechnique makes use of the following movement principle: There is a counter–direction to every movement. If one body part is sent in one direction, then a different body part will be directed in the opposite direction. The counter–direction is the less obvious of the two. To understand the implications of this, it will help to return to the toolbox introduced in Historical Context chapter (Individual Approach), which contains answers to the following three questions: 1) Why do I use (counter) directing? 2) What are the possibilities of (counter)directing? 3) How do I (counter)direct effectively?

why > Counter–directing is an alternative to gripping, i.e., an alternative to creating stability by using over–tensed muscles. Over–tensing muscles to create stability, especially once the weight of a body part is outside the central body axis, tends to block movement and results in dancers using excessive force to continue moving. By working without a fixed center, one can establish a shifting, dynamic balance found in a continuously counter–directed movement. Directing and counter–directing implies a conscious distribution of weight in space, even on a microscopic level. The space outside the body is always connected to the space inside the body. Directing body parts in space means sending energy into a designated direction. The overall motivation for doing this is to open the dancer to the widest spectrum of movement possibilities, enabling a greater availability to movement.

what > The scope of directing and counter–directing covers a spectrum that includes understanding basic spatial directions into which dancers may send their energy, to increasing the distance between different parts in the body, to directing and counter–directing the bones away from the joints (POV). Sequential thinking supports refined movement coordination by counter–directing slightly before directing, and thus helps to trick gravity.

how > To put the potential for counter–directing in relation to space into practice, dancers must understand basic anatomy. Mental parameters such as 'fuck it' or 'working against false assumptions' (i.e., working against what dancers might believe to be their own physical limitations) will help them to become more effective and make optimal use of directing and counter–directing. Physical parameters such as reducing unnecessary tension, popping, or falling horizontally help students to direct and counter–direct effectively. All physical and mental parameters are also considered movement principles.

scanning > The 'why, what, and how' only become functional when scanning is applied. By choosing where to focus attention and how to solve problems, dancers and students become proactive and nurture their own development both mentally and physically.

Strictly speaking, there are no basic movement forms or elements in Countertechnique. Since Countertechnique is not about learning steps or shapes for choreographic use,

The Countertechnique Toolbox

availability to movement

why >
basic principles of (counter)directing

(counter)directing instead of gripping

dynamic balance

widening

what >
directions and
counter–directions

lengthening

(pre-)popping

how >
physical parameters

sequential thinking

distance

acknowledgment of weight

POV

horizontal falling

**scanning
(you)**

seeing

how > double presence

mental parameters

space analysis

how >
body in space

false assumptions   fuck it!

smile

inter-connectedness

spatial trajectories

bones

how >

joints   basic facts of anatomy

muscles

helpful assumptions

exercises and movement combinations are vehicles used to train the mind and body in order to prepare for rehearsal and/or performance.

A class can theoretically be based upon any movement style as long as the aim is to prepare the body and increase its use to maximum potential. Anouk van Dijk, however, has developed specific exercises over the last twenty years in which the principles can be physically practiced and experienced directly and immediately. Many short exercises warm up and coordinate the rotation of the legs at the beginning of class, even before standing in first position. Another distinct characteristic is a preference for movements that require constant shifts of weight and falling in space. With these movements sending energy, directing and counter–directing can be felt most intensely. Falling horizontally and catching the weight propels the body for-

ward, creating a pulling quality and allowing the body to change directions at all times. Actively rotating the legs in- or outwards, increases the spontaneity of direction changes. In Countertechnique, a lengthier and more expansive movement combination in the second part of the class involves enchaining movements of individual body parts. The body is never moved as a whole, but part–by–part. Dancers coordinate the movements of body parts in sequence. If a dancer, for instance, wants to do a backward turn, he or she would move the hip first, thus triggering the movement. Only then would he or she send the leg and then the trunk in the same direction while counter–directing the movement in the other direction with, for instance, the shoulder.

In the next chapter, the three sections of a class will be elaborated upon.

Gerald Siegmund, Anouk van Dijk

TEACHING: PRINCIPLES AND METHODOLOGY

CONCEPTUAL BASIS

Countertechnique is taught to help dancers' bodies become stronger and freer, and to enable more risk–taking while dancing. At the same time, Countertechnique enables dancers to use their bodies more safely by engaging the mind. Students are trained to become aware of what is happening technically inside their dancing bodies. Simultaneously they engage with the space surrounding them, refining awareness of how their dancing relates to and influences the environment—whether it be the studio, stage, or in everyday life. Once consciously engaged with their surroundings, a student's physical state and way of moving will change in turn.

Countertechnique has been developed by Anouk van Dijk for professional dancers who are trained in contemporary techniques and/or ballet, for members of her company, and for dancers all over the world. The technique was developed to serve professionals who need a balanced muscular training, and who need to release tension in order to prevent injuries in training, creating, rehearsing, performing, and touring. "The aim," as Anouk van Dijk says, "is to become an open vessel when you are performing on stage."

In 2009, Codarts in Rotterdam put Countertechnique into the curriculum for a four–year test phase, so students of all levels now have classes. What students need to understand, above all, is the difference between mimetic function as in traditional dance classes (wherein their images are corrected with help of a mirror) and applying a principle. In Countertechnique, students are not expected to simply repeat what they are being told by teachers, instead they should actively engage with Countertechnique information and integrate it into their own practice. Countertechnique only begins to work when the dancer is dialoguing between body and mind. Since it is not a style but a system of movement theory, the information should help a student in ballet classes as well as in modern or contemporary classes.

Countertechnique classes are group classes. Personal needs, however, will be incorporated into the group work by providing various intellectual or physical exercises that can cater to the needs of a particular student.

The underlying principles of Countertechnique can be understood quickly. The timeframe, however, needed until professional dancers can successfully apply these principles is considerably longer. Dancers of Anouk van Dijk's company speak of three years needed to incorporate the principles and employ them naturally.

Dancers who study Countertechnique need not have learned a specific technique or have taken a specific type of class prior. Certain basic skills that are common to most dancers, however, can be helpful in the learning process. Students should have analytical skills for studying the organization of the body. They need a good sense of coordination and a certain amount of strength and flexibility. Experience in Alexander Technique is helpful in understanding the influence the mind has on the body and, more specifically, for grasping the principle of directing. On a more practical level, Anouk van Dijk answers the question about the conceptual basis for teaching by saying: "Wanting to figure out what makes your life as a dancer easier is helpful as well!"

Since Countertechnique implies mental work and is process–oriented, results are highly individual. First–year students at Codarts, with no previous experience in Countertechnique, were not taught a regular Countertechnique class. Instead Anouk van Dijk and her artistic assistant, Nina Wollny, gave a Practical Tools Workshop. This workshop was held for two weeks, five days a week, three hours a day, and aimed at introducing the students to the basic Countertechnique principles.[6] In the various phases of the awareness exercise[7] no corrections were given; instead, suggestions were made. "Look around," or, "Try not to search for what you see but simply register it." After the exercise, the purpose was explained to the students: "It helps you to open your mind for one particular piece of information at a time. It also helps you to consciously shift your attention to another piece of information." Feeling the floor underneath the feet, walking, and running–through–space exercises were followed by lying on the floor and trying so send body parts into space using the Nine Point Technique. After having engaged the students physically, Anouk van Dijk continued to talk to them about specific anatomical features. "Where is the shoulder girdle attached to the skeleton?" Answer: "Only at the sternum, which means that the shoulder blades can move over the rib cage and are not attached to it." Knowing how this functions changes the use of the arms and shoulders. Only towards the end of the workshop did Van Dijk and Wollny engage students in small move-

---

6 See chapter "Context and Ideology", "Intent".
7 See Extra Material on DVD 2.

ment combinations to integrate awareness, spatial direction, focus, and anatomical knowledge. After a week of the workshop, the first results were visible. Combinations were executed with more lightness and less forcefulness. Movements looked bigger and freer.

As has been pointed out in regards to the concept of scanning, students are encouraged to take ownership when training their bodies. Countertechnique's approach to the work aims at students eventually teaching themselves. When dancers take responsibility for their own training, the daily ritual can become a research area for enhancing one's own mental and physical abilities. Eventually assuming the role of self–training will change the relationship between the dancer and others.

Because Countertechnique is about applying principles rather than imitating forms, it should be emphasized that the training method is entirely process–oriented. A class is not aimed at teaching choreographic skills nor does it encourage generation of choreographic material. At the same time, however, students learn that they can employ the principles creatively, using them improvisationally or in stricter choreographic strategies as well. Not focusing on an end–result has many implications. In the Countertechnique class at Codarts, the second–year students are kept moving almost constantly. Tasks are given so they can experiment with various approaches and test information for themselves. They must draw conclusions about what works for them. In order to help them apply what has been learned, Anouk van Dijk will remind students of a particular piece of useful information given in one exercise and then refer to it in a later exercise in the same class. Instead of repeating the exercise, the same information is transferred to another exercise. Students learn that the underlying principles can be applied to other exercises and eventually to other technique classes as well.

Not being product–oriented also means changing the nature of the information given to students. Instead of correcting physical behavior, Anouk recommends that Countertechnique teachers look for the causes behind harmful habits. Referring to the Practical Tools Workshop mentioned above, the example about the relation between the shoulders and the ribs is telling. Think of a student who sticks out his or her ribs: this blocks arm and shoulder movements, requiring more energy and strength than necessary. Instead of telling the student to hold the rib cage in, which means the student should comply to a certain 'correct' image, the question for the teacher is: Why is he or she doing this? Presumably the student sticks the ribs out to widen the rib cage. The next step would be to offer an alternative approach. One solution the teacher might offer is to inform the student that widening can be achieved more effectively by acknowledging the three–dimensional volume of the rib cage, by allowing the back side of the rib cage to open and widen. Allowing the shoulder blades

to slide over the rib cage and to the side will also provide space for the ribs on the back to move and expand. This piece of anatomical information can change the way a student will realize the widening of the rib cage, eliminating blocking or preventing injury.

Since teachers educated by Anouk van Dijk also use the toolbox, they have many ways to answer students' questions. If, for example, the widening–the–back solution from above did not help the student, the teacher will likely open another 'drawer' in the toolbox and work further away from the problem area; this could be literally inside the body, a more mental approach, or a complete change of perspective to distract the student from his or her preoccupation and worry. As Anouk van Dijk says: "The solution often lies far away from the problem area." After class students often approach Anouk van Dijk with their problems, asking her for advice to alleviate pain. Her advice is usually a suggestion on how to change the way they approach to certain movements.

PEDAGOGICAL METHODS

A teacher structures a class in accordance with the strengths and knowledge available in any given group, and material is added in accordance with the group's progress in grasping both the physical work and the conceptual basis.

A class consists of three parts. After several years of working on class structure, the class (as it is taught today) begins standing center floor. (Anouk calls this a 'standing up class', i.e., in contrast to many contemporary techniques that start on the floor.) Also no barre is used. From the beginning, dancers must find support in a dynamic balance between directing and counter–directing while moving freely through the room. From the first exercise, Countertechnique works on directions in space. By starting class standing center floor rather than lying down or at the barre, dancers' senses are aroused in a proactive way, making them more aware of the space around them. "See what is really there, really see it," as Anouk van Dijk says. Or, as she says at the beginning of class, "Look at the city," thus asking students, for a moment, to simply and directly acknowledge what is outside the window.

The Countertechnique class has a fixed order of exercises, which Anouk van Dijk calls the *skeleton*. In the first section, all exercises are the same and are presented in (almost always) the same order. Not all exercises are used in every class, however, as there are too many and time does not allow. A selection is made based upon the students' level, and to support the build–up of a specific class. While exercises may vary in the rest of class, the first part each day is similar and lasts about thirty minutes. These exercises and combinations should become routine so students can focus on details involved in finding alignment and energy flow. Once dancers know these exercises, they can use them whenever needed. Anouk van Dijk finds this self–supporting aspect of Countertechnique to be crucial.

The three–part structure of the class, which lasts for at least ninety minutes, is as follows. Although it is a standing up class, all spatial levels are addressed while traveling through space:

→ **Part I** The first half hour of a Countertechnique class consists of slow and fluid movements. The last exercise in this section is called the *walks*; it emphasizes upright traveling and involves a continuous transfer of weight through space. Thus the walks are a transitional exercise: simple in form, preparing the body and mind for the next level.

→ **Part II** This section begins with *Big Shifts/Temps lié* or *Pre-falling*. The second half–hour consists of, again, familiar exercises. However, small variations are introduced in order to either wake up short–term memory, to dose complexity depending on the dancers' level, or to prepare technical difficulties for the last part of the class. Pre-falling is also a transition exercise; it introduces falling horizontally through space while distributing the weight of various body parts in opposing directions. The energy of the falling momentum is suspended over several steps and is finally stopped by taking one big step, either stepping up and over, or down and under. This coordination enables the dancer to 'over–shoot' his or her falling momentum and bring the body into balance without using the extra strength that normally would be needed. Becoming smart in falling and traveling will make dancing less exhausting; it will appear more dynamic even though dancers are using less effort.

Towards the end of Part II, in the *Fall Allongés*, different elements are combined for the first time: horizontal falling and transferring of weight while traveling through space is now combined with rotation of the legs and with independent head and upper body movements. Either the feet or the head can lead a body shift into space. The second part of the class finishes with battements.

→ **Part III** The last part of the class goes to the full extremes in movement; all skills must be put into practice. Starting with the *Big Move Combo*, the exercises now travel through the entire space. In the Big Move Combo, the emphasis is on the flow initiated from the feet, from the body weight, or body parts. It uses turns, balances, unexpected direction changes and combined upper/lower bodywork. In the previous sections, separate movement elements have been prepared—an intricate shift of weight, upper body and arms coordination, etc.—and in the Big Move Combo these elements are brought together. Now an intricate

weight shift includes an upper body movement as well, and a turn or sudden level change. The Big Move Combo is the most challenging exercise in the class, and will be worked on for two to three classes in a row. When parts of the exercise are mastered, they are then replaced by new elements. Over the course of a week, the Big Move Combination might change completely. Part III also includes jumps to strengthen the hamstrings and, for example, at the end, the *duckies* can be added—an exercise that strengthens the muscles around the knees and the sides of the back. Either that, or other repetitive strengthening or stretching exercises, are used according to the dancers' needs. For a detailed plan of a lesson, please refer to the example provided on the DVD 1.

The training method depends on the type of Countertechnique class being taught. There are five types of classes, each one aimed at honing different skills:

→ The *flow class* is a basic Countertechnique class in which the dancer is introduced to the distribution of weight in space by emphasizing fluid upper body and horizontal falling exercises. In the flow class, the dancer can experience the intricacies of counter–directing more immediately than while standing center floor.

→ A *pump class* expands on the basic flow class by adding strengthening exercises that focus on muscular quality in the movement. Repetition is used to build strength.

→ Similarly, the *stamina class* uses repetition to increase stamina. The stamina class uses less strengthening and more jumping exercises than a pump class.

→ In a *stretch class*, the emphasis is on various means of stretching and the pace of the class is slower than that of a pump class. In order to have students stretch correctly, specific explanation is given and the exercises are interrupted by talking. Stretching is therefore taught in intervals.

→ Finally, in the *translation class* there is a lot of talking. It aims to illuminate the Countertechnique principles in relation to classes or techniques taught by other teachers, and to provide students with alternative explanations for corrections they are given in other classes. The aim is also to help deepen students' understanding—not to bombard them with more information.

Every Countertechnique technique class starts with physical work. The movement phrases are learned via imitation in order to teach skeletal anatomy or a progression of exercises. How Countertechnique actually functions should be deduced by students' experiences, using trial and error, throughout the various exercises. At the beginning, no analytical information is given. More underlying information is provided, gradually, as exercises are repeated every day. Too much analysis in early on has proven to be ineffective. It is important that students don't loose their joy of movement and the excitement of taking risks—even if they don't fully understand the coordination. Gradually, suggestions are made to alter movement patterns. Verbal reflection is offered after the student has physically and pragmatically engaged with the material.

As opposed to the Practical Tools Workshops, a Countertechnique class uses very little improvisation. Countertechnique also offers partnering workshops and compositional classes with a concentration on artistic process. Thus the learning path progresses from simple to difficult, from individual body parts to the entire body, on to the body doing different things at the same time using space multidirectionally. This may eventually generate movement that can be used for choreographic purposes.

Since Countertechnique also has a purely theoretical component, teachers must have a grasp on group dynamics and foster a positive atmosphere so students are able to become their own 'research object'. Teachers who are able to create a class that is 'cool' and who give people a good feeling will help students to let go of fear. This implies that teachers must pay special attention as to how they address students and to the way they phrase observations and corrections. It is important to be supportive, not to sound dogmatic. To help students, teachers need listening skills to fully comprehend students' questions and problems. Those who want to become certified teachers must have physically and mentally mastered Countertechnique.

Rhythm is used to support motor skills acquisition. A typical Countertechnique class, however, begins without music or counting. Only after a while will music or counting be incorporated to support increasingly complex movement patterns. Whether working with a percussionist or using contemporary pop or rap music, the rhythm is changed regularly to keep students attentive. Counting more quickly, more slowly, or changing the meter will alter the dynamics and the speed of muscular reaction in the body. Too complex and irregular rhythms are not used lest they distract students from active scanning. Both in the Practical Tools Workshop for beginners and in the partnering workshop there may be music, but counting is kept simple.

A Countertechnique class does not teach or engage with artistic process. Studying Anouk van Dijk's choreographic material, however, can be advantageous to creative work since the movements entail more extreme changes of directions and specific coordination than might be found in a regular class. For that reason, Van Dijk's repertory is taught to upper level students in Rotterdam; learning choreography demands applying the principles—or the movement coordination simply will not work. This experience can help students when applying the principles to basic movements in class. As a dancer once said, "In Anouk's choreographies I cannot cheat."

In preparation for teaching, the teacher must decide what type of class he or she wants to teach. Preparation requires an appropriate choice of exercises, and the teacher must also develop a skeleton (a framework of exercises). If a teacher, for example, wants to give a pump class, he or she puts together a series of existing exercises that focus on the strength of the back and legs, or might develop new exercises. These exercises, both slow and fast, will include strength training for the hamstrings and strengthening the sides of the back as well as equal distribution of stress throughout the body. The class takes place mostly standing in the first part, and becomes faster in changing levels and directions in the second and third parts. Movement phrases build up systematically; they are graded according to complexity.

A teacher must also decide which key elements are going to be introduced; it is impossible to work on all the Countertechnique principles within the time frame of a single class. Therefore, in the first slow section of class, one or two key elements will be introduced, which might, for example, be a mental tool, a particular distance, or a way of sequential thinking. A key element is one that determines how a movement is actually performed. The teacher then selects a few supporting key elements that feed into the main key element; all the principles in Countertechnique complement and support each other.

In the class featured on the DVD in this book, the first two key elements introduced are widening and lengthening (in reference to distances). Pre-popping is introduced as the next key element. Then, widening, lengthening, and pre-popping are combined and spatial trajectories are added. In combination, they influence how movements are executed. The students are reminded of these key elements during the remainder of class. There are many ways these key elements can relate to the movement phrases: one could, for instance, keep the key elements widening, lengthening, and pre-popping, but change the movement phrase to which they are applied.

Using the key elements as a guide in how to work movement phrases, each class is constructed around a theme that determines the movement quality. In a flow or stamina class, a teacher might decide to work on head rolls while changing directions, for example. The pace and number of exercises are dependent upon the type of class being taught, but the theme of the movement phrases can remain the same. Important, in this context, is the notion of variation. Sticking either to a type of class, a key element, or a theme while altering the parameters of any given aspect means that it can be approached from various angles. Countertechnique is a modular system and can be adapted to the specific needs of the dancers.

Although a Countertechnique class follows a 'no non-sense get up and do it' approach, the teacher is careful in vocabulary choices, avoiding terminology that can be misunderstood. Giving feedback while working on an exercise is an integral part of the class. Often Anouk van Dijk asks the students: "How did it work for you?" "Was there a difference?" "Why do you think we do this exercise?"—thus encouraging students to verbalize experiences and problems. Students often have false assumptions about their bodies and their physical capabilities; they might think of themselves as, for example, having no turn-out or no plié. What they think they can or cannot do often is the result of their interpretation of information given by teachers. Misunderstandings arise in the chain of acquiring information, interpreting information, and applying it; false assumptions will eventually have to be addressed so students can develop and explore their true potential. A student might think he cannot move his head because he has a tight neck, but after learning where the head/neck joint is located, the weight of the skull becomes available for movement. With the use of the direction and its counter-direction (which distributes the weight in space), the student is able to move his head more freely. On one hand, feedback may happen after any kind of exercise, as in the above example. On the other hand, students often approach Anouk van Dijk after class to ask questions about a particular exercise and how they should approach it.

Given the need to verbalize experiences, the teacher's role in communicating ideas, principles, and content is essential. Since Countertechnique also has a theoretical component, in-depth explanations about the principles will come at some point in class. Verbal explanation is needed for the students to understand the difference between a more conventional way of doing an exercise and doing it according to the principles of directing and counter-directing.

Countertechnique concepts are implied in the choice of words that teachers like Anouk van Dijk and her colleague Nina Wollny make. Instead of using the verbs 'to focus' or 'to concentrate', which imply the notion of a center, they choose phrases like 'put your attention to', or 'allow yourself to'. These phrases imply an engagement without expectation. Similarly, saying 'suspend' rather then 'reach' helps students think in spatial directions rather than in terms of muscular tension. Language triggers physical action—much more so than students are aware of—which is why Anouk van Dijk and Nina Wollny ask students to verbalize experiences. Van Dijk and Wollney assist the student in finding the proper terminology so both the verbal and physical experiences develop side-by-side. The teacher's role is to share information so as to improve students' movement skills both on a physical and mental level. He or she is there to guide, offering suggestions instead of corrections.

At first, a teacher concentrates on teaching steps and basic elements that make up the skeleton of the class. This is one of the reasons why, at first sight, Countertechnique classes exude a formal and even strict atmosphere. But, as Anouk van Dijk explains, she personally tries to establish an objective foundation for working with students so as to distract them from personal obsessions, prejudices, and fears. Clear and objective information added to the skeleton of the class provides students with a neutral grid upon which they can experiment and learn how to approach their work differently.

In Countertechnique classes, no imagery or metaphors are used to stimulate the imagination. What students have to visualize, above all, are anatomical relations between various bones and spatial directions. Using imagery in the physical learning process would stipulate specific content and thus encourage a way of thinking that favors a result—an image is quickly perceived to something that should be achieved—and would be a diversion from process-related thinking. The teacher does not use personal metaphors to share information either, since personal metaphors are likely to cause misunderstandings with students from different cultural backgrounds.

Countertechnique classes are not 'hands-on' classes. Information is communicated by verbalization and physically demonstrating when the body is directed and when not. Touching students may, however, occur when discussing anatomical detail. Anouk van Dijk uses her hands to encourage students to feel the results of directing and counter-directing. Once a student has felt the difference, applying the principles will be easier. This only happens once the student is familiar with the exercises, however, not before.

In summary, one can say that in a Countertechnique class, movement acquisition happens in two phases. First dancers learn exercises by copying them, which creates a class structure. The teacher demonstrates the exercises full-out with all the directions, length, ease, and risk. At the beginning, demonstrating how Countertechnique functions will convey more to dancers than a lot of words. Before dancers can have an idea about the principles, teacher demonstrations provide inspiration. Once familiar with the exercises, the real work begins. In the second phase, information from the Countertechnique toolbox is gradually introduced. Anouk van Dijk, as well as her colleague, Nina Wollny, guide the students through both theoretical insights as well as through the practical experience. The intention is to introduce theory in an informal and playful way, step-by-step. After all, it should not be forgotten that the main goal of Countertechnique is to keep—and often retrieve—the joy of dancing by absorbing new and often complex insights into how the body works. In this way, joy and interest in exploring can continue to grow throughout a dancer's career.

Gerald Siegmund, Anouk van Dijk

CONCLUSION

With her down–to–earth, common sense approach, Anouk van Dijk says, "It is only dancing, not world politics." This does not imply, of course, that she doesn't take her work seriously. What's at stake, in the on–going development of her work, is to take pressure off both the moving body and the mind so dancers remain open for movement and continue to enjoy dancing. Countertechnique intends to make a dancer's life, and that of students wanting to become professional dancers, easier. She hopes that both her research into the efficient functioning of movement and the system she has been developing since 2002 will help future generations of dancers to enjoy a long and healthy career.

LINK

For further information about Anouk van Dijk, her company, and Countertechnique see: **www.anoukvandijk.nl**

BARBARA PASSOW
JOOSS–LEEDER
TECHNIQUE

LABAN
LONDON

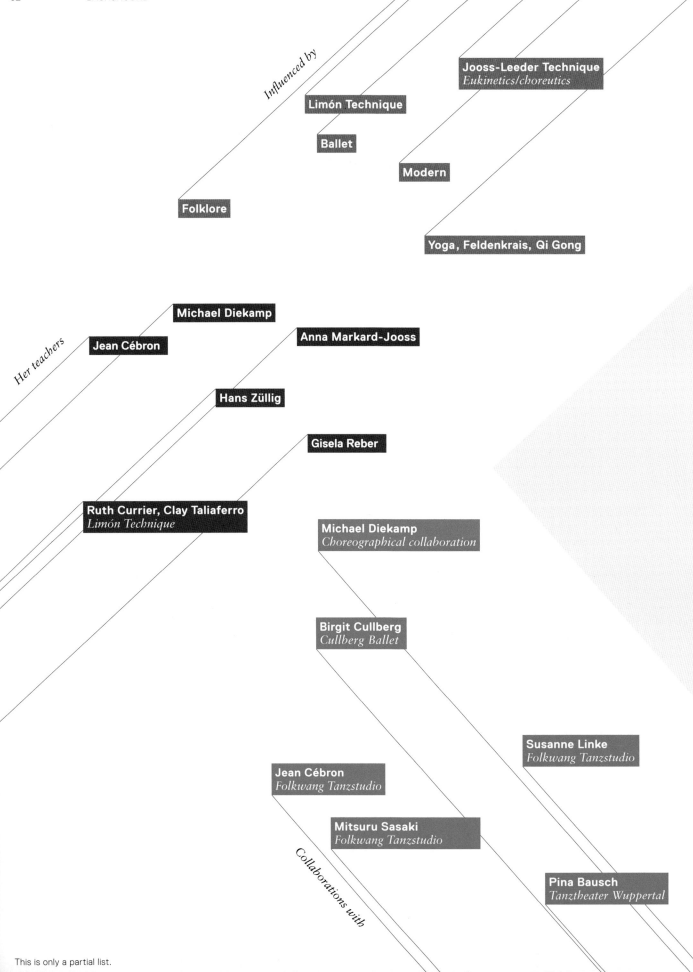

Influenced by

Jooss-Leeder Technique
Eukinetics/choreutics

Limón Technique

Ballet

Modern

Folklore

Yoga, Feldenkrais, Qi Gong

Her teachers

Michael Diekamp

Anna Markard-Jooss

Jean Cébron

Hans Züllig

Gisela Reber

Ruth Currier, Clay Taliaferro
Limón Technique

Michael Diekamp
Choreographical collaboration

Birgit Cullberg
Cullberg Ballet

Susanne Linke
Folkwang Tanzstudio

Jean Cébron
Folkwang Tanzstudio

Mitsuru Sasaki
Folkwang Tanzstudio

Collaborations with

Pina Bausch
Tanztheater Wuppertal

This is only a partial list.

BARBARA PASSOW —

JOOSS-LEEDER TECHNIQUE

Research team at LABAN, London: Barbara Passow,
Dr. Claudia Fleischle–Braun, Wiebke Dröge, Dr. Patricia Stöckemann,
Reinhild Hoffmann, Anna Markard

AUTHORS
Wiebke Dröge, Claudia Fleischle–Braun, Patricia Stöckemann

INTERVIEW
Edith Boxberger

STUDENTS
of the dance theater bachelor's degree program (second–year): Yolanda Aladeshelu, Sarah Armstrong,
Anna Bergstrom, Fabian Brandt, Typhaine Delaup, Charlie Dixon, Rachel Graham, Karin Floengard Jonsson,
Samuel Jordan, Sara Kemal, Leonie Nadler, Aimee Parsons, Eleonora Pennacchini, Marcella Piscitelli,
Artemise Ploegaerts, Caroline Roussy, and Elisabeth Schilling

BARBARA PASSOW (*1949)
trained under Hans Züllig as a dancer at the Folkwang University of the Arts Essen from 1968–1972, also completing a one–year dance education program specializing in dance for children and amateurs. In 1979 she was
awarded a scholarship by the state of North Rhine–Westphalia that enabled her to travel to New York for a year
where she studied Limón Technique intensively. She worked as a dancer at the Cullberg Ballet under Birgit Cullberg
in Stockholm from 1972–1984, at the Tanztheater Wuppertal under Pina Bausch, and at the Folkwang Tanz
Studio under Susanne Linke. Since 1986 she has taught modern dance at various universities and dance companies
(Bremen Theater, among others) and workshops for professional and non-professional dancers, as well as working
as a dancer and choreographer with Michael Diekamp. Since 1995 she has taught at the Palucca Schule Dresden—
Hochschule für Tanz.

Barbara Passow Interviewed by Edith Boxberger

RESPECT AND RISK

/ **Which techniques and teachers were formative in your career?** I studied at the Folkwang University from 1968 until 1972. The main subjects were ballet, modern, and folk dance. It was important for me to have experienced folk classes at the start of my career, and important that I didn't have so much classical training, for example, because I would have been too focused on the technique. I, unfortunately, only had contact with Kurt Jooss in the entrance examination, not in classes, as he had given up teaching by then. But I studied with his daughter, Anna Markard, for two years, then with Hans Züllig, who was a lead dancer in Jooss's ballets and later a teacher at the Folkwang University. And I studied with Jean Cébron, who preserved the Jooss–Leeder method. I also experienced Jean Cébron several times when he gave classes at the Palucca Schule in Dresden as a guest teacher. This allowed me to see the Jooss–Leeder Technique with a fresh perspective, which was very impressive and enriching.

An important teacher was my later husband, Michael Diekamp, who had worked closely with Jooss. He passed his teaching exams when I was training, and he was my teacher from then on. He also taught the companies in which we danced; teaching was his thing from the start and he consistently pursued this path. We were both involved with the Cullberg Ballet in Sweden for two years from 1972 to 1974. Back then, I definitely wanted to train more and Michael Diekamp wanted to teach, so we often went into the studio and worked for a long time after rehearsals. This meant that I developed in-depth knowledge of the technique, even more than at the school, I think.

We both then worked in Wuppertal with Pina. My husband stayed for three years before he went to Stuttgart to teach at the John Cranko School. I stayed for four years and then went to the Folkwang Tanzstudio after a study trip to New York. Even during these years, there were times when we worked together. We also choreographed together later in Bremen. I did not have Kurt Jooss as a teacher myself, but my husband taught me a lot about Jooss's way of thinking.

The work with Pina was an essential influence. She had a very strong, educated sense of what was authentic and what was not. Did any of it rub off on me? I think so: the alertness for wrong tones, sensing what is harmonious and what isn't, and putting oneself completely into something. Pina was not an easy personality to work with, but I would never have wanted to miss the experience. I learned an enormous amount from her.

/ **Which techniques did you learn in America and what influenced you there?** I received a scholarship in 1979 and went to America. As I was already involved with the Folkwang Tanzstudio, I split the scholarship and went to New York twice, for about four to five months each time over the summer to concentrate on modern dance. One had to enroll in a school at that time. I was at the Graham School first, but it wasn't my thing. I looked elsewhere, and even did ballet for modern dancers, but it was the Limón Technique that really interested me. This work, and in particular how one dealt with weight, simply fascinated me. I took classes with Ruth Currier and also worked intensively with Clay Taliaferro, a former dancer with the company. Alongside the Jooss–Leeder Technique, Limón was the other technique that was important for me.

I think everything one does leaves traces. I did yoga and came into contact early on with the Feldenkrais Method—and I might have been able to get to know Moshé Feldenkrais in America as I was there at the same time, but I didn't. Body–awareness techniques were not so in fashion then as now, and rather coincidentally I came across his book *Awareness Through Movement*. What impressed me, among other things, was the fact that he let the body actually perform an exercise, yet it was only performed in the mind. I was completely fascinated by the fact that the mental exercises gave measurable results. I think that dancers have still not grasped the momentousness of this.

/ **What areas do you emphasize in your educational work?** First, it is obviously about training the body, but it is very important to me, that students start early on to dance 'beyond' the technique. Technique is only the basis, and then it starts to get interesting. I try to teach that. I work a lot with images, as it is simply easier to grasp some things via an image than through an explanation of many details. Dynamics are, for me, the primary means of expression—like the salt in the soup—as well as the spatial orientation, both of which are emphasized in the Jooss–Leeder Technique. I personally get a lot of pleasure out of rhythm complexity.

And it is also about training the mind. Nurturing dancers is a big part of it—it takes a lot to train dancers. You actually work on this from all sides, but it is not possible for a single teacher to cover all facets satisfactorily, so I often tell students to take the key points from all their teachers—the things any given teacher can really teach—collect them, and then, at some point, it will all be there.

/ **How is your work influenced by different experiences?** One teaches what one has learned in the course of one's life—one's dancing life, that is— and what one considers valuable. There have been many influences, and what was important to me has become a building block in my work. My experiences with yoga and Feldenkrais certainly flowed into my work. I often start with yoga exercises or with dynamic yoga positions in order to open up the body. The Feldenkrais Method influence references a different awareness and respect for the body. All this, along with the dance techniques I learned, are building blocks that influence my work, and upon which something new and very individual emerges.

/ **What should training not be?** I don't necessarily use ideals, but instead try to lead students to the place where they recognize their limits, respect them, and maybe push them back. I don't think one can ask any person to go further than his or her own limits. It is problematic if you hold a picture in front of a student and say, 'you must be like that,' as it is important that students have a positive image of their own bodies and don't think, 'everything about me is wrong.' Respect for the body, for what each one has been given, is important. And then work with it, see what is possible.

/ **What is the basis for your teaching the Jooss–Leeder Technique?** First, I don't teach the Jooss–Leeder Technique, but my classes are based on the principles and themes that were important in that work—for example, labile turns, tilts, pelvis circles, impulses, and step phrases. My work is a creative process in which these themes are always processed in new combinations. Then there are Jooss's two major areas, namely eukinetics and choreutics. Eukinetics queries the *how* of a movement—the dynamics—and choreutics asks *where*, namely the spatial reference. This analytical approach trains the eye enormously and opens up infinite possibilities to invent movement. I think this is what is really special about this work.

The Jooss–Leeder work was never a fixed technique, it is about awareness. I know that my husband and former Folkwang students arranged a meeting with Kurt Jooss in order to work on an inventory, a catalogue as it were; the meeting was due to take place the summer Jooss died. I don't think he wanted the meeting. When you look at Jooss's choreographies, one is immediately struck by the incredibly differentiated rhythmic structures. Musicality and rhythm are very important for me too.

The artistic aspect of the work is also important for me. In classes, I point out that the stage is the goal—it is the step beyond technique that brings one to the dance. I use a lot of images because I have myself experienced how many problems can be solved with an image. It is

important for me that one handles the body carefully, respect it, but at the same time always take risks.

/ **What forms the relationship between teacher and students, in your view?** It is wonderful if there is an open and trusting relationship between students and teacher, when one can pass on one's knowledge and experience and have it land on fertile ground. The teacher must be strict to a certain extent, draw clear limits but deal affectionately with the students. You definitely have to create a climate that is free from fear, in which it is okay to make mistakes. But there is obviously a difference if I am teaching a class of fifteen-year-old students or adult dancers. In the first case, I am more the authority figure, and intentionally so. But generally speaking, I am very close to my students.

/ **What relationship do you see between the Limón Technique and the Jooss–Leeder work?** I think, above all, it is the play between weight and the moment of weightlessness, giving into and resisting it, which is present in both styles. It is certainly more central in the Limón Technique with all these swings; swinging means giving in to gravity, falling, and getting up again, i.e., fall and recovery. I find both techniques dramatic, both want to nurture dancing people rather than dance technicians. Both techniques are influenced by great musicality and have an awareness of movement quality that I have not found in other techniques.

/ **How do you prepare your classes?** It varies a great deal. My husband went into a class with three exercises…the starting exercises. I can't do that. I prepare myself relatively well, a whole class more or less through to the end. But when I see that someone doesn't understand something at all, I go into it and, in the best case, make an exercise out of the mistake. I go with it. When you absorb the energy of a class, it often goes in a completely different direction, but I often come back to what I wanted at the beginning.

/ **Has your teaching changed over time, and how?** My teaching has become much richer over time; there are many more facets to it. I can now play with the individual elements; I have more of an overview. And if I discover something that is new to me, it will naturally be reflected in my classes.

/ **And how has class preparation changed over the years?** I no longer prepare totally different classes for different levels, (amateur work and professional work), but create a class that I can vary, make easier or more complicated. I used to develop a different class for each level, now I simply modify it, take something away or add to it. The classes develop in totally different directions over time, however.

/ **When do you consider that a movement is successful?** I think when you have grasped the essence of a movement, when you fulfill exactly what is intended with it. There is a quote from Kurt Jooss in which he talks of the rough road of the intrinsic, the essence. Students often don't go fully into a movement, but merely hint at it. Or they do something with too much energy. They should only use the amount of strength needed for a particular movement, no more, just the appropriate amount. We spoke earlier about limits that should be respected, but one has to get close to these limits in order to experience them. Sometimes you actually have to almost fall over in order to see how far you can go. I often notice that students don't go far enough, don't immerse themselves in the movements—that they don't try to fathom what is in the movements. Tasting movement…it is something very sensual to taste a movement.

/ **What do you see for the future of this technique? Where can it go, and in which contexts?** This technique is not taught in many places…by a few people at the Folkwang University, mainly Lutz Förster, who in turn has been influenced by his work with Hans Züllig. There is a school in Santiago de Chile that works with the Jooss–Leeder principles. Both the founder of that school, Patricio Bunster, as well as its current director, Raymond Hilbert, have worked at the Palucca Schule for years. Bunster taught the Jooss–Leeder principles in–depth before Michael Diekamp came to Dresden. And there are a few choreographers who are trained in this work, for example the ballet director from Wiesbaden, Stephan Thoss, who was a student of Patricio Bunster.

Simone Michelle—a former member of Ballets Jooss and assistant of Sigurd Leeder—taught the Jooss–Leeder Technique at the Laban Centre in London until 1991. Nowadays, students busy themselves with Laban Movement Analysis categories in choreological studies. Eckard and Loni Brakel run a private school in Hanover, both of them were at the Folkwang Tanzstudio and worked with Kurt Jooss for a long time. They have dealt intensively with this work and pass on their knowledge in their space. I teach mainly at the Palucca Schule, but also to amateurs, and now and again in the theater—for example, I regularly train the Bremen Theater dance company.

The great value of this work is, for me, in the awareness it creates of movement qualities as well as in spatial references, in the conscious handling of eukinetics and choreutics. I very much hope that this reference system will be important for future dance generations, maybe with a new look.

/ **How has dance technique changed in recent years?** It is becoming increasingly demanding, increasingly more virtuoso. The students' technique is always getting better. With all the emphasis on technique, the soul sometimes gets forgotten—and that is a great shame. I want to always sense the dancer as a whole person.

/ **Are there any new influences on your work?** I currently have little opportunity to absorb new influences. My husband used to teach modern dance teachers at the Palucca Schule, and this was an important source of inspiration. I have also tried taking part in the workshops or classes given by our guest teachers in order to get new stimuli and not to get too wrapped up in my own material. Alan Danielson was very important, and Risa Steinberg is a wonderful teacher—both in the Limón tradition. Sometimes it is only a gesture or a movement detail that one takes in and develops further. I would have liked to have done more Contact Improvisation and Release Technique, but it didn't happen.

/ **What would you like to pass on to the next generation?** I am very grateful to have been able to take this route, first as a dancer for a long time, and now as teacher. It is a wonderful profession, a wonderfully productive job in which one also has the chance to work on one's own personality. You discover a lot about yourself. The level of technique is very high and you need to have a good body and mind in order to be able to earn money in this profession. Knowing what I wanted from the start felt like I had been given a gift. When one has a goal, and pursues it with dedication and full concentration, really wants something, then the sacrifices don't feel like sacrifice at all—what is better than that? I think that when one can answer the question, 'why do you want to dance?' by saying that one has to, then paths will open up. The will that is necessary to follow this route appears to me to be a very important prerequi-site, alongside all the others. And one can only handle what is often very difficult work if one is passionate about what one is doing.

Wiebke Dröge, Claudia Fleischle–Braun, Patricia Stöckemann

INTRODUCTION

The research project investigating the Jooss–Leeder Technique[1] was conducted at LABAN in London, with Barbara Passow, as part of the Historical Project module. The second–year Bachelor of Arts in Dance Theater students not only were exposed to dance history, they were also able to improve their technique through intensive training in a selected modern dance style, as well as being afforded the opportunity to learn repertoire by a dance–theatre pioneer, Reinhild Hoffmann.

Seventeen students opted for the Jooss–Leeder Technique as taught by Barbara Passow. The fifteen teaching units were closely intertwined with Reinhild Hoffmann's rehearsals. Following each technique class, Hoffmann, a choreographer and opera director, rehearsed an excerpt from the opera *Dido and Aeneas* (music by Henry Purcell) that she had staged at the Bremen Theater in 1984.

LABAN was an ideal location, not only because of its educational focus on contemporary dance and its advantageous location; students from a number of countries identified strongly with the project, they were highly motivated, and showed an eagerness to work during both the training and rehearsal phases. The great teamwork and organizational preparation, as well as the project's integration into the LABAN curriculum, were factors that contributed to an intense and effective working atmosphere.[2]

In preparation for the project, a meeting was held with Barbara Passow and Anna Markard, Kurt Jooss's daughter. The London project team included Passow and Reinhild Hoffmann, as well as Wiebke Dröge, Claudia Fleischle–Braun, and Patricia Stöckemann.

---

1 Whether this is a 'technique' or a 'technology', a knowledge–system or an elaborated 'working method' will become clear over the course of the essay. The term 'dance technique' encompasses sequences of movements specific to dance (including partial movements) and skills oriented towards overall concepts. These can be extrapolated from the experiences gained from teaching and performance, and the physical laws underlying them, as well as from an individual movement style. See Robert Prohl/ Peter Röthig et al. (Editors): *Sportwissenschaftliches Lexikon*. Schorndorf: Hofmann Verlag, 2003, pp. 588–592.

2 At this point we would like to give our special thanks to Colin Bourne, Naomi Lefebre Sell, Amy Knauff, Rosmary Brandt, and the musicians James Keane, Robert Coleridge, Gian Franco Biasiol, and Oli Newman.

About our research working methods:

In order to get an impression of Barbara Passow's teaching approach to the Jooss–Leeder Technique, during the first several days we focused our investigations on making phenomenological notes about the technique and determining the distinguishing characteristics of Passow's teaching methods. After the first week of classes, we questioned students about their impressions of the physical–kinesthetic and kinetic–awareness approaches as we wanted to include their reactions in our analysis. We used a student questionnaire to minimize anticipated language issues, which also encouraged students to reflect independently.[3]

During our stay in London we had many opportunities to speak with Passow and Hoffmann about their teaching experiences at LABAN, and about the characteristics of the Jooss–Leeder Technique. The complex weave of autobiographical influences and individual aesthetic preferences became apparent in our discussions. Core elements in teaching content were influenced and determined by Passow's personal creative processing and handling of the movement material, by the Jooss–Leeder Technique's principles, as well as by her assessment of the student group and institution. Considering the above variables, Passow's methods and teaching style cannot be seen as a simple reproduction of the Jooss–Leeder Technique that she learned as a student at the Folkwang University of the Arts Essen and in collaborations with Michael Diekamp in particular. We presume that her teaching is ultimately defined by her own dance experiences as well as by experiences she had in artistic, performing, and teaching contexts. Thus the knowledge she gained and processed as dance student, dancer, and teacher is integrated into her entire 'body (of) knowledge' and can be observed in her teaching style.

Modern dance classes in the Jooss–Leeder tradition taught students (taking part in the three–week training program taught by Passow) how to achieve good centering and differentiation in movement quality, as well as providing them with a rhythmic–musical and motor–qualitative 'feeling for form'. This implicitly provided a comprehensive and balanced training.

3 The questionnaire was composed of thirteen questions in English. The students come from seven countries; answers were written in English.

For the following report, Claudia Fleischle–Braun and Patricia Stöckemann dealt with the historical and biographical contexts. Claudia Fleischle–Braun described the conceptual foundations of the Jooss–Leeder Technique and its movement forms. Wiebke Dröge carried out an extensive examination of Passow's teaching methods.

Claudia Fleischle-Braun, Patricia Stöckemann

HISTORICAL CONTEXT

TIME, PLACE, AND SOCIO-POLITICAL CONTEXT

In order to put Passow's educational background and her teaching methods into context, the following offers a brief summary about the historical development of new dance in Germany and the creation of the Jooss–Leeder Technique.

After the First World War, Rudolf von Laban returned to Germany from Switzerland. In 1920 Kurt Jooss became Laban's student in Stuttgart. The new German dance (called 'free modern dance') they practiced was part of a reform movement, and was driven by cultural reactions to developing social concerns (known as the *Lebensreformbewegung*). Free modern dance was already an important element in Expressionism's avant-garde, and well on its way to becoming established institutionally. For four years Jooss worked closely with Laban—a visionary mastermind of new German dance—both as a dancer in Laban's works and as a choreographic and teaching assistant.

The development of modern dance in Germany paralleled the body-culture (*Körperkultur*) movement and *Lebensreformbewegung* (both of which were critical of modern civilization); they shared a holistic vision of humanity that included visionary living concepts renouncing industrialization and the mechanization of life. Modern dance defined itself as being the artistic avant-garde; the practitioners not only rejected the ballet, they considered their dance to be a countermovement.

Using systematic research and analysis of human movement, Rudolf von Laban created a theoretical basis for a new dance and gymnastics movement. Using Labanotation (invented by Laban and developed further by his employees Dussia Bereska, Kurt Jooss, and Sigurd Leeder) it was possible for dances and choreographic creations to be analyzed and notated as a score. Laban's notational system and analytic approach, which differentiated between teaching spatial ideas and specific movements, enabled the systematic description of physical, expressive movement by observing the spatial–temporal process as well as the rhythmic–dynamic form. This notational system was used not only for artistic and choreographic work and profes-

sional dance instruction, it also established the foundation for future dance education, dance teaching, and dance therapy. (Kurt Jooss and Sigurd Leeder were partners and, together, a driving force in the development and systemization of pedagogical concepts as a part of dance education.)

Kurt Jooss (1901–1979) and Sigurd Leeder (1902–1981) met in Hamburg in 1924. Based upon their individual artistic experiences and insights, they developed educational concepts and methods. The Folkwang School in Essen, which Jooss cofounded in 1927, aspired, from the outset, to offer an interdisciplinary education that would transcend artistic boundaries.

Jooss and Leeder's lesson plans were based on Laban's teaching of choreutics and eukinetics; Laban's principles and concepts were transformed into etudes and movement exercises. Jooss and Leeder also taught theory. They focused (more abstractly) on historic and contemporary dance forms and integrated gymnastics, ballroom dancing, as well as the reading and writing of dance notation into the teaching plan.[1]

Laban's theories about space assisted teachers and pupils in understanding the body's relationship to space and in analyzing the body's spatial orientations. The theories divided a movement combination into time, energy, and space components—and enabled differentiation between specific dynamics inside the phrase.[2] This created a more objective, object-oriented, and analytical approach to teaching modern dance technique—as opposed to a subjective, individualistic, or stylistic approach.

In 1933 Jooss left Germany with his dance troupe. In 1934 he and Leeder founded the Jooss–Leeder School of Dance in Dartington Hall in Devon, England, and the Ballets Jooss a year later. After the war, these two congenial artists, teachers, and friends parted ways.

In 1947 Leeder founded his own school and a studio-based dance troupe in London. In 1960 he went to Chile to reorganize the Dance Department at the Universidad de Chile in Santiago. After his return to Europe in 1964, he and Grete Müller ran a school in Herisau, Switzerland. The school in London, meanwhile, continued and was run by his students and employees, Simone Michelle and June Kemp, until 1965. Afterwards, Michelle joined the Laban Art of Movement Studio in Addlestone, Surrey, and taught the Jooss–Leeder Technique at London's Laban Centre of Movement and Dance from 1974–1991. During the research project with Passow, the center's students were given the unique opportunity to experience the style and

1 See Jane Winearls: *Modern Dance. The Jooss–Leeder-Method*. London: Billing & Sons, 1958, and also Grete Müller: *Sigurd Leeder. Tänzer, Pädagoge und Choreograf. Leben und Werk*. Herisau: Verlag Appenzeller Medienhaus, 2001.

2 See Table 2: Eight Movement Qualities in the section Understanding the Body / Movement.

3 Quoted from: Birgit Rüstroer: 'Ein Interview mit Michael Diekamp'. In: Gesellschaft für Tanzforschung (Publisher): *Jahrbuch* 1995, Volume 6. Wilhelmshaven: Florian Noetzel Verlag, 1996, pp. 62–70.

approach to dance that had played a central role in the Laban Centre's early history.

In 1949 Jooss responded to a call from Essen and resumed his position as director of the Dance Department (which he had originally founded) at the Folkwang School. As before, he promoted dance education that was appropriate to the times: He wanted to systemize the aesthetic and technical foundations, and envisioned an institution wherein ballet and modern dance were taught as independent but equal disciplines. It was also important to him that the entire spectrum of dance culture be made accessible to, and experienced by students. In 1961 the school was finally able to get masterclasses in dance (classes and/or courses for especially gifted students taught by experts) up and running again—from which the Folkwang Ballet emerged. Jooss remained the Dance Department's director (which had, in the meantime, become accredited as the Folkwang University), until his retirement in 1968. He was succeeded as Dance Department director by his long-time companion, Hans Züllig (1914–1992).

BACKGROUND: BIOGRAPHIES AND ENVIRONMENT

Barbara Passow describes her husband, Michael Diekamp, who died in 2007, as her most important teacher. From him she learned most of what now distinguishes her teaching and educational activities at the Palucca Schule Dresden. Diekamp completed a five-year dance and dance–teaching program at the Folkwang School in Essen between 1956–1961, during which time he became engrossed with the working methods. He held Jooss in high regard because "it [was] unthinkable for Jooss to imprint his style onto his students. The point for him was always to awaken and foster the dancer's personality, not to constrain it in any way."[3] Diekamp considered Folkwang's exceptional strength to be its fundamental openness and flexibility in being able to adjust instruction to individual students.

After his studies, Diekamp remained an additional two years in Essen as a member of the masterclasses that Jooss had founded. Diekamp eventually left Folkwang to dance as a soloist in Mannheim and, later, in Cologne. After two years, however, he returned to the Folkwang Tanz Studio as a repertoire soloist and completed additional dance–teaching training. During this time he met Barbara Passow, whom he would later marry. After a professional stage career in Dortmund, with the Cullberg Ballet Stockholm, and the Tanztheater Wuppertal, in 1977

Diekamp began teaching at the John Cranko School in Stuttgart. In 1986 he became the training director at the Bremen Theater, and in 1994 was offered a position at the Palucca Schule Dresden. After retirement, Michael Diekamp continued to teach movement theory in Dresden until his sudden death in 2007.

Reinhild Hoffmann, who studied under Kurt Jooss in Essen from 1965–1970 at the Folkwang University—and who is considered one of the pioneers of German dance–theater—said of Diekamp that he, "counts among one of the very few Folkwang students who understands how to carry Jooss's body of thought further in teaching," and who made it his business "to find one's own movement language by coming back to the body" and not to simply "fabricate an action."[4] As characteristic of her time at Folkwang, Hoffmann says that Jooss encouraged her to be extremely detailed and analytical about dancing, and notes that it was important, for Jooss, to awaken "the consciousness for 'why do I move?'" She adds, "When that is finally clear, you are freed from all styles, and can invent movement yourself."[5]

Passow began her dance education at the Folkwang University Essen in 1968—after Jooss's retirement as director—under Hans Züllig and Anna Markard. She also completed a one-year teacher training parallel to her dance studies, and took her final exams in 1972. (Her further professional artistic and teaching career has been outlined above.)[6] She also received a teaching appointment as lecturer at the Palucca Schule Dresden when Diekamp took on the professorship in modern dance there.

Founded by Gret Palucca in 1925, the Palucca Schule Dresden played an important role in modern dance's development. Patricio Bunster (1924–2006) was lecturer for modern dance and choreography from 1979–1984. A dancer, choreographer, and teacher, Patricio Bunster, a native of Chile, was a soloist for the Folkwang Theater Essen from 1951–1953, and had studied with Sigurd Leeder in London from 1953–1954. Bunster helped to spread the Jooss–Leeder Technique in Chile and Latin America, both as instructor for and director of the Dance Department at the University of Santiago, Chile, from 1954–1973, and again with numerous activities upon his return in 1985.

In 1961 Kurt Jooss brought Jean Cébron to the Folkwang Ballet Essen as a choreographer and soloist. Cébron had studied with Leeder in London and worked with Jooss in Santiago, Chile, in the years following the war. Cébron's duets with Pina Bausch and his group works formed the experimental profile of the Folkwang Ballet at the time. After teaching stints in Stockholm and Rome, he returned

4 Ibid., p. 62.
5 Quoted from: Hedwig Müller / Ralf Stabel / Patricia Stöckemann: *Krokodil im Schwanensee. Tanz in Deutschland seit 1945.* Frankfurt: Anabas Verlag, 2003, p. 189.

6 See Passow's biography on the title page of the project, as well as Edith Boxberger's Passow interview.

to the Folkwang University in 1976 where he served concurrently as training director for the Folkwang Ballet and the Tanztheater Wuppertal, both of which were, at the time, under the direction of Bausch (1940–2009). Lutz Förster—who, after completing his dance education in Essen, began his professional career in 1975 with Bausch at the Tanztheater Wuppertal, and now, since 1992, is director of the Folkwang University Dance Department—describes Cébron as a "master of movement analysis." Förster names both Cébron and Hans Züllig as formative teachers.[7]

RELATION TO OTHER ART FORMS

Both Jooss and Leeder considered it important for students to have insight into other art forms; both worked in educational environments offering students involvement with a variety of artistic media beyond dance that included music, theater, visual arts, film, design, etc. And both Jooss and Leeder were artistically gifted and multi-talented: Jooss began music and acting studies in Stuttgart in 1920 before going on to study dance with Rudolf von Laban; Leeder was active not only as a dancer, but also as a painter, costume designer, and stage technician.

Jooss subscribed to the idea of a dramatic dance theater. His choreographic works show human behavior and social milieus in a stylized form.[8] For his famous work, *The Green Table*, he and his company received first prize at the 1932 International Choreography Competition in Paris. Jooss saw the intersecting of art forms, i.e., between dance, drama, and opera as being important,[9] and his artistic approach was clearly linked to Expressionism. His choreographies presented subjective impressions of the world—using time and space abstractly, his works were an interpretation of his impressions and transformed his message into a narrative form.

Affinities and equivalents can be found in the visual arts. For example, as of 1927 in Essen, Ernst Ludwig Kirchner (1880–1938) drew sketches for paintings, among which was the *Farbentanz* ('dance of color') that was eventually realized in the Folkwang Museum's ceremonial hall. Kurt Jooss's dance works also have a powerful expressionistic aesthetic based in Realism, similar to Kirchner's work and to paintings and sculptures of other Expressionists like Otto Dix (1891–1969), George Grosz (1893–1959), Edvard Munch (1863–1944), and Ernst Barlach (1870–1938).

In the 1960s and 1970s, Jooss was a pioneer in contemporary dance theater in Germany. He was guided by a new interpretation of dance through multimediality, and led the way with his aesthetics and staging of dance.

RELEVANT THEORETICAL DISCOURSES

Expressionist art and the German new dance movement evolved from a renunciation of conventional notions about art at the time, and both were closely intertwined with the *Lebensreformbewegung*. Ballet's rigid form was burst open in a myriad of ways—by the sheer joy of experimentation. Because representatives and proponents of the classic and modern approaches to dance all needed to formulate and clarify their ideas, a demarcation between the two camps was both understandable and necessary. In retrospect, Jooss and Leeder's integrating mindset, as manifested in their teaching approach, was ahead of its time and remains relevant. From a cultural and historical point of view, further research must consider where modern dance fits into the history of art in society's Modern era. The understanding and relationship of 'traditional' versus 'modern' should not only be recalibrated in the era of 'Modernism',[10] but contemporary choreographies should also be taken into consideration.

Jooss and Leeder, both as choreographers and teachers, sought an interface between modern dance and ballet. For both men, however, it was also important to maintain the independence of both dance forms in the curriculum. The various dance forms or techniques, as well as the characteristics that define them, had to be taught separately in order for dancers to be able to understand any specific style(s). With this in mind, it makes sense when Passow points out that Jooss–Leeder Technique is in no way a synthesis of ballet and modern dance—as has often been written elsewhere.

On the other hand, Jooss's historic aesthetic was based upon crossing and overstepping boundaries. When a piece called for it, Jooss included ballet elements, ballroom dancing, and historic dance forms. The label 'hybrid dance form' applies not only to the traditional Jooss–Leeder Technique, but also to the present–day work taught by Passow at LABAN.

7 See Tonja Wiebracht: '"Doch eines fehlt dem neuen Tanz in Deutschland: Die konsequente Systematisierung der Tänzererziehung." Die Folkwang Hochschule wird 80.' In: *Ballett Intern*, 4/2007, pp. 4–8, here p. 5.

8 For more about his artistic approach, see the monograph by Patricia Stöckemann: *Etwas ganz Neues muß nun entstehen. Kurt Jooss und das Tanztheater*. Munich: K. Kieser Verlag, 2001.

9 About this, see the catalog of works published in Stöckemann 2001 (pp. 443–461).

10 See remarks by Gabriele Klein: 'Was ist modern am modernen Tanz? – Zur Dekonstruktion dualistischer Tanzverhältnisse'. In: Gesellschaft für Tanzforschung (Ed.): *Jahrbuch* 1993, Volume 4. Wilhelmshaven: Florian Noetzel Verlag, 1993, pp. 61–72.

CURRENT PRACTICE

Jooss and Leeder's enduring legacy was the introduction of Laban's elaborate model for movement analysis into a comprehensive dance education curriculum. Laban's ideas were transformed into an efficient method in accordance with dance pedagogy. The technique they developed is well suited as company training, which explains why Passow is a regular guest instructor at the Bremen Theater.

The Jooss–Leeder Technique remains an important instructional component at the Folkwang University, in particular in postgraduate studies for dance teaching. Current instruction, by various teachers who all are closely associated with the Tanztheater Wuppertal, sets new accents in modern and contemporary dance. Nonetheless Lutz Förster still finds advantages in the original Jooss–Leeder approach and says: "Applying eukinetics helps establish dynamic differentiation; applying choreutics leverages plasticity and three–dimensionality."[11]

New accents in pedagogical methods are in keeping with Jooss's approach. For him, technique was not an end in itself, rather it existed "for the sake of the aesthetic," and is "determined and created by it. The aesthetic, however, changes with the zeitgeist, and thus the technique must change, must modernize with the times."[12] Not only was the founding generation of German dance–theater-makers taught in this spirit; generations of well–known contemporary dancers and choreographers developed their technical roots and personal dance styles during their education at the Folkwang University or during engagements at the Folkwang Dance Studio—and they have passed these basics and styles on to others.

One can assume that dancers' and/or instructors' knowledge is passed down in a variety of artistic and teaching contexts, and that such knowledge is filtered through the vying priorities of teaching institutions. An instructor's personal processing, integration, and choice of focus inside a dance technique are factors in how information is transferred generationally.

Nowadays, the Jooss–Leeder Technique is taught primarily by former graduates of the Folkwang University in private dance and ballet schools throughout Germany. One good example is the Brakel Dance Academy in Hanover, established in 1969. Loni Brakel–Harmssen and Eckard Brakel, the founders, were previously associated with Kurt Jooss's masterclasses and, later, the Folkwang Ballet.

After Sigurd Leeder's death in 1981, his school in Herisau, Switzerland, continued under the direction of Grete Müller (with support from Christine von Mentlen). Even today, the school (now known as the 'Dance Space Herisau — Space for Dance, Movement, and Performance', run by Mentlen and Claudia Roemmel) offers courses and advanced training in dance and performance based upon, among other things, choreutics and eukinetics.

In the Dance Department at the Academy of Christian Humanism University in Santiago, Chile, Raymond Hilbert, as Patricio Bunster's successor, continues teaching in the Jooss–Leeder tradition. Hilbert studied with Bunster at the Palucca Schule Dresden in the 1970s. From 2000–2004, Hilbert was a professor for modern dance at the Palucca Schule, before following his teacher's example and moving to Chile.

INDIVIDUAL APPROACH

Assessing the history of the Jooss–Leeder Technique, its approach, and how it is taught, fundamental and integrative concepts are recognizable. This technique does not rely on a fixed or formal, stylized movement vocabulary: the exercises and movement sequences are structured, analyzed, varied, and organized around choreutics and eukinetics. These two core disciplines provide students with a means to systematically explore articulation and modulation of the body and to incorporate these ideas into their own work.

Barbara Passow reiterates that the Jooss–Leeder approach is not a teaching concept set in stone, rather dancers and instructors educated in the Jooss–Leeder Technique are particularly capable of realizing their own educational ideas because they have explored, and continue to explore, theoretical parameters that determine the shape and form of any movement. Instructors are also able to choose their own style, can select teaching content and methods that set goals, and gear learning to a group's particularities— thus providing a teacher with options for direction and leadership.

The Jooss–Leeder Technique is Passow's foundation for teaching professional modern dance classes, for training professional dance–theater companies, and in her courses and workshops for amateurs.

RELATION TO OTHER DANCE AND MOVEMENT TECHNIQUES

We are able to characterize Passow's movement style as follows: qualitative characteristics are seen in an organic flow, there is a preference for swinging movements and a play between the workings of gravity, elasticity, and cushioning of weight that can be found in regaining balance. Furthermore, movement phrasing is articulated such that gentle, flowing movements and transitions using accented pauses can, for instance, be connected with extended

---

11 Quoted from Wiebracht 2007, p. 5. Along with Prof. Lutz Förster, Prof. Malou Airaudo, and Prof. Rudolpho Leoni, today's Folkwang faculty also includes Stephan Brinkmann, who studied modern dance with Jean Cébron, Hans Züllig, and Lutz Förster, among others.
12 Quoted from Stöckemann 2001, p. 230.

stretches and falling momentum. Swinging and falling movements use cushioning and rebounding to catch the weight, for the body to re-establish balance. While finding this balance, or a higher stretched position (sometimes in conjunction with an elongated *suspend*), a playfulness might be recognized along with control. Utilizing the torso's plasticity is another aesthetic feature: Arm movements away from, and back toward the body draw clear lines of movement and/or traces in the space. An awareness of both form and precision is also manifested in spatial referencing via the use of dimensional and transverse spatial lines. Movement combinations involve all the sides of the body equally.

This allows us to draw the following analogies and recognize the influences of other dance and body–work techniques: Passow's teaching is remarkable in how reminiscent it is of Limón Technique—not only by how body weight is dealt with as well as in pronounced rhythmic articulation, but also in selected exercise elements and movement structures. Passow sees this correspondence not only as a result of her own intensive experience with the Limón Technique, but also because both Limón and Jooss–Leeder Techniques demand strong kinesthetic experiences and incorporate swinging dynamics, playing with balance, and the intermittent loss of control.

Similar to the Limón Technique, there are also analogies to ballet training, which (to a certain extent) provide a frame of reference. This is apparent in, among other things, use of terminology and how the class is organized.

As mentioned, Passow was most influenced by Michael Diekamp in regards to her teaching methods and approach to the Jooss–Leeder Technique. His teaching was characterized by a systematic 'working–through the body', and by lessons that were clearly structured and focused on specific content.

Beyond this, Passow often allows elements from body–awareness and alignment techniques (yoga and stretching, Feldenkrais and others) to flow into the initial phase of class, thus providing students the opportunity to prepare themselves both mentally and physically for the complexities of the training that lie ahead.

Claudia Fleischle–Braun

CONCEPT AND IDEOLOGY

IMAGINING THE BODY

The body is viewed as a sensitive and expressive instrument whose articulation and transformative abilities must be developed. This notion derives from Jooss's basic understanding, expressed thusly, that "the language of formed and inspired movement" is what raises dance to a theater art.[13] Passow identifies with Jooss and Leeder in that expression, for her, is less a matter of feeling than one of a harmonious movement. All three want(ed) to train dancers comprehensively; an all–around training should help dancers employ differentiated reactions. Dancers should master a complete scale of movement if they are to create art that reflects the human soul, which is why they should learn to play their bodies like an instrument—experiencing all tonal qualities and possibilities for expression, and "achieve a unity between movement and themselves"[14] while doing so. Jooss and Leeder varied between using dancerly–tools that were unconscious and conscious so as to avoid the danger of becoming too intellectual. Passow is also dedicated to such thinking: It is important for her that the dancers are able to resonate in class, which she describes as, "seeking the movement's essence within themselves, perceiving and being open to the experience, to experience joy, passion, feeling, and to remain aware of the unconscious in dancing."

The ideal dancer is therefore able to perceive and resonate, to find fulfillment in dancing, is endowed with a body that is harmoniously balanced, has well–trained coordination, is willing to take risks, and is present. This body is prepared for all the technical demands made upon it, and can bring expressive nuance into movement.

Passow's training aims to provide dancers with an opportunity to grow beyond their bodies' capabilities and to exude presence beyond their kinesphere. Dancers should give the impression their bodies are able to reach into the space and, in a certain sense, are able configure the space using the principle of 'counter–tension'.

When assessing a person's potential for a career in dance, one of Passow's criteria is an aesthetic physique combined with the learned skills of coordination, musicality, and versatility.

Because Jooss–Leeder Technique takes movement across the spectrum of human expression, and wants as much variety as possible in movement dynamics and qualities along bipolar scales, Passow's training offers a multitude of nuances for movement execution without masculine or feminine connotations. Her movement sequences' aesthetic radiates elegance and lightness, despite the permanent interplay of body weight and body tension. In terms of gender, this focus on the entire body, on all–around physical coordination, on the play with directionalities and spatial levels, on big movement combinations and powerful stops that radiate out into the space—all in combination with rhythmic changes—make this technique equally interesting for both genders. Nonetheless, the movement vocabulary includes smooth arm gestures, swings, and flowing movements with differentiated torso articulation that are typically characterized as feminine—an assessment that both male and female students shared in the final discussion.

The relationship to space is based on Rudolf von Laban's detailed teachings about space and form. In all of Passow's exercises, the body has clear spatial alignment; the exercises often accentuate an expansive physicality through stretching, and participants aspire to a maximal movement range with proper alignment throughout. Shapes that open and close often provide clear contrasts in the range of the movement (narrow–wide). The body is pliable in its three–dimensionality, and movements are identifiable by clear lines of alignment and directionality. There is full use of all spatial axes and directions, as well as various levels both in the movement and in the dancer's immediate environment, i.e., the kinesphere.[15] This also includes systematic diagonals in the spatial and body alignment.

Kurt Jooss defined the relationship between dance and music in a several ways. While he understood music primarily as dance's catalyst, he also understood dance as being equally independent from music. The correlation between movement and music plays a large role in Passow's training: A particular emphasis during the London project

13 From 'Credo der Folkwang–Tanzbühne', quoted from Stöckemann 2001, p. 171.
14 Sigurd Leeder: 'Über Prinzipien der technischen Erziehung.' In: Müller 2001, p. 17.
15 For spatial references see also the corresponding explanations in the following section Understanding the Body / Movement / Movement Characteristics and Physicality, under keyword 'space'.

was mindfully dealing with musical structures and their congruent realization in movement, and she took pains to ensure that the music and the exercise sequences and/or movement combinations were in sync rhythmically. Musical accompaniment was usually live, piano or percussion, and required a great deal of coordination from both the musician and the dancer to achieve a nuanced dialogue between rhythm and phrasing.

Musical parameters often provided a catalyst for modulating various qualities of a movement phrase or motif.

Occasionally Barbara Passow accompanied movement sequences vocally, either onomatopoetically or by singing words. Introductory movement sequences that started on the floor, however, were usually done without music, enabling the dancers to focus on physical processes and, more importantly, on their own breath rhythm.

The rhythmic correlation between music and movement is important in the Jooss–Leeder Technique. The movement combinations' structures contained various tonal qualities; changes in rhythm, meter, and tempo occurred often. Passow targeted the use of musical accompaniment for the following:

→ To support and strengthen the respective rhythmic and dynamic phrasing needed for the movement's motif and/or exercise sequence;

→ To transform musical structures into dancing, whereby music is the configuring medium (regarding, for example, rhythm, dynamic, and mood);

→ For cooperative interaction, whereby the individual as well as the interplay between dance and music determined the class dynamic or general mood.

When creating movement combinations in class, Passow also uses a variety of music styles (classical, Latin, folk, world, jazz), played either live or prerecorded, in order for students to become familiar with a myriad of music styles.

INTENT

Jooss–Leeder Technique conditions the body, trains movement skills, and strengthens an individual's will to express emotion. In her classes, Passow wants to nurture the dancing personality, to make it capable of experiencing and creating. One of the most important things for her is that students are lively, moving, and inspired as they dance, and that they can perform with clear and differentiated articulation. This reflects her psychophysical approach to modern dance.

"In Passow's class I gained quite a lot of clarity in the space, and timing with the music." *Anna Bergstrom, student*

A movement sequence's performance quality is demonstrated by clarity in shape, precise execution, and in its three–dimensional spatial form, as well as by lively, rhythmic, and dynamic accentuation and phrasing. The same is true of the correlation between movement and the intended expression. Highly developed kinesthetic differentiation is required to make a movement sequence coherent (in regards to the respective movement approach and the energetic momentum and/or impulse).

Making movement coherent is dependent upon interpretation, which is rooted in the intention, the idea, and thus in the movement material itself. Crucial is an appropriate personal modulation of movement sequences, 'authenticity', and 'believability'. For Barbara Passow this means "dancing without empty phrases."

These were also key elements used by Jooss and Leeder to judge a work artistically. Their writings make multiple references to the 'essentiality' that must come across at all times, and that is vital for a dancer's interpretation. During a lecture–demonstration, Michael Diekamp described a central tenet of the Jooss–Leeder Technique as follows: According to Kurt Jooss, the dancer's and choreographer's task is to "to continually find the *real*, the *essential* movement through rigorous self–critique and uncompromising discipline…to search for the *essence*."[16] Passow remains committed to the same ideal and goal.

16 See Michael Diekamp: 'Kurt Jooss: Seine Pädagogik und tänzerische Schulung.' In: Gesellschaft für Tanzforschung (Ed.): *Ausdruckstanz in Deutschland – Eine Inventur. Mary Wigman–Tage 1993.* Wilhelmshaven: Florian Noetzel Verlag, 1994, pp. 126–131, here p. 178.

17 According to the 'Grounded Theory' approach.

Exceptional in this technique, as taught by Passow, is the individual 'qualitative' (usually energetic potential) that is created and expressed in performance—one that must come from the dancers themselves. LABAN students also rated this component as important. They provided the following written answers to questions as to when a person, as dancer and observer, can speak of successfully executing this dance technique (see table 1).

Passow's concerns also include the dancer's presence. Presence emerges when authenticity and liveliness configure, when a dancer concentrates on the task at hand, is in the moment, has an inner focus. These affect how a movement is executed and can be seen by an audience. Furthermore, 'extending to the periphery' gives the impression of a dancer being connected to the space beyond the body's limits. This creates an immediate energy and communication between the dancers as well as between the dancers and the audience—which is further strengthened by focus and/or direct eye contact.

Table 1: Students' answers to 'This is it'

'MEMO' CATEGORIES GENERATED [17]	STUDENTS' ANSWERS
Dancer–Subject: Inward–Outward Believability	"It's about the soul, like everything in dance." "Believing in what you and we are doing."
Individual movement expression about qualitative implementation	"For me, the rhythm that she asks us to emulate gives us the sense of the movement and the energy that we can put into it." "To set accents and make individual decisions."
Movement precision and movement control (calculated risk): Balance Stability	"Precision, playing with body weight, and having the capacity to drop and catch weight at any point." "To be controlled in 'letting go' and being alive." "Connection to gravity (weight) and center." "To be grounded and strong in the lower body." "Relaxed limbs, strong core."
Movement qualities	"Released quality, mainly a fluid flow with some contrasting rhythmic moments." "The use of dynamic elements, particularly swings." "Swings incorporated in various ways, somehow almost in every movement." "To go with the rhythm of the movement." "An organically moving body, movement that works along with the breath." "Suspend and release." "Release of weight."
Coordination of body parts and the whole body	"The coordination between arms and legs." "To connect the upper body to the arms."
Torso maneuverability	"Curves, moving released weight through space." "Curves. / The curved, rounded back."
Relationship to music	"Music is really important in this technique. It provides the impulse; movement and music are very closely related."
The body's relationship to space	"Clear arm directions and gestures." "Peripheral and transversal pathways." "Intelligent spatial awareness and use of the kinesphere and planes." "Seeing other dancers find the planes and the curve of the upper back."

Claudia Fleischle–Braun

UNDERSTANDING
THE BODY/MOVEMENT

PREREQUISITES

The Jooss–Leeder Technique is suitable for dancers with varying degrees of experience and can thus be taught at every instructional level. The level of difficulty can be adjusted, allowing a teacher to respond to a group's particular circumstances and requirements. Passow is experienced in teaching a variety of proficiency levels, from students on their way to becoming professional dancers or teachers, to novices interested in dance with varying levels of experience (or none at all). The Jooss–Leeder Technique is also appropriate training for professional dance–theater companies as it encourages better movement interpretation and compositional possibilities.

A longer period of study is necessary to learn and physically incorporate the Jooss–Leeder Technique's basic principles and differentiated movement approach. The compact fifteen–day course at LABAN, for example, with two hours of training daily, provided the second–year dance students with an overview. Thanks to their previous training in Laban movement analysis and daily ballet and/or modern or contemporary dance training, they were able to quickly pick up the occasionally complex movement combinations. These combinations required whole–body coordination, an aptitude for motor learning, and good movement recall. Execution was relatively good; that said, long–term training is necessary if students are to develop awareness of and sensibility for the breadth of qualitative–dynamic execution and expressive means that the technique offers. According to Passow, four years of training are necessary for a basic education.

In Passow's opinion, professional dance training should incorporate good awareness of alignment and body consciousness, along with good physical and constitutional conditioning. Furthermore, strength should be trained sufficiently, for example, and include holding–power and elasticity. Good flexibility, especially in the torso, is another prerequisite. Further prerequisites include whole–body coordination trained in a variety of ways, as well as a feeling for rhythm, the ability to orient oneself in space, and balance. The ability to pick–up and recall material is also important. Thus knowledge acquired in basic ballet training (for example, about class structure, awareness of body placement, and balance) are as helpful as are spatial orientation and technical dexterity—all of which can also be acquired through analytical movement training (for example, Laban). Other skills include being able to modulate movement by using basic elements such as strength, time, and space, as well as being able to consciously mold subtle dynamic and rhythmic nuances.

The chances of injury are low because of the class structure and the attention given to individual participants' physical conditions. Mindful and appropriate functional–physical movement execution is strongly emphasized.

MOVEMENT CHARACTERISTICS AND PHYSICALITY

Movement quality characteristics that define the technique are presented in the following structural analysis. The movement repertoire's basic technical structure, as taught by Barbara Passow in the Jooss–Leeder style, will also be presented by way of example.[18]

Movement sequences in standing or in other positions (i.e., sitting) contain the following whole–body activities:

→ Rising and lowering (high–deep);
→ Leaning forward and pulling back (forward–backward);
→ Weight–shifting and leaning to the sides (left–right);
→ Contracting and expanding;
→ Widening and narrowing;
→ Torsion;
→ Strew circles (scattering) away from and scoop circles (gathering) toward the body, performed by the extremities.

Changing shapes while standing, with weight on one or both legs, happens in various ways. Observed movement organization reveals that whole–body movement sequences dominate, whereby movements of individual body parts can be simultaneously executed (for instance, steps and/or weight–shifting (back–and–forth) in combination with arm movements on the various spatial levels).

Movements include bending and stretching in the vertical, shifting the center of gravity; with resultant steps and large falls, the center of gravity changes and locomotion is initiated.

---

18 For the movement sequences' structuring and description, the following were of assistance (among others): Claudia Jeschke's suggested categories in 'Inventarisierung von Bewegung'; see also Cary Rick: *Tanztherapie. Eine Einführung in die Grundlagen*. In cooperation with Claudia Jeschke. Stuttgart/ New York: Gustav Fischer Verlag, 1989, as well as Claudia Jeschke: *Tanz als Bewegungs-Text. Analysen zum Verhältnis von Tanztheater und Gesellschaftstanz (1910–1965)*. Tübingen: Max Niemeyer Verlag, 1999.

19 See Winearls 1958, p. 27.

Barbara Passow's exercises and movement combinations are characterized by a clear relationship to the space. The following features are found in the spatial relationships:

→ *Dimensional planes:*
Movement sequences are executed with a clear spatial alignment in both the dancer's positioning and the direction of the dancer's body inside the kinesphere or in the space. Diagonals, along with the laterals (the high–deep dimension), sagittals (the backward–forward dimension), and the horizontals (the side–side dimension) are used systematically. Changes in frontal positioning using torsion and turns are an important part of the exercises.

→ *Preferred spatial level:*
Most of the class takes place in standing. Elevated positions (for instance, standing–leg elevated onto ball of the foot with the gesture leg in attitude) and jumps are also common elements; lower levels and floorwork are seldom used.

→ *Extent and/or range of movement in space:*
The spatial range (narrow–wide) is a distinguishing feature because extensions and stretching often occur at the end of fall– and swinging–elements, or might be used as a transition to torso bends or waves. Large peripheral movements performed by the extremities with clear directional alignment (trace forms) and that incorporate the full kinesphere also belong to the movement repertoire (i.e., eight swings, scoop spirals, and strew spirals).

→ *Use of spatial levels:*
Exercise sequences incorporate all spatial levels (i.e., sagittal, lateral, and horizontal).

→ *Spatial diagonals:*
The spatial diagonals (i.e., diagonals drawn from corner–to–corner within the Laban cube) are important orientation points for falling and balance, labile (off–center) turns, and tilts. These demand more balance since the body is taken off the vertical axis and away from its normal level.

→ *Movement design and/or patterns in the space:*
Movement of the extremities and the torso trace either straight, open half–circle, round, or S–shaped gestural paths (i.e., trace forms) in the space. These trace forms are found, for example, in forward–moving arm circles performed by both arms, in a falling movement with centrally aligned scooping eight swings, in a stretched–out starting position with both arms executing downward scoop swings followed by a torso bend that leads the body into a stretched high–

diagonal, and lateral torso swings with and without torsion.
These basic forms were also used as patterns for spatial pathways while moving through the space (for instance, walking with and without frontal changes, walking forwards and backwards along small half–circles).

→ *Symmetry and balance in the form:*
These movement sequences take body symmetry into account either by using mirror–inverted repetition of the series or repeating the sequence on the other side.

Furthermore, other types of spatial reference appear in movement sequences and are described as 'free flow', 'bound flow', and 'guided movement' in the Jooss–Leeder Technique.[19]
In relation to the body's architecture and movements within the kinesphere, a movement's point of origin can be either 'central' or 'peripheral', which will affect the shape:

→ *Central* movements originate either at the body's center or in a joint at an extremity (pelvis or shoulder), and flow outward towards the periphery. Examples: Forward impulse movements that correspond to a gymnastic 'body wave'; central arm movements like eight swings in front of, or close to, the body; guiding the pelvis and arm on the central level when walking backwards along a circular path. Movement flow is swaying or wave–shaped.

→ *Peripheral* movements originate in the limbs (i.e., extremities), or in regions of the body at a distance from the center. Examples: A flexible torso with arm gestures on various levels (partner exercise); curling and uncurling the spine in all directions; inward and outward rotation of the arms at pelvis level; arms per-forming frontal strew circle and a transition to torso circles. Movement flow is generally direct and continuous.

The relationship between the initiation of any given movement and its qualitative character should occur by using a wave movement of the entire body and/or torso, and an impulse movement originating in the pelvis:

→ *Wave* movements are created with a shifting of the pelvis or part of the spine (forward, backward, or to the side), and are characterized by a successive, flowing progression along the torso through the spine, as well as in the movement's continuation through the arms and legs. Wave movements can also be executed as isolated movements, such as wave movements of the arms.

→ *Impulse* movements originate with energy that has been collected in the body's centers: for example, in the pelvis with a strong contraction of the abdominal side muscles, and then released explosively. This might trigger a sudden and vehement wave movement that seizes the entire body and continues with reduced intensity, velocity, and energy out into the limbs. Impulse movements can also be initiated by a limb (i.e., arms and legs).

The end points of the extremities (i.e., fingertips, the hands' edges, and tops of the feet), as well as the inner and outer sides of arms or legs can lead a movement, just as certain parts of the torso and/or sections of the spine can also serve as pivot and fulcrum points. Frequently used pivot points for torso bends are the sternum (for example, when curling forward), and, for bending backwards, near the vertebrae's spinous processes at the lower part of the scapula. Overall, other fulcrum points can also be imagined, for example, around the waist or the lumbar region.

Articulation and mobilization of the upper body and/or torso happens in distinct ways:

→ Facing forward and with weight–shifts;[20]
→ Twists: rotation around the body's longitudinal axis, inward and outward;
→ Curves: forwards, to the side, backwards;
→ Tilts: flexible and stable upper–body tilts;

→ Rounded: arching and contracting movements;
→ With dynamic variations, for instance successive swinging with elastic rebound, or stopping and falling (drop).

Torso curving and tilting, as well as contractions, can basically be executed in all directions while in a deep knee bend, standing on the balls of one's feet, or while standing on one or both legs.

Particular emphasis was placed on bending the chest during the technique training at LABAN. Bending and/or tilting of the torso can be partially executed and may only involve the upper or lower torso, for instance, or alternatively may include the whole torso (for instance, in a large trunk bend). The pivot point in this case is at the intersection of the sacrum and lumbar spine. This movement can progress successively either rolling up or down, or as an intra-corporeal coordinated movement with a multitude of energy influences and dynamic shadings.

Movement combinations are designed with regard to the joints' anatomical differences and to the elastic characteristics of the muscular system (which includes connective tissues, tendons, and ligaments). Efforts are made to improve overall flexibility in order to optimize the range of harmonious movement. The training has a special effect on movement elasticity, as well as on neuromuscular interaction and the elasticity of muscles, tendons, and ligaments. It promotes inter- and intramuscular coordination,

20 Shifts can be initiated from other body parts besides the torso (from the pelvis, chest, head, or legs, for instance).

21 See also further above in this section about the topic of the upper–body's articulation and mobilization.

and, additionally, regulates muscle tonus and can correct muscular imbalances.

Much emphasis is placed on the respective inner and outer strength in the dynamic execution of a movement's shape. Muscular strength is only one factor with respect to this: One must also include gravity and other kinetic moments of force. Regulation of muscular tension happens in relation to gravity, for the most part. Dancers strive to use these forces as economically as possible when dancing, and with a minimum of muscular strength so movement looks as effortless as possible. Movement is initiated by carefully measured changes in tension, and modulated by muscular elasticity.

An entire scale of muscular tension is employed during class, and attention is paid to differentiating the energetic and dynamic changes of a movement sequence.

In order to protect the vulnerable lumbar and cervical spine regions, it is essential to strengthen muscles in the torso, i.e., to build up adequate tonus. Dancers are made aware of this in conjunction with alignment and posture work, aided by the notion of counter–tension, i.e., the 'stretching–triggering' resistance emanating from the floor. Strengthening the body's midsection is also achieved through the repetition of tilts and turns, stable and labile (center and off–center) body positions. Special attention is paid to this during exercises in preparatory classes so that muscular imbalances (which are often the cause of pelvic misalignment) are reduced, and so that optimum physical flexibility is reached while maintaining respect for the anatomical and physiological. Furthermore, other strength characteristics, in particular elasticity and maximum strength (especially of the entire leg) are improved by training the all intra- and intermuscular coordination.

Weight–shifts, steps, falls, hops, and rebounds are executed with the assistance of body weight in particular; these are used as transitions to other positions and changes in space. This employs the body's changing center of gravity and counter–tension, and exploits kinetic energy. The transition to locomotion, for example, is preferably achieved through weight–shifting in falling steps and/or leaning, which is particularly noticeable when walking backwards along a curved path.

Using body weight when executing falls requires a carefully measured reduction in muscular tension, which implies sinking directly to the floor along the line of gravity with a wide step to the side, or spiraling to the floor. Floor elements such as rotations (i.e., rolling over the pelvic girdle in a sitting position, or a crouching somersault) and jumps *à terre* and back to standing in conjunction with acrobatic elements (i.e., a handstand) are additional options to reach a new position.

For jumps performed in combination with forward locomotion, in addition to the active stretching and elastic–springing of the knee, a counter–tension is produced: this counter–tension is achieved by dancers imagining that the top of the head is being pulled upward with a magnet, or as if it is attached to a string. When the dancer is off the ground, such imagery produces a characteristic lightness and effortlessness.

The use of body weight is the most prominent feature of swings, which can be taught in a variety of ways. The execution of a pendulum swing, for instance, is facilitated by an accelerated fall that is followed by a deceleration when moving back upward.

Overall, the following swings or swinging movements can be distinguished:

→ Pendulum swings
→ Active swings
→ Curving swings
→ Eight swings
→ Spirals

The torso swings used during the London project were executed with a high curvature, meaning the pivot point was around the sternum or in the area near the upper thoracic spine.

The end positions of the swings were often varied; variations in phrasing were accomplished by relying on differentiated use of muscle tension and elasticity—both of which influenced the phrasing and the visible intensity of strength.

The term center is used in Jooss–Leeder Technique as follows:

It describes the body's center—approximately corresponding to the body's center of gravity—as residing in the middle of the body (two finger–widths below the navel). This center serves as an 'initiator' for whole–body movements and drives actions, shape changes, and/or locomotion (central movement qualities). However—as mentioned above—points along the extremities, i.e., on the body's periphery, can also initiate movement (peripheral movement qualities), just as individual body centers (for example, the pelvis) can trigger movement in isolation or be used as a catalyst for movement.

Playing with balance and off–balance, and with the destabilization of balance is important. The following possibilities are utilized:

→ Tilts: leans and bends of the whole and stretched–out body (with the pivot point along the sagittal axis);

→ Stable and flexible upper–body tilts:[21] for example, lunges with a stretched–out upper body, or a fall and recovery with various upper–body positions.

→ Stable and labile turns: centered turns (deep and high; inward and outward) and deep and high off–center turns.

Generally, well–developed midsection tonus is necessary for the leans and tilts.

A lunge can, for instance, lead to a stable balance through a weight–shift, or falling out of balance after a stretched–out lean, and then returning into an upright position, can be a play with weight and balance (i.e., fall and recovery). These falls can be executed with various degrees of muscular tension and in a variety of directions. A feeling for or awareness of the body's center is critical for performing the falls.

Expanding the spectrum of rotations around the body's longitudinal axis can be accomplished with labile (off–center) turns, for example, with a tilt to the side or with various upper–body positions, performed either deep or high, as well as with spirals upward performed in a variety of body positions.

Movement sequences are accentuated and presented rhythmically[22] in a variety of ways during Passow's classes:

→ *Initial accentuation:* sources the movement's impulse and uses muscular energy.
Examples include quick thrusts or impulse movements, or sudden torso bends or upper–body contractions.

→ *Terminal accentuation:* is intentional, purposeful, direct, and increases the tension.
Examples: Abrupt, successive bending of the arms after a torso swing; holding the gesture–leg in attitude after leg swings forward and/or backwards; ending a series of jumps with a two–legged jump in which the legs are brought up into a 'crouched' position.

→ *Transitional accentuation:* as a balanced relationship between weight–shift and muscular energy; this has the swinging character with relative relaxation, includes activation and an increase in tension, and then resolves.
Examples: swinging arm movements while walking; frontal swinging arm movements that lead over the head (i.e., a throwing gesture); flowing arm movements that alternate sides (arm lifts).

Rhythm is an important component in Barbara Passow's instruction. In the warm–up phase, movement sequences are usually directed vocally, without musical accompaniment, and linked to the dancer's own breathing. Passow wants to direct attentiveness inward, to get the students to concentrate on the development of the lesson. Exercise sequences and movement combinations through space are accompanied by live music, meaning that the movements are, for the most part, clearly set to and defined by the rhythm.

Tempo changes also contribute to rhythmic phrasing. Passow pays close attention that the tempo correlates to the rhythm of the movement, and to students' performance level.

"There is the use of weight, but the use of lift as well. And then it is partnered with a difference in dynamics that are in one exercise: being really smooth and soft, and you then must suddenly get heavy." *Samuel Jordan, student*

The relationship between energy–defined and dynamic components is made clear by examining the Jooss–Leeder movement principles. During our working meetings in London, Barbara Passow explicitly referred to Jane Winearls's compendium about the Jooss–Leeder Technique. Winearls gives us the following descriptions:[23]

1. Tension and relaxation:
   – Tension as outward expansion results in lightness.
   – Tension as inward contraction results in strength.
   – Relaxation as inward deflation results in heaviness.
   – Relaxation as outward release results in softness.

2. Weight and strength:
   – Little resistance: movement is light.
   – Great deal of resistance: movement becomes strong.
   – Great deal of support of the weight: movement becomes heavy.
   – Little support: movement becomes gentle, delicate, soft.

---

22 Jane Winearls 1958, p. 22, wrote here of "basic rhythms".
23 See Winearls, 1958, pp. 17–21 and pp. 84–91.

24 See Winerals 1958, p. 84, and Müller 2001, p. 38. The movement qualities that apply to the Jooss–Leeder Technique are not identical with Rudolf von Laban's eight elemental Effort Actions. See Rudolf von Laban: *Der moderne Ausdruckstanz.* Wilhelmshaven: Heinrich-shofen Verlag, 1981.

3. Movement phrasing—eight fundamental qualities: The basic components for a movement sequence's variation on qualities and dynamic modulation are energy, the movement initiation, and speed. Eight fundamental movement qualities can be derived by combining the components' characteristics. A movements' dynamic shadings and phrasing can be derived by using these combinations, as listed in Table 2 below.

In summary, Passow's training program contains the following fundamental types of movements:

→ Whole–body movement shapes initiated centrally and peripherally, as well as isolated partial–body movements;
→ Torso mobility: torso bends and leans, as well as successive rolling upwards and downwards;
→ Weight–shifts and releases in various directions and levels;
→ Stability/Instability: fall and recovery movements, flexible and stable leans, tilts, center and off–center turns;
→ Foot positioning, gesture leg movements, and attitudes;
→ Step movements and sequences (with directional changes and frontal changes);
→ One and two–legged jumps and/or landings;
→ Falls and changes in body position (floorwork);
→ Swings and swinging movements;
→ Waves and impulse movements.

A wide range of exercise sequences and complex movement combinations can be created by selecting movement forms and motifs from the various element groups. These represent a systematically structured exercise program in which the dance's expressive quality is experienced by accessing a spectrum of variations as well as precise execution.

Beyond acquiring these qualities and skills through the involvement with the Jooss–Leeder Technique in Passow's classes, students are also made aware of fundamental technical movement principles; for example, alignment and centering, pelvis positioning, outward rotation in the pelvic joint, stable–labile (center and off–center), economy of movement, etc. In class students are able to experience the key features and peculiarities of this technique, and able to understand analogies by learning various ways of executing different movements (for instance, different types of curves or approaches to contractions, regulation of tension, and understandings of release).

Table 2: Eight Movement Qualities[24]

| Movement qualities | ENERGY/INTENSITY | | SPATIAL INITIATION/DESIGN | | SPEED/TIME | |
	strong	weak	central	peripheral	quick	slow
1	strong		central			slow
2		weak		peripheral	quick	
3	strong			peripheral		slow
4		weak	central		quick	
5	strong		central		quick	
6		weak		peripheral		slow
7	strong			peripheral	quick	
8		weak	central			slow

Wiebke Dröge

TEACHING: PRINCIPLES AND METHODOLOGY

CONCEPTUAL BASIS

Barbara Passow's pedagogical goal is to develop awareness by cultivating physicality, taste, and musicality. This comprehensive approach can be traced back to Rudolf von Laban:[25] "It is that person of clear mind, deep feeling, and strong desire who consciously seeks to attain a harmoniously balanced and yet limber whole that is nonetheless aware of the interdependence of all its moving parts."

Teaching both amateurs and professionals, Passow's instruction encompasses a broad spectrum in dance education. Jooss–Leeder movement themes are interwoven with elements from Limón Technique to achieve a characteristic movement aesthetic. The following themes outline the basic pedagogical framework:

→ Swings: pendulum swings, centrifugal swings, eight swings;
→ Accents: initial, transitional, terminal;
→ Leans, tilts;
→ Diagonals;
→ Turns: labile (off–center), stable (center), rising, sinking;
→ Jumps;
→ Impulse movements, waves;
→ Hip circles;
→ Scales, main movement directions, levels;
→ Foot–work, step forms;
→ Combinations, etudes.

These themes are the foundation for a learning process that is long–term in scope. During the three–week workshop, specific themes were worked through in a proficiency–oriented, predetermined teaching model in classes that built upon one another. Following Kurt Jooss and Sigurd Leeder's approach, Passow demands continual work on movement themes. "The goal is an optimal and comprehensive training for the body—the dancer's artistic instrument—with an honest, exact, and human mindset rather than making provision for a standard technique."[26] The

movement themes should help the student develop the material; the student's continued growth was important to Jooss as well.[27] Passow—with her personal interpretation of the technique and integration of the Limón Technique and elements of yoga—remains true to Jooss in this respect. She handles the movement themes in a specific way; from this the characteristic form of the Jooss–Leeder Technique evolves.

"It's not about *what* my body can do.
It's about *how* my body can move."
Marcella Piscitelli, student

Teaching skills, based on the movement themes (as outlined above), are connected to choreutic and eukinetic parameters. The movement technique builds on basic principles of alignment,[28] whereby balanced hip placement and alignment of the feet are particularly important. The dancer configures and plays with shifts of the body's center of gravity in a physical and rhythmic way. For swings, momentum is an important criterion. The high center, marked by the sternum, is also significant. The breastbone is understood to be a strong expressive medium; the upper torso is set into motion through the spine's rounding or sideward bending around this high pivot point. As all themes are taught with rhythmic–musical design, dance is always considered to be (and experienced as) integrated, and never as a sequence of isolated movements.[29]

With respect to form, Passow addresses the various ways a student can perceive movement and takes an individual's body structure into account when observing movement execution. From her personal point of view (as a successful professional performer and teacher), the statement, "I often see people working against their bodies," expresses the motif behind her approach. In this respect, her teaching speaks to the individual, to the person who dances, and against artificiality. By incorporating the widest range of movement qualities into formal combinations, the dancer should be able to engage with the movement themes through dance. This process promotes an approach of 'not exactly knowing, yet taking the risk to go beyond one's own knowledge' in movement. By the same token, the students' rhythmic–musical sensibility is also trained. The goal is to make the body, as an instrument, available in such a way that dancers can use the movement themes as a foundation from which they might develop and implement their own artistic ideas.

25 See Rudolf von Laban: *Die Welt des Tänzers. Fünf Grundgedanken.* Stuttgart: Walter Seifert Verlag, 1922, p. 3.
26 Tonja Wiebracht in Wiebracht 2007, p. 5.
27 "With his vision, Jooss never claimed to have developed a perfect, definitive movement vocabulary or an all–encompassing

technique, just as he never thought about codifying or setting one in stone. Doing so would contradict his attitude of dance as 'a living art form,' whose technique changes 'just like every other form of art.' Rather, Jooss hoped that his 'system would forge ahead and develop (and) would be able to change along with

the changing times.' Jooss was open to other dance styles from the start." (Stöckemann 2001, p. 236). See also: Historical Context.
28 *Alignment* here is understood as José Limón defined it: "Alignment is the correct, balanced placement of all parts of the body in their relationship to one another, originating

Target group: Barbara Passow teaches her version of the Jooss–Leeder Technique primarily to students at the *Palucca Schule Dresden—Hochschule für Tanz*, as well as to ambitious amateurs who regularly take classes with her. Group classes (as opposed to private instruction) make the most sense. The teaching can be varied in its degree of difficulty by increasing or decreasing the complexity of coordination along with the demands for flexibility, balance, strength, speed, and rhythm. Passow recommends four years of intensive involvement with the technique for dance career. Generally, the incorporation of so many different components will depend upon various factors—such as previous training, talent, and training frequency—meaning that a specific time frame for learning must be determined on an case–by–case basis. Previous knowledge of ballet and modern dance are helpful.

Noticeable progress was made during the fifteen–day workshop in London, including improved differentiation in the execution of movement phrases and more volume was seen in swings, steps, and suspensions. Movement expression also changed to a stronger, more outwardly directed presence.

The approach to the work employs mimetic learning, i.e., emulation. It is thus configured as a mirroring activity through which predetermined dance forms, phrases, and exercises are learned and embodied. Passow demonstrated and discussed a many–layered ideal, using internal and external images to orient the dancers. Partner work and small improvisational explorations provided experiential leeway that fostered technical improvement and strengthened sensitivity for movement. The class is teacher–centered. Learning is product–oriented in terms of movement acquisition, while the development of the dancer's self–image is clearly process–oriented.

Passow keeps an eye on the individual and the collective state of the class, and takes this into consideration when making decisions about feedback, demands, forbearance, and motivation. By paying attention to each dancer, she functions as a partner on the student's learning path.

Her approach to work requires that the students, for their part, be willing to put effort into learning, actively cooperate, and to conform to the given teaching structure. Passow is always physically present in her students' learning process. She is more than a witness to her students' processes in picking up movement; she consciously, actively, and sensitively engages in a learning process wherein she is extremely present and in which (depending on the situation) she alternates between personal attention, joining her students in the exercise, and concentrated observation. Passow supports her students, using her presence to help them to find and maintain focus.

PEDAGOGICAL METHODS

The lesson structure, as seen during the London project,[30] consisted of six sections (with a total of nine to eleven exercises) plus a combination that, in part, included elements from the current learning unit:

1. Movement in place; steps including torso and arm movements
2. Moving sideways through the space
3. Diagonals
4. Frontal circles, i.e., strew and scoop circles
5. Combinations of the above exercise elements
6. Jumps across the diagonal
7. Combinations

This more or less traditional class structure was varied by interspersing partner exercises, among other things. Training was successively and progressively structured according to the thematic emphases named above.

From a scholarly perspective, this technique specifically addresses rhythmic ability as a subsection of 'coordinative abilities':[31]

→ The ability to perceive rhythm through an individual's motor abilities (kinesthetic) and realize such through the following approaches:
  › Demonstration of new movement sequences using individual phrases, initially without music.
  › Recognizing dynamic structure to improve the execution and quality of movement sequences.
  › Determining and training quantitative and qualitative attributes.
  › Attuning what is heard to one's own motor rhythms in movement, with frequent repetitions to music, among other things.
  The body should adapt a rhythmic flow to the music.

→ Variation of specific rhythmic processes according to dynamic, temporal, or spatial criteria.

from the skeleton and its muscular support." See on this Daniel Lewis: *Illustrierte Tanztechnik von José Limón*. Wilhelmshaven: Florian Noetzel Verlag, 1990, p. 207.
29 Additional teaching goals can be deduced from the technique's central movement characteristics; see the section Movement Characteristics and Physicality under Understanding the Body / Movement.
30 See the DVDs and Class Plan on DVD 1.
31 *Coordinative abilities* is the "collective term for the conditions determined by information–reception and information–processing processes necessary for realizing movement." According to Hirtz, coordinative abilities include balance, responsiveness, rhythmic ability, being able to spatially orient oneself, and kinesthetic differentiation. Hirtz in Prohl / Röthig 2003, p. 308.

→ Making movement sequences more complicated, or expanding them, with respect to coordination; integrating sequences and rhythmic changes into movement combinations.
Increasing complexity and demands for precision in a movement sequence (stability) will make the exercises more complicated. Adding coordination requirements will increase virtuosity and adaptability.

Passow's rhythmic phrasing incorporates the upper torso by use of swings and tilts, and includes the arms. The step sequences through space come about half–way through the class, at the latest. Training usually begins with floorwork, including breathing exercises and elements of yoga, which serves to mentally prepare students and is not directly related to the exercises that follow.

After the warm–up phase on the floor, most of class takes place with students standing center floor, in rows. Movement sequences, in general, are characterized by a clearly defined beginning and end, with accents. Special attention is paid to spatial alignments. Spatial lines and pathways (ornaments) are clearly defined, for example, as 'round', 'eight circles', 'circle with loops', or 'straight'. Dealing with the frontal, sagittal, horizontal, and transversal body levels is deliberate, exact, and distinct. Phrases on the lower spatial levels (floorwork) are more sporadic and used to connect contrasting elements within a combination, and are not exercises in and of themselves.[32]

The overall impression of the Jooss–Leeder Technique, as seen in Passow's teaching, is one of a dancer usually standing upright, who makes extensive use of the space with marked articulation of the arms and torso.

Passow repeats each of the nine to eleven exercise sequences six to ten times. Because of her intensive pre-structuring, there are few pauses for students other than water breaks, moments of waiting for group performance, or during explanations and critique. From a physiological standpoint, the amount of repetition should improve muscular stamina. Improving aerobic fitness is a possible byproduct, although not aimed for, per se.

Work–load patterns can only be deduced by observation. The individual movement sequences are as follows:

→ Mostly whole–body exercises, or combinations using parts of the upper–body and the lower extremities;

→ Movement execution using a medium muscle tonus or a temporally structured change in tonus (i.e., contraction, hold and extend, swing and coming back to standing);

→ Increasing holding power, for leg–work in particular;

→ Targets maximum movement range for suspensions and swings;

→ Often characterized by extensive use of the space.

This combination of exercises puts demands on a wide range of muscle groups and the cardiovascular system.

Overall, the learning path described above leads from easy to complex. Passow increases or reduces complexity depending upon the teaching situation. Either individual phrases are practiced and then connected to a sequence, or partner exercises assist the student in understanding the movement or help develop the movement quality. Students work freely in the space in these moments, as an exception, and are allowed time for research.

Passow's teaching trains skills typical to ballet and modern dance techniques; for instance, motor retention, transferring movement sequences to the opposite side of the body, and muscle elasticity in the form of strength for leg lifts, jumps, and holding power. The latter is especially important for torso and pelvis stabilization and thus for alignment.

Variety in the methodology can be observed in how Barbara Passow communicates movement content, and less in the class structure. Her instructor–centered style requires a range of personal skills. Because the teacher is always the role model, he or she must have incorporated the Jooss–Leeder Technique at a professional level. The teacher additionally needs good demonstration skills along with an ability to verbally describe an exercise and convey rhythmic structure. This means having a keen sense of observation: being able to precisely differentiate is important inasmuch as a student's mimetic success is dependent upon adequate correction by the teacher. Thus the observer/teacher must be able to recognize the dancers' rhythmic execution independently from that of

32 Passow pointed out that many decisions about class content occur in conjunction with the overall curriculum at the Palucca Schule Dresden. Concentrations or adjustments arise from conversations with other teachers about the current learning curve of individual classes, or might arise from reactions to repetition of content, for example with the floorwork that, as the case may be, is covered in other classes and thus must not be repeated in the Jooss–Leeder class. This shows that the analysis of techniques and teaching decisions must be seen within a larger context, i.e., that of the overall teaching institution. The question is to what extent various content and teaching concepts influence one another within a dance educational context.
33 Visual and auditory impressions cannot be separated from one another when perceiving music and movement simultaneously. Furthermore, the auditory experience is more dominantly processed and determines the observer's experience of rhythm. "This may be based on the fact that—in contrast to visual perception—every auditory perception is only possible in connection with a temporal component (Neumann, et al 1986) and

the music, as far as possible.[33] Above and beyond this, a teacher must have knowledge of music theory for handling rhythm, meter, and beat. This applies to both the selection of prerecorded music as well as for communication and cooperation with live musicians.

Rhythm overall has a formative influence on motor learning. All dance exercises have a rhythmic design. The rhythmic phrasing, in combination with the music, creates the framework for the potential embodiment of movement qualities. Proper execution of rhythmic structures has great significance in the Jooss–Leeder Technique as taught by Barbara Passow. She preferably works with accentuation, intonations, and suspensions within the on– and off–beat rhythmic structure and in accordance with the music. The musical structures illustrate the dynamic and temporal design of movement, and vice versa. The goal of this restrictive approach is to develop a feeling for rhythmic structures and to recreate such structures in movement—and thus the development of (what is understood as) musicality in the dance. In contrast, the dialogue between dance and music in Passow's purely choreographic work is much more open and multidimensional. With the exception of the quiet beginning of class, which addresses breath rhythm, Passow works by talking, using onomatopoeia, or with music.

The overarching class content, along with musicality in movement, are those listed above. These are connected with central and peripheral movement initiation, body levels, spatial levels, and spatial directions. Specific movement phrases that train these elements are taught so that they build upon one another. The phrases have an inner relationship to one another: on the one hand, sequences combine, bit by bit, various technical elements and body areas with one another in the respective building–up exercises. On the other hand, elements from these exercises are integrated into the combination at the end of class. Intermediate phrases with specific movement motifs are repeated and practiced separately, and usually in a simplified form. In addition, the phrases are either related to one another by similarity in musical structure, or in that one phrase is a variation

of another. Movement requirements increase during the course of the class, in accordance with the learning path, going from simple to complex.

A notable aspect of the teaching concept is the impressive "running the gamut" (direct quote from Reinhild Hoffman, who also observed classes in London) in movement themes based on the variable parameters of space, time, and dynamic (and the corresponding complex possibilities for combining these elements). This 'running the gamut', in the sense of working through everything,[34] is accompanied by an appropriate choice of music and conscious use of rhythmic and musical variations.

Teaching this dance technique requires a basic understanding of art, one that touches upon the correlation between the individual dancer's subjective expressive will and formal–aesthetic design principles. Becoming proficient in the technique takes place primarily by repeating exercise sequences and combinations that the dancers fill with personal expression. Only then do the movements become performative and expressive, i.e., become dance. Kurt Jooss, described them as, "…one and the same: a technical exercise and a dance piece to music."[35]

The class delivers the groundwork for mastering technical skills needed for performance. The Jooss–Leeder Technique conveys good centering, differentiated movement quality, and, at the same time, a rhythmic–musical and

thus the perceived auditory structure can more immediately trigger the percipient's ideomotoric mechanism due to its dynamic properties, which are lacking in the perceived visual structures." (Klaus Wiemann: 'Rhythmus wahrnehmen—realisieren—lehren.' In: Kottmann, Lutz / Schaller, Hans-Jürgen / Stibbe, Günther (Ed.): *Sportpädagogik zwischen Kontinuität und Innovation.* Schorndorf: Hofmann Verlag, 1999, pp. 164–176).

34 The training here consists of working through particular movement themes and—connected with this—particular skills. In this respect, it leads to an application–oriented, generalized knowledge. Students become flexible in dealing with the material and their understanding is therefore deepened.

35 Kurt Jooss (1976) quoted from Stöckemann 2001, p. 230.

motor–qualitative 'feeling for form'. This is implicitly connected with a comprehensive and balanced physical training for dance. Additionally, it provides good preparatory training for companies in rehearsal. The artistic processes lie in the preparation of the body, as an instrument, to execute movements with clear and precise forms using a wide

binations that are rich in variety is, from the beginning, a form of dancing and performing with a clear focus.

Movement research and improvisation are important elements of the Jooss–Leeder methods.[36] These are, primarily, either a topic found under movement theory or stand–alone subjects within a dance education. In the observed technique classes at LABAN, London, improvisation was only used occasionally, for example, to find arm variations during a series of jumps.

Movement themes mentioned at the top of this section are used in preparation for teaching. Passow's work is to design, select, and specify exercise sequences and movement studies. She develops variations appropriate to the group's current learning curve, using a repertoire that has been built up over decades.

For self–assessment and feedback, Passow makes notes afterwards. The Jooss–Leeder Technique, as she teaches it, is conceptually open in regards to the order in which themes are taught. The notes allow her to maintain an overview regarding thematic material, and focuses therein, that have been dealt with.

The method of communication contributes a great deal to the overall image of the Jooss–Leeder Technique as taught by Passow. The technique is easily understood and 'visible' on a superficial and formal level. In order to comprehensively describe her working methods, we need to take a deeper look into Passow's knowledge.[37]

During the London teaching, we observed that Passow—aside from her use of basic ballet vocabulary—manages to communicate without specialized terminology or jargon; for the most part she was able to communicate what is essential to her with precision, authority, and presence. In a dance history context, she shares this with her longstanding, close relationship to her teacher Michael Diekamp—namely, the transmission of an imminent body of knowledge as both dancer and teacher. Years spent studying various body techniques as well as experiential knowledge

range of rhythmic–dynamic qualities, and to fill movement with personal emotional and expressive will. Further, movement should be projected, going beyond the dancer's body, out and into the space. In Jooss–Leeder training, artistic nurturing, learning, and development begin in class. The individual incorporates a dancer's habitus through mimesis. The acquisition and practice of standard, formal etudes (each with a different focus), and movement com-

36 See statements by Michael Diekamp in Diekamp 1994, pp. 126–131 as well as in Rüstroer 1996, pp. 62–70, among others.

37 In order to work out what is 'her own', the research team used dyadic conversation techniques. These were to guide Passow toward an inner relationship to herself (dyadic) and to the work methods that she uses and also bring forth her intuitive self–knowledge. (Dyadic conversation techniques aim towards an appreciative questioning

and investigation. They are also known under the term Appreciative Inquiry (AI), among others. The goal is to address the level of intuition behind the structured answer. The personal potential in this is appreciated as a valuable source of knowledge.)

indwells Passow, the dancer. Beyond this, she demonstrates the social interactions of embodiment and to embody. Passow, as dancer and teacher, consequently represents a style of composition and expression of particular cultures, as well as a diversity of techniques and internal and external approaches toward them.[38] In teaching, she conveys her work and its related historical and content–driven context through herself—as body knowledge. Especially due to her choice of teaching methods, i.e. imitation, the transfer of knowledge occurs to a large extent from body to body. Passow is not just imparting this dance form, she herself is the intermediary—on the levels of body, language, voice, person, inner bearing, and outward appearance. The dance vocabulary, as understood by Michael Diekamp, her husband (who had, in turn, learned from Kurt Jooss), has multidimensionally written itself into her consciousness and onto her physicality, and is intertwined with other experiential fields. Fueled by her passion for the dance, she shares an embodied realm of experiences with students by opening herself, and her physicality, for productive dialogue. All of this is palpable when she teaches. Passow used teaching methods that have significance and meaning for herself, in combination with the respective teaching approach and role.

When we speak of a transfer of information from body to body, then the technique becomes both the contents and the means of communicating: this happens in a bound, formless, and quality–related way. In the case of Passow's teaching, multi-sensory information speaks to the dancers in their corporeality and as social beings.

Barbara Passow begins her training in silence, with students lying on the floor. Her voice is nearly a whisper, so gentle it is almost as if she is asking for entry into another world, asking herself for permission into her store of knowledge, finding her way into the swing of it and setting up a connection—as if she must first find her way into 'transmission mode'.[39] "Starting with the swings, something gets going in me," is how she described it during a conversation. The swings awaken her desire to dance and bring her in touch with her energy ('gut instinct'). The swings create a strong dynamic that, for Passow, means, "Joy and giving oneself completely to the movement." Her movement motifs are characterized by rhythmic accents and beat changes (regular–irregular). A gut feeling, "the joy of contrasts," as she puts it, leads her through the class, whereby she makes use of her differ-

entiated and experienced handling of rhythmic movement sequences.

Selection of and decision for a particular series of rhythmic structures comes from her inner logic, mitigated by what Passow finds appropriate for her students. Rhythmic structures, especially strong accentuations and drawn–out phrasing, are her personal contribution to the Jooss–Leeder Technique. The joy of dancing, passion, rhythm, and expressive power are expressed as qualities within the technique's language. Beyond this, Passow establishes an experiential platform that places the Jooss–Leeder Technique in a larger context for the students.

On a sensory level, students employ sight, hearing, and touch for learning. Information is processed kinesthetically and aurally. Passow utilizes her voice to a great extent; along with speaking, she also makes vocal sounds with surprising effect. Her voice goes deep, occasionally becomes loud, and can generate long drawn–out or accentuated 'a' and 'o' sounds with abandon that resonate from her abdomen and chest. These sounds help students to experience their own movements more intensively. Passow is asking that the movement be filled with feeling and expression. Her voice reflects the movement's dynamic—similar to what has been reported about Kurt Jooss in this respect.[40] With its robust vitality, her voice serves as an inner 'dancing along', and assists students in finding impressions for movement.

In the students' questionnaire, the following comments were found: "She often uses her voice—especially a change in tone—in order to accentuate the desired dynamic." "She often uses (body)noises, which I find extremely helpful." "She often gives corrections through vocal expressions." Through her multifaceted vocal presence, Passow also conveys: "This is about something! What we are doing here is important."

Emotional feeling is also reflected on another level, without Passow explicitly intending it. When questioned about Passow's feelings for movement, students replied: "The movement leads the body, not vice versa." "Alongside the exercises Barbara tries to create an atmosphere with movement." "Because of what is sometimes a big difference between letting go and finding a fixed position, I feel powerful and free simultaneously." "Sturdier, like I thought I was going to a wedding." "Lively, vibrant, expressive, strong." "I like the flow." "Relaxed, stretching flow." "Space in the body." "I like the sensing of weight in

---

38 "Both ballet and expressionistic dance connote a 'body knowledge in movement' in that they draw on performance rules and strategies in moving oneself within the 'cultural memory' in order to symbolically express both oneself and culture by means of operating with symbols." (Nicole Faust:

Körperwissen in Bewegung. Vom klassischen Ballett zum Ausdruckstanz. Marburg: Tectum Verlag, 2006, p. 131.)

39 *Transmission mode* refers to which channels of communication are used to convey and to receive. Here the teacher opens up to an inner and outer responsive willingness, both for herself and the group.
40 See Stöckemann 2001, p. 361.

the swings." "I most enjoy the letting–go." "Risk, energy, flow." "I sense the air, lightness, and freedom."

Students also described to what extent Passow communicated the technique's concepts, beyond the exercises, and how she configures her relationship to the students: "She creates an inviting and human atmosphere." "She is never aggressive." "She is direct, spirited, and philosophical concerning the body." "I feel accepted." "She offers support in finding individuality." "She tries to convey an atmosphere in the movements." "Her teaching is clear, yet very challenging." "She is good at providing every individual with specific corrections." "She differentiated in details." "She gives very clear and direct feedback, which was the most important part of the communication of this technique for me." "She says exactly what the focus is in this special exercise." From their answers, it becomes clear that the individual and the details are what matters. To that end, precision also is a part of finding individual expression. The students additionally perceive themselves and their learning paths as important and valuable. In this respect, the learning processes and handling of feedback fosters a democratic notion in a teacher–centered class.

Imagery is used for teaching. Associative images improve students' impressions of movement, for example: "Stand like a tiger ready to pounce," for the body's presence and readiness for action; "Jump over a puddle," for the movement's range; "Ikea shelf cross," for the diagonal connections in the body and their extension into the space; "A car with good road handling," for a good connection to the floor when moving across it. Metaphoric imagery is also used, for instance: "Radiate beyond the skin," and "A waterfall is running down your spine." Four images appear repeatedly and have clear connotations, targeting the main points of reference for the Jooss–Leeder Technique as taught by Passow—alignment, momentum, and space:

→ The body's center of gravity is defined as residing two finger–widths below the navel and imagined as a "buoy in the water that bobs on the surface, securely inside of you."

→ The image of 'the line of the vertical axis extending far out into the space' is also continuously present, for instance when coming back to standing from swings and tilts.

→ During a swing's falling momentum, students should imagine a Ferris wheel or a rollercoaster; the goal is to create momentum and falling movement, to allow for acceleration and letting go of the upper torso.

→ The imagery for deep bends is *thinking of the space*: "You enclose a living space with your body" in the form of an imagined spherical continuation of the body (a ball for forwards, a snail's shell for backwards). This helps expand movement as well as the perception and presentation of the imagined space.

The following student statements complement observations about her imagery, the body, and hands–on: "She uses a lot of images/impressions and her body." "She uses images in order to explain the quality, the shape, or the initiation of a movement." "She presents images for a better understanding of movement." "Images in order to understand the movement's phrasing, rhythm, and shape." "Sometimes she describes a feeling." "She teaches a lot through her body." "She gives hands–on corrections, which I find very useful." "She touches in order for us to feel the right things." "Sometimes she touches body parts to research their relevance for a specific movement." As an aid for spatial and dynamic orientation, Passow also uses images of objects, like a book placed between the hands for parallel arm movements, or a jacket that is thrown off as the arms begin a swing.

Wiebke Dröge

CONCLUSION

The Jooss–Leeder Technique, as taught by Barbara Passow, is a teacher–centered training that strongly relies on deductive learning based on a movement's outward appearance. Through the type of communication, however, it also conveys more than just the shape of the movement itself: It transports humanistic values like acceptance, the importance of the individual, and enjoyment of the dance. Barbara Passow's strong mental, physical, and tangible presence fosters this. It can be deduced from students' statements that the Jooss–Leeder Technique's characteristic movement forms, in combination with the typical rhythmic accentuation and drawn–out phrasing, predominantly generate positive emotions in the dancers. The transference of dance knowledge is, in this respect, also accomplished.[41]

The Jooss–Leeder Technique, as taught by Barbara Passow, works through individual movement themes and their associated spatial, temporal, and dynamic design parameters—and thus remains true to the goals and aspirations of Jooss and Leeder. Musicality is trained when rhythmic–musical design is physically reproduced; this supports a consequential dialogue between music and dance that is hardly considered in most other contemporary dance techniques. Passow's personal presence (as described), together with her embodiment of the technique and the quality of her communication, have a direct influence on the movement materials and the students' awareness. Both the uniqueness as well as the significance of this technique lies in the blending and intertwining of these aspects.

41 "The psychological relationship to the physical movement is probably even more remarkable in the field of eukinetics than in choreutics…That feelings and emotions are connected with very specific spatial directions and movement approaches, that there is a 'type of psychological spatial harmony that corresponds with the physical', are principles upon which Jooss's artistic and pedagogic work is based." (Stöckemann 2001, p. 232).

LITERATURE

Diekamp, Michael
'Kurt Jooss: Seine Pädagogik und tänzerische Schulung'
In: Gesellschaft für Tanzforschung (Ed.): Ausdruckstanz in Deutsch-
land – Eine Inventur. Mary Wigman–Tage 1993
Wilhelmshaven: Florian Noetzel Verlag, 1994, pp. 126–131

Faust, Nicole
**Körperwissen in Bewegung: Vom klassischen Ballett
zum Ausdruckstanz**
Marburg: Tectum Verlag, 2006

Gorgas, Gabriele
"Schatten Rosen Schatten"
In Dresden starb 68-jährig der Tänzer,
Tanzpädagoge und Choreograf Michael Diekamp
http://www.tanznetz.de (as seen on 7 February 2010)

Jeschke, Claudia
**Tanz als BewegungsText: Analysen zum Verhältnis von
Tanztheater und Gesellschaftstanz (1910–1965)**
Tübingen: Max Niemeyer Verlag, 1999

Keller, Reiner
**Bericht über eine internationale und interdisziplinäre Tagung
der Sektion Wissenssoziologie & Soziologie des Körpers
und des Sports**
Universität Koblenz-Landau, 2009
http://www.uni-koblenz-landau.de/landau/fb6/sowi/soziologie/mi-
tarbeiter/sozio-profs/keller/keller-bericht-korperwissen.doc/view
(as seen on 3 March 2010)

Klein, Gabriele
**'Was ist modern am modernen Tanz? –
Zur Dekonstruktion dualistischer Tanzverhältnisse'**
In: Gesellschaft für Tanzforschung (Ed.): Jahrbuch 1993, Volume 4
Wilhelmshaven 1993, Florian Noetzel Verlag, pp. 61–72

Laban, Rudolf von
Der moderne Ausdruckstanz
Wilhelmshaven: Heinrichshofen Verlag, 1981

Laban, Rudolf von
Die Welt des Tänzers: Fünf Grundgedanken
Stuttgart: Walter Seifert Verlag, 1922

Lewis, Daniel
Illustrierte Tanztechnik von José Limón
Wilhelmshaven: Florian Noetzel Verlag, 1990

Müller, Grete
**Sigurd Leeder: Tänzer, Pädagoge und Choreograf
Leben und Werk**
Herisau: Verlag Appenzeller Medienhaus, 2001

Müller, Grete
'Demonstration der Sigurd-Leeder-Methode'
In: Gesellschaft für Tanzforschung (Ed.):
Ausdruckstanz in Deutschland – Eine Inventur
Mary Wigman-Tage 1993
Wilhelmshaven: Florian Noetzel Verlag, 1996, pp. 108–113

Müller, Hedwig | Stabel, Ralf | Stöckemann, Patricia
Krokodil im Schwanensee: Tanz in Deutschland seit 1945
Frankfurt: Anabas Verlag, 2003

Prohl, Robert | Röthig, Peter u.a. (Ed.)
Sportwissenschaftliches Lexikon
Schorndorf: Hofmann Verlag, 2003

Rick, Cary
Tanztherapie: Eine Einführung in die Grundlagen
In cooperation with Claudia Jeschke
Stuttgart / New York: Gustav Fischer Verlag, 1989

Rüstroer, Birgit
'Ein Interview mit Michael Diekamp'
In: Gesellschaft für Tanzforschung (Ed.): Jahrbuch 1995, Volume 6
Wilhelmshaven: Florian Noetzel Verlag 1996, pp. 62–70

Stöckemann, Patricia
**Etwas ganz Neues muß nun entstehen:
Kurt Jooss und das Tanztheater**
München: K. Kieser Verlag, 2001

Wiebracht, Tonja
**'"Doch eines fehlt dem neuen Tanz in Deutschland: Die konse-
quente Systematisierung der Tänzererziehung."
Die Folkwang Hochschule wird 80'**
In: Ballett Intern, 4/2007, pp. 4–8

Wiemann, Klaus
'Rhythmus wahrnehmen—realisieren—lehren'
In: Kottmann, Lutz | Schaller, Hans-Jürgen | Stibbe, Günther (Ed.):
Sportpädagogik zwischen Kontinuität und Innovation.
Schorndorf: Hofmann Verlag, 1999, pp. 164–176

Winearls, Jane
Modern Dance: The Jooss-Leeder-Method
London: Billing & Sons, 1958

LINKS

www.dartington.org/archive/display/T/AD
www.folkwang-uni.de
www.tanzakademie-brakel.de
www.tanzraum.ch

Wibke Hartewig

OBSERVATION TECHNIQUES

MOVEMENT ANALYSIS FOR CONTEMPORARY DANCE TECHNIQUES

"The head will follow. If you simply leave it behind in the space, it will come along because of its natural weight." A., following the Countertechnique teacher's directions, is focused on his cervical vertebrae, sensing movement in his back as it progresses upwards and toward his head.[1] Meanwhile, B., who is dancing next to A., is wondering whether or not gravity is applied the same way it was in yesterday's Release Technique training. Today's Release class, by teacher C., is being observed by dance scholar D. who wants to find out which movement characteristics occur automatically during the ongoing improvisation: D. is investigating the influence of improvisational techniques on movement aesthetics. At the same time, she is doing groundwork for E., a dramaturg, who wants to incorporate a similar form of live improvisation in his newest choreography; the two of them will discuss the impact of using such a scene in a finished work. Later, F. will be sitting in D.'s seat, taking notes about the characteristics of the Jooss–Leeder Technique training, working on a document for the Leeder Archive about how this technique is being passed on. While this is happening, G. is observing H., her student, do pliés as he has knee problems.

Dance movement is observed for myriad reasons by a number of people with different levels of expertise. Those who are observing might not consider what they do to be movement analysis. When a dancer takes up a teacher's corrections, is that movement analysis? What if said dancer unconsciously breaks down the combination into parts so as to be better able to grasp it? Or is an analysis happening when a dancer, during an improvisation, exercises self–observation in order to play with movement parameters? Ultimately, every dance teacher conducts some type of movement analysis during a class, an analysis that is fused with teaching methods and one that is also conveyed to the students. Accordingly, the ways of observing movement in contemporary dance training are as hybrid and dependent upon the personalities involved as is the field of teaching contemporary dance.

A contemporary dance technique[2], because it is concerned with and of itself, might make the impression that analytical methods are part of the work—especially in techniques wherein the body's anatomical and physiological elements are resourced, referred to by name, and called upon during class. At the same time, what are known as somatic techniques, like Body–Mind Centering, Alexander Technique, Feldenkrais method, and Klein Technique, represent a special case: They explore and encourage personal investigation that foster (self)awareness of the body and movement processes.[3] Contemporary dance training—whether it be a somatic work, improvisation, or modern and postmodern dance—includes any number of techniques that engage conscious analysis in varying degrees.

Besides movement observation inside the dance, methods for movement analysis exist that are more geared toward theoretical analysis. This essay is about these methods;

---

1 The technique named here, by way of example, was chosen from the techniques discussed in detail in this book.

2 About the definition of 'dance technique' and the characteristics of contemporary dance techniques, see the introduction by Ingo Diehl and Friederike Lampert.

3 See essay by Irene Sieben about somatic techniques.

4 See introduction by Ingo Diehl and Friederike Lampert as well as the results of the research projects in this book.

methods that are characterized by analytic processes that make movement accessible for discussions within a context broader than practical exploration done while dancing, the pure perception or correction of movement, and its analysis for the purposes of imitation. These methods were created in order to reflect upon movement from an outside perspective. They have an inherently systematic approach oriented to extracting particular insights.

The following discusses what movement analysis processes can look like, which analytic methods are often used for dance, and how they work for contemporary dance techniques.

To start: What characteristics of contemporary techniques must the analyst consider? Contemporary dance is a hybrid form. Depending upon the respective artist and/or teacher, it is an amalgam of various and sundry movement experiences that are expressed as the individual's technique—meaning there is no uniform movement vocabulary or terminology that can be drawn upon for description. Similarly, there is no uniform concept about movement—i.e., in relation to a particular hierarchy for using body parts, to the space and the floor, or to rhythm—to use as a starting point, such that, theoretically, all types of movement can be used equally. Correspondingly, every contemporary dance technique sets its own focal points and priorities. Because the technique must define and position itself, it is usually strongly (self)reflective, conscious of the provenance of its elements, and possibly comments upon this provenance and makes it a subject of discussion.[4]

Movement analysis methods must thus be flexible in their approach to extreme differences in movement phenomena, i.e., be applicable independent of a particular aesthetic. The analyst should be able to independently select which aspects of movement to be focused on depending upon the technique's special characteristics: Do hand movements, for example, play a large role? Are movements executed in strong relation to the space? Is the focus on dynamics and use of energy?

The analytic method should also match the interests of the analyst, not just be appropriate to the specific subject of study. An analyst using a contemporary movement observation technique should engage in self-questioning on multiple levels, analogous to a contemporary dance technique's introspective nature.[5] It is helpful to ask oneself the following questions at the beginning of every analytic process:

→ What is my interest? What specific questions do I want to answer?
   What hypotheses do I wish to assess over the course of the analysis?

→ What previous knowledge (including body knowledge), experiences, and
   expectations am I bringing into this process?

→ Which movement phenomena do I want to investigate? Which of these
   presents the best example for my study goals? What are the specific historical,
   ideological, conceptual, etc. contexts?

None of these questions can be answered independently from the others. Any one of them could serve as the initial question for the investigation; the respective answers reciprocally bring both answers and questions better into focus.

5 The demand for critical reflection of one's own actions is a part of most analytic methods developed for dance and theater studies in the last several decades. It ultimately results from a reasoning rooted in postmodern, (post)structuralism theories of the 1970s and 80s—similar to many concepts of contemporary dance artists. For movement analysis see, for example, Claudia Jeschke: *Tanz als BewegungsText. Analysen zum Verhältnis von Tanztheater und Gesellschaftstanz (1910–1965)*. Tübingen: Max Niemeyer Verlag, 1999, p. 42; for performance analysis see, for instance, Guido Hiss: *Der Theatralische Blick. Einführung in die Aufführungsanalyse*. Berlin: Dietrich Reimer Verlag, 1993, pp. 7–81; for both see, for example, Peter M. Boenisch: *körPERformance 1.0. Theorie und Analyse von Körper- und Bewegungsdarstellungen im zeitgenössischen Theater*. Munich: epodium, 2002, pp. 22–85.

And finally:

→ Which analytical methods best fit my interests and research subject?
How can I fine tune the methods to match both my interests and the subject?

→ To what extent are this method and my overall approach historically informed?

In order to find the appropriate movement analysis method, one should be aware of the methods' idiosyncrasies: The potential for providing insights depends on the methods' respectively unique perspectives on movement.[6] Every analysis method reveals different things.

What does the matching of a movement analysis method to a particular question and a movement phenomenon actually look like? Let us return to the situation presented at the start of this essay. Dance scholar D. is interested in how certain improvisation techniques form movement. Her question is: Which recurring movement features occur automatically when the dancers improvise on the basis of Release Technique as taught by C.? D. is analyzing dance from the viewpoint of a scholarly observer and dramaturg who, among other things, is interested in aesthetics. She has already investigated various other improvisation techniques, is familiar with C.'s work, his concepts about the body, movement, and dance training, and she knows which dance techniques are referenced in his work.[7] This knowledge leads D. to assume that the improvisation mode specifically affects the movement flow, the movement's energetic–dynamic structure, the dancers' physical tonus, and where the impulse for movement comes from as well as the relationship between the dancers—a hypothesis that also has influenced the observational model she constructed for the analysis.

D. has decided to work with the **Inventory of Movement (Inventarisierung von Bewegung—IVB)**, a movement analysis method developed by Claudia Jeschke in Germany in 1999 that was designed to assist dance and theater scholars.[8] IVB appears to be well suited to D.'s objectives because it allows an overview of fundamental movement patterns to be notated without having to record details of the movement sequence chronologically. So, not least, the choice of method takes the improvisational character of the event into account. The method is also well suited for opening up movement to a theoretical discussion inasmuch as it allows movement to be transcribed into the written word, not (necessarily) into dance notation or other visual or digital mediums.[9] This makes the method relatively accessible, and it can also be learned quickly. The IVB system contains those features required for the analysis of contemporary dance techniques: It is flexible, adaptable, and requires critical reflection. This is due, in no small part, to the fact that the method was developed with an eye towards early forms of so–called contemporary dance at a time when these began rapidly developing in very different directions.

IVB can be used to investigate every type of human movement. It approaches movement as a motor process; the descriptive vocabulary is taken directly from the body's motor functions. IVB thus works with a neutral language inasmuch as it remains independent of dance style, genre, or a particular aesthetic. The observer puts himself into the dancer and imagines the movement's execution from the dancer's point of view; he thus uses the movement's *production* (not its result) to conceptualize the body, space, and time.[10] IVB differentiates between four basic motor activities that—it is assumed—

6 For example: Which observer perspective is being taken? How do the methods deal with the special characteristics of movement, i.g., with the interplay of body, space, and time, with movement as a process, with the physical understanding? How can movement be transferred—at least temporarily—into a different medium (be it verbally, visually, or numerically) in order to make it accessible to discussion? (About the particularities of 'reading' movement vis-à-vis other media in general, see Wibke Hartewig: *Kinästhetische Konfrontation. Lesarten der Bewegungstexte William Forsythes*. Munich: epodium, 2007, pp. 20–32.)

7 It is self–evident that movement analysis cannot occur in a vacuum, i.e., that a movement event must always also be considered with respect to its conceptual, historical, ideological, aesthetic, etc. context.

8 Jeschke 1999.

9 While IVB does offer the possibility to note an overview of the observed movement characteristics with the assistance of special symbols, this is nothing more than an additional methodological option.

10 In this manner, the observer's kinesthetic empathy is also addressed.

comprise every movement: 'mobilizing', 'coordinating', 'supporting', and 'regulating'. These activities are each assigned a series of observation criteria.[11] The analyst watches the interaction of the activities, focusing on which motor phenomena are present, how they are connected, and which motor systems and concepts come together. IVB offers a structured framework full of descriptive vocabulary; the person using it must select from the options and combine elements in order to establish what items will be observed. The descriptive vocabulary is understood to be incomplete and open to diversification and enhancement, which is what makes it so flexible: On one hand, it can be fine tuned to the technique's characteristics and, on the other, it can focus on describing only the motor structures relevant to the respective question. The conscious positioning of the observer (i.e., grappling with the questions mentioned above), is thus a vital prerequisite and explicitly part of the system.[12]

D., from the introductory example, has put together an observation model based on IVB's ideas and vocabulary that she is now using to target individual movement characteristics. Her questions, working hypotheses, and the technique observed are reflected in this model in various ways: For instance, she is paying close attention to the area of energy and use of strength (i.e., regulating), the form of support, the movement flow (an aspect of mobilizing), and combines these with non-IVB observation criteria like 'impulse for the movement', 'direction of view', and the 'use of the laws of physics'. She has also expanded the IVB criteria by including observation items about how the dancers interact with one another. During the observation, she ignores all gestures that can be traced back to the individual dancer's personal movement vocabularies and, instead, concentrates on movement characteristics that are similar among the improvising dancers.[13] After that, she examines how the individual characteristics are connected and which general rules of movement can be deduced from these connections. Finally, she asks herself about the relation between motor patterns and the chosen improvisation technique.

D. can now further use these results by, for example, comparing them with results from her analyses of other improvisation techniques. Or she can discuss with choreographer E. how this type of movement would work in a scene of his piece, what affect it might have on the audience, and which associations it might evoke. Movement analysis and interpretation are thus two separate steps in IVB.

While IVB integrates flexibility into its methodical approach (and thereby includes the critical reflection of the analyst), this is not necessarily the case for other movement analysis methods—which can be traced back to the time when they were created and thus reference a corresponding view of (dance) movement. However, nothing speaks against using such methods to examine contemporary techniques, providing the essential positioning has been determined beforehand—i.e.: Which method matches my questions? What questions can be answered by the method? How can and must the methods be adjusted to meet the object and goals of the observation? This implies the analyst understands that the method is a collection of options and observational instruments from which he or she can select; the selection, however, must be made with the knowledge of any given method's formative context.

Kinetography Laban/Labanotation and **Laban Movement Analysis (LMA)**, for example, are some of the most commonly used notational and/or analysis methods; IVB also counts them among its predecessors. Beginning in the 1920s in Germany, Rudolf von Laban designed a dance notation system known in England as *Kinetography* and in the

11 See Jeschke 1999, pp. 52–57 and the accompanying booklet for a table of these criteria as well as detailed explanations with additional descriptive vocabulary.
12 Among the direct predecessors to Inventory of Movement are the movement analysis methods of *Movement Evaluation Graphics* (MEG), developed cooperatively by Jeschke and Cary Rick (Cary Rick/Claudia Jeschke: 'Movement Evaluation Graphics'. In: Rick,

Cary. *Tanztherapie. Eine Einführung in die Grundlagen.* Stuttgart/New York: Fischer Verlag, 1989, pp. 23–89). MEG will not be addressed in further detail here as it is used primarily in dance therapy.
13 This describes one of many ways to use IVB; detailed descriptions of other applications can be found in Jeschke 1999, pp. 58–181 and Hartewig 2007, pp. 128–288.

U.S. as *Labanotation*, where it was further developed, simultaneously with Kinetography in Europe. After World War II in the U.S., Laban's student Irmgard Bartenieff took his notational system and ideas and merged them with the Laban-based *effort/shape* theory to create *Laban Movement Analysis*.[14]

Laban–based methods are closely intertwined with choreutics, Laban's 'spatial harmony theory of dance' (*Raumharmonielehre des Tanzes*): Space and movement are inseparably related to one another and mirror each other—an assumption that was very much in keeping with its time and the holistic view of the world. Laban perceives movement as having its own dynamic, as a phenomenon that exists independent of the context of traditional dance forms. Respectively, his analytical method is directed toward all forms of movement. It examines the movement *process*, whereby the focus lies on the spatial pathways, which are known as 'trace forms' (*Spurformen*). This puts the focus on the movement's geometric content, the 'living architecture' that it creates in the space and which can be described using the model of the kinesphere.

Laban also systemized the qualitative aspects of movement in his *effort* theory, developed later. He assumes that a particular inner effort triggers a certain physical and emotional reaction. Accordingly, a feeling and/or an inner intention attend every movement and are expressed in the movement's respective dynamic and rhythmic quality. He describes these qualities as a series of effort patterns that combine the factors of space, weight, time, and flow in a different way in each case.

Laban Movement Analysis first examines movement in separate categories, namely body, effort, space, and shape (BESS), and then looks at how these interact. Use of the body and changes in body shape, use of space, and movement effort are not just described, they are also assigned certain characteristics that reflect the dancer's inner world. These characteristics cannot, ultimately, be perceived by an outside observer and thus remain an interpretation. Accordingly, movement is not just being observed, but also interpreted at the same time.[15]

Using LMA, movement can even be analyzed without knowledge of Laban's notational language, although its concept is based on Kinetography. In contrast, a purely notational–based movement observation targets other objectives and insights.[16] Following Laban's original intention, the goal of Kinetography is to record movement as completely as possible, thus to document the dance in order to archive and reproduce it.[17] In contrast to IVB or LMA, Kinetography is initially descriptive and not devised to make movement accessible or available to a theoretical discussion.[18] The structure of the notational language allows the person doing the notation to take on the dancer's perspective: The body is viewed from behind and symmetrically divided on paper into a left and right half; from bottom to top, the system of lines describes the body's movement through space and time. For the dancer and the person doing notation, the body's left and right sides correspond to one another, their spatial perception is identical. Despite the purely abstract symbols, it is thus fairly easy for someone experienced in the notational language to quickly note the movements and to re-translate the notes into movement. Over time, the catalogue of symbols that Laban originally created with a view toward German free dance (*Ausdruckstanz*) has been expanded, and the notational form has been modified for various

14 Laban analysis is especially widespread in the United States and England. While German dance universities focus solely on the teaching of Kinetography (LMA is mostly taught in private courses), LMA is the standard for analysis in dance and dance studies institutions in the Anglo-American world. (About Laban, see Rudolf von Laban: *Choreutik. Grundlagen der Raum-Harmonielehre des Tanzes*. Wilhelmshaven: Noetzel, 1991; Rudolf von Laban: *Die Kunst der Bewegung*. Wilhelmshaven: Noetzel, 1988; see the literature list for more information.)

15 Because of this feature, LMA is used in dance therapy in particular: Movement characteristics are linked to particular psychological attributes. See, for example, Susanne Bender: *Die psychophysische Bedeutung der Bewegung. Ein Handbuch der Laban Bewegungsanalyse und des Kerstenberg Movement Profiles*. Berlin: Logos Verlag, 2007.

16 Writing movement always also includes its analysis: The movement must be mentally broken down into recordable units and the person doing it must decide what is to be written and how it is to be accomplished. This

person follows a particular impression about movement inherent in the respective notational form. Thus a notational language can also be called a method of movement analysis.

17 The secondary idea to use this notational language—similar to musical notation—as a tool for composition has rarely been used in practice.

18 By way of contrast, *Motif Notation* (also known as *Motif Writing* or *Motif Description*), a simplified form of Labanotation, developed by Ann Hutchinson Guest, offers a notational form for selected movement features that can be customized to record movements for

ends so that now, using Kinetography, even the most diverse movement phenomena can be recorded.[19]

Kinetography Laban is excellent, for example, for documenting the sequences from the Jooss–Leeder Technique as presented in the imaginary scene at the beginning of this essay: Both the dance form and the notational language focus on spatial and body geometry, and the notational language needs only be slightly modified to match the movement phenomena—which is hardly surprising, because Laban's notational language and the dance technique sprung from the same environment.[20]

Movement notation can also serve analytical evaluation beyond the purposes of documentation. The advantage over the spoken word is the visual depiction of the examined phenomenon that can better translate the movement's visual characteristics. Furthermore, this depiction—depending on the notational language used—can allow for better recognition of patterns that can be used analytically. This is especially true of the **Eshkol– Wachmann Movement Notation (EWMN)**, which, along with Kinetography Laban/Labanotation and *Benesh Movement Notation*,[21] is currently the most commonly used form of dance notation. Noa Eshkol and Avraham Wachmann introduced EWMN in 1958 in Israel. Their goal was to be able to record every movement of the human body, (not necessarily movement in dance), independent of emotional or stylistic expression.[22] The method focuses on mechanical aspects of physical movements. The body is abstracted from an anatomical viewpoint, and body parts are imagined as lines between two joints or connected to a joint. Movement means change in the joints: This can be recorded as coordinates located on the surface of a sphere upon which the free end of the respective body part moves. Movement can therefore be described quantitatively and abstractly without a specific dance vocabulary.

In contrast to Kinetography Laban, EWMN was specifically developed as an instrument for composition, not primarily for documentation purposes.[23] Accordingly, this notation system is more systematic than that of Laban and uses a more manageable number of symbols.[24] Because it is more abstract, however, it is also further removed from the movement phenomenon's visual form. Labanotation (thanks to its 'proximity to the movement') thus allows faster notation, reading, and dancing from the score, while EWMN (thanks to its systematization and clarity) is not only good for composition but can also be used for further movement analysis. Reoccurring structures, clusters, and patterns can be easily recognized and compared so that regularities in movement sequences can be formulated and interpreted respective to the research goal.[25]

Along with notational dance languages, **filmic and digital media** also provide forms of visualizing movement. The following presents a few short, exemplary descriptions of individual projects—in most cases, these are not methods for movement analysis, but tools that can be used for analysis, tools that are gaining relevance in movement research and have their own underlying concepts of movement observation. Film and video recordings work well for visualizing movements as they provide immediacy through visual and kinesthetic proximity to the subject. They are often used for documentation purposes.

use as a memory aid and basis for discussion. See www.lodc.org, Language of Dance (LOD), about Guest's analytic method that works with Motif Notation, among other things.
19 See, about the history of the notational language, Henner Drewes; *Transformationen. Bewegung in Notation und digitaler Verarbeitung.* Essen: Die blaue Eule, 2003, pp. 75–80.
20 The close connection between Laban's movement analysis ideas and Jooss–Leeder Technique can clearly be seen in the training for this technique; see, for instance, Barbara Passow's class on the accompanying DVDs.
21 *Benesh Movement Notation* is not dealt with further here as it was developed for ballet notation and its perspective is generally derived from this dance style. Emio Greco provided an interesting example of how Benesh Notation can also be used to document certain forms of contemporary dance with his project Capturing Intention; see Emio Greco I PC/Amsterdamse Hogeschool voor de Kunsten (Ed.): *Capturing Intention. Documentation, analysis and notation research based on the work of Emio Greco I PC.* Amsterdam: Emio Greco I PC and AHK, 2007.
22 About the characteristics of EWMN, see Drewes 2003, pp. 69–75/88–111.
23 Noa Eshkol actually choreographed a series of dances with her language. Notational scripts and performance videos of these dances can be found, for instance, under www.ewmncenter.com/133376/Dance-Suites.
24 This is not least due to the underlying knowledge about physical mechanics: The description allows the exclusion of all of those things that are automatic givens about the anatomical conditions and the body's functions.
25 EWMN has also been used to diagnose autism in infants and for the scientific analysis of animal behavior; see Drewes 2003, p. 103.

Techniques like *Motion Capture* record movement and translate it into data in such a way that it can be analyzed by computer; the material can be re-animated at any desired level of abstraction. Multimedia formats, in turn, link documents so that movement can be viewed repeatedly from different perspectives with a click of the mouse, and these various perspectives compared directly to one another on the screen—thus presenting manifold points of view.[26]

A series of multimedia projects in the form of CD-ROMs/DVD-ROMs or online platforms are dedicated to archiving and imparting the movement and choreographic concepts of individual artists or dance techniques. These projects also exploit media potential in order to illustrate movement–analytical thought processes. Among the most famous is William Forsythe's *Improvisation Technologies*—the imaginary geometric forms upon which the dancers orient themselves when dancing are traced as white lines and forms by computer animation and then placed on top of the filmed movement sequences.[27] Forsythe's follow–up project, the interactive online platform *Synchronous Objects*, can be understood as the documentation of a movement analysis study of a group choreography's structure.[28] Using similar graphic means, it makes the 'cues' and 'alignments' visible that interconnect dancers during a performance of Forsythe's piece *One flat thing, reproduced*. This is based upon empirical data that has been gathered by questioning the participating dancers. This allowed the choreography's operating rules, which could never be described from outside, to be determined from the inside.[29]

Both *Improvisation Technologies* and *Synchronous Objects* have been used in dance classes: With assistance from these digital tools, certain forms of movement observation—especially spatial awareness and awareness of connections between dancers—can be trained in order to be used in practical (improvisation) exercises and thus be transferred into physical processes.[30]

In contrast to these projects, Henner Drewes and Claudia Jeschke are developing software inside the scope of the *Visualizing Dance Archives* project at the University of Salzburg that will provide an instrument for movement analysis.[31] The software allows motor and kinesthetic information from a wide variety of dance documents to be translated into three–dimensional movement sequences. Unlike 3D–animation software such as *DanceForms*,[32] this program will specifically support movement research and analysis, and assist in the reconstruction of movement in particular. The vision is to create a movement archive in which, bit by bit, body positions and movement sequences can be saved, separated into dance styles, techniques, or choreographic signatures.[33] Using these building blocks, users can then choose, combine, and change details within the dance simulation they have just constructed. The instrument could also be used to recognize gaps when reconstructing dance sequences and to design transitions for these gaps through creative trial and error. An archive with this potential would not only be extremely useful for scholarly research and reconstructing historic dances, it could also be employed in contemporary training when dancers need to be aware of historic interweaving of movement materials. They could, then, through experimentation with the animated sequences, experience these in their own dancing.

All observation methods discussed thus far are characterized by the fact that they look at the visible movement phenomena, meaning those attributes that are visible on the

26 The DVD-ROM / DVD / Book project *Capturing Intention* by Emio Greco I PC, for instance, explores such a form of multi-perspective archiving of a workshop by the choreographer pair; Emio Greco I PC / AHK 2007.
27 William Forsythe: *Improvisation Technologies. A Tool for the Analytical Dance Eye.* (CD-ROM with booklet) Karlsruhe: ZKM, 1999.
28 www.synchronousobjects.osu.edu.
29 Building upon *Synchronous Objects*.

Forsythe and his colleagues are currently working on a notational system for dance as part of their Motion Bank program—thus ultimately their own movement analysis method. See, for example, www.kulturstiftung-des-bundes.de / cms / de / sparten / film_und_neue_medien / motion_bank.html.
30 Anouk van Dijk, for example, uses Forsythe's improvisation techniques in her Countertechnique (see chapter in this book) in order to physically explore various spatial di-

rectional possibilities. Furthermore, Forsythe's colleagues teach practical dance workshops based on these multimedia tools.
31 *Visualizing (the Derra de Moroda) Dance Archives,* www.movement-notation.org / VisualizingArchives.
32 *www.credo-interactive.com / danceforms.*
33 The project is initially focusing on the visualization of material from the Salzburg Derra de Moroda Dance Archive's collection of 19th century dance. They hope to con-

body's surface and can be perceived by an outside observer. However, there are also movement analysis methods dedicated to internal movement processes, for instance the broad field of **biomechanics**, which is playing an increasingly important role in dance training.

Biomechanics, a branch of biophysics, examines the mechanical conditions behind human movement.[34] It was primarily developed in the 1970s as an independent scientific discipline. While it initially found application in sports and industrial sciences, it soon made inroads into orthopedics. Biomechanical analysis defines the body as a mechanical apparatus, as a collection of rigid segments connected at the joints. Every movement can be divided into separate joint movements for investigation. The biomechanical perception of movement as a change in position of a point on the body, a body part, or the entire body in space within a certain time period is correspondingly mechanistic. Simplification is necessary in order to make the human body's highly complex movement processes measurable and calculable. Movement is thus transformed into quantitative and descriptive data.

Biomechanical investigation includes anatomical, physiological, and body–mechanical knowledge that is separated into three main fields of analysis: (1) movement description, (2) analysis of muscle activity and muscle function, and (3) analysis of forces that impact the body.

Producing, recording, and evaluating biomechanical data requires special measuring instruments from simple inclinometers and accelerometers (manual and electronic) to extremely complex technical procedures that can only be accomplished in appropriately equipped laboratories. The most common methods in the latter category are *Motion Capture*, used to record and reconstruct movement as well as to calculate extrapolated values like speed and acceleration; *electromyography*, used to research muscle activity; *dynamography*, to record the forces impacting the body (pressure distribution measurements using force platforms, for instance); and *dynamometry*, to measure muscle function and muscular strength production.[35] These procedures are often used in combination, and the data are synchronized in order to create a complex profile of movement's cause and effect.

Biomechanical analysis becomes interesting for the dance when considering the optimization of individual movement processes, an efficient training design, health, and injury prevention (like it is used in its main areas of application in sports, sports sciences, medicine, and physiotherapy). Biomechanical knowledge about ideal movement execution, on the one hand, and knowledge about one's own movement processes (including the physical requirements), on the other, can assist dancers in improving their technique and allow for the best–possible utilization of individual abilities. The dancers, their teachers, physiotherapists, or dance medicine physicians can recognize vulnerabilities and trace the origin of problems in particular movements and thus appropriately adjust training and prevent injury.[36] Accordingly, biomechanical methods are especially relevant for dance techniques that are geared towards shaping and reproduction of certain movement processes.

As opposed to competitive sports, dance practitioners still have problems in doing biomechanical movement analyses that include all the measurement processes. Expensive instruments and elaborate measuring techniques require financial resources, experts, and laboratories that are usually only found at universities, in hospitals, or rehabilitation

struct movement archives for other dance forms as well.

34 About biomechanics, see Yiannis Koutedakis/Emmanuel O. Owolabi/Margo Apostolos: 'Dance Biomechanics. A Tool for Controlling Health, Fitness, and Training' and Margaret Wilson/Young-Hoo Kwon: 'The Role of Biomechanics in Understanding Dance Movement. A Review', both in: *Journal of Dance Medicine & Science*, Vol. 12, No 3, 2008, pp. 83–90/109–116.

35 For a detailed description of these methods see Koutedakis 2008, pp. 83–85 and Bettina Bläsing: 'The dancer's memory. Expertise and cognitive structures in dance'. In: Bläsing, Bettina/Puttke, Martin/Schack, Thomas: *The Neurocognition of Dance. Mind, Movement and Motor Skills*. Hove/New York: Psychology Press, 2010, pp. 79–81.

36 Much biomechanical information has been obtained over the course of sports science investigations. However there are now also studies about all these fields of application that deal especially with questions relevant to the dance. For instance, individual movement sequences (i.e., plié, balance, and jumps) or stress on individual body parts (i.e., the ankle joint) have been analyzed. For an overview of specific studies, see Wilson 2008, pp. 111–114 and Koutedakis 2008, pp. 85–88. However, further research is necessary for problems specific to dance.

centers. Simpler and (in part) manual instruments are, however, also available at larger dance institutions.[37]

The *knowledge* gained from biomechanical research, however, has already made its way into many contemporary dance techniques, especially those techniques that base their understanding of movement and forms of conveyance explicitly on information about the human movement apparatus. An example of this would be *Axis Syllabus*, a movement and movement observation training developed by dancer and choreographer Frey Faust. It uses the practical application of anatomical, biomechanical, and physical knowledge during class to find and train 'healthy' (meaning with respect for the body and its movement principles) movement solutions.[38]

Cognitive research has its own viewpoint toward movement that, in turn, has a special effect on dance training—combining experimental psychology with biomechanical analysis methods. At Bielefeld University, for example, neuroscientists and movement scientists have joined dance practitioners to explore questions about the structure of human movement, especially researching movement control and acquisition. A project team directed by Bettina Bläsing, specifically researching dance movement, was able to show that subjects with greater dancing abilities had more differentiation and were more strongly function–oriented in the mental representation of movement processes in long–term memory than was the case for novices or beginners.[39] These results, along with further studies,[40] suggest how a mental dance training might look like when adapted to an individual's unique movement memory. Research in Bielefeld also reconfirmed that when one trains a movement process mentally, one also trains motor execution, and vice–versa.[41] In addition to knowledge about the body's anatomical, physiological, and mechanical properties, knowledge about cognitive and neuronal regulation can also be used to make dance training more effective for the teacher's and dancer's respective goals, and to optimize physical processes.

Observation Techniques: This overview has characterized movement analysis as a process that can be supported by a series of trainable 'techniques', each of which represent their own specific view of movement and provide the appropriate observation tools. The individual method must be chosen by the observer and fine–tuned to the dance technique being examined, the individual goals, and the overriding analytic strategy. Analyzing movement is thus a creative process in and of itself. This essay only presents a selection of the most common movement analysis methods—they can be combined and further developed.[42] Analysis itself can also create and form movement knowledge, as well as movement processes.

My thanks to the experts Bettina Bläsing, Henner Drewes, and Claudia Jeschke, all of whom responded to questions about various analytical methods.

37 There are, additionally, initial attempts to develop measuring instruments that dancers can use in their everyday lives: for instance, a force platform in the form of a 'force mat' that the owner can easily roll up and store after measuring the pressure dis-tribution on the soles of his or her feet during a relevé. A prototype of such a mat has been developed by the *Ambient Intelligence Group*, which is part of the excellence cluster *Cognitive Interaction Technology* (CITEC) at the Bielefeld University.
38 An anatomical–physiological type of observation is increasingly characterizing contemporary dance training; it is firmly anchored in many techniques that take a somatic approach (see the essay by Irene Sieben). Gill Clark's teaching can be exemplary here for the specific work with anatomical knowledge; see Gill Clarke—Minding Motion / Concept

and Ideology and her class on the DVDs. In contrast to other movement analysis methods, anatomy classes are almost universally a part of dance universities' curricula.
39 To get these results, the researchers compared the biomechanical data of executed movements with data that provided information about the mental representation of the process in the subjects' long–term memory; see Bläsing 2010, pp. 87–92.
40 See, for instance, Thomas Schack: 'Building blocks and architecture of dance'. In: Bläsing et. al., pp. 11–39.
41 Martin Puttke—dancer, dance teacher, ballet director, and cooperation partner of Bettina Bläsing—has already integrated a corresponding, self–developed mental training form in his ballet teaching; see Martin Puttke: 'Learning to dance means learning to think!' In: Bläsing et. al., pp. 101–114.

42 The questions used as the basis for the research projects collected in this book provide a good example of how elements of different observation methods can be combined and used to create a movement–analysis framework. Observations that resulted are primarily documented in the sub-sections of Movement Characteristics and Physicality. (See Diehl's/Lampert's introduction about the creation of the question catalog.) Based on the research projects, it also becomes clear that movement analysis is just one building block for analyzing dance training and the interpretation of a dance technique: Methodological, didactical, historical, conceptual, ideological, social, psychological, etc. aspects must additionally be researched and considered with respect to their effects on the movement and its aesthetic—which occurs exemplary in this publication.

LITERATURE

Bläsing, Bettina
'The dancer's memory: Expertise and cognitive structures in dance'
In: Bläsing, Bettina I Puttke, Martin I Schack, Thomas
The Neurocognition of Dance. Mind, Movement and Motor Skills
Hove/New York: Psychology Press, 2010, pp. 75–96

Boenisch, Peter M.
körPERformance 1.0. Theorie und Analyse von Körper- und Bewegungsdarstellungen im zeitgenössischen Theater
Munich: epodium, 2002

Dahms, Sibylle (Ed.)
Tanz
Stuttgart: Bärenreiter-Verlag, 2001

Drewes, Henner
**Transformationen:
Bewegung in Notation und digitaler Verarbeitung**
Essen: Die blaue Eule, 2003

Emio Greco I PC I Amsterdamse Hogeschool voor de Kunsten (Ed.)
Capturing Intention. Documentation, analysis and notation research based on the work of Emio Greco I PC
Amsterdam: Emio Greco I PC and AHK, 2007

Forsythe, William
Improvisation Technologies: A Tool for the Analytical Dance Eye
(CD-ROM with booklet) Karlsruhe: ZKM, 1999

Hartewig, Wibke
Kinästhetische Konfrontation. Lesarten der Bewegungstexte William Forsythes
Munich: epodium, 2007

Hutchinson Guest, Ann
Labanotation: the System of Analyzing and Recording Movement
London/New York: Routledge, 2005

Jeschke, Claudia
Tanz als BewegungsText: Analysen zum Verhältnis von Tanztheater und Gesellschaftstanz (1910–1965)
Tübingen: Max Niemeyer Verlag, 1999

Jeschke, Claudia
Tanzschriften: Ihre Geschichte und Methode
Bad Reichenhall: Comes Verlag, 1983

Koutedakis, Yiannis I Owolabi, Emmanuel O. I Apostolos, Margo
'Dance Biomechanics: A Tool for Controlling Health, Fitness, and Training'
In: Journal of Dance Medicine & Science,
Vol. 12, Nr. 3, 2008, pp. 83-90

Laban, Rudolf von
Kinetografie. Labanotation: Einführung in die Grundbegriffe der Bewegungs- und Tanzschrift
Ed.: Claude Perrottet, Wilhelmshaven: Noetzel, 1995

Laban, Rudolf von
Choreutik: Grundlagen der Raum-Harmonielehre des Tanzes
Wilhelmshaven: Noetzel, 1991

Laban, Rudolf von
Die Kunst der Bewegung
Wilhelmshaven: Noetzel, 1988

Preston-Dunlop, Valerie I Sanchez-Colberg, Ana (Ed.)
dance and the performative. a choreological perspective – Laban and beyond
London: Verve Publishing, 2002

Puttke, Martin
'Learning to dance means learning to think!'
In: Bläsing, Bettina I Puttke, Martin I Schack, Thomas
The Neurocognition of Dance. Mind, Movement and Motor Skills
Hove/New York: Psychology Press, 2010, S. 101–114

Rick, Cary I Jeschke, Claudia
'Movement Evaluation Graphics'
In: Rick, Cary
Tanztherapie. Eine Einführung in die Grundlagen
Stuttgart: Gustav Fischer, 1989, pp. 23–89

Schack, Thomas
'Building blocks and architecture of dance'
In: Bläsing, Bettina I Puttke, Martin I Schack, Thomas
The Neurocognition of Dance: Mind, Movement and Motor Skills
Hove/New York: Psychology Press, 2010, pp. 11–39

Wilson, Margaret I Kwon, Young-Hoo
'The Role of Biomechanics in Understanding Dance Movement: A Review'
In: Journal of Dance Medicine & Science,
Vol. 12, Nr. 3, 2008, pp. 109–116

LINKS

Bewegung und Notation (Henner Drewes)
www.movement-notation.org

Dance Notation Bureau Homepage
www.dancenotation.org

Eshkol-Wachman Movement Notation Center
www.ewmncenter.com

Inside Movement Knowledge
www.insidemovementknowledge.net

International Council of Kinetography Laban/Labanotation
www.ickl.org

Labanlab – Interactive Labanotation Tutorials
www.dance.ohio-state.edu/5_resources/labanlab/index.htm

Open Benesh
www.dancewrite.com/OpenBenesh

Synchronous Objects for 'One flat thing, reproduced'
by William Forsythe
www.synchronousobjects.osu.edu

The Benesh Institute
www.benesh.org

The Language of Dance Centre
www.lodc.org

Visualizing (the Derra de Moroda) Dance Archives
www.movement-notation.org/VisualizingArchives

Irene Sieben

WORKING SOMATICALLY

SUPPORTING TECHNIQUES FOR CONTEMPORARY DANCE

/ "It's only when you know what you're doing that you can really do what you want."[1] /

This statement, by Moshé Feldenkrais, challenges us to take responsibility for our actions. It sounds provocative. Who knows *what* they are doing and *how* they are doing it at each moment of their lives? And what should dancers know about the *how*? Feldenkrais, a physicist and behavioral researcher, believed in the genius of each person, yet he was also aware of disruptive factors: repressive upbringing and habits formed by orders and regulations, role models, social norms, ideals of beauty, and traumatic experiences. These inhibit further development and restrict perception. In artists and creative contemporaries, he observed how lifelong learning formed flexible minds. He saw this not only in the brilliance of their performance, but also in the exciting way of learning that allowed for mistakes and questions: "Do not avoid errors, but rather use them as alternatives for what you feel is right and their roles may soon be interchanged." And who knows exactly whether what they currently think of as *wrong* isn't, in fact, *right*?[2]

These considerations are fundamental for would–be dancers in increasingly more open training systems. The language of movement must be reinvented and refreshed repeatedly over the course of a career. Why do I move? What moves me? These questions are not always asked at the start of a dance career because of the need to work on strength, balance, flexibility, coordination, and virtuosity. The dancer's instrument, the body, is being finely tuned—but to what pitch? What is the objective? It is good to know that each dance technique and each training practice influences the body image and creates wiring in the nervous system, and that mindsets then determine muscle tone—and that this fuses with habits we have brought with us from childhood, which is both baggage and opportunity.

LETTING GO HELPS

Only when injuries present career obstacles are dancers required to separate routine habits from intelligent habits, like separating the wheat from the chaff, and thereby neutralize their bodies. This means freeing the body from unnecessary tension and mental barriers and sharpening perception for the realities of the dance world.

Not all teachers have a well–founded knowledge of the structure and functioning of the body. Gill Clarke, for example, is convinced that the "grammar of controlling the body in space and time"[3] is necessary in dance. Clarke says that releasing unnecessary tension leads to a release of energy that gives shape and direction to the body in space. "Every muscle that doesn't help, hinders," says Bonnie Bainbridge Cohen, while André Bernard suggests a "smarter not harder" approach. Susan Klein, who helped

1 Moshé Feldenkrais: *The Master Moves.* Capitola/CAL: Meta Publications, 1984, p. 68
2 Moshé Feldenkrais: The Elusive Obvious. Cupertino/CAL: Meta Publications, 1981. p. 94

3 Gill Clarke in Irmela Kästner: "Denken manifestiert sich in Bewegung." In: *Tanz-Journal,* 1/2003, pp. 32–33
4 Susan Klein in Irene Sieben: "Knochenarbeit." In: ballettanz, 10/2005, pp. 74–75.
5 Sieben, loc. cit.

6 Amos Hetz in Uta Ruge: "Das expressive Selbst – ein Prozess." Im: *FeldenkraisForum,* Nr. 65, 2/2009, pp. 13–14.
7 Jarmila Kröschlová: *Movement Theory and Practice.* Sydney: Current Press, 2000, pp. 11–12.

Trisha Brown avoid giving up dancing at the age of fifty-five, believes that strength training is unnecessary. "We don't have to do exercise to get our muscles to work (...) We are *too* strong, actually. The outside muscles have to release, so you can get into yourself, to the inner muscles and to the structure, the bones."[4] It is the lack of understanding of aspects of function and energy that Klein believes is the main reason why dance, in comparison to other art forms, "is an immature art form, because dancers are immature, they are children, nineteen-, twenty-years old," which makes dancers "like artists in the circus,"[5] —a conclusion that gives food for thought.

BASIC LAWS

Somatopsychic or *psychophysical* learning methods have become common among experts for the practices highlighted below. These methods are all based on improved perception of the quality and efficiency of doing. They encourage self–regulation (homeostasis). In dance, they are known as body therapies, perception techniques, or somatics. By experimenting patiently and just letting things happen, these therapies allow one to discover something on one's own. They entered postmodern dance as Release Techniques. Contact Improvisation uses somatic strategies, for example, as do Anna Halprin (Life Art Process), Frey Faust (Axis Syllabus), the Hawkins Technique, John Graham (Gentle Dance), and what is known as floorwork. The essence of exploring basic motor principles distinguishes these processes from those with more directive practice concepts that are highly effective for many dancers, for example, Gyrotonics, Pilates, Spiraldynamik, etc. These will not be discussed further here.

The creative researchers discussed below have passed on, as general knowledge, what they themselves experienced in the 'world of movement'. This world of movement implies the room for maneuvering inside the space and time that is the basis not only of day–to–day doing, but also the highly specialized action in the arts, and dance in particular. They believed that change—even social change—takes place first in oneself. Each one of these pioneers was interested in a person's potential; they thought and practiced holistically. Body and mind and thinking and feeling were an inseparable whole for them. They were interested in obvious aspects: kinetic intelligence; gravity; avoiding wear and tear through economy; coordination; and facility. They developed rules for posture through better alignment. They focused on the motor patterns of young children. Correction, which often has drastic consequences for dancers, was replaced by self–correction. Instead of exercises copied and repeated mechanically, these researchers explored methods based on self–awareness, touch, and using the senses to understand anatomical, biodynamic, and evolutionary correlations. They used mental pictures that made it possible to rehearse entire choreographies in the mind.

AWARENESS AND PRESENCE

All somatic methods understand awareness to be the highest function of the human brain. It leads to considered movement, movement that does not focus on the goal but on the path. The Israeli, Amos Hetz, stresses it is the poet and the observer in us who is being addressed, rather than the survivor.[6] For dancers, awareness also means presence. Jarmila Kröschlová (1893–1983) called this state of heightened body sensitivity 'enlivened immobility'. She compared a dancer before a performance, who is fully alert kinesthetically, to a roe deer that has picked up a scent. "We sense her body endowed with life from inside."[7] She wrote three books about her investigations into human anatomy and the synthesis of body, mind, and psyche. As a Czech citizen, her legacy is hardly known in Germany. Her knowledge lived on in Rosalia Chladek, who, as a dancer in the German–speaking world, used Kröschlová's work as the basis for her own dance system, which does not involve watching and imitating but rather an independent search for the physical laws of movement.

In an era in which neurosciences are booming, and speed and energy expenditure are accelerating in line with the 'higher, faster, further' motto, it is not just in dancers' lives that somatic practices are becoming more important. Natural scientists' image–guided procedures are now making switching operations, and thus mental flexibility, visible; for example, how impulses from particular areas of the muscular system are passed along. The brain's development is seen as an integrative and continuous process within a large network that has no higher command center. Through computer–assisted analyses, kinesiology nowadays is re-opening the field where the pioneers once worked and recognized that every thought and feeling has an impact on the constitution, and embodies itself. More sophisticated research is being carried out into questions about perception (i.e., the function of the senses in the coordination of movement), the role of equilibrioception and with it the vestibular system in the inner ear and kinetics, and how strength and movement in the gravity field have affected the evolution of humans and animals.

A LOOK BACK

The findings of Charles Scott Sherrington triggered a revolution in perception. In his book, *The Integrative Action of the Nervous System,* from 1906, the neurophysiologist highlighted the significance of proprioceptive sensibility in self–awareness, and discovered that the synapse was the junction of two nerve cells. The kinesthetic sense, also known as the sense of movement, expanded the spectrum of the five senses and caused a cultural explosion. The ideas of François Delsarte (1811–1871) about the emotional origin of every gesture had already spread across Europe and the U.S. by the end of the 19th century. The forerunners of free dance—Isadora Duncan, Ted Shawn, and Ruth St. Denis—relied as much on his holistic teachings as did Bess Mensendieck and Geneviève Stebbins (the initiators of breathing and body exercises), and F. M. Alexander and Émile Jaques-Dalcroze (the latter's 'educational establishment' for rhythm in Hellerau thus becoming a breeding ground for artistic reform). Kröschlová and Chladek were deeply involved in cultivating dance in Hellerau. At the same time, Rudolf von Laban was at work in his Arts School on Monte Verità, the cradle of German expressionist dance. Psychoanalysis gave the soul a voice. Education reformers freed themselves from authoritarian shackles, and the gymnastics movement pursued its vision of harmoniously training the body. This formed the basis for the development of new body concepts, and what body therapist Thomas Hanna called 'somatic culture'.[8] We do not know how things would have developed without National Socialism in Germany, as Elsa Gindler's research material was destroyed during the bombing of Berlin. William Forsythe is now based at the Festspielhaus Hellerau, which was built in 1911 and has been beautifully restored. Forsythe, who speaks of the materialization of the dancer's body through the mind, makes idiosyncratic use of Laban's space harmony theories (Choreutics) in his choreographies. Such is history.

The most important somatic movement methods used either in modern–day dance teaching or that are historically relevant are discussed below. They can also be found as independent subjects in dance training course around the world. Although somatic movement methods work well in treating injuries or as therapies, their potential for teaching artistic development in dance as well as self–development should not be underestimated.

8 Thomas Hanna quoted in Helmut Milz: *Mit Kopf, Hand, Fuss, Bauch und Herz – Ganzheitliche Medizin und Gesundheit.* Munich: Piper, 1994, p. 77.
9 *"Welcher 'Schwung' fürs Tanzen und Springen und wie wenig wirklicher Schwung bei*

der täglichen Arbeit.": Elsa Gindler quoted by Sophie Ludwig: *Elsa Gindler – von ihrem Leben und Wirken. Wahrnehmen, was wir empfinden.* Hamburg: Christians Verlag, 2002, p. 98.
10 *"Sie müssen verlernen, was sie gelernt haben, und das ist das Schwerste, was es*

gibt. Was wir gelernt haben, scheint stärker zu sein als unsere eigene Natur, die dadurch verdrängt wird.": Elsa Gindler quoted in Charlotte Selver in Peggy Zeitler (Ed.): *Erinnerungen an Elsa Gindler.* Munich: P. Zeitler, 1991, p. 70.

WORK ON THE HUMAN BEING Elsa Gindler, Heinrich Jacoby

Elsa Gindler (1885–1961) first demanded quietude (*Stillwerden*) from her pupils in 1917. She wanted them to "accept and recognize what we are feeling and sensing," as the body is "one large experiential organ." Having taken Hede Kallmeyer's 'harmonious gymnastic' courses in Berlin, Gindler encouraged people to develop sensory awareness and interest in themselves by getting to know themselves on a deeper and more authentic level. She did not need a method or a theory. Instead of exercises, she called her approach 'experimental self–observation'—coming to terms with the dynamics of gravity, with habitual thoughts and tensions, and work on the human being. "What 'drive' for dancing and jumping, and how little real 'drive' in everyday work."[9] Although her teaching was improvisational and radical in the freedom she took, Gindler influenced the arts in the same way as psychoanalysis, Gestalt therapy, concentrative movement therapy, and the work of pediatrician Emmi Pikler on child development. She never corrected her pupils. The essence of her 'experimental arrangements', which went far beyond movement exercises, can still be seen today in exchanges of experience in working groups. The participants determine a theme and do not follow a set pattern.

Gindler was heavily influenced by the musician and gifted researcher, Heinrich Jacoby (1889–1964)—and he by her. He called 'receptive' listening, looking, tasting, and touching 'antenna–like behavior' and propounded 'self–re-education' in order for a person to become aware of restrictive behavioral patterns and thereby recognize what proves to be correct, how it comes about, and why. Only experience counted for Jacoby, not knowledge. After turning away from Dalcroze, he concentrated (like Feldenkrais later) on the relationship between movement, fear, and perceived inability rooted in early child–rearing errors that hinder the blossoming of talent. This gave Gindler's intuitive body–work analytical dimensions, including one of practical self–help in an era of war and persecution. For Jacoby, 'functional questioning and task–setting'—for example, when speaking, playing music, and drawing—was also part of working on oneself when carrying out simple actions such as walking, standing, sitting, and lying down, as well as when experiencing load, thrust, and gravity.

Elsa Gindler shied away from working with people who had been conditioned by dance techniques. "They have to forget what they have learned, and that is the hardest thing to do. What we have learned appears stronger than our own nature, and our own nature is repressed by it."[10] Working with Gindler, the dancer Gertrud Falke was lucky to experience how effort can be "reduced to its most simple form." Kurt Jooss brought Falke to Dartington Hall where he had resettled. Falke established 'awareness' as a new subject at the Jooss–Leeder School, where she taught: "…the sensing of the self is no technique and is nothing dramatic. It is very simple, and therein lies the difficulty."[11]

Other Gindler students also fled Germany. In the USA, Charlotte Selver developed Sensory Awareness, influenced by the philosopher Alan Watts and Zen philosophy. Gindler's spiritual legacy can also be found in Israeli dance. Lotte Kristeller passed on her knowledge to Amos Hetz, who is still incorporating her particular use of balls, batons, contact, and peripheral seeing in his playful exercises today.

11 *"…daß dieses Sich-selbst-Spüren keine Technik ist und auch nichts Dramatisches. Es ist sehr einfach, und darin liegt die Schwierigkeit.": Gertrud Falke Heller in Zeitler,* loc. cit., p. 83.

ALEXANDER TECHNIQUE Frederick Matthias Alexander

Frederick Matthias Alexander (1869–1955) discovered that a tiny change can have a great effect on the relationship between the head, neck, and back—and in doing so found the key to the effortless 'use of myself'. This can silence the 'inner noise' that occurs in the nervous system through overly tense muscles. Plagued by permanent hoarseness, the Australian actor observed himself using mirrors. He determined that when reciting his lines, he pulled his head back and depressed the larynx; in doing so, he shortened his whole body. This mechanism was based on a startle reflex (found in fetuses) and the source of fear, stress, and strain later in life, one that could create patterns and bad habits. Discovering the dominance of the head in the hierarchy of the body proved to be critical to Alexander's relearning, and his reaction to it was revolutionary: "He realized that he didn't have to *do* something different, but to stop doing what he was doing."[12] Instead of correcting oneself or learning to do the right thing, he prescribed for himself *non-doing, inhibiting*. This allowed him to rehabilitate the small muscles at the base of the skull, to poise the head and to leave it alone/balanced freely on the atlas and axis.

The next step toward a more useful body mechanics came from directional *self–checking*: neck free, head forward and up, back long and wide—with the emphasis on thinking. Alexander called the dominance of the head *primary control*, "because in unraveling the muddle of misuse, it is the first factor to be dealt with, and it sets the conditions for misuse in the rest of the body."[13] He also discovered he could not trust his sense of feeling while doing; perception is therefore unreliable and goal–oriented (or end–gaining, as he called it) behavior was counterproductive. Giving up goal–oriented thinking is also a challenge for dancers, and almost no other somatic approach has won so many fans. The Alexander Technique can be used at any time—in everyday life, when training, when experiencing stage fright, and on stage—in accordance with the 'head leads, body follows' principle.

Alexander rejected the use of specific exercises. He was convinced that they only reinforced unconscious patterns. Instead, students learn through subtle use of the skilled practitioners' hands, who themselves use touch to practice what they preach (a basic rule for Alexander teachers): for example, not pulling back and shortening the muscles in the neck when getting up from a chair.

The technique, which took sixty years to develop, has had a broad impact. The poets George Bernard Shaw and Aldous Huxley practiced it, as did the philosopher John Dewey, who got to know Alexander during the First World War and wrote the foreword to three of his books. The neurophysiologist Sherrington saw his research from 1906 about the reciprocal relationship of muscles put into practice. "Excitation and inhibition of the muscles work together to create a harmonious chord in a healthy functioning human body."[14]

IDEOKINESIS Mabel E. Todd

Even the voice teacher Mabel E. Todd (1874–1956) preached 'action without action'. Her observations on the efficient working of our 'living machine' are profound, whether she describes the arch of the foot and the pelvis like an engineer or bridge–builder, or compares the quality of a movement with natural phenomena: a good movement "happens the same way it rains, snows or hails."[15] Her metaphors, simple and complex at the same time, first appeared in her 1937 book, *The Thinking Body*. This book became a

12 Marjorie Barlow: *The Teaching of F. Matthias Alexander. The annual F. M. Alexander memorial lecture, 9 November 1965, at the Medical Society of London.* London: STAT books, 1993. Gedächtnis-Vortrag 1965. Eberbach: Edition Kavanah, 1991, p. 19.

13 F. M. Alexander quoted by Barlow, loc. cit.
14 Sir Charles Sherrington quoted by Michael Gelb: *Körperdynamik.* Frankfurt a. M.: Runde Ecken Verlag, 2004, p. 61.
15 Mabel E. Todd: *The Thinking Body.* London: Dance Books, 1937/1997 p. 281.

16 André Bernard/Wolfgang Steinmüller/Ursula Stricker: *Ideokinese. Ein kreativer Weg zu Bewegung und Körperhaltung.* Bern: Hans Huber Verlag, 2003, p. 41.

bible for generations of dancers and movement experts, and has not been bettered by any other work on bio-dynamics, anatomy, or kinesiology since. Todd, an American, established her work at U.S. universities using images, which became an early form of mental training. She used this strategy herself; she aligned the skeleton as near to the central axis as possible when learning how to walk again after falling down the stairs.

Metaphoric images are messengers between the planning and the acting parts of the nervous system. They help coordinate the muscles. Energy is activated through imagination; the nerves send an impulse to the muscles and no energy is wasted in doing so. A muscle that has been prepared by thought responds efficiently, which means that a person does not have to worry about the details in a movement sequence. This strategy is a source of strength for dancers and athletes, as it is often the prolonged and incorrect use of 'flawed designs' that result in futile action.

Starting in the 1970s, Lulu Sweigard, Barbara Clark, Irene Dowd, and André Bernard (1925–2003) took Todd's work in a highly artistic direction and renamed it ideokinesis. Bernard said that the art is, "to become the image", i.e., not to interfere with images so that they can have an effect—"Think it, imagine it, let it happen."[16] And he recommends not saving good movements for particular occasions, like dancing, for example, but to use them in the 'dance of everyday life'.

Images have to be dynamic, sensory, and unusual—the brain needs a strong impulse so a person moves in an efficient rather than strained manner. As Bernard puts it, movement should make the 'bait' bite into the 'fish' (the nervous system). When you visualize something, you sense and feel it at the same time. Todd noticed, as did Gindler, Frederick Matthias, and Gerda Alexander, that motor imagery and focusing on anatomical interactions cause involuntary changes in muscle tension. Basic knowledge of anatomy and the mechanics of the body helps visualize nine lines of energy through the skeleton, supports the balance effect with tactile assistance, and selects the most effective image from the rich collection available: the head *becomes* a balloon, the chest a breathing umbrella, the body a crumpled suit whose creases are smoothed out, while the head of the femur rolls into the socket like a golf ball into the hole.

The Graham dancer Erick Hawkins introduced his colleague André Bernard to ideokinesis in the 1950s. While Bernard's work remained close to that of Todd and Clark, Joan Skinner (who also danced with Graham) developed her own method called the Skinner Releasing Technique, which aims at demolishing physical barriers and conventions in dance, and expands ideas by using animated images from nature in a multidirectional fashion. Ease, effortlessness, and transparency emerge in a 'liquefied' body. These Image Actions play freely with a large catalogue of movement qualities: "Melting like butter or wax, floating like dust particles that glow in a ray of sunshine…"[17]

EUTONY Gerda Alexander

Regulating muscle tone through flexibility became the focus of research in Eutony (in Greek *Eu* = good, harmonious, measured; *Tonos* = tension, tone). Gerda Alexander (1908–1994) discovered that a balance between rest and activity could lead to efficient movement, affect the ability to form relationships, and promote personal creativity. As a rhythmist, two of her teachers were followers of Dalcroze: Otto Blensdorf and Peter Petersen. Her method was developed in Germany and later, after fleeing from Hitler, in Scandinavia. Alexander knew that muscle tone, as a regulator of physiology, is controlled, above all, by the vegetative nervous system. She recognized its influence on the

17 *"Schmelzen wie Butter oder Wachs, schweben wie Staubpartikel, die in einem Sonnenstrahl leuchten...": Bruno Stefanoni in Irene Sieben: "Innere Bilder in Bewegung setzen." In: Tanz aktuell, 6/1989, p. 13.*

psyche and discovered that thinking and feeling one's way clearly into the skin, the organs, the bones down to the marrow, and into the inner space of the body has a profound effect on the balance of tension in the muscular system and the soul's mood. She described the ability to be in the 'reality of the moment' as 'presence'.[18] She used lever and micro-movements, developed control positions to enable assessment of mobility, created physical exercises involving balls and chestnuts, marked traces in space using parts of the body, and had students use clay to make 'body image tests' that could detect body parts that the student was 'blind' to. The transport of weight by the bones, the bulwark against gravity, is investigated to determine tone regulation. "The involuntary extension of the skeletal muscles is not only activated by the feet, but by every and any point of the body. I have called this proprioceptive reflex 'thrust'."[19] This reflex, according to Gerda Alexander, is the source of effortlessness in dancing.

Regina Baumgart, for example, uses eutonic principles in her ballet classes for contemporary dancers, and does not believe in pressure, fear, or coercion: "Everything gets very tight with too much exertion in ballet. Getting rid of this expands the range of movement expression. I say, for example: 'Strip away the skin! Observe the inner space!' If you give your weight to the earth when aligning yourself, then the skeletal muscles tone their counter–pressure. These are logical principles. If dancers grasp this, they become different dancers. They understand that they can influence themselves…The more flexible the muscle tone, the more differentiated the quality of expression."[20]

The proximity of eutony to dance is mirrored in improvisation and artistic movement. 'Thinking ahead through sensing' or 'sensing ahead through thinking' leads to deeper experience. No other method has dealt so profoundly with the transfer of muscle tone—from dancer to audience, from mother to child, from teacher to pupil. "Gerda Alexander introduced intuitive phenomena to muscle tone regulation and adaptation that can, today, be explained by mirror neurons."[21]

FELDENKRAIS METHOD Moshé Feldenkrais

Moshé Feldenkrais (1904–1984) was the only scientist among the pioneers. A Russian Jew, he was a physicist and engineer who carried out systematic experiments. Five of his six books that have been translated into German are works of popular science and highlight, in an autobiographical way, research into the physiology of movement that he carried out on his own body. He attained the black belt rank in Judo and, even though he was involved in the first nuclear fission experiments in Paris, did not spend his life in the laboratory. His awareness was sparked through a knee injury. He used self–experiment to develop his method, which focuses on learning organically. Key elements are an understanding of movement functionality and reducing strain in order to increase sensibility. From young children, he observed how people learn for themselves through trial and error, and thus propel their development forward. He found the key to the survival techniques—which emerge in the body as fear, fight, and flight phenomena—in evolution. He used principles from mechanics, thermodynamics, cybernetics, and brain research to underpin the dynamics of posture, the relationship to gravity, and the 'reversibility of movement' (a phrase he took from his study of physics and which refers to effortless control of the body) as being the most important factors for body efficiency. He agreed with Mabel Todd on many things, although he only read her book toward the end of his life. In his nearly 3,000 brilliantly developed group lessons in Awareness Through

18 Gerda Alexander quoted by Karin Schaefer in Michael Fortwängler / Karin Schaefer / Wolfgang Steinmüller: *Gesundheit – Lernen – Kreativität. Alexander-Technik, Eutonie Gerda Alexander und Feldenkrais als Methoden zur Gestaltung somatospychischer Lernprozesse.* Bern: Hans Huber Verlag, 2001/2009.

19 *"Die reflektorische Streckung der Skelettmuskulatur kann nicht nur von den Füßen, sondern von jeder beliebigen Stelle des Körpers ausgelöst werden. Diesen proprioceptiven Reflex habe ich als 'Transportreflex' bezeichnet.":* Gerda Alexander: *Eutonie.* Munich: Kösel, 1976, p. 41.

20 *"Bei der hohen Anspannung im Ballett wird alles schnell eng. Sie wegzunehmen, erhöht das Spektrum des Bewegungsausdrucks. Da sage ich beispielsweise: Streich mal die Haut ab! Nimm den Raum im Innern wahr! Überlässt man bei der Aufrichtung das Gewicht zur Erde hin, tonisiert ihr Gegendruck die Skelettmuskulatur.*

Movement, he leads us through rolling, crawling, creeping, and on all fours, through the jungle of movement development on the trail of unusual variants—always searching for pleasure and ease, for inner order in the chaos of diversity, and also for that which disturbs, the 'parasitic'[22] movements.

For Feldenkrais, dealing creatively with mistakes went so far as to consider wrong and right as simply two of many possibilities. The more of these possibilities we have, the better. Freedom of choice is key to deciding whether we get into trouble or not. Learning means understanding the unknown. He believed that novelty in every lesson—as opposed to always practicing the same thing—was key to the formation of new synapses.

Preparing movement in the mind or imagining entire classes are part of the toolbox for learning. The strategy is unique: Feldenkrais deconstructs the elements of each movement into small puzzle pieces and then reorganizes them so that the goal, which might engender ambition and stress, is invisible to students. The finished puzzle only appears as the main event at the end, and often in significantly improved ways of moving.

Feldenkrais developed the lessons from his own work to create the hands–on work called Functional Integration. A student's potential is discovered by using precise and accurate contact, and movement. Instead of looking at what does *not* work, one looks at what *is* working. When searching for alternatives, Feldenkrais applies technical tricks and chooses detours from the usual strategies in at least thirty positions, from lying, kneeling, squatting, and sitting up to standing, walking, or even to balancing on wooden rollers.

Feldenkrais owes his fame to his background as a natural scientist and to the renowned students from politics, music, acting, and dance—including David Ben Gurion, Yehudi Menuhin, and even Peter Brook.

LABAN/BARTENIEFF MOVEMENT STUDIES Irmgard Bartenieff

Based upon laws of motion that enable analyzing and understanding of movement, Irmgard Bartenieff (1900–1981) developed concepts that, for example, include grounding oneself, the intention of voluntary actions, and ideas regarding the relationship body parts have to one another. She was inspired by Rudolf von Laban, with whom she had studied in the 1920s; both had a dance background but were wholly interested in movement processes. When Bartenieff left Germany for New York in 1936, she used Laban's ideas of space, effort, shape, phrasing, and a person's ability to be spontaneous in order to research (as a dance therapist and physiotherapist) a corrective exercise system that would become known as the Bartenieff Fundamentals. Her neurophysiological and anatomical knowledge, along with her interest in the developmental motor skills of babies, helped her clarify not only the dynamic but also the emotional aspects of posture—ranging from the transport of weight when changing levels to movement initiation. She discovered that improving neuromuscular facilitation, sequential courses of movement, and connecting individual body parts to each other, and to the body as a whole, produced an amended self–image. Function and expression, stability, mobility, and grounding come together. Laban/Bartenieff Movement Studies, when expanded through theme–based improvisation, help a person to experience, observe, shape, and essentially understand movement.

Das sind logische Prinzipien. Wenn das die Tänzer verstehen, stehen sie am Ende anders da. Sie begreifen, dass sie selbst Einfluss nehmen können. [...] Je flexibler der Tonus, desto differenzierter die Ausdrucksqualität.": Regina Baumgart in Melanie Suchy: "Die Lehrerin Regina Baumgart." In: *tanz*, 4/2010, p. 72.

21 "*Gerda Alexander setzte mit der Tonusregulierung und Tonusadaption intuitiv Phänomene ein, die heute durch die Spiegelneuronen erklärbar sind.*": Karin Schaefer/Wolfgang Steinmüller: "*Somatopsychische Lernmethoden im Dialog.*" *FeldenkraisForum*, Nr. 67, 4/2009, p. 7.

22 Moshé Feldenkrais: *The Potent Self: A Study of Compulsion and Spontaneity*. San Francisco: Harper&Row, 1985.

KLEIN TECHNIQUE Susan Klein

The dancer Susan Klein (b.1949) began developing her technique in New York in 1972, having been greatly influenced by Irmgard Bartenieff as well as by German expressionist dance. Klein studied Bartenieff's Fundamentals meticulously and discovered the 'hollows' that emerge with slight hip flexion in the groin area when the iliopsoas is activated. She has since worked with the support and leverage power of the bones, thrust and counter–thrust, and the duality of forces. Like Laban and Bartenieff, she believes that the pelvis is the center of energy and the chest the center of expression.

A knee injury led to her discovery that the hamstrings are often permanently strained. These muscles, between the sit bones and lower leg, became the focal point for her work, as did the nape of the neck for F. M. Alexander. Dancers in particular enjoy practicing her technique, as the hanging over of the spinal column, head down with knees stretched (flexibly)—repeated very slowly and in silence—is often painful for non-dancers. Hand-picked exercises use instructions that include anatomical facts and emphasize the links between the bones, the articulation of the joints, as well as the relationship between the skeleton to the earth. For Susan Klein, this provides the space to support and discover each student through contact, something she calls *body felt sensation.*

Klein sees herself as rooted more in Movement Re-education than in Release Technique. She is an 'indirect' teacher and enjoys talking at length, which leads to lively philosophical discussions with the group. Notable students of Klein have included Stephen Petronio and Trisha Brown.

BODY–MIND CENTERING (BMC) Bonnie Bainbridge Cohen

Bonnie Bainbridge Cohen (b.1941) also references Irmgard Bartenieff, although Cohen's experiential realm extends far beyond those of all the other pioneers, and delves into the tiniest details. Her Body–Mind Centering (BMC) method, which has been continually developed in the U.S. since the 1970s, uses movement, touch, the voice, and the power of imagination.

Bainbridge Cohen trained with the Graham dancer Erick Hawkins. She was an occupational therapist and studied yoga, martial arts, Ideokinesis, and the Kestenberg Movement Profile. She learned Neuro Developmental Therapy with Karel Bobath and Berta Bobath, a student of Elsa Gindler, and then transformed the developmental movements into a creative form of yoga called Developmental Movement Patterns. Acute illness gave her insights that would inform her study of various body systems. She called it "an experiential journey into the alive and changing territory of the body,"[23] and felt privileged not to have to prove anything scientifically—even when she delves into the bone marrow or the mitochondria of the cells or when simulating the developmental processes of the embryo. No other method so meticulously highlights the primitive reflexes, righting reactions, and equilibrium responses so well that even adults can access their potential quickly.

Cohen asks: How does the movement quality change when we send the mind (perception, thoughts, feelings, and consciousness) into bones, muscles, organs, fluids, glands, the brain, or nerves and embody these systems? The relationship to Gerda Alexander is obvious, and the relationship to Moshé Feldenkrais's work is in the relearning of early patterns. Once the anatomical and evolutionary correlations have been meticulously worked out both cognitively and sensorily, BMC follows through with improvised

23 Bonnie Bainbridge Cohen: *Sensing,
Feeling and Action. The Experiential Anatomy
of Body-Mind Centering.* Northampton/
MA: Contact Editions, 1993, p. 1.
24 Cohen, loc. cit., p. 118.

research. Cohen assumes that each cell has its own 'mind' as part of a massive hologram, and she even talks with brain researchers about this. She is convinced the first year of life determines the way the relationship between perception (how we see, hear, and sense something) and motor processes (how we act in the world) is expressed, and whether we have choices when solving problems. When she learned that the spinal motor nerves in the fetus mature before the sensory nerves, she knew, "that one needs to move before one can have feedback about that movement."[24] Every experience, therefore, creates the basis for subsequent experiences. Perception requires movement.

But there is a deeper form of knowledge lying beneath conscious knowledge, namely the unknown. Cohen learned from the Japanese healer Haruchika Noguchi, with whom Feldenkrais also had lively debates in Japan, how to unleash the autonomous nervous system and thereby create involuntary self–regulating movements. This is called Kadsugen Undo. Authentic Movement, i.e., improvisation with eyes closed and an observer, is based on similar knowledge. Janet Adler developed this into a dance therapy practice, Cohen into a further form of BMC that she calls 'more fun than serious'.

Cohen's magic attracted whole generations of dancers who integrate her valuable knowledge into traditional training worldwide. The co-inventors of Contact Improvisation—Steve Paxton, Nancy Stark Smith, and Lisa Nelson—feel supported and inspired by her. They have been publishing Cohen's latest findings in the American journal *Contact Quarterly* in an interview format since 1980, and also published her book entitled *Sensing, Feeling and Action*.

FRANKLIN METHOD Eric Franklin

The Swiss–American Eric Franklin (b.1957) studied dance and sports science. He was a student of André Bernard and Bonnie Bainbridge Cohen, among others, in the 1980s and 90s. He mixes elements of ideokinesis and BMC with findings from sports science. He takes the results around the world (to dance company training programs and universities) with the goal of improving specific aspects such as plié, en dehors, and alignment, and also to work on optimal rebound when jumping, higher leg work, and balance while turning. He calls this Applied Somatics or Mental Motor Imagery.

His motto is, "Embodying the function improves the function,"—meaning one must first *think*, perceive, feel, and understand, and then *do*—and, ultimately, do all of the above at the same time. Anatomical models and metaphoric images play an equally important role—as does touch and the power of Mood Words, which are short formulas repeated in the mind that not only silence the inner critic but also allocate direction and space in order to conserve energy. Dancers who apply Franklin's method experience how the body follows the mind, and vice versa.

LITERATURE

Alexander, F. M.
Der Gebrauch des Selbst Basel: Karger, 2001

Alexander, Gerda
Eutonie Munich: Kösel, 1976

Bainbridge Cohen, Bonnie
Sensing, Feeling and Action: The Experiential Anatomy of Body-Mind Centering Northampton (MA): Contact Editions, 1993

Barlow, Marjory
Die Lehre des F. Matthias Alexander Gedächtnis-Vortrag 1965 Eberbach: Edition Kavanah, 1991

Baumgart, Regina in Melanie Suchy
"Die Lehrerin Regina Baumgart" In: tanz, 4/2010

Bernard, Andrè | Steinmüller, Wolfgang | Stricker, Ursula
Ideokinese: Ein kreativer Weg zu Bewegung und Körperhaltung
Bern: Hans Huber Verlag, 2003

Brooks, Charles
Erleben durch die Sinne, Sensory Awareness Munich: dtv, 1991

Clarke, Gill in Irmela Kästner
"Denken manifestiert sich in Bewegung" In: Tanz-Journal, 1/2003

Doidge, Norman
Neustart im Kopf: Wie sich unser Gehirn selbst repariert
Frankfurt a. M.: Campus, 2008

Feldenkrais, Moshé
Die Feldenkraismethode in Aktion: Eine ganzheitliche Bewegungslehre Paderborn: Junfermann, 1990

Feldenkrais, Moshé
Die Entdeckung des Selbstverständlichen
Frankfurt a. M.: Insel/Suhrkamp, 1985/1987

Feldenkrais, Moshé
Bewusstheit durch Bewegung
Frankfurt a. M.: Insel/Suhrkamp, 1968/78

Feldenkrais, Moshé
Abenteuer im Dschungel des Gehirns – Der Fall Doris
Frankfurt a. M.: Insel/Suhrkamp, 1977

Fortwängler, Michael | Schaefer, Karin | Steinmüller, Wolfgang
Gesundheit – Lernen – Kreativität, Alexander-Technik, Eutonie Gerda Alexander und Feldenkrais als Methoden zur Gestaltung somatopsychischer Lernprozesse
Bern: Hans Huber Verlag, 2001/2009

Gelb, Michael
Körperdynamik: Eine Einführung in die F. M. Alexander-Technik
Frankfurt a. M.: Runde Ecken Verlag, 2004

Hanna, Thomas
Beweglich sein ein Leben lang Munich: Kösel, 2003

Hartley, Linda
Wisdom of the Body Moving: An Introduction to Body-Mind Centering
Berkeley (CA): North Atlantic Books, 1989/1995

Hetz, Amos in Uta Ruge
"Das expressive Selbst – ein Prozess"
Im: FeldenkraisForum, No. 65, 2/2009

Hüther, Gerald
Bedienungsanleitungen für ein menschliches Gehirn
Göttingen: Vandenhoeck & Ruprecht, 2005/2001

Jacoby, Heinrich
Jenseits von begabt und unbegabt: Zweckmäßige Fragestellung und zweckmäßiges Verhalten, Schlüssel für die Entfaltung des Menschen Hamburg: Christians Verlag, 1983/1994

Kennedy, Antja
Bewegtes Wissen: Laban/Bartenieff-Bewegungsstudien verstehen und erleben Berlin: Logos, 2010

Klein, Susan in Irene Sieben **"Knochenarbeit"** In: ballettanz, 10/2005

Klinkenberg, Norbert
Moshé Feldenkrais und Heinrich Jacoby – eine Begegnung
Berlin: Heinrich Jacoby-Elsa Gindler Stiftung, 2002

Kröschlová, Jarmila
Movement Theory and Practice Sydney: Current Press, 2000

Ludwig, Sophie
Elsa Gindler – von ihrem Leben und Wirken: Wahrnehmen, was wir empfinden Hamburg: Christians Verlag, 2002

Moscovici, Hadassa K.
Vor Freude tanzen, vor Jammer halb in Stücke gehn: Pionierinnen der Körpertherapie Hamburg/Zurick: Luchterhand, 1989

Peters, Angelika | Sieben, Irene
Das große Feldenkrais Buch
Kreuzlingen/Munich: Hugendubel/Random House, 2008

Shusterman, Richard **Leibliche Erfahrung in Kunst und Lebensstil**
Berlin: Akademie Verlag, 2005

Stefanoni, Bruno in Irene Sieben:
"Innere Bilder in Bewegung setzen." In: Tanz aktuell, 6/1989

Todd, Mabel E.
Der Körper denkt mit: Anatomie als Ausdruck dynamischer Kräfte
Bern: Hans Huber Verlag, 2001 (Translation of **The Thinking Body**)

Todd, Mabel E.
The Thinking Body London: Dance Books, 1937/1997

Selver, Charlotte in Peggy Zeitler (Ed.)
Erinnerungen an Elsa Gindler: Berichte, Briefe, Gespräche mit Schülern Munich: P. Zeitler, 1991

Sherrington, Charles Scott
The Integrative Action of the Nervous System
1. Edition 1906, 2. Edition New York: Ayer Co Pub, 1973

LINKS

Alexander Technique
www.alexander-technik.org

Body-Mind Centering
www.bodymindcentering.com
www.contactquarterly.com
www.moveus.de

Eutony
www.eutonie.de
www.regina-baumgart.de

Feldenkrais Method
www.feldenkrais.de

Franklin Method
www.franklin-methode.ch

Gindler/Jacoby
www.jgstiftung.de
www.sensoryawareness.org

Klein Technique
www.kleintechnique.com

Laban/Bartenieff Movement Studies
www.laban-ausbildung.de
www.laban-eurolab.org

Skinner-Releasing
www.skinnerreleasing.com

Patricia Stöckemann

DANCE TECHNIQUES AND LIVES — DISCUSSIONS
ABOUT GERMAN EXPRESSIONIST DANCE

THREE INTERVIEWS WITH: ANN HUTCHINSON GUEST, ANNA MARKARD AND REINHILD HOFFMANN, AND KATHARINE SEHNERT

Expressionist dance not only defined an epoch, approaches developed by the early teachers are still being used by some dance educators today—approaches that are comparable to those used by contemporary dancers today. This series of structured interviews with experts investigates the influence of dance techniques on the lives of these experts. Their very personal accounts provide insight into the way they pass this knowledge on and how they use it themselves.

Participants

Ann Hutchinson Guest (* 1918) was an internationally recognized expert on dance notation (in particular, Labanotation). **Anna Markard*** (* 1931, † 2010) was the daughter of Kurt Jooss and Aino Siimola, and a trustee of her father's work. **Reinhild Hoffmann** (* 1943) is a choreographer and one of the protagonists of German dance–theater. All three trained in the Jooss–Leeder modern dance technique at different times and places.

Kurt Jooss (1901–1979) laid the foundations for what would become the German school of modern dance at the Folkswang School, which he established with Sigurd Leeder (1902–1981) in Essen in 1927. Mary Wigman's (1886–1973) pedagogical work before and after the Second World War ensured that that their legacy would continue. **Katharine Sehnert** (*1937) came to Berlin in 1955 to study at Wigman's studio and is one of the last students to have trained with Mary Wigman personally.

Interviewer
Patricia Stöckemann

ANN HUTCHINSON GUEST ON THE JOOSS–LEEDER SCHOOL OF DANCE IN ENGLAND

London, 8 May 2010

╱ **When and how did you first encounter Jooss–Leeder Technique? Who were your teachers?**
I went straight from boarding school to the Jooss–Leeder School of Dance in Dartington in January 1936, at the age of seventeen. The school year had already begun, which is why I had to catch up on the missing material by attending a summer course in 1936. I had 'script', as the subject was called at the Jooss–Leeder School, on my first day of training. I didn't discover the official term *Labanotation* until later in New York. As I'd very much enjoyed studying math at school, the notation system's logic appealed to me.

Although the school was called the Jooss–Leeder School of Dance, Jooss himself taught little; he looked after the dance company and was on tour with his troupe most of the time. Leeder was the most important teacher at the school. He taught third–year students when I arrived. Lisa Ullmann taught second–year students, and Marlisa Bok was responsible for first–year students. Teachers of the respective school years taught all the subjects, like technique, eukinetics, choreutics, and improvisation. Friderica Derra de Moroda came once a year to teach Hungarian and Russian folk dance to third–year students.

We saw little of Jooss, as I said. I remember a few classes he gave during the summer course of 1936—they were an excellent introduction to various forms of waltzes. I wish I had written down all the variations he taught. In another class, which was a more general class, I recall he started with practical work then continued on to theoretical considerations. His English was wonderfully fluent and one thought led him to the next, and one theme led him to the next. It was always interesting and fascinating.

*Anna Markard took part in this discussion shortly prior to her death on 18 October 2010.

Sigurd Leeder was an unusually precise and inspiring movement teacher. He was always searching for new images and words to elicit particular movements from students and he used these images with great sensitivity in his classes. He also had a sense of humor and brilliant choreographic skills, though it has to be said he was a better choreographer for the classroom than for the stage. We had to choreograph our own dance every term, which was great, and Jooss was very good at giving feedback to students.

There were also 'awareness' classes with Gertrud Heller–Falke, a German dancer whose awareness work was based on Elsa Gindler's methods. I found her classes very interesting. We lay on the floor and tried to feel if our alignment was genuinely straight and correct, and if we were genuinely relaxed. We concentrated our awareness on all parts of the body: feet, legs, pelvis, etc. We stood with our eyes closed and felt the body in a different situation before we gradually started to walk through the space. Other tasks were then given. The disadvantage for me was that these classes were in German; although I had learned German in school, I didn't understand everything.

/ **Was any ballet taught at the Jooss–Leeder School in Dartington?** Ballet was a dirty word when I was at the school—it was frowned upon. Ballet was taught once a week before I came, but then the class was scrapped…unfortunately. There was no training of the body as an instrument, which I would have personally liked. I had high shoulders, for example, and special exercises could have been used to do something about them…or my knees, which were not properly stretched. I only became aware of this when I studied ballet with Margret Craske in New York. When I performed a battement tendu, she said, 'Stretch your knee.' I think someone should have been able to tell me that during three years' training in Dartington! On the other hand, at the Jooss–Leeder School I experienced the most wonderful exploration of what movement can be. I remember Jooss being asked what a wrong movement is, to which he answered, 'There are no wrong movements, every movement can be right. It depends on the context.' When you learn ballet, there is always a 'wrong' and a 'right'.

/ **But later, in the 1950s, Jooss added ballet to the class roster at the Folkwang School, and put it on par with other subjects.** It is probably true that Leeder was the one who didn't want ballet on the schedule in Dartington, but ultimately no one at the school wanted it.

/ **How was the body trained at the Jooss–Leeder School of Dance? Were there gymnastics classes?** No, we had choreutics and eukinetics, and also technique classes in which, for example, special foot-work was taught—like walking with a spring in your step—or stable and off–center turns were trained. Or Leeder developed an exercise, a study, when he saw that something wasn't working. And the wonderful thing about these studies was that they became ever more comprehensive over the course of a term. We repeated them time and again, as if we were perfecting a dance. Each year group had to perform the study as well as their own dance at the end of the term. The technique itself was based on Laban swings, eight swings with the whole body, or just with the arms, or the arms working in opposition to the body—in all these combinations. This certainly improved one's technique.

/ **But not enough?** Not for me. I was seventeen and rather immature. I came from a boarding school where everything was regulated, and I had an English stepfather who was very strict, so my self–confidence wasn't very high. I somehow had to move on from all that. I discovered Martha Graham in New York and studied with her I liked her work a lot. It was so challenging. The Jooss–Leeder work was not in the same vein. And I had to learn ballet to get a job, so I studied ballet intensively over many years. When I started teaching, I only taught ballet and Labanotation, never modern dance really. But I believe that my understanding of other dance forms was enriched by the knowledge of the movement possibilities I acquired at the Jooss–Leeder School of Dance.

/ **Where and how did all that you learned have an impact?** When I left the Jooss–Leeder School of Dance, I was best trained in Labanotation. I had added an extra year to the three-year training course because Jooss asked me if I would notate his ballets, *The Green Table*, *The Big City, Ball in Old Vienna*, and *Pavane*. Jooss paid me absolutely no attention when I wanted to hand him the finished score for *The Green Table*. It was only years later, after the war, that I learned from him how much he liked the notation because it was simple and clear, and it served as an *aide mémoire* for those who were familiar with the work.

I returned to New York in 1939 and opened the Dance Notation Bureau—with others, but without any money—on the recommendation of John Martin, the American dance critic, who gave us his full support. We earned money from teaching, and it continued like this for years. We did everything out of love for what we were doing.

/ Would you define 'Jooss–Leeder' as a Technique? Yes, because the movement categories that the students have to master—above all choreutics and eukinetics—are clearly defined, and one must learn all the swing sequences. It is good training. The dimensional scales—the A scale and the B scale—produce rich, three-dimensional movements.

/ In your opinion, what are the most important basic principles? I think eukinetics. Studies were developed that highlighted contrasts in the various qualities of dance—we called it 'central–peripheral', later it was called 'direct–flexible'. Then there was 'quick–slow' and 'strong–weak'. If a dancer applies this, then he or she goes from one quality to the next. Leeder was very inventive and interested in the origin of a movement. He called it a 'point of interest' when one imagined, for example, that a light was shining on the underside of the arm, and that this part of the body was receiving more energy and thus producing a movement. He loved that.

/ Where can one see the influences of the Jooss–Leeder Technique at work today? Simone Michelle taught the Leeder Technique at the Laban Centre for many years, and she was a student in Dartington when I was there. When she retired the subject was no longer taught at the Laban Centre as there was no one who had been trained in it and could teach it. Leeder opened a Leeder School with Grete Müller in Switzerland in the 1960s. Grete Müller continued running the school on her own after he died, as well as the Leeder Archive with all his records and notations. Grete never made this material available, however. Only when she died did those who were then in charge of the school and the estate make the material available to interested parties before it was handed over to a Swiss archive. I was also invited to view the material. There were wonderful notations and I was able to get copies of them; I busied myself with them and then taught the Leeder Technique when I was invited to give classes. There was a great response to these studies every time, and people have come to love them. A great deal more should be done with them, but there aren't many people around any more who can do that.

/ You talk about the Leeder Technique. Can one separate the Jooss Technique from the Leeder Technique? No, not really, except for the studies that Leeder developed—which is why I talked about the Leeder Technique here.

/ Is the Jooss–Leeder Technique not taught at the Laban Centre in London nowadays? I believe they teach Laban's 'effort–shape' concept there, but that is something else, as it originally served a different purpose. Laban applied eukinetics when he worked with factory workers: The opposite of strong is weak. But you don't want any weak workers, so he changed 'weak' to 'light touch', so that you kept something strong. I remember that Jooss very much regretted the change from central and peripheral to direct and indirect. Although it again makes sense—it is different to central and peripheral, i.e., whether a movement emerges from the center or from the periphery. I also find these changes a shame, but they are a part of history.

/ How relevant is Jooss–Leeder for the future? The Jooss–Leeder Technique could be relevant. Students loved it whenever I taught the studies to advanced students, or at the Royal Academy of Dance—in part because it is something different. It should be kept alive and available. It cannot be declared as an independent dance form, but one can get to know it and learn to value its content.

ANNA MARKARD AND REINHILD HOFFMANN ON THE JOOSS–LEEDER TECHNIQUE

Amsterdam, 20–21 February 2010

/ How did you come to study the Jooss–Leeder Technique?
/ **Anna Markard** I have danced for as long as I can remember although my parents—Kurt Jooss und Aino Siimola—vehemently tried to dissuade me from becoming a professional dancer. They saw the difficulties I would face, and they knew how tough a dancer's life is. But I begged them. I was still at boarding school in Surrey, and I was allowed to go to London once a week to participate in Sigurd Leeder's open classes. I was a chubby teenager and jumped around in his professional class, but I could do everything and one year later I was training formally with Leeder. Then my father agreed to become head of the dance department at the Folkwang School again. I figured I could do my pliés there as well as anywhere, so I went to Essen in the summer of 1949. I had no idea that I would become a Folkwang student.
/ **Reinhild Hoffmann** I completed training at the *Berufsfachschule für Gymnastik und Tanz Härdle–Munz* (a vocational school for gymnastics and dance) in Karlsruhe in 1965. But I wanted to be a dancer, so once I'd finished my exams I went to the Folkwang School. Kurt Jooss was director at the time, and it was the only state school that focused on German modern dance

alongside ballet training. Folkwang was also an educational center for all other art forms, and it had always been my wish to go Essen and attend the Folkwang School.

/ Your father was your teacher in Essen, Anna; you no longer had Sigurd Leeder, as he stayed in London.

/ **AM** Yes, and Hans Züllig. It was a real thrill for my father to have acquired his former pupil, Hans Züllig—who had since become a great soloist—as a teacher at the school. I found it very important to learn the discipline that ballet requires. One has to understand the situation in Essen–Werden in 1949: There was no link to a major city, Essen was totally destroyed and very unattractive, as was all of Germany a few years after the end of the war. Jooss wanted ballet teachers for the Folkwang School, as he believed that dance training could not focus on modern dance alone. He wanted the program to include difference dance techniques, and each technique should be on an equal footing with the other. He managed to win Laura Maris from England for the ballet component of the program. We owe her a great deal indeed. It was the start. I belong to this experimental generation, and I was, at the same time, a pupil at the Folkwang School.

/ Which other teachers were important for you?

/ **AM** We had a Frau Hartung for character dance. Folk dance didn't come until a few years later.

/ **RH** You were my teacher for modern dance technique the first two years, Anna, then came Trude Pohl for composition, Gisela Reber for folklore and Diana Baddeley for script (Kinetography). Space awareness and movement quality were trained in the modern dance classes; we learned how to analyze movement in the Kinetography classes. We learned musicality and about specific, ethnic characterization in folk dance classes; in composition class we learned to discover our own movement. Hans Züllig was my teacher for modern technique in years three and four, and Kurt Jooss for eukinetics and choreutics. Kurt Jooss gave movement combinations for us to explore in terms of space, time, effort, and movement approach. This is how we learned how to describe movement.

My ballet teacher, Irén Bartos, was very important for me. I was not the ideal ballet dancer as I didn't have the feet for it, but she observed my modern work, appreciated it, and tried to get the best out of me.

/ Anna, you trained at the Folkwang School and then continued your studies abroad.

/ **AM** I was still far from being a dancer. I was fortunate to get to know Nora Kiss at a summer course in Switzerland. Nora was a famous teacher in Paris at the time, and for me there was no question about it—I had to go there. I went to Paris to Madame Nora, took classes

with her, and observed what she was doing. After two years, Madame Nora put an additional beginner's course on the class roster that I was allowed to teach. She tested me every evening: How would one correct that, and that, or what does one need to master a particular technical challenge? I was introduced to the essence of ballet in the most wonderful way and really educated—and I learned how to work hard. I returned to the Folkwang School later and became an assistant.

/ **RH** I would also like to mention that meeting Rosalia Chladek was very important for me during my time at the Folkwang School.

/ **AM** Chladek also taught at the Folkwang School, on a course-by-course basis.

/ **RH** That is interesting as Chladek's system is based on movement analysis; for example, it questions how the body functions in an off-center or tense state. Or, how does movement progression change when different approaches to the movement are taken? Kurt Jooss was open to other techniques. He often invited guest teachers and choreographers to the Folkwang Dance Studio, for example Vera Volkova for ballet. She mostly came to conduct examinations and was a legend in the school—she exuded a great authority and a great aura.

/ **AM** Jooss asked Vera Volkova if she would be willing to run the school with him. Both of them spoke often about the link between ballet and modern. For Volkova, modern dance was a wonderful contrast, and thus complementary—which reassured those of us who were teaching. Vera Volkova worked at the school for ten years, conducting examinations and teaching advanced students for a couple of days each year.

/ How did the Jooss–Leeder Technique influence your work? It's clear that you were very much influenced by other techniques and teachers.

/ **AM** I loved the work at the Folkwang School. I really wanted to work more on this material and in this spirit—I did not go my own way. I was passionate about teaching, and I discovered this passion early on, but over the past thirty years I have been coaching rather than teaching.

/ **RH** I was deeply influenced by composition class where I was required to look for my own forms of expression from the first class onward.

/ Where, and how, did what you learned have an influence?

/ **RH** I learned that the interplay between space, time, and effort (choreutics and eukinetics) offers limitless possibilities for expression. This knowledge helped me in particular as a choreographer, as well as in my work directing opera and music when studying roles with the performers.

/ **What is taught in choreutics? And what is taught in eukinetics?**

/ **AM** Choreutics is about developing an awareness for what one does in the space and how one uses the space—it is about clear spatial awareness. Eukinetics is about the dynamics of the movement.

/ **RH** Every dancer works with them. Awareness helps a dancer to develop a more differentiated approach. One need not be permanently engaged in a theoretical discourse about the principles—but adopting a more aware approach enriches one's choreographic work. We thus have a tool available when creating choreographies, when teaching, and when dancing.

/ **Would you describe Jooss–Leeder as a technique?**

/ **AM** Definitely, yes. Technique is the way one masters the trade. Teaching technique means helping young dancers to forge their instrument. It is about mastering and becoming aware of the body. Technique is about all of that, but it doesn't exclude fantasy. One needs fantasy to achieve technique: imagining how something *should* be is also very helpful when learning or developing technical skills.

/ **RH** I would agree with that and add that the Jooss–Leeder Technique is not a technique with a fixed movement vocabulary, it is more about inviting teachers to develop their own material to train the body.

/ **AM** The Jooss–Leeder Technique has no set movements that everyone must learn and can perform, although there are principles that, when understood, repeatedly lead to certain movement qualities being taught. In ballet, for example, there is a jumping technique that can be used and which doesn't need to be developed again. The same is true of balance, one learns balance in ballet. Going off–balance and finding it again is our modern task. Technique is about finding a lively and new form, and playing with the principles.

/ **RH** If one has a fixed movement vocabulary, as in ballet, then an ideal of the perfect performance exists, for example of an arabesque or attitude—one has to conform to a particular form. If one goes off–balance in modern technique, one is floating, falling, and giving in to gravity. It is not about shape at this moment, it is about quality. I haven't found the kind of endless play with losing and regaining control found in the Jooss–Leeder work in any other technique.

/ **AM** But what does the Jooss–Leeder Technique mean, in fact? We teach technical challenges like swing, impulse, falling, etc.—namely, typical movements that don't exist in ballet. Then you get choreutics coming in from one side, and eukinetics from the other. This means the technique we are discussing informs both muscles and skills, while at the same time it teaches spatial awareness and precision through choreutics—as well as analysis and dynamics through eukinetics. So we really do cover a wealth of material.

/ **You have both spoken about how important ballet is for you. Does one need to study both ballet and Jooss–Leeder in order to become a well–trained dancer?**

/ **AM** I believe in cooperation between both techniques; both are enormously challenging. If students want to become dancers, they need to be trained in order to be able to adapt to any choreographer's style. To prepare for this task, young people need two techniques that are complementary but have different values.

/ **RH** At the *Tänzerkongress* (dancers convention) in 1928, Kurt Jooss called for equal treatment of ballet and modern. In my mind, one could already see a dovetailing of the two disciplines if one looked at Hans Züllig and later Michael Diekamp's classes.

/ **Does the Jooss–Leeder Technique have any basic principles in the following areas: methodology, didactics, physical learning, and artistic practice?**

/ **AM** We started thinking about the partnership between ballet and modern more in–depth after 1950. We organized the modern work a bit more and decided to focus in the beginner classes on purely dimensional movement—saved going on the diagonal, working off–balance, and also working with the torso in which one has to lose one's placement until the advanced classes. We thought—and Volkova disagreed with us to a certain extent—that ballet placement was so important that one couldn't simultaneously learn placement *and* how to lose it! But I must add that the Folkwang students were not teenagers—most were already eighteen years old—and one can't work with eighteen–year–olds the same way as with twelve–year–olds. The entrance audition was not about a proportion (like whether the legs or torso are a bit short), it was about motivation and recognizable talent such as musicality, coordination, and understanding of movement. Everything else had to be demonstrated in the probationary period. By this I mean that the methodology had a great deal to do with the age of the students.

/ **RH** Attaining a 'dance moment' in the class and then leading dancers into a movement sequence was part of the methodology used in modern dance training. First, individual motifs of a movement sequence were worked out before they were put together. There were musical and rhythmic tasks involved and the performance of different movement qualities. I don't often see this 'classic' progression in a modern dance class today.

/ **What are the most important basic principles for you?**

/ **AM** All those that we have already mentioned. I can't say spatial principles are more important than dynamic principles or musicality.

RH You can't separate one element from another. As already mentioned, it is the interplay between the three elements—namely effort, time, and space—or, in other words, between choreutics and eukinetics.

/ **Has teaching changed over the years and generations?**

/ **AM** Yes, very much so. Nowadays I only speak about rehearsal work with dancers in the theater. Dancers' skills have become much greater and their horizons wider over the last few decades. At the start of the 1970s, students still emerged from school with some blinders. There were dancers who believed they would lose everything they could do if they allowed themselves, even for a moment, to give in to weight, to sink. Today's dancers are open; their training has been more versatile or they have learned a lot in rehearsals with different choreographers. Dancers always learn a lot in rehearsals. A great deal has changed and lots of things have become much easier, but virtuoso technique has increased to such an extent that it is difficult to train dancers for a piece like *The Green Table*. They often fail to understand how difficult it is to master this work, although there are no striking variations in it. Restricting oneself and serving a choreographic work are things that are often very difficult to teach.

/ **What has changed in the approach to the Jooss–Leeder Technique as far as you are concerned?**

/ **AM** The approach has nothing to do with it, that is something else completely. We also have no time to develop things from the ground floor up—not even to name them. We have to use movement that has already been composed, learn it, then make it one's own. That is separate from technique, unfortunately.

/ **RH** It is different with one's own ensemble, where one builds something up slowly, piece–by–piece. The questions for me back then were: How to integrate dancers in the creative process? How does one motivate them to grapple more precisely with a theme, and on a more theatrical basis? The process wasn't always easy, as the limits during discussions were often exceeded. You say, Anna, that bravura—virtuosity—has become so important. We wanted to get away from that back then. When I worked with LABAN students on a section from my choreography *Dido und Aeneas*—which I created twenty-five years ago—most of them had difficulty performing a simple movement correctly. There is a moment in the piece where a female dancer begins curled–up in a seated position, opens up into the space, and then notices something, which initiates a walk across stage. Just finding this motivation was extraordinarily difficult for her. But such a simple movement can only come from one's power of imagination.

/ **AM** I am thinking how my father composed—the statement was the most important thing for him. He sought a shape for a theme—a language, as he called it. That had nothing to do with a formal, technical exercise sequence, however—for example, there are 'eight swings' in all variations in the Jooss–Leeder Technique, but when you watch Jooss's choreographies, there isn't a single eight swing, or even a half of one. That may be a simple example, but the vocabulary used when working on the principles isn't a choreographic vocabulary—the choreographic vocabulary emerges anew every time.

/ **Where can we still see influences of the Jooss–Leeder Technique, in your opinion?**

/ **AM** There is 'effort/shape' in America, that is not the same, but eukinetics plays a big role in it. Laban himself created 'effort' and 'effort/shape'. My father was irritated that Laban did away with the clean eukinetics/choreutics separation and mixed the two. These values will not be lost, even when there is little work done with them nowadays. Forsythe, for example, works as a choreographer with choreutics and has created new configurations.

/ **RH** What's important today is that one keeps talking about the technique, and one obviously listens when Forsythe says something about it. It is through him that young people, who now have new media at their fingertips, are most likely to have access to it. Forsythe ignores eukinetics, because, for him, the work is more about choreutics. I have heard from dancers and choreographers that they intentionally avoid dealing with eukinetics, as they fear too much expression and interpretation in movement.

/ **AM** That is a misunderstanding.

/ **RH** Exactly, as it has nothing to do with expression in the narrative sense, rather it's more akin to phrasing in music.

/ **And who is still working with the method?**

/ **RH** Barbara Passow was a discovery for me. I only knew Michael Diekamp, who taught the Jooss–Leeder Technique. Barbara carries on with this knowledge and legacy in her own, profound way. She is a teacher who still includes all the principles in her classes.

/ **AM** Jean Cébron is no longer active and has no successor, although he enjoys tremendous respect. Lutz Förster probably learned a lot from him; although I don't know how Lutz teaches, I can only assume that he carries something of the technique forward.

/ **How relevant is Jooss–Leeder for the future?**

/ **AM** Very, to my mind, because the Jooss–Leeder Technique is such an open system, there are no specialists and no institutionalization. There was always a highly talented individual who at some point in his or her time worked further on these things—but other than Barbara Passow, I don't know of anyone at the moment.

Choreutics and eukinetics are no longer kept up and taught at the Folkwang, which I see as a real failure..
/ **RH** Is it not the case that a talented choreographer is needed who deals with the technique? Jooss was a teacher, had established and run a school, but he was at the same time a creative person, a choreographer. This is what's needed so that it is not only carried on in amateur work.
/ **AM** That's true. It only needs guided teaching of the qualities and principles that Jooss and Leeder worked out for dancers, for professionals, so that they have the opportunity to use these qualities and principles creatively. Choreutics and eukinetics, as individual subjects, were scrapped at the Folkwang University and that is a shame. They could have been kept as courses in the curriculum, not only for beginners but also for advanced students. Who now knows that dealing with the three elements—time, effort, and space—covers everything?

/ **How do you assess the current relevance of the Jooss–Leeder Technique?**
/ **AM** Very high, and precisely today as virtuosity and the 'higher–faster–further' motto are so important. One should return to fine qualities and sensitize—heighten the awareness of the instrument and spatial correlations.

KATHARINE SEHNERT ON MARY WIGMAN AND HER TECHNIQUE

Cologne, 20 March 2010

/ **How did you come to Mary Wigman's studio?**
As a child, I went to dance–based gymnastics classes in my hometown, Erfurt. All the teachers were Wigman students who had trained in Dresden. My parents wanted to send me to ballet because of my musicality, but there were only ballet classes for children at the local theater and the ballet teacher was so strict and terrifying that I never wanted to go back. When it came to training, I wanted to go to Wigman. I already knew the name. I wrote to her and received an invitation to attend an entrance audition.

I was seventeen when I arrived at the school, very shy and rather naïve, nothing like seventeen–year–olds nowadays. After taking many deep breaths, I rang the bell and a young boy—a real youngster—opened the door: pale, in make–up and with black–rimmed eyes. I thought, 'What kind of creature is that?' He took me to the office, to Nora, the secretary, who pointed the way into the hall. Shy in front of people, I didn't have the confidence to go into the studio so I stood stiff as a board in the doorway. Then Mary was suddenly in front of me—she was so old, she looked like a grandmother—I'd never seen such a woman. Her face was, of course, very wrinkled. She wore make–up, had wild red hair, and was dressed

from head to toe in black. My first thought was, 'I want to get out of here.' (*laugh*) I was really scared. The students in the room continued improvising while I stood in the doorway for the entire lesson. No one took any notice of me. When the class was over, Mary came to me and said, 'Are you…' and everything changed. My first impression of her disappeared the moment she spoke and was nice to me. In class, she was still very strict, in fact, ruthless. And she grew fierce if she thought a student wasn't giving his or her all! There were slaps on body parts where she thought the student could work a bit harder.

As was common at the time, different improvisation tasks were given as part of the entrance audition, including the 'heroic lament'. Back then, this was something funny and boisterous. I received a letter a short time later saying I could start at the beginning of the next school year. Before the school year began I took part in the annual summer course at the Wigman Studio in Berlin—the classes were always full of American students. I began as an official student in September 1955.

/ **Which teachers and colleagues were important to you, aside from Wigman?** We had another two teachers at the Wigman Studio and a few guest teachers. The technique teachers were Til Thiele, who had worked with Marcel Marceau for a bit, and Manja Chmièl, who worked more with dynamics and her own temperament. I had Dore Hoyer as a guest teacher—she was a friend of Til Thiele and would come to the Wigman studio when in Berlin in order to be coached by Til. In Til and Manja, I had two very good technique teachers with different personalities. Mary taught the artistic and creative subjects. Because we were normally free after two o'clock—unless we had rehearsals for études that we had to show the next day—I always went to ballet in the afternoon. I used to go with Gerhard Bohner—who trained as a guest at the Wigman School—to Sabine Ress in East Berlin before the Wall went up. Once the Wall was up, I took classes with Tatjana Gsovsky.

/ **You later became one of Wigman's assistants, didn't you?** When she needed me, yes, which was very sporadically. I obviously needed to earn money once I had finished training, so I took run–of–show contracts in the theater. But I didn't really want to work in the theater. What one had to do as a dancer in the theater was not consistent with my idea of being a dancer. And then we founded Group Motion relatively quickly to try out our own dance ideas—but the Wigman Studio remained my home. I didn't have my own rooms, as I couldn't afford them—just a bed. I would stay in the studio from morning to evening and take classes well after I had finished training. And when required, if someone was absent, I jumped in.

/ **Why did you continue to use Wigman's method or technique?** Wigman's teaching method was so open—constantly changing and in a state of flux. When I started studying, one still thought one was entering a world of late expressionism. But that changed quickly, as we didn't want anything more to do with pathos and feelings. We still moved in this way, but we already had a completely different approach, a completely different attitude to movement. And we worked on becoming more technical. That was also the reason why I took ballet classes. This escape from pathos also led to our taking off the long skirts in class, at least in technique classes, simply so that you can see the legwork. And we no longer shied away from lifting the leg as high as we could back then (*laugh*). Producing or even paying attention to such technical skills were not at all important for Mary—she was looking for something completely different. We also cut our hair and wore tight–fitting tops. We focused on the body and tried to shape it into pure movement, pure shapes.

/ **How would you describe Wigman's influence on your work?** I think it is definitely there, because everything I did afterward was built upon it. You got the basics from her: namely what it means to dance, what comprises movement, how you recognize its structure, its dynamic, where movement comes from, and what it can express. That is what we learned from her. The body was seen and addressed holistically. And wherever one went in the course of one's life, you could build on this training, which meant finding one's way relatively quickly in any other technique. You may not have been fully faithful to the style, but you knew straight away that something 'comes from there' and that something 'goes there', and so it was easier to grasp a movement sequence quickly.

This is how it was when I went to the then dance mecca, New York, and trained at the Limón Studio. There I thought, 'Oh, the swing! That was a part of Wigman's teaching, and here is an entire technique built on it! The people can't do anything else. They can't vibrate or glide because they only move in their swing–fall–break way.' I thought that we had had the best training with Wigman because we experienced a wide range of movement; it was up to the individual how far he or she fleshed it out or used it.

We used to hold it against Wigman that she had not developed a system, that she had not systematized her teaching methods. What one learned depended upon the respective teacher and how this teacher had internalized the material and passed it along. Every class was different. And if you were not in class or did not give one hundred percent, then you missed something. That was also a good lesson: Always get fully involved with everything available, have one-hundred-percent presence.

/ **What does Wigman mean for your work today?** I have internalized it all to such an extent that I really couldn't say whether this or that movement comes from Wigman. But this approach was never part of the training anyway. For Wigman, it was about developing the student's own creative potential, and of course, about training the body so it functioned as an instrument. That was her concern—that the student master and control the body as an instrument, even in seemingly un-controlled movements, and knows at all times what he or she is doing, along with why and how it is being done. So I cannot say at all, when I develop move-ments, that this or that movement is a Wigman move-ment. It is now my movement, though it has, in a sense, been nourished by Wigman's 'mother's milk' (*laugh*).

I have tried out a lot, for example I have also done Graham. One asks oneself, 'Is that my thing? Can I identify with it?' And then one does something else. There may be other elements that have flowed into my work, but again, these have been discovered and made into my own. I am not oblivious to outside impressions, but I have worked continuously on this analytical path, on this consideration of movement, and I have therefore drawn a certain line through time, regardless of the current *zeitgeist*. I was always more interested in creating and the creative process than in the end–result. I have never worked toward a certain end–result but constantly tried to discover where the logic in the movement lies, and what emerges from it. That also harks back to Wigman's legacy.

/ **You also taught and still teach. How would you describe the connection with the Wigman legacy?** Here, too, I have always tried—apart from in my techni-cal training—to get students to recognize correlations and relationships. Why is someone doing this movement, now, exactly? And what does it produce? What could follow? I teach awareness of what one is doing, not just copying movements. A dancer has to find his or her own way to this technique and ask themself what he or she wants with it. We never worked with etudes, and also never used a mirror. There was no mirror in the Wigman Studio. I had one in my studio, but it was always covered (*laugh*). When I see people training today, they all stand in front of the mirror—even the teacher looks into the mirror—and the students stand behind and copy. I find this a terrible way to communicate.

/ **Would you describe what you teach as being 'in the Wigman tradition'?** No. I would never call it that. The tradition in which one teaches something is not at all important. There are no Expressionist dancers any more, as time has moved on. And back then, when it was still called Expressionist dance, it was contemporary dance as it existed in its own era. Each era has its own terminology and imagery. The tools of the trade are always the same, to a certain extent, because the body is always the same. The craft has to be mastered and perfected, but the artist's creativity exists in the spirit of the age, in the here–and–now, so today's artists have their own impressions or their own mental states and feelings. If I learned gliding or jumping (and bouncing) with Wigman, then these are the tools that I use in class, but I use them in conjunction with the knowledge I have today.

Anatomical and medical knowledge was not relevant for dancers back then. We didn't take any notice of the anatomical realities of the body, for example, like the position of the pelvis in certain movements. Nowadays people have an enormous body of knowledge—also about the neuromuscular system. I would be limiting myself enormously if I were to work now as I did fifty years ago—that would be terrible. That would not be very inventive, nor very Wigman. She wanted things to develop on their own, which is why she didn't develop a system like Graham's, whose technique spans the globe. Wigman's teaching method is, indeed, not well known today because of the lack of any system.

/ **Would you call Wigman's working method a 'technique'?** We did speak of technique back then. But the term 'technique' has changed in meaning for me. Back then, technique simply meant learning the craft. Nowadays, the word 'technique' is used to describe a particular system, something that is fixed. In this sense, I can obviously not say that Wigman's working method was a technique. With Wigman one researched and tried out the various possibilities and qualities of, for example, basic movements like walking and turning. When I work with dancers today, and get them to perform a movement that, for me, is normal—for example, a movement starting from the center—then they actually ask me 'And where should the head be? And where should the hips be?' They see everything from the outside, so to speak, the arm moves like this, the head like this—but they don't see where the movement starts and that it can trigger a wholly organic movement sequence. Then I stand there and think: So what, indeed, are the hips doing? What is the head doing? We also observed shape, and there was a lot of work on coordination. But there were also organic movements that followed an internal logic.

/ **That is not the case today?** Not really. The dancers are much, much better technically—that much is certain. I sometimes ask myself, 'How does the body manage to do what these dancers are doing?' But I see almost everything done with the same energy, the same dynamic. Dancers should always be involved in what they are doing, but I don't think that they do so at all now. The speed dancers must maintain means that they can only strive to make their dancing more or less technically clean (*laugh*), they can't tune the tech-

nique to their personalities. Yet the dancing is so virtuoso that I stare open–mouthed and think, 'Wow!' Yet after ten minutes I fall asleep because it's just rote.

/ **So the question again: Would you describe Wigman's working methods as a 'technique'?** Til Thiele taught technique differently than Wigman, and Manja was different again. Wigman built on what other teachers had discovered from our bodies, so to speak. She genuinely only worked with basic movement forms and principles, which meant that the working method was exercise–based, whereas today it is more goal–oriented in that one has to reach a specific outcome as quickly as possible. With Wigman, one always repeated a movement until it was clear what one had to do, what the phrasing was, and what energy was needed, until one had internalized it. Whenever needed, the movement could then be referred to, and that is maybe the method, the way of working.

There was the spinning on the spot, which was one of Wigman's specialties, revolving around one's own axis without letting the head lead, something that didn't exist in any other dance technique, in my opinion. She had a way to do this that was based on a foot movement. You started practicing slowly, then did it quicker and quicker. It was the same procedure for everything else. For jumps, we started with some foot–work, and then launched ourselves into the air. The jumping class was always on Wednesdays, the turn class on Mondays. Wigman's classes were exercise classes rather than technique classes, which we had with Til und Manja. Wigman's classes were exercise classes in the truest sense of the word: We worked on a single movement form—jumping, vibrating, turning, gliding—for one-and-a-half hours.

/ **Are there any basic principles underlying Wigman's methodology, pedagogy, didactics, physical learning, aesthetics, and artistic practice?** I have already said something about physical learning and artistic practice. We discovered themes through practice. Everything else was learned through improvisation and composition. We were given composition tasks that mostly had to do with spatial principles. How does one place people in the space? Which movements make sense at particular points in the space? One has to take into account that when I was training with Wigman in the middle of the 1950s, she was already seventy-years old. Her main focus was on space. Even in her exercise classes she made a big point of working with space, that the dancer be aware of space and the point in space, that focus was used. She worked a lot with focus, such that it didn't stay with the person but became 'depersonalized', i.e., a gaze went beyond one's own gaze. I think that's something that has since been lost. We also worked a great deal with the back, with an awareness of the back.

/ **Which basic principles/qualities are especially important in the Wigman technique?** All of them (*laugh*). Over the years my respect and reverence for the body has only grown stronger. I am more and more amazed by what the body can do. The fascinating thing about dance, for me, is that there are infinite possibilities for development, that one continues to locate the next layer of the onion, always finding something new, new knowledge, new ability, and that the body stores so much that can emerge later and can be called up. I find that extremely fascinating. I see absolutely no difference between a person moving in everyday life or in the studio or on stage. I learn so much from nature, for instance when I am watching birds, what they do with their heads because they can't move their eyes. One can learn so much by observing.

I think that the critical thing I learned is that one has to find the path from 'expressing oneself' to 'being it'. I don't know if I can give a good example of this in practice. Let's take a flower. I portray a flower, and I do so as if I were a flower and my arms are the leaves, my hands the flowers, and this flower grows and grows. Or I try to portray the essence of a flower in dance, and I ask myself what is being a flower actually all about, at which point I then perhaps think about the basic human principle about growing and dying. This particular energy develops until a certain highpoint and then it disintegrates. I don't want to portray what a flower could be, but want to be this flower, the flower 'principle', with every movement. I am the movement, I am here. And that is what dance is.

/ **Has the Wigman Technique changed over the years and generations?** Of course it has changed. It would be a bad thing if it hadn't. I am kind of the last generation, if you will. When there is no longer anyone else who has experienced Wigman directly, I think this knowledge will disappear. All the efforts to document her work—film, photos, notation, and movement descriptions—will never cover everything. Video loses the three-dimensional aspect; words can only come close to describing a movement, and you cannot convey feeling in notation. That is also a characteristic of dance—it is fleeting and refuses to be held down, refuses to be made into museum material (*laugh*). And why should one want to desperately hold onto it? That said, we can listen to music from previous centuries, and can look at paintings by old masters—it's a shame this isn't possible with dance.

/ **Have you continued, developed, expanded, or modified aspects of the Wigman Technique?** Yes I have, but not in the sense that I have eliminated those movements that are out of date or that I have tried to bring movements up to date, rather this happened in practice more than by thinking about it. I am still alive,

and I change and will hopefully continue to do so. And I have already said before that one learned certain tools of the trade from Wigman, and that one is always developing and fine-tuning this equipment. One increasingly learns how to master it and increasingly understands what is behind it, and this is something that cannot be led by the mind.

My experience and encounter with Butoh was extremely beneficial, as I discovered my roots in something foreign, so to speak. It was on this path to somewhere else that I suddenly realized that my training had been the best.

/ **Why Butoh and not Graham?** Graham wasn't dance, as far as I was concerned, as everything happened on the floor (laugh). Butoh has a great deal in common with modern dance. There are many parallels in the working methods and movement concepts. The training I had with Min Tanaka in Japan in 1988 was energetic and powerful, and this is how it was at the Wigman Studio too. We only moved through the space. Even with Wigman, there were no standing exercises or floorwork. We sat on the floor only when we stretched, there was no floor technique. Min Tanaka called his training 'bodyweather', which means that the state of the body is different every day, like the weather outside is always different. One has to deal with every type of weather: one can't say, 'I don't feel like it today and so I am not going training.' As is always the case, sometimes the sun shines, sometimes there is a storm, and sometimes it's foggy. In Japan, I learned to work with the weather and to use it as material, and this approach coincided with all my other experience, as did this permanent moving 'through the space', and the one hour purely spent jumping. It was just like that in the Wigman Studio. Crazy.

I spent an afternoon improvising with Kazuo Ohno. He sat in a chair, read aloud, and we were given a cup of tea and a cookie. We sat at his feet, as we did with Mary. Mary also sat in her chair and told wonderful stories, read a poem out loud, and we all sat around her and listened and then improvised the poem. It was the same with Kazuo Ohno. He was very touched by the fact that I'd come from Wigman, and my time with him completed the circle after all my wanderings across America, England, and wherever else I had been. A real knot loosened up in me. I only did solos after that, and I once again achieved a proper, more sophisticated access to movement.

/ **Where have the specific characteristics of the Wigman Technique, and of her teaching, left their mark?** Gundel Eplinius was a professor in the dance department of the university in Hanover for a long time and taught 'Wigman'. She came from Wigman's school in Leipzig and had systematized the technique a bit. She taught all the basic movement material. The dance department was closed a few years ago. It is also possible that Corrie Hartong taught a lot of Wigman in Rotterdam after the war, and let's not forget Hanya Holm in New York. The way Wigman dealt with the space also had an impact on the staging styles of opera and theater directors, like Sellner, Rennert, and Ruth Berghaus. Elements of Wigman can also be found in ballet.

Wigman is also still present in the reconstructions of her dances, but I generally find these reconstructions unacceptable. One only sees what has been copied from video and you end up with something so wishy–washy. I can only accept those dances reconstructed by Fabian Barba. He came to grips with the technique and didn't just take the movements from the video; he delved deep into the Wigman's ideas.

/ There has also been no institutionalization of this method or technique, right? No, and Wigman didn't want that either. She always thought that it would be at the expense of individualism. She preferred that personalities work in her spirit, but not necessarily in her way.

/ And if someone asks you to teach a Wigman class, what would you teach? I would also have to ask myself—after fifty years—what is memory of Wigman and what is, in fact, my own experience? The memory and my experiences overlap, so what is from Wigman and what is from me? There are many aspects of Wigman's teaching that were important for others, but I don't necessarily remember those things at all. Memory is selective, and one doesn't continue with things one never liked.

/ Were there any other activities that supplemented your training, i.e., theory, other physical practices, or analytical processes? I felt stimulated by the new music (neue Musik). Music was like a guide for me, especially Anton Webern's music, in how he reduced music to fundamental elements, its essence. That was our goal: If one was thinking about something particular, one searched for a movement for as long as it took, a movement that corresponded with what one wanted to say. This sometimes took weeks, even though the dances back then were very short— two and three minutes. When I did my first five-minute dance, it was considered much too long. I worked mainly with musique concrète, as it gave you a lot of freedom. One could hold a dialogue with the music, work with it as a partner.

And then Informal Painting emerged, which was no longer a reproduction of nature but the portrayal of an internal attitude. This type of painting was not about feelings, however. On stage, lighting could create a particular space that was important for the mood, a particular color represented a particular expression or idea. Movement, color, and lighting had to be harmonious.

/ That applied to your work with Group Motion, right? Yes, but it was also part of our training and work in the Wigman Studio.

/ Did you work with modern music there? Yes, for example with Bartók, Hindemith, and Ravel. Ulrich Kessler was our constant accompanist, and he also played freely. We never worked with classical music. My first dances with Wigman were to free jazz and Webern.

/ Is today's teaching coupled with a particular artistic practice? When I returned from Japan and did my first solos, I was immediately labeled as a Butoh dancer. I was always described as a Butoh dancer and I could only say that I wasn't a Butoh dancer! I am also not an Expressionist dancer. I am just a dancer. Where I get my inspiration is completely irrelevant, but even the Goethe Institute pigeonholed me the same way. Being pegged is always double–edged. The Wigman Technique was developed further in America, for example, it is not something that is rigid or systematized— and it has influenced my pedagogical and artistic work.

/ How did Wigman's relevance change after the Second World War? I never experienced Wigman before the Second World War. There was a resurgence of ballet after the war, particularly in Berlin under Adenauer's government. Expressionist dance was forgotten overnight. That was Dore Hoyer's dilemma, and also Manja Chmièl's, who had the same artistic potency as Hoyer. Manja was caught between two generations and never really had her moment in time.

/ And how relevant is this technique today? One can still use some aspects of the technique today. Perfection and speed has made a great deal of what happens in dance very physical. Moving away from this, and thinking about movement and the content of movement, would be a good way of redressing the imbalance. It is not a matter of putting more feeling into movement, but adopting the movement as one's own, so that one brings oneself as a person into the movement. This way of working should be given more weight in my view, so that the audience once again enjoys seeing the person as well as the dancer on the stage.

/ What are your hopes for the future? That the qualities we possess are recognized, and that we are not labeled as antique…that dancers and others become aware of these qualities once again, and integrate them into dance.

Irmela Kästner

P.A.R.T.S. — CONTEMPORARY POSITIONS

TEACHING TECHNIQUE IN CONTEMPORARY DANCE TRAINING *Brussels, 10 March 2010*

The Flemish choreographer Anne Teresa De Keersmaeker founded the Performing Arts Research and Training Studios (P.A.R.T.S.), a training institute for contemporary dance, in Brussels in 1995. Nine generations of students have since passed through the school. Many of them have made a name for themselves as dancers and/or choreographers and are part of a new generation of artists who are leaving their mark on contemporary dance around the world. Young dancers from all parts of the globe apply to the school. P.A.R.T.S. sees itself as a location for lively artistic exchange and change.

As part of the *Dance Techniques 2010* research project, the author and journalist Irmela Kästner talked with the teachers and colleagues whom the director of the school believes have played, and are playing, a key role in shaping the young history of the school. The teaching concepts, and how P.A.R.T.S. approaches dance technique, was of particular interest.

Participants
Steven de Belder
Coordination of Research Cycle, Theory

David Hernandez
Contemporary, Improvisation, Composition, Rhythm

Mia Lawrence
Coordination of Training Cycle, Yoga

Janet Panetta
Ballett

Chrysa Parkinson
Co-Coordination of Research Cycle, Contemporary

Theo Van Rompay
Deputy Director

Salva Sanchis
Coordination of Research Cycle, Contemporary, Choreography

Moderator
Irmela Kästner

/ This discussion focuses on pedagogical concepts in contemporary dance training. How is the training at P.A.R.T.S. designed? What is your approach to teaching?

/ **Mia Lawrence (ML)** I focus on helping students express themselves honestly, whichever art form they choose, so that they create a link to their individual creativity—in this case through the body.

/ **Salva Sanchis (SS)** My involvement with dance is based mainly on my interest in technique. Teaching has become an essential part of my own research as a dancer and choreographer.

/ **Chrysa Parkinson (CP)** I have a background in ballet and modern dance that I later complemented with various body techniques. I am neither a choreographer nor a teacher—I see myself as a performer. My interest in technique is based on precision: precision relating to the *how* when working with the material, in terms of both the choreography and the performance. My teaching ultimately aims to identify a person's own artistic approach, and what the physical, stylistic, and aesthetic implications are. The question, 'How far can I go as a performer?' is always in the background.

/ **Janet Panetta (JP)** A technique enables you to imagine what you can do and what you would like to do. It tells you about yourself. If it can't do that, then it is not a technique. Unlike creativity, technique is, for me, something that you can teach. I have been teaching professionally since 1974 and have witnessed so many changes in the dance world that I find it extremely interesting that I still belong to it. Despite my ballet, and later modern and postmodern background, it has never appealed to me to teach ballet to classical dancers.

/ **David Hernandez (DH)** Teaching has always been my way of learning. I started as a musician—theater and dance came later. All these art forms were somehow part of a whole. Technique, for me, quite simply means how you do things; a technique should open up many paths and not just enable you do to one thing in a very particular way. A technique lesson should be interesting and illusive—and also demand the impossible. I always see things in a historical context. Nowadays, it is no longer about teaching people a particular aesthetic or ability. We are the next generation. The ball has been passed along to us—where do we run with it?

/**Theo Van Rompay (TVR)** The key for Anne Teresa De Keersmaeker is to translate experiences from her own artistic work, knowledge from her own training, and the art you see on stage today, into a training program. She also asked choreographers like Pina Bausch, Trisha Brown, and William Forsythe for advice at the start. However, the people who are actively involved in this project, as Anne Teresa intended—with everything that they have assembled and amassed over the years— are the essence of the school. P.A.R.T.S. was not the result of a theoretical concept.

/ **Is the training aimed at a specific job description, a particular job title, for the school's graduates?**
/ **DH** Thankfully we don't have that kind of label, and that is precisely what is nice about this place. Otherwise we would have had a real problem in terms of the debate about whether you can teach art.
/ **TVR** An interesting question that we, of course, asked ourselves when we extended the program from three to four years (*in 2000, author's note*). The program was broken down into a two–year Training Cycle and a subsequent two–year Research Cycle in which students had to choose between two directions, 'dancer' or 'choreographer'. It took us less than a year to realize that it was impossible for us to develop separate programs, however, and there was absolutely nothing that would not have been equally important for both. So we scrapped this division and now let the students choose from the entire spectrum of their own priorities and determine their own course of studies.
/ **DH** Coming back to the job description—if you look at it in a historical context, then a label that you put on it today should be valid in ten years' time. You can't take that for granted, however. And a choreographer is definitely not made in a school.
/ **JP** You don't know that. You can't predict the future, regardless of how well informed you are about the past and present. We never know what is coming and where it is coming from. If we were training dancers for a particular company, then predictions would be possible. But things have fundamentally changed.

/ **With regard to technique within contemporary dance training, what do you understand by the term 'contemporary'?**
/ **SS** Contemporary technique means contemporary teachers means contemporary experience means individual experience. Students nowadays no longer say that they are taking a class in a particular technique, but with a particular teacher.

/ **Do you mean that contemporary is synonymous with individual?**
/ **SS** Individual, but not isolated. Everything is linked. That is how I see it, which is different to fifteen years ago.
/ **CP** No form can claim a reality for itself. There are, for example, artists whose work is based on anatomical, Western medical research. Some ask questions about aesthetics or political contexts. Others delve into their own bodies. The poles today are essentialism and relativism. You try to move between these two extremes.

/ **American modern dance techniques still determined the teaching profiles of many schools until recently. Nowadays, Graham, Limón, Humphrey, even Cunningham, appear to be truly out.**
/ **JP** No, that isn't true—they are not out in the U.S. One of the most important schools in New York introduced the Cunningham Technique into its program for the first time last year. A bit late, actually a bit of a shock.
/ **TVR** When Anne Teresa De Keersmaeker decided in 1995 to introduce ballet and contemporary training into her program and throw out all modern techniques like Limón, Cunningham, or Graham, we were not aware of the remarkable standpoint she took at that time. There were ballet schools that offered a bit of modern, and there were postmodern institutes like the School for New Dance Development in Amsterdam that had scrapped ballet and in many cases modern dance, too. We took an extreme route and threw out the middle. That was no verdict on style. But there are only seven hours in a day.
/ **CP** And now one of our students from last year is doing a Mary Wigman reconstruction.
/ **TVR** That's funny.
/ **DH** Time is an important aspect for me in connection with this question about what is contemporary technique: The time it takes to develop a format, to teach one's own process and material to others. And the distance. Sometimes I only have an inkling of what I am doing; I give the students a direction, and get something back. It is a continuous two–way process nowadays in which the teaching develops in contemporary dance.

/ In your contribution to the book *P.A.R.T.S. — Documenting Ten Years of Contemporary Dance Education,* you speak, David Hernandez, about the contradiction between ballet and Release Technique. Where is this contradiction exactly?

/ **JP** I don't think there is a contradiction. I don't know of any teaching that encourages you to be restrained… not as a final goal. The title 'Release' alone drives me crazy. You should always be 'released.' If you look at really good ballet dancers, they are not suffering, they are 'released' in what they do.

/ **DH** At least those you like to watch and who last longer than ten years. Sometimes I get the impression that there are people who simply have it in their blood. Maybe that is the difference: training nowadays is no longer just for those people who walk in and can do it.

/ **JP** I was very fortunate with my training. My teachers were, of course, horribly strict compared to today, but they taught us how to make even a dry technique, like the Cecchetti method, really dance. I recently had a discussion with a ballet teacher about basics like the demi-plié, how important and interesting it is to remember the basics. 'How old are your students? They should know what a demi-plié is at twenty-one!' the teacher said. But it is not about a position; it is about function and recognizing where something comes from and where it is going.

/ **CP** For the benefit of understanding: The title Release Technique originally meant letting go of movement patterns, it didn't mean being relaxed. I think that there is a contradiction between techniques that create patterns and techniques that release patterns. But it is a useful, not a negative, contradiction that tells you how to coordinate yourself.

/ **JP** Your body gives you patterns too.

/ How and where does precision, which has already come up several times, come into it?

/ **CP** You should be able to do a movement in exactly the same tone, time, and space, and with the same effect, as you intended.

/ Does that mean that movement is also functional for the body?

/ **CP** Precision doesn't necessarily mean healthy.

/ **JP** You can choose not to be healthy to your body.

/ **SS** It does overlap. If you want to be efficient, it tends to be healthier.

/ **CP** In performance situations, you are always faced with the decision of doing something that is 'bad' for the body.

/ **DH** That reminds me of my earlier days with Damaged Goods. Meg Stuart and I knew that Release Technique had started a process in the body that helped us do even contorted movements without killing ourselves. By contrast, we now often have students that barely have any patterns to release. This is possibly why ballet is being embraced again after being rejected for a while.

/ What role do techniques like yoga, which I would like to call mental techniques, play?

/ **ML** Students see it as a purely physical technique. I also teach a very physical Asana practice that focuses on the alignment of muscles and joints, but also on relaxing the mind. I'd like to come back to something Janet said earlier, that you can't teach creativity. It is often mental patterns that block creativity, a lack of self–confidence, negative opinions of oneself. Yoga can be a way of unraveling these thought patterns, so that the obstacles are seen on a more conscious level and finally disappear.

/ Eastern philosophy—Anne Teresa De Keersmaeker is known to reference Taoism in her work— as opposed to Western science. The contextualization of an analytical, anatomic approach was just mentioned. How does this impact dance?

/ **CP** Much of the Release Technique is based on rehabilitation and therefore focuses on Western medicine and uses the same language, namely Latin. This helps people learn about and articulate the body. On the other hand, I am aware that there is a mechanism that imagines and considers physical experience through the filter of Western medicine and beds it in a context that is more a hindrance than a help—the more so as it releases a certain anxiety. The authority of medical language has a very mysterious relationship to the body.

/ **DH** I've almost stopped using that language.

/ **JP** It came into fashion at some point. It was also necessary, if you remember that everything beforehand was imagery. It opened the floodgates to a lot of interpretation. Dancers and athletes knew so little about their bodies.

/ **DH** Dancing hurts, that is my personal opinion. There is good and bad pain. You used to take a hot bath and return to class the next day. Nowadays you carry out anatomical self–analysis.

/ **CP** And you didn't have a career after the age of forty-five either.

/ **JP** Oh, yes you did!

/ **DH** For some people. At the same time, you can't divorce the demand on the body from the aesthetic. Not many people burn themselves out on stage anymore. If that is the idea of dancing, then it will be easier to dance until forty.

/ **CP** We must be careful not to demonize something that is also useful.

/ There was talk of imagining what you can do and would like to do. Does language play a role in the visualization of skills?

/ **ML** We were the first generation to dive so deeply into an analytical process based on anatomy. I can remember that I couldn't even move my little finger without knowing where the movement came from. I couldn't improvise without my brain not only observing, but also directing it. That lead to a new awareness, not only physical but also psychological. We have gone so far in this direction that we have to find a way back.

/ **JP** It was a necessary step. Anatomy was necessary.

/ **DH** And it is still necessary. Coming back to my article, which you mentioned earlier, one quote that I included from Gertrude Stein said that a person 'is an outlaw until he is a classic, there is hardly a moment inbetween...' This also applies if you want to find a language to teach new approaches and ideas; teaching is a tricky matter nowadays.

/ **JP** When I look at the students here—they are chosen because they are among the best. I mean that they are very, very good. Some already have degrees, and they know it means something to have been accepted here. We often have to teach them in the first year that what they have learned so far wasn't necessarily the best. That confuses them and they lock themselves up in their bodies, but everything comes back. And then you see the whole process open and in front of you; that has an impact on creativity. It is my goal to convert knowledge into physicality until new knowledge manifests itself physically. How that looks in detail at the end, I am unable to say.

/ The idea that teaching is important for one's own artistic research is interesting.

/ **SS** It is enormously important for the students in this training program to sense that the teaching is alive. It isn't a presentation of something that was once valuable; it is current, now. And because everything is in motion, it cannot be perfect. I teach to make things clear to myself, and these things are taught to others by becoming clear to me—it's a reciprocal process. I can try out things in the lesson that I can't try out in a goal–oriented rehearsal. My expectations are different each time, but both are complementary.

/ **ML** Yoga and ballet have a set form. Contemporary dance doesn't. The process—I don't want to call it research—which I follow every day in my yoga teaching practice is based on a form that has been around for three or four thousand years. I stopped teaching contemporary classes when I stopped dancing myself. It would not have been a problem to continue, I had enough material, but it no longer felt as it should, namely alive in every moment. Our generation did not start teaching to become teachers, they started teaching while they were still actively involved in the process.

/ **JP** And something else: We all love and are fascinated by this art form. Each student comes to the lesson with their individual personality and their own approach. If that didn't interest us, if we were not thrilled by this give and take, we wouldn't do it. We shouldn't do it.

/ **ML** And we want to share that with each other.

/ **JP** What we all share is the ability to strip something down to its bare minimum and make it new and exciting time and again. This is something the students should also learn. Artificiality interests no one.

/ I am interested in how repertory teaching influences technique classes.

/ **Steven de Belder (SDB)** It is meant to influence technical training as part of a process that the students take into their own creations. Connections can possibly be seen between a technique and an artistic process, and how they come together in a historical context.

/ **DH** Repertory teaching has changed a great deal since the school opened. Back then you dedicated yourself to the works of choreographers you considered particularly important: Trisha Brown, William Forsythe, and Anne Teresa De Keersmaeker. I always thought of it as a trip into the past that you forced on people for a moment. The focus was not really on students' own work.

/ But P.A.R.T.S. performed works by Brown, Forsythe, and, of course, by De Keersmaeker publicly.

/ **SS** What do you mean by that? 'Of course by De Keersmaeker?' There's no 'of course' about it.

/ Do you want to say that the school does not aim to train dancers for the Rosas dance company?

/ **SS** Exactly. That is definitely not the case.

/ **ML** It is not intentional. It is just that recently she (*De Keersmaeker, author's note*) likes the people coming out of the school, so she takes them.

/ **SDB** It is a question of efficiency; and it's actually logical for her as a choreographer to benefit from having her own school—but that is not what we are working toward.

/ **JP** Repertoire is a good thing; it gives you an idea of what it means to work with people. It makes you aware that learning does not end when you leave the school, it is just beginning.

/ **ML** Repertoire is used, for all intents and purposes, as material for teaching technique. Teaching covers a lot more than pure technique; it is about working with a specific approach to the body, to phrasing, and to inter-action. A lot of it is already history—it was developed be-fore the students were born. It therefore calls for another type of physicality and opens up new paths. Dancing in a group of eight or ten people is a particular experience that is not on offer in a technique class. Composition tools are also taught. In *Set and Reset (by Trisha Brown, author's note)*, the students learn the structures in order to work with them rather than copying the piece exactly.

/ **SDB** Also, the repertory pieces by De Keersmaeker tend to be older, whereas her way of working today has developed and is quite different. We will be teaching a workshop based on one of her very recent works, *Zeitung*, for the first time next year.

/ **Does that mean repertory is a part of teaching composition?**

/ **ML** It is all interlinked, all feeding into each other. De-finitely more than it did ten years ago.

/ **CP** You can sometimes coordinate technique training and repertoire. Sometimes they work in opposite directions. Students learn how to integrate different in-formation.

/ **DH** Repertoire is an intersection of composition, technique, and theatricality, which converge in a creative whole. Of course people come here because they have seen performances by Rosas. But what has devel-oped here has mainly to do with the fact that Anne Teresa is very interested and curious; she is always taking on new people, wanting to know how they work, what they bring, and she gives them a chance to work here. Something develops that is also relevant for repertoire.

/ **CP** It would be interesting to ask Anne Teresa this question, as her work is clearly more influenced by the people that teach here, and her dancers, than our work is influenced by her. It has something to do with her sensitivity—a sensitivity to the ability to express, which is more important to her than technical virtu-osity. That also decides who gets to work here.

/ **Does De Keersmaeker choose the teachers for the school?**

/ **CP** Not on her own, but she has a large influence on it. And she has a personal, creative relationship with all the people sitting at this table.

/ **Are repertory and lessons in dance theory and dance history complementary?**

/ **SDB** Not enough. We should invest more in this. Give more context instead of just being inside. Fourth–year students are currently working on the perfor-mance of *Drumming*. Instead of creating a new work, they are concentrating fully on rehearsing and performing an existing work and in doing so have the opportunity to go much deeper into it, particularly as there will be eight to ten performances of it in the theater.

/ **Do you mean that historical and theoretical knowl-edge produces a better dancer?**

/ **ML** You are influenced by everything, all the time.

/ **JP** And what influences you determines who you are.

/ **CP** Artists are created by their environment in exactly the same way that they create their environment; it is tricky not to build a hierarchy out of the incoming and outgoing information. You have to allow artists to build their own hierarchies.

/ **SS** You should avoid having expectations as to what form any influence should take. What is certain is that the students are being influenced, even when they fall asleep in theory class.

/ **ML** When I look at our auditions today—the infor-mation that the eighteen, nineteen-year-olds bring with them is very different to four years ago. They used to come into contact with this information for the first time here. We have to develop the program further for this reason alone.

/ **To what extent have the students changed?**

/ **CP** They are trained differently. The training that is given in other institutions has changed rapidly over the last ten years.

/ **DH** There have been important developments in this respect. Brussels had a handful of influential com-panies that were touring the world, but no dance com-munity. That has changed, however, not least with the founding of this school. Artists settled here, and graduates of the school started teaching in the city, so more and more of this other information is spreading.

/ **How is the Training Cycle different from the Research Cycle?**

/ **JP** It is the students who are mainly different. They have changed. You know them better and you react to them differently.

/ **CP** Their expectations of the school are different.

/ **ML** And the training itself is different. The classes are shorter in the Training Cycle, one-and-a-half hours each of ballet and contemporary training every day. In the Research Cycle, the students themselves determine how they want to train their bodies.

⁄ **Is there an age limit for admission?**
⁄ **SDB** Twenty-four for the Training Cycle, twenty-six for the Research Cycle. We like to have a certain homogeneity in the group.

⁄ **What is the biggest challenge for you as teachers?**
⁄ **DH** I find it interesting and difficult to deal with the change of attitude that I encounter time and again in many students. First, they are begging to get into the school, then, after a short period of adjustment, there is suddenly no pleasing them any more. It appears to be a necessary process that I try not to let affect me, but at the same I don't want to ignore it. The pushing and pulling is all part of it and if it stops, then I am doing something wrong. In any case it stops me from feeling too secure.
⁄ **JP** I think that each generation is becoming increasingly narcissistic. I try to make it clear to my students from the start that teaching cannot revolve around them individually. They can't tell me what they think and feel about each small step before they have understood what it is I want to teach them. I can only say, 'Come and tell me in two years' time what you think about a tendu.'
⁄ **CP** As I am a performer, I always tell the students that, as dancers and performers, they have to develop their own voice—and then I suddenly realize that they are using exactly this to resist the choreographic process they are in! They hold back. But a personal voice means giving your all, exhausting the full context of a choreographic situation so that the personal voice emerges clearly at the end. It is about pushing back the boundaries. I realize that I also must expand the complexity of what I am talking about to my perception of technique. Based on an understanding of how intricately artists articulate themselves, you should encourage them to commit themselves as fully as possible, and not restrict them.
⁄ **SS** I am obsessed with precision. In situations where you can almost smell that extensive work on technical details is being questioned, it is a challenge for me to involve students in the work without confrontation. I am not championing any Eastern doctrine here, like practice and practice again; you don't need to understand anything. The school is not at all Eastern in this sense.
⁄ **JP** But that is not Eastern—it is old Western.
⁄ **ML** Resistance used to be a very big challenge for me before, when I taught more. As you get older, you learn how to deal with it differently; it makes you think.
⁄ **SDB** I can only speak from an organizational perspective. The biggest task is finding a balance, for example in the Research Cycle. You encourage the students to develop their own paths and goals, and they are

given a say in the way they are assessed. It is a move toward more independence. On the other hand, they are still in a school environment and we tell them what is good for them; they are not self–determined artists. And with twenty-four students, restrictions are necessary.
⁄ **SS** We are currently in the middle of auditions and I again realize that we teach an elite. Not *the* elite, but an elite, and that colors our entire discussion here. These students have drive. They will go take their own paths anyway.
⁄ **CP** The standard of the students certainly promotes the development of each teacher. That is how intense—how tight—and strong the exchange is here.

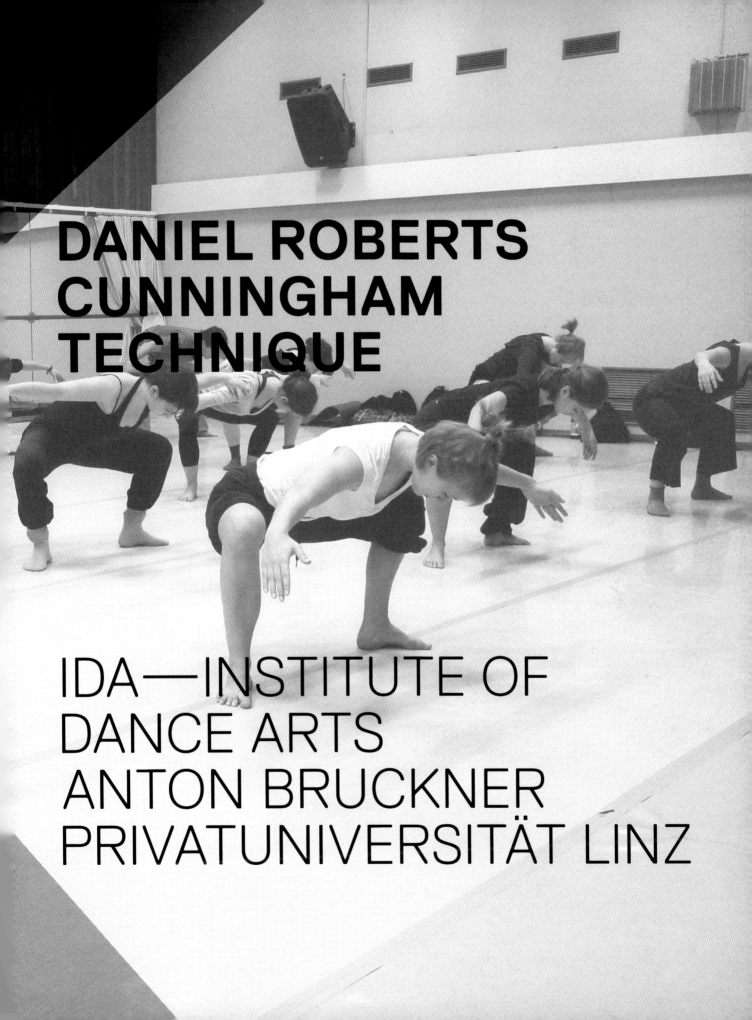

DANIEL ROBERTS CUNNINGHAM TECHNIQUE

IDA—INSTITUTE OF
DANCE ARTS
ANTON BRUCKNER
PRIVATUNIVERSITÄT LINZ

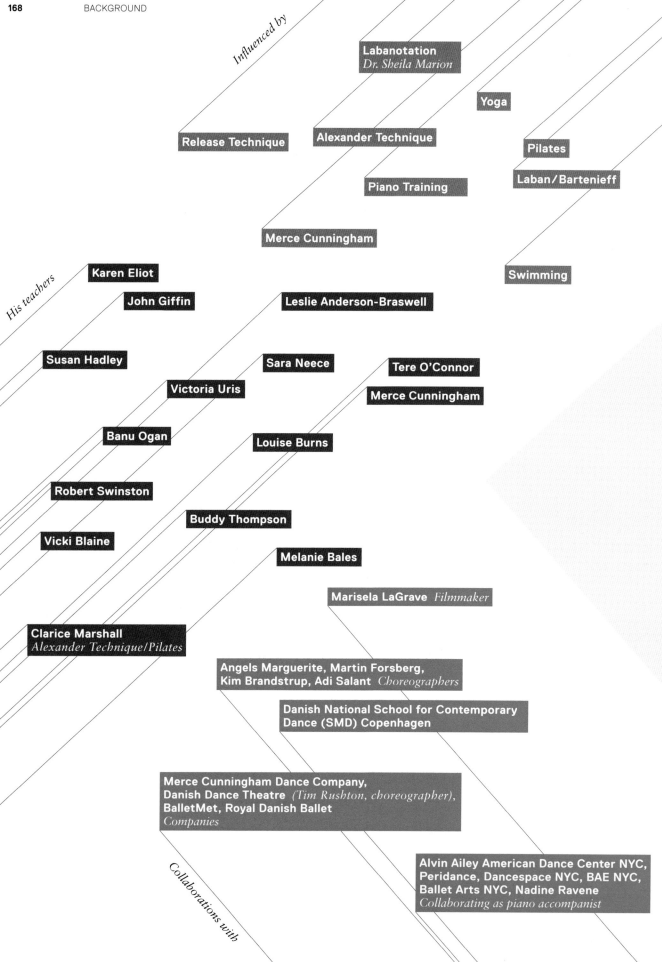

Influenced by

Labanotation
Dr. Sheila Marion

Yoga

Release Technique   **Alexander Technique**   **Pilates**

Piano Training   **Laban/Bartenieff**

Merce Cunningham

Swimming

His teachers

Karen Eliot

John Giffin   **Leslie Anderson-Braswell**

Susan Hadley   **Sara Neece**   **Tere O'Connor**

Victoria Uris   **Merce Cunningham**

Banu Ogan   **Louise Burns**

Robert Swinston

Buddy Thompson

Vicki Blaine

Melanie Bales

Marisela LaGrave *Filmmaker*

Clarice Marshall
Alexander Technique/Pilates

**Angels Marguerite, Martin Forsberg,
Kim Brandstrup, Adi Salant** *Choreographers*

**Danish National School for Contemporary
Dance (SMD) Copenhagen**

**Merce Cunningham Dance Company,
Danish Dance Theatre** *(Tim Rushton, choreographer)*,
BalletMet, Royal Danish Ballet
Companies

**Alvin Ailey American Dance Center NYC,
Peridance, Dancespace NYC, BAE NYC,
Ballet Arts NYC, Nadine Ravene**
Collaborating as piano accompanist

Collaborations with

This is only a partial list.

DANIEL ROBERTS — CUNNINGHAM TECHNIQUE

Research team at the IDA—Institute of Dance Arts, Anton Bruckner
Privatuniversität Linz: Daniel Roberts, Dr. Sabine Huschka,
Prof. Rose Breuss, Dr. Henner Drewes

AUTHORS
Sabine Huschka
Insights into 'DanceForms' by Henner Drewes

INTERVIEW
Edith Boxberger

STUDENTS AND GUESTS
of the bachelor's and master's programs in contemporary stage dance: Katja Bablick, Juan Dante Murillo Bobadilla,
Andrea Maria Handler, Philine Herrlein, Blazej Jasinski, Tamara Kronheim, Dorota Lecka, Petr Ochvat, Amandine
Petit, Anna Prokopová, Arnulfo Pardo Ravagli, Aureliusz Rys, Olga Swietlicka and the physiotherapist/contemporary
dance teacher Johannes Randolf

DANIEL ROBERTS (*1977)
grew up in Pittsburgh, Pennsylvania, and started playing the piano at the age of seven. He was piano accompanist at
various ballet schools. He studied ballet and modern jazz at the CLO Academy in Pittsburgh then took a Bachelor
of Fine Arts in Dance at the Ohio State University, with a specialization in performance and Labanotation. Roberts
received a scholarship to the Merce Cunningham Studio in New York and apprenticed with the Merce Cunningham
Dance Company (MCDC). He joined the company in 2000 and danced in a vast amount of repertory, including films
about Cunningham (for example, in *Merce Cunningham: A Lifetime of Dance* in the reconstruction of *Totem Ancestor*).
He left the MCDC in 2005 and taught Cunningham Technique at the Danish National School of Contemporary
Dance in Copenhagen. He is currently rehearsal director for Danish Dance Theater. Daniel Roberts has taught the
Cunningham Technique at The Place (London Contemporary Dance School), at the Royal Academy of Dance in
London, at the National University of Arts in Korea, and at various companies, dance schools and festivals in Europe,
Russia, the U.S., and Asia.

Daniel Roberts Interviewed by Edith Boxberger

LIVING INSIDE THE INSTRUMENT

/ **What was your education in dance? What techniques did you learn, and in which context?** I grew up in Pittsburgh where I first studied in a school with two very inspiring teachers. One of them, Leslie Anderson, was a former dancer with the Dance Theatre of Harlem who had come back to Pittsburgh to teach ballet. The other, Buddy Thompson, had studied at the Alvin Ailey School and also with Luigi—he taught Luigi jazz. In 1995 I went to Ohio State University in Columbus, which has a wonderful dance faculty. I had a wide range of teachers—someone from Cunningham, from Mark Morris, from Paul Taylor, Pina Bausch, etc. I just fell in love with the class of Karen Eliot, a member of Merce's company in the 1980s. There was grace and clarity—as John Cage would say—in the way she presented the technique, of her interpretation and understanding of it. There were some things so pure but open at the same time.

At university I studied also with a lot of New York Release–based teachers. Choreographers came in for residencies who would teach for a period of time—for instance Tere O'Connor taught a Release Technique–based class. He had a wonderful way of using time—maybe it was influenced by the way Merce Cunningham used time in choreography, but Tere was using it with a different movement vocabulary.

I also studied Labanotation at Ohio State, and discovered a solo of Merce's called *Totem Ancestor*—the only notated Cunningham score. I reconstructed it for a research project and the head of the notation department, Dr. Sheila Marion, wanted me to make it into a big performance project. Eventually I went to Merce's studio and worked with Merce one–on–one. When Charles Atlas was making his documentary on Merce, I was asked by Robert Swinston (Merce's assistant at the time) to dance *Totem Ancestor,* and in return they gave me a scholarship for a half–year at the school.

/ **So it was a direct way into the Cunningham studio?** Yes, and I worked with many different teachers there, people who danced with Merce. At the end of that half–year I was made an apprentice for the company. Being an apprentice is a way of learning the material, and if someone gets injured, then you step into the company. The Cunningham studio developed a little group called the 'rugs': Repertory Understudy Group. During the day we learned the repertory and did small performances—it is the most demanding job you could ever have. Robert Swinston oversaw the group; he was my main teacher. He

handled the finer details of the work. It was like: What is this? Why isn't it working? He was very tough, very demanding.

I got a lot of corrections from him. Maybe because he thought I was talented, maybe because he thought I was stubborn, maybe because…whatever. But then I realized it was because he wanted something to come out in me. And he wanted enthusiasm for the work and the training, and the discipline. I think that is so important now, and I really want to convey that as a teacher: Passion and discipline has to be there because our world as dancers does not get any easier. You never get to a point really, like, 'Okay, that's it, now I have made it, now I can relax.' It just keeps intensifying, so you need a little voice inside of you to be, like, 'What was that? How can I make that better? What is the meaning of that?'…to keep questioning.

In New York mostly I took ballet classes with Jocelyn Lorenz and Sara Neece, a ballet mistress for William Forsythe—both supported what I was training at Cunningham. From time to time I took a jazz class to get out of the Cunningham and ballet studios, to open up a little bit. I was not inspired to take other contemporary classes in New York at that time; it just was not physically stimulating to me. I really wanted to dance for Merce.

/ **What attracted you so strongly to Cunningham's work?** Before I started dancing, I was trained as a pianist. I came to dance as an accompanist for dance classes. For me, most important thing in Cunningham Technique is musicality, rhythmic and music awareness, virtuosity, and efficiency and passion. I feel there is a tremendous inherent passion in the technique and in the work. The technique is hard. The class is hard. You have to have a desire to do it—otherwise it turns into shapes in space. For me it is really important to have had the experience of dancing the choreography, dancing the repertory, to inform how I teach the technique. Otherwise it becomes somewhat two–dimensional: shape, position, shape, position. Having danced the repertory, I see much more of a three–dimensional view of how things flow, how to problem–solve, of how dynamics and the individual dynamics are involved.

Dancing Merce's work taught me a lot about phrasing and musicality. Former teachers said, 'Why would you not choose to work with more musical choreographers, like Mark Morris, who works with music visualization and counterpoint?' For me, Merce's is the most musical work alive because *you* are an orchestra. The legs are doing a seven, the torso is doing a three, and you are travelling on a diagonal, and then it changes to a 4/4, and then you are not dancing to the music and have to rely on your sense of time and other people.

What the body goes through to make that happen, to make those changes clear, is fascinating. You are not on autopilot, you are always going deeper and deeper and deeper. What is it? How can it be different? Now I am injured, so how do I make this work in this way? Now I am feeling bad, how do I bring myself up to make it happen or get through it? It is that wonderful thing of living inside the instrument.

/ **What do you like, and what do you not like, in technique training?** I don't like vagueness in training, I like a clear approach: This is the outline of the class, these are some learning outcomes from the technique, this is what we will study in the class. I like a clear use and clear description of the body. So I don't like a 'whatever' approach to training dancers—whatever happens. I think the more you can bring dancers in touch with their bodies and with what they are doing every second, and enable them to call upon that, the stronger they become. I like to develop their awareness of themselves and of other people, and keep their eyes going, which is the most important thing for a dancer. The eyes: what you pick up, what you see, what stimulates you.

I love to see the dancers come in the next morning and they are tired, and they start working again, going to that motivational place where they are training for themselves. When there are people who are more adult, who have more training—like in this class here—they can give themselves to the complexities more quickly. I can see they are interested in their process, and that invites me to bring in what I can because they are ready to listen.

It is not just me at the front of the classroom barking out orders—we are trying to learn, also, how to take class. Closer to the professional level, I love seeing how people problem-solve, how they bring their unique musicality and sense of phrasing to what they do. I am never bored because there is not one way to solve a problem, and it is beautiful to see that.

/ **What is important for you when teaching a technique class?** For me as a teacher, musical support is very important. When I came here I said I had to have musicians or I would not come. That is a requirement. I think it is very important for dancers to have live music for class; it challenges their ideas of phrasing. When a musician is present and involved in their personal sense of time, it brings a live element to the physicality and the energy for the class is much stronger. People listen differently with live music than recorded music, and it facilitates my teaching. There are tons of exercises in the class; to play around with an iPod or a

CD would be futile, I would spend the whole time at my iPod, not looking at the dancers.

I like percussion, in all the variations between African instruments and Indonesian instruments. There is a direct rhythmic clarity, and one doesn't get involved melodically. With piano music, I am a bit more specific because it is not enough to just play ballet music for the contemporary class. On my own time, I play a lot of romantic music from the late 19th century. If musicians can use this type of music in the right way, then it can work. I also like musicians who have a clear touch to the piano—perhaps confidence is the right word.

/ **Is there anything you learned from Merce Cunningham about teaching?** I did not teach very much then. When I left the company I asked Merce's permission to teach the technique. He said, 'Yes, and I am glad that you asked me.' He gave me some tips for teaching—clarity is very important, and you have to be able to inspire people to want to do the work. Good points—very simple, very direct.

/ **What is required to teach this technique?** You have to be honest, and to be able to create an environment where we can look at what is functioning for our bodies and what is not, and at what functions for further advancement. If we look at placement and alignment in a way that is functional and not representational, there has to be an openness in the classroom. I am demanding, but I also have to be able to let students open up and experiment. Being honest with my corrections, my approach, about what I want, and what I expect will create ground for them to navigate. If I was ambiguous and said nothing, just gave the exercise, I think it might put people into a sometimes too-questioning place in their head. There has to be a point where we can reflect and criticize—criticize as in: This is working, this may work better, this might not work, whatever…let's try.

/ **What qualifications does one need to teach this technique?** I think it is important to have danced the repertory. I know people will disagree with me, and there are lots of people in the world teaching this technique without having had that experience, but that's my gut reaction. It informs how you teach the technique differently, for one thing. The second thing would have to be a desire to see the individuality of the students. The technique is not a form that we follow, it is how the information comes to the students—it teaches them how to use the directions given and turn it into dancing, make it into movement. To be an inspiring dancer and person is also vital to teaching; there has to be some visual or verbal inspiration.

/ **How do you define the relationship between yourself and the student?** I do believe that someone needs to be in charge and make decisions, and say, 'This is what we are going to do.' But it's not a one-way system; it is me being in there with them, moving and figuring out how the movement could go deeper, or how it could be more analyzed, or what movement difficulties might come about from physically figuring it out. When I'm going through it, I have that same appetite. So I feel we are doing the work together, that I am actively looking at where everybody is in this process.

I try to make myself very available. At the school in Denmark, I try to make an open-door policy to come and talk about things because there is not always time in the classroom. I try to learn from my experience and use the demanding passion I got from studying with Robert, and then take the caring, listening, looking at it in a different way from Karen, who taught me from the beginning and was very supportive and very communicative about what was working or what was not working. I try to wear both of these hats because it is very important to have a dialogue with people about where they are in their training.

I make the students at the conservatory in Copenhagen keep journals about their training, and I collect the journals a few times during the semester. The students write about their corrections, ideas about movement, philosophies, etc. It is another way for them to cognitively tune in. Sometimes I read something and am surprised; I would never guess this student was having this thought process when I see the work in class. And when I meet with them, I say, 'I read this and now that I see you, maybe you could think about it and make it more visible.'

In work that is physically as well as mentally demanding, that sort of dialogue is needed, especially for education. Professionals, they go a bit their own route, but young dancers need that reflective view—that three-dimensional view of themselves to be able to be inside the body. And they need to have the critique as well as their own perception about their development.

/ **How do you prepare for class?** I come with a program to class. Sometimes I have elaborate ideas before I come in and then I see where the dancers are—and that what they need is not necessarily what I'd planned, so I modify and that is fine. If I see their relevé work is a little bit weak, and I really wanted to focus on more extensions, then I adapt or I combine. The exercises, though, are sort of codified. There is a structure one can play off. I have done so much that I can go in and do theme and variation. For the bigger phrases across the floor, slow movement, big jumps, or fast jumps, I put a little bit more 'how I want this to be done' because I want to explain it efficiently and quickly, and be ready for the questions that will come at me.

What I have learned from Merce directly…he used imagery at times to convey what he wanted from movement, and he used a lot of animal references. I use a lot of ballet terms, like Robert did, which is sort of taboo in some branches of the Cunningham family. Merce was looking at it in a different way. He took the elements, of course, from his studies in ballet and Balanchine, but in Cunningham Technique they were not tendus but leg brushes or foot brushes on the floor—basically the same thing using a different language. For the sake of time and getting people to quickly recognize something they may already know, I use ballet terms.

/ **Are there other experiences you use for teaching?** I call upon my own studies in Alexander Technique and Pilates. In Pilates, I can make connections between exercises I learned in this technique to the motions I do. Merce's technique focuses on the spine—a lot of coordination of the spine—and this refers clearly to Alexander Technique. I studied regularly with a wonderful woman in New York, Clarice Marshall, a Pilates and also an Alexander teacher. She combined the two brilliantly. She was an accomplished dancer as well as pedagogue, so she was very informed.

Alexander Technique and Pilates helped me understand my body and to counteract some harsh effects of Merce's technique. Like, given an extreme position, how do I get there without such a muscular reaction, or what is the skeletal approach to solving an extreme position and then coming back to a neutral place. I had a nice base to draw upon, from a deeper perspective of the spine. I did yoga also. I find some references to yoga in Merce's material with the stretches. And I use my music training all the time. I talk about musical terms, Italian musical terms, and musical forms—and I talk about them a lot. I think you have to use whatever is there to inspire you, what is coming from the music.

/ **Music and dance are deeply connected for you?** I can be very picky about what I want musically because it intrigues me. I am very stimulated by music and sound as a source of either making up my material or of enhancing what I am doing. I think all dance students should study piano because a physical and mental relationship is developed. It is not just listening; a dancer is active and making something happen to the body, and then recognizes—*physically* recognizes—tone. That is wonderful.

I can tell the people who are musicians, the dancers who have trained in music—they come easily to understanding rhythmic structure in my class. Nine out of ten people who have studied piano, singing, or something like that have an idea of structure and space and know how to play with it.

⁄ **Did your teaching change, and how?** When I
moved to Copenhagen in 2006, coming from New York,
I had that New York attitude, 'Get through it, get
through it, go, go, go!' And people either went with it
or they were afraid. I think, over time, I have found a
way to keep a healthy amount of aggressiveness for
the purpose of pushing people, and to be a little bit more
sensitive to my environment—a reflective view that the
way I was taught is not the only method. I take more time
to think, 'What are ways of inspiring myself to go deeper
in my work? How do we go further? How do we evolve?
How can we get better at conveying information and
executing directions?'

⁄ **Are there new influences on your work?** I am
always influenced. I watch a lot of other people's classes,
which I recommend for teachers to do all the time.
Something always comes to me, 'Oh, I like that! And
how could I incorporate that into what I do?'
I watch anything— but I don't like gurus, like, 'I have
the way and I have all the secrets for you, and you follow
me!' We are much more multilateral in training now.
We have to look at each other, take many different things,
and go in—and not just be 'one way'. I don't train
people just to go to the Cunningham studio—that would
be futile now. I want them to be able to take the wonderful things Merce has laid out, and take these things to
their work, to whatever level they go to next.
    We now have a lot of somatic influences on how we
look at the body and how we work. We are sometimes going in to go out, rather than taking the outside form
and putting it onto the dancer. At this stage, with a highly
developed intellect looking at the body, any extreme is
dangerous. We have to go forward with the ideas, taking
both the somatic and the technical into question.

⁄ **What do you see as the future for this work?**
I hope the Cunningham studio continues in New York.
The principles of clarity and movement awareness for
the dancer should stay. A dancer is raw in that class: you
come in and there is no barre, there is nowhere to hide,
and you have to address this. This element builds a lot of
strength, mentally and physically. I think Cunningham
Technique is wonderful for conservatory educations, universities. There can be some value in it for companies—
depending upon the company, what they have done before, and whether it is applicable for their repertory. For
workshops, I think it is too complicated.

⁄ **What do you want to deliver to students today?**
I want them to find that elements like musicality, virtuosity, alignment, and consciousness of body and space
will add to whatever work they choose to do. And to
say, 'Wow! This technique really made me aware of all of
those ideas!' And to understand that the technique builds
a strong dancer, mentally and physically.

Sabine Huschka

INTRODUCTION

/"The training of a dancer is important, and this training will hopefully benefit the dancer's ability to learn and adapt to various movement challenges. It will challenge dancers to function and be creative within a form such as the one I teach…When people come to my class, I want their priority to be to organize themselves in time and space."[1]/

The research project in Linz was carried out in two phases, from 19–23 October 2009 and from 30 November–4 December 2009, under the motto of discovering something new. In practice, this afforded students a new and fresh perspective on their own movement repertoires. At the same time, new collaborative possibilities were established between departments inside the institute. During both sessions, practice and theory nurtured each other in a lively fashion: Daniel Roberts's workshops were rife with serious student discussion and the time between discussions was filled with theory and in–depth debates about Tanzplan Deutschland's catalog of questions. The 'journey' was taken up in the spirit of Cunningham's creative credo: something new can be discovered when its intrinsic possibility *is realized*.[2] Daniel Roberts (a longtime Cunningham dancer) achieved precisely this as IDA dancers (second–year bachelor's in contemporary stage dance and third–year master's program students) used the intensive two-week workshops and master classes to explore their own kinesthetic spectrum. The project gave students an opportunity to confront, in a concentrated situation, key issues about the meaning and purpose of dance technique, and it provided a rich learning experience for all involved.

A supplementary seminar given by Henner Drewes provided productive theoretical stimuli by enabling students a more in–depth look at the principles behind Merce Cunningham's movement organization and compositional

---

1 Daniel Roberts in discussion with Sabine Huschka in December 2009. Unless otherwise stated, all other quotes from Roberts in this text come from the discussions the author had with him during this research project.

2 Sabine Huschka: *Merce Cunningham und der Moderne Tanz. Körperkonzepte, Choreographie und Tanzästhetik.* Würzburg: Königshausen & Neumann, 2000, p. 378.

technique. This was made possible by *DanceForms—Software for Visualizing and Chronicling Choreography* program, which students were able to access and use to design movement. Sabine Huschka was on–site in Linz to discuss, with the students and research team, key issues about the technique, its principles, and in situ teaching. The participants were thus able to reflect on their personal experiences with the technique as well as to discuss their personal encounters with the Merce Cunningham Technique during classes.

The drummers who accompanied Roberts's classes (musicians from the *Institut JIM für Jazz* (Jazz Institute) at the Anton Bruckner Privatuniversität Linz) must also be mentioned. They responded to complex rhythmic needs—including drawn–out notes and irregular time signatures—with spirited and dedicated improvisations.

Dancing, thinking, and writing were all utilized to facilitate the creation of new movement and the exploration of a contemporary dance technique that, in its approach to movement and the body, was considered by all participants to be a state–of–the–art contemporary technique. In practice, this meant that those involved in the project (Daniel Roberts, Rose Breuss, the students, Johannes Randolf, Henner Drewes, and Sabine Huschka) discussed each item on the Tanzplan catalogue of questions that applied to working phases and formats; the writing tasks were divided according to knowledge and interest. In addition to the intensive preparatory phase with Rose Breuss (supported by Sabine Huschka), in–depth and open discussions between Daniel Roberts, Rose Breuss, and Sabine Huschka provided particularly rich source material, and many students contributed detailed reflections.

What follows are impressions and insights from the research process. Texts that evolved from this process—answers, comments, experience reports, and reflections—were consolidated and edited by Sabine Huschka.

Sabine Huschka

HISTORICAL CONTEXT

TIME, PLACE, AND SOCIO-POLITICAL CONTEXT

Similar to other modern dance techniques, the Cunningham Technique was developed as an individual training regiment with the goal of creating an aesthetic spectrum of movement for the body. Created by Merce Cunningham (1919–2009), the technique is based on a functional and physiological understanding about the interplay between joints and muscles, and on notions about subjecting divergent positions of the limbs to changing tempos, rhythms, and spatial directions. While training in tap, modern

dance, and ballet, as well as during his first engagement with the Martha Graham Company (1939–1945), Cunningham doggedly pursued questions about performing radically different styles of movement. With his logical and functional approach, Cunningham—despite ideological and aesthetic barriers that typified American dance–theater in the 1940s and 50s—wove the opposing principles of modern dance and ballet into a movement complex. The goal was, within a structured time–space continuum,

to establish a complex of coordinates between divergent movements that could be physically explored.

The Cunningham Technique was, initially, created as a personal exercise and training program, and used by Cunningham's dancers, as of the early 1950s, as a systematic training format that should help them learn his choreographic material. At Black Mountain College during the 1952 summer session, backed by his first influx of financial support, Cunningham established the Merce Cunningham Dance Company (MCDC)—with Carolyn Brown, Anita Dencks, Viola Farber, Joanne Melsher, Marianne Preger, Remy Charlip, and Paul Taylor. A pedagogical format was developed within the context of his choreographic work.[1] Teaching the technique became increasingly important for Cunningham in subsequent years in his studio in New York (established in 1959), because, among other reasons, it provided him with personal income.

The technique remains in a transformative state until today; this being a process that happens from the inside–out, and by which the technique has become more and more differentiated with time. Principles and exercise sequences emerged from Cunningham's choreographic work, which, determined by the aleatoric composition process[2] (i.e., a composition process based on chance operations as practiced by the composer John Cage and others), confronted dancers with technical challenges that bordered on the impossible. Cunningham's entire body of work was influenced by innovations in film, as film recording techniques enabled Cunningham to modify spatial–temporal concepts in respect to the phenomenon of motion. In the early 1990s, Cunningham began using *DanceForms*—a software program using animation to generate choreography—as a supplement to aleatorics.[3]

Cunningham taught twice–weekly in his New York studio until shortly before his death at the age of ninety. Extracts from his technique classes, which can be seen at www.merce.org, give insight into his teaching style and

1 Vincent Katz: *Black Mountain College*. Cambridge/MA: MIT Press, 2002.

2 From the early 1950s, Cunningham choreographed movement motifs, phrases, and sequences, as well as the shape of his pieces, using elaborate random processes. These transformed the role of the choreographer by employing a self–perpetuating and playful logic. Chance operations overrode decision–

making and the personal taste of the choreographer. This compositional process treats movement as an abstract dimension and confronts the body with the 'impossible'. For details, see Huschka 2000.

philosophy on the body and movement. The combinations and rhythms have, without doubt, become ever quicker and physically more demanding since its beginnings and the establishment of his company. The Cunningham Technique is characterized by a clearly recognizable and virtuoso movement style, one that can—as it is based on complicated coordinations, mental and physical concentration, and spatial and rhythmic elasticity—be described as 'intelligent' and 'transparent to the mind'.[4]

Thus at the core of the technique, evidenced both historically and conceptually, lies the notion of constant change—indeed, eminent changeability. Changeability is the technique's quintessence, its motive, and its impetus (also referenced in the title of Cunningham's notation book, *Changes*[5]). Cunningham Technique does not set mastery as a goal; it fosters a mental and physical willingness to change. Accordingly, one can understand why Daniel Roberts—even after five years as a member of the MCDC (2000–2005), and since the beginning of his professional teaching career at the Danish National School of Contemporary Dance in Copenhagen—returned regularly to the studio in New York, taking classes with Cunningham until his death. Roberts was eager to broaden his knowledge and stay up on changes and developments—i.e., be informed about Cunningham's new movement material, compositional options, and about new timing and rhythms. Only by attending classes in the New York studio could Daniel Roberts experience and understand the on-going developments being made to existing sequences and movement principles, and follow refinements in coordination as well as in temporal nuances. Changeability is the rule in Cunningham classes and presupposes that dancers, teachers, and students be mentally prepared to embody change. In this context, Cunningham Technique constitutes a sophisticated and lively body of knowledge.

BACKGROUND: BIOGRAPHIES AND ENVIRONMENT

In a technique with such a unique history, a good teacher should have many years' experience with source material, as only through embodiment can skills appropriate to the principles and the details be acquired. Daniel Roberts's training and career as a member of the MCDC is a good example: He became enthused about Cunningham Technique while studying dance at Ohio State University, impressed by the clarity and grace he saw in his teacher and former Cunningham dancer, Karen Eliot. Here, Roberts

discovered the passion for movement that is key to the Cunningham Technique's aesthetic and philosophy.

Simply being a dancer in one of the most important modern dance companies in recent history, however, does not mean a person is predestined to become a teacher—regardless of how much repertory and refined knowledge has been acquired. A teacher needs more: He or she must have interest and curiosity in the technique's details, as well as in the underlying philosophy and material that will and would be danced.

Beginning with a scholarship at the Merce Cunningham Studio, and later as an apprentice with the company, Roberts was able to explore the technique's options and principles in-depth. Roberts is an enthusiastic and dedicated teacher, and says becoming a teacher was something he had always envisaged. In both spontaneous and structured time with students, Roberts especially enjoys teaching movement phrases and exercises in new ways, and in finding new approaches. His teaching is accompanied by an insatiable 'appetite for movement',[6] something that could have been said about Cunningham as well.

RELATION TO OTHER ART FORMS

Although Roberts's teaching concentrates on the physical experience and the all-important role of the functional body, it is characterized by a subtle musicality. The Cunningham Technique is structured by (and remains lively due to) complex and constantly changing rhythms as well as by the variability of movement material. The nature of the movement lends itself to temporal structuring, and a dancer's intrinsic musicality will influence how the movement is performed—all variables in Roberts's teaching. He only uses live music for class; Roberts, a trained pianist, accompanied dance classes for many years. He creates and teaches combinations that encourage students to find their own dynamic motivation for tempo changes and rhythms, as well as to learn how to embody movement. Live music, either percussion or piano, first clarifies and illustrates the rhythm, i.e., it fosters a kinesthetic sensibility for the movement sequence. The entire class is accompanied by various styles of music with many changes in rhythm, which helps the dancer coordinate and perform the movement with more energy.

From a historical viewpoint, John Cage's composition methods, philosophy of music, and general influence were crucial to Cunningham's handling of movement material as well as to how he formed his aesthetic for the stage.

3 See: Vaughan, David (Moderation): "Cunningham and his Dancers. Transcript of a Discussion with Carolyn Brown, Douglas Dunn, Viola Farber, Steve Paxton, Marianne Preger-Simon, Valda Setterfield, and Gus Solomon," In: *Ballett Review*, 3/1987; Vaughan, David: *Merce Cunningham Fifty*

Years. New York: Aperture, 1997.
4 See: Noel Carroll/Sally Banes: "Cunningham and Duchamps." In: *Ballett Review*, 2/1983; p. 73.
5 Merce Cunningham: *Changes. Notes on Choreography*. Published by Frances Starr. New York: Something Else Press, 1968.

6 Susan Leigh Foster: *Reading Dancing. Bodies and Subjects in Contemporary American Dance*. Berkeley/Los Angeles: University of California Press, 1986, p. 32.

The long–term partnership between Cunningham and Cage, who were committed to dance and music as both performance and 'temporal' arts, resulted in the radical notion of treating time as an autonomous and structural element in which movement was intrinsically a part. Time became an independent variable that could be used freely in composition.

Cunningham's work with Cage is also central for Daniel Roberts.[7] Roberts, without limiting himself to twentieth century music, shares Cunningham's appreciation of Erik Satie. Depending on how the movement is structured, Roberts makes use of jazzy pieces or waltzes, something by Prokofiev, or even romantic music in class.

RELEVANT THEORETICAL DISCOURSES

Zen philosophy directly influenced Cunningham's philosophy of movement and physicality, and his dance aesthetic.[8] Early members of the company, like Marianne Simon,[9] have emphasized the mental training involved in the technique: A dancer concentrates solely on how the movement is being done, which requires full attention being given, in the Buddhistic sense, to the body at every moment in time.

Unlike Cage, Cunningham did not talk about Buddhism, nor did he follow Daisetsu T. Suzuki's lectures in New York in the 1950s with Cage's enthusiasm. The influence of Eastern philosophy can only be clearly found in Cunningham's compositions: When drafting movement sequences, he explored choices by using dice[10] and the *I Ching*, the oracular Chinese book of 'changes'[11] with its sixty-four hexameters.

CURRENT PRACTICE

Teaching Cunningham Technique, or any technique that a dancer has learned intimately, is only one career option after leaving the professional stage. Other possibilities, like choreographing one's own work or supporting the administration and organization of a dance company, are also valuable options. There are few MCDC dancers who have chosen Roberts's route, i.e., teaching Cunningham Technique outside of the New York studio context. Among these are Jeanne Steele, who teaches at The Place in London, Cheryl Therrien, who teaches at the *Conservatoire National Supérieur de Musique et de Danse* in Paris, Banu Ogan, who teaches at the Juilliard School in New York, and Tom Caley, who teaches at Stockholm University. No Cunningham dancers are teaching in Germany, as far as we know, at least not in the professional training sector. (We have no information about private studios or other areas of amateur dance.)

Cunningham Technique is employed intensively and effectively by various choreographers and dance companies, including Richard Alston in London, Ton Simmons in Holland, and by the Rambert Dance Company, which has integrated parts of the technique into its training program.

INDIVIDUAL APPROACH

Roberts has taught Cunningham Technique to dance companies throughout Europe in Sweden, Denmark, Iceland, and Holland, as well as in Russia and Asia. For companies whose members are ballet trained, the technique is easier to learn and particularly effective.

For Roberts personally, training in Cunningham Technique is valuable time spent increasing awareness of his own body and exploring functional movement principles; it opens him physically and mentally as well as helping to expand his own range of movement. This attitude impacts his understanding of himself as a teacher: Alongside learning technical skills, students are confronted with mentally, emotionally, and sensually constructed learning processes (whereby clear and disciplined expectations are indicated), requiring that the dancer not shy away from unfamiliar territory or the seemingly impossible, but rather face it.

7 John Cage: *Silence. Lectures and Writings.* Middletown (CT): Wesleyan University Press, 1973.
8 Sabine Huschka: "Subjekt-Körper-Leere: Diamanten. Merce Cunningham zum 90. Geburtstag". In: *corpus*, 12/2008, www.corpusweb.net (accessed on 08/27/2010).

9 Comment from Simon in: Vaughan 1987, p. 29.
10 Huschka 2000, pp. 358–422.
11 Frank Fiedeler: *Die Monde des I Ging. Symbolschöpfung und Evolution.* Munich: Eugen Diederichs Verlag, 1988; Daniel Charles: "Au-delà de l'aléa. Jenseits der Aleatorik." In: Barck, Karlheinz/Gente, Peter (Ed.):

Aisthesis. Wahrnehmung heute oder Perspektiven einer anderen Ästhetik. Leipzig: Reclam Verlag, 1991, pp. 322–331.

RELATION TO OTHER DANCE AND MOVEMENT TECHNIQUES

Cunningham Technique is practiced daily, much like a ritual, in order to prepare the body for learning choreography—as is common with other modern dance techniques and in other companies. A daily class in Cunningham Technique, however, contains constant differentiation and continually changing nuances. Cunningham Technique has aesthetic links to ballet and elements from Graham Technique. Complicated ballet–based and differentiated leg–work is paired with a large range of movement options in the upper body. This is characteristic in that organizational principles found in leg–work are carried over to the torso's movement potential. The directional variations of the torso—upright, curve, tilt, arch, and twist— operate as the five ballet positions. These five positions are both combined in sophisticated ways and contrasted temporally and spatially. Although clear spatial structures are suggested, a classical geometric division of space is not employed. In Cunningham Technique, use of directional vectors involves segmented mobilization of the entire spinal column. The spinal column can be mobilized in three areas (and each can be activated independently) to achieve spatial diversity as well as a general increased flexibility of the entire spinal column. Compared to ballet and Graham Technique, the Cunningham body becomes more supple and stabilized through a strong center within a relaxed body alignment. In contrast to other modern dance techniques, the body is always trained in standing and there is no floorwork.

Sabine Huschka

CONCEPT AND IDEOLOGY

IMAGINING THE BODY

The Cunningham Technique was revolutionary; the first to concentrate on and train 'movement articulation' as something not intended for expression or emotion. As the technique is free from all psychological or spiritual motivation, it excludes any aesthetic and philosophical principle that aims for a 'natural' moment in movement—i.e., it excludes any principle that modern dance and its theoretical constructions in their different forms might turn into an aesthetic role model.[12] For Cunningham, the extent of the body's energy is outside any symbolic framework or topology. To evoke energized moments, one must conceptually go beyond existing models of the body.

The technique's distinctive style supports the complex and intricate spatial–temporal spectrum of articulation (which is moderated by strength). This constitutes the central tenet—a secular concept—of working "with the possibilities of the human body in movement" and "nature in its fields of application, if you like,"[13] as Cunningham said in his 1986 interview with Jacqueline Lesschaeve. The focus is on exploring a kinesthetic radius and movement configuration. This approach couches a utopian view of the body—and its inexhaustible potential for new movement.

Daniel Roberts's teaching is based on yet another premise: He teaches material that students can grasp immediately while simultaneously leading dancers into situations that are 'not yet possible'. Each dancer must first pick up the material, and then form it with some fluidity. Dancers learn to take their own physique into account, knowing that limits are to be pushed; this encourages them to move differently as well as to attempt more complex coordinations. The decisive factor is philosophical; a dancer's awareness is boosted through physical means, by use of foreign or imposed input—as opposed to 'going into oneself'.

To support this process, unfamiliar aspects are intentionally included in training as modifications to the routine. Roberts uses changes in nuance and modifies rhythm each time to confront students with challenges and gaps in his or her movement knowledge. It is therefore relevant for dancers to ask, "How can you do a movement that

you've done over and over again and think you have it perfect, or whatever—and do it in a way so it becomes awkward again, to discover it anew?"[14] The technique's objective is not mastery of the body in the sense of being able to use the body as an instrument, or even to demonstrate knowledge of movement; rather, mastery emerges in accepting changeability and is evidenced in the performing body's spatial and temporal structuring of movement.

In Cunningham Technique, the body alone stimulates perception and awareness. Habitual and personal experience, emotional and psychological memories, or emotional articulation are not starting points for working on technique. The body is better viewed as a utopian and individual world, filled with potential and capable of learning how to constantly perform new, unfamiliar, constructed, and sometimes inorganically created movement. The body becomes an agent for the embodiment of an aesthetic.

Roberts's workshops demand a high level of concentration from students, as well as discipline, an ability to focus on the matter at hand, and a constant orienting of thoughts toward the possible. Students at the dance institute in Linz reflected on Roberts's classes in more precise terms. Dorota Lecka said: "In the Cunningham class, the body needs to be very well trained, while the technique itself requires dancers to have a high level of self–awareness about their own bodies. Self–awareness is important not only for executing the technique, but also in order to have a conscious presence while performing, to be able to become a medium, a channel through which certain information is being transferred. To emphasize it again, 'I am not my body.'" And within this paradoxical movement experience, she sees "an image of calm un-calmness" at work.

Gender–specific connotations in the movement or a gender–specific classification of certain movement sequences do not figure into the Cunningham Technique. As the body is a neutral instrument that can achieve any movement possibilities, it is consequently viewed as gender–neutral.

Cunningham Technique teaches space–time skills—and therewith, the transformation of a movement's energy. In this sense, Roberts's teaching, like Cunningham's, demands virtuoso craft through an ever–fluctuating stasis. The spinal column does not function as a fixed axis, rather it actively and dynamically creates a metastable balance in the body. This makes it possible to change vectors by directing limbs into space. The body learns how to work with the greatest possible movement spectrum, in both a kinesthetic and sculptural sense. This results in a transformation and increased experiential depth that only reveals

12 See, among others, Rodger Copeland: *Merce Cunningham. The Modernizing of Modern Dance.* New York / London: Routledge, 2004.
13 Merce Cunningham: *Der Tänzer und der Tanz.* Ed.: Jacqueline Lesschaeve. Frankfurt a. M.: Dieter Fricke Verlag, 1986, p. 168.

14 Merce Cunningham in *The John Tusa Interview.* [Transcript] 2008, www.bbc.co.uk/radio3/johntusainterview/cunningham_transcript.shtml (accessed on 12/10/2009).

15 Merce Cunningham: "The Function of a Technique for Dance." In: *Contact Quarterly. A Vehicle for moving Ideas,* 7/1982, pp. 7-9.
16 Cunningham, loc. cit., p. 6.

itself in a concept in which the space is open and available—in accordance with Einstein's perception that "there are no fixed points in space"—a spatial concept that is shaped by time. The Cunningham Technique, in fact, intensifies how time and space are combined in movement. Dancers change quickly from one place in space to the next, changes often being carried out simultaneously by several body parts or rhythmic modulation.

The second key movement principle in Cunningham Technique is an isolation technique; the legs, upper body, pelvis, arms, hands, head, and feet are moved independently of each other, in different directions and different time phrases. Movement sequences taught by Roberts—fast, sometimes abrupt, but occasionally with some drawn-out changes of position—demand a high level of concentration. Students must constantly reorient themselves in both the room and inside their personal kinesthetic body space, and they must be able to find their balance amidst continual changes of tension in the body. This requires special attention to the spatial design of the movement, which, according to several students in Linz, is achieved by sight as well as by focusing on all other parts of the body. Students learn to coordinate the body in multifarious ways and, in doing so, always use the space as a directional framework.

Roberts teaches isolation by means of specific movement sequences, and talks about specific body parts involved in a movement sequence. For example, Roberts might ask students to turn with a relaxed upper body, the arms deviating outwards on either side (away from each other) and to let the leg accent the movement. The movement sequence therefore involves body parts moving simultaneously in different directions; each body part should move as if it has its own pair of eyes.

One general observation is that the relationship to space is always established and formed from an upright position. Cunningham Technique includes no floor exercises, referencing an anthropological perspective that the human body is identified by its upright position.[15] Some students had the impression they were embodying dignity.

Each combination—and some are very complex—is characterized by a sculpting of the body. Shapes are created by precise spatial positioning of various body parts. In order to do this, accurate placement is trained, which requires an awareness about appropriate amounts of tension, as well as about position and alignment of individual limbs in space. Upper and lower body movements are considered two separate spatial zones; separating them enables a free and fluid space for the upper body, 'above' the rhythmically driven leg-work and step combinations.

A space-time relationship in the dancing is visible to an observer. It is key that dancers understand the "correct, vertical position of the body"[16]—based on kinesthetic energy principles—as well as understanding the biomechanical principles that the technique is grounded in. Only with this understanding can one realize a movement repertoire that is directionally and spatially differentiated. Dancers work intensively on maintaining a controlled stability, using body weight to manage balance. Other exercises require directional and spatial expansion, demanding a great deal of muscular strength. Moving the body with clear directional orientation through space, and along equally clear pathways, yields a feeling for the volume of a body in motion. Space is thus structured by continuous movement, rather than by fixed positions in space. Each shape should be a living and breathing shape. In his classes, Roberts speaks of a dialogue between the body and the space that is continually reinventing itself.

Daniel Roberts's training defines the musical shape of the movement; an intrinsic sense of body rhythm is developed, trained, and promoted by rhythmic changes in movement sequences. A clear and virtuosic elegance was recognizable in the dancers' bodies. This elegance concords with another fundamental principle of the Cunningham Technique: Referencing the dance scholar José Gil, musicality, as expressed by the body, represents the 'float' in Cunningham's movements, endowing them with a flowing yet easily recognizable temporal gestalt.

Training awareness for temporal gestalt was often done in silence. The students worked either alone or with others in these phases. Interestingly, Roberts also prepares his classes, for the most part, in silence; he first sets movement phrases to music during class, with live accompaniment. Timing is adapted to suit the movement. Roberts gives the musicians a time signature before each phrase, and determines a combination's meter and rhythm in the moment. It is essential, for him, that exercises have a clear musical and temporal structure. Roberts uses about thirty movement exercises in a ninety–minute class, which also explains why he cannot use prerecorded music. He talks to the musicians during the entire class and appreciates the creativity, interpretation, and improvisational skills that are reflected in their music when observing the students. Roberts understands a technique class supported by musicians to be a joint artistic process. The students in Linz appreciated the live music; they emphasized the positive influence it had on their movement execution as well as on their personal comprehension of the logic behind the exercises, and said the music aroused emotional, mental, and even visual impressions.

Roberts's experiences of working with different musicians and musical styles explain this strong connection. He describes a musical accompanist in Denmark who had a wonderfully sharp sense of timing:

/ "He was a very odd man and brought electronic music into the class that he had made on his computer. He played guitar, piano, and anything that was sitting around. He had a real mind for what sound is and what is interesting to listen to and how that affects the body. So he had a real connection to the work that I taught. He was my favorite because he was investigating his own compositions within the ideas of the dance class." /

Most of the musicians that accompany Roberts's dance classes come from a jazz background and have well–honed instincts for improvisation. A pure jazz accompaniment is not perfect for the classes, as Roberts feels too much swing is imposed upon the movement phrases. He also almost avoids using classical music (as in traditional ballet classes), although, for some parts of the lesson, it does help students establish a stronger emotional connection with the movement. A mix of styles is best.

17 Anne Seymour: "Foreword", in Anthony d'Offay: *Dancers on a Plane: Cage– Cunningham–Johns*. New York: A. A. Knopf in association with Anthony d'Offay Gallery, 1990, p. 11.

INTENT

The art of the Cunningham Technique lies in dancers being able to use personal dynamics to move fluidly through a complex framework of directions and time signatures while remaining engrossed in the act of performing. In Cunningham Technique, the moving body needs—and is promised—a specific type of awareness. For Linz student Dorota Lecka, this showed up from time to time as follows: "What I particularly admire about the experience is a certain distance toward one's own body and emotions, while, at the same time, the ability to access information, wisdom, and beauty, which enriches everyone, even if it is beyond our conscious understanding." As a consequence, dancers are aware and alert at any given movement when performing. Skills, therefore, are found in a wide spectrum of movement that, in accordance with an understanding of dance as art, embraces all forms of movement.

As Anne Seymour writes in *Dancers on a Plane*, Cunningham Technique is about "a process of personal discovery, and the ideal is to work with movements as if becoming aware of them for the first time."[17] This way of recognizing and becoming aware of one's own movement, whereby a specific presence is generally identified in movement performance, is regarded, from a philosophical point of view, as both a path to be walked and a hike. Becoming aware of one's own movement always leaves, in its wake, processes of distancing oneself from oneself and becoming a stranger to oneself. It is in these processes that something first reveals itself. Dorota Lecka describes her experience as follows:

/ "Movement sequences are complicated and fast, and, to be able to perform them with exact musical timing, one's mind needs to be prepared and trained to stay calm. The only way to learn and afterward perform all of those sequences is with a deep awareness of mind and body, often because changes in directions, speed, and levels require you to be awake and aware both inside and outside. I often experienced myself 'observing myself while moving,' witnessing my own performance where I could literally see myself as if observing myself through somebody else's eyes, as if my eyes would double up and my focus would divide itself in two. One pair of eyes would remain a part of the moving body, looking outward, while another pair would be looking more inward. It is about the absence of mental and emotional identification with the body, which creates a time shift between awareness and memory of the movement sequence, and the actual body performing it." /

This awareness of movement, intensified by a conscientious attitude in training—i.e., keeping one's attention focused on the body—gives rise to a specific performative quality. This quality assures vital and lively dancing; and an unlimited, essential, potential for temporal–spatial design.

Sabine Huschka

UNDERSTANDING
THE BODY/MOVEMENT

PREREQUISITES

Any form of previous dance or physical training is a plus when learning Cunningham Technique. Some ballet or other modern dance background can be particularly helpful, as is experience in techniques that train coordination and stamina, like yoga or Pilates.

Students Handler, Kronheim, Rys, and Bobadilla stress that a ballet background is helpful to understand placement, i.e., the biomechanical organization of the body, positioning of limbs (and their constant repositioning), as well as shifts in body weight during directional changes. Previous modern dance experience will assist the dancer in combining upper body and leg movements common to the Cunningham Technique, particularly in regards to torso mobility and the multifarious specified zones.

Good stamina makes it easier for dancers to master the physical demands of the technique—although this is true for all types of dance. The Linz–based physiotherapist Johannes Randolf[18] believes there is too little stamina training in most techniques, although stamina in particular is indispensable for an injury–free dance career. Without stamina, the body cannot compensate for the physiological demands of the Cunningham Technique, thereby leaving dancers at greater risk of small injuries or irritations.

As to the most basic motor and coordination skills, experience in gymnastics or martial arts can be helpful as these disciplines teach both eye–body coordination, stretching, and precise movement execution—all of which are of particular importance for Daniel Roberts's Cunningham classes.

Roberts consciously avoids making any statements as to the ideal physique for Cunningham Technique. As to the physical or movement prerequisites for a dancer, in Roberts's opinion, the issue is how interested and open students are for 'problem solving' (as described above). Students in Linz also supported this; they emphasized that it is precisely an 'alert mind' that helped them perform their best when the pace of learning new exercises accelerated. The better one can recall exercise material, the better one can concentrate on mastering rhythms and movement qualities.

Having well–developed leg and foot muscles, a strong back, good turnout, extensions, and flexibility is beneficial. From a physiological viewpoint, it helps to have flexible connective tissue, i.e., ligaments, tendons, and muscles; natural elasticity means that an individual need not go beyond physical limits.

Basic motor skills especially relevant to the Cunningham Technique are strength, stamina, and speed—in equal measure—and coordination in particular. Roberts's training requires the dancer to have enough physical strength to perform constant repetitions. Having good coordination skills makes it easier to mentally incorporate continual rhythmic and direction changes. If dancers do not have these skills, then, in certain circumstances, visualization exercises can help to compensate. These, when 'looped', spark a correlation between the image and the movements to be performed. Stamina training—such as running, Nordic walking, or swimming—is well suited to provide an appropriate break from the interval training outlined above, and for allowing the body to recover from the substantial physical demands. Other techniques such as Pilates, Gyrotonic, or Gyrokinesis are equally suitable in this respect, as all of them train muscular strength that underpins demands made by intricate and difficult coordinations. Musculature should maintain a balance between tension and relaxation, and elasticity.

Training in Feldenkrais, Body–Mind Centering, or yoga will help the body to recover, releasing both mind and muscles from the high degree of concentration and tension. Linz students also felt that meditation or visualization techniques were helpful for learning the Cunningham Technique, as these methods refresh the mind and foster a visual understanding for movement detail.

The adagio combinations in which the students, standing on one leg, repeatedly work the gesture leg through different positions from passé into développé before guiding it downward to repeat the movement, require a great deal of physical strength. Added upper body actions like curve, arch, and tilt increase the level of coordination required. As the students Handler, Kronheim, Rys, and Bobadilla state, good contact with the floor is necessary in order to perform these exercises well; the foot must be rooted and the standing leg connected to a strong center. A strong center is key to understanding the gestalt of a moment, to giving it life and form, and enables the dancer to perform in–the–moment.

The high level of precision demanded by the Cunningham Technique quickly exposes weaknesses, whether they be rhythmic, coordination, or physical uncertainties—or even mental blocks that prevent dancers from remembering

18 Johannes Randolf teaches contemporary dance at the IDA and also works as a physiotherapist.

exercises. This explains why some students say there are few ways, in this technique, to compensate for uncertainties. Injuries can occur because of excessive cognitive as well as physical expectations. Inadequately trained ankles increase the risk of injury, as extensive jumping exercises require a high level of stability. This is exacerbated by the fact that all exercises are done, on principle, in standing (i.e., no floorwork), meaning there is potential for knee and leg–joint injuries. Daniel Roberts occasionally compensates by including floor exercises.

MOVEMENT CHARACTERISTICS AND PHYSICALITY

Cunningham Technique, as taught by Daniel Roberts, involves whole–body activity in which all parts are mobilized. However, in terms of dexterity, fine motor skills for the torso, legs, arms, and feet are trained more intensively than those of the hands. Therefore, an ability to mobilize and coordinate individual body parts efficiently, and in accordance with one's own strength, is essential. At the start of class, the entire body is warmed up using torso swings and turns to activate the center; other body parts are gradually engaged.

The wide range of exercises used at the beginning of class serves to activate the spinal column and as a basis for flexibility and coordination skills. A comprehensive mobilization of the spinal column, as well as increasing its range of motion, is important. The spinal column not only keeps the body upright, it also determines the amount of mobility—which, in turn, determines the body's range of directional and spatial options. This is successively expanded in training. As all body parts can initiate movement and a stable center is crucial. The lower pelvic region must be able to adjust to constant weight shifts found in off–axis shapes. Having total and segmented mobilization of the spinal column (in the chest, abdominal, and lumbar regions) allows dancers to guide the torso through different levels and axes like a kaleidoscope.

Dancers must thus learn to activate the body segmentally during movements that simultaneously contract, lightly pulsate, and rotate. Muscular flexibility and strength is required for stretching, bending, and elongating torso movements performed to both fast and slow rhythms. This also emphasizes the significance of Roberts's exercises at the start of class, which are primarily leg exercises, as these teach students how to support and stabilize the body.

Roberts pays particular attention to foot articulation. As training primarily involves stabilizing, mobilizing, and locomotion using both legs—including walking and lots of jumps—positioning and strength in the feet are extremely important. Given the speed of the exercises, which involve constantly changing directions and rhythms, it is helpful to root and locate the body by means of a conscious awareness of the relationship between the feet and the floor. The foot is usually the first body part engaged in a clear shift of weight.

But as Handler, Kronheim, Rys and Bobadilla note, the head can also initiate movement and, thanks to a flexible axis/spinal column, send the body into the space. A whole–body approach thus dominates when performing exercises, even when it appears as if individual movements (like curving the lower back) are only initiated locally. Of course, all body parts are connected, meaning an impulse from one will engage others.

The high level of coordination demanded by the technique presented a real challenge for some Linz students as they had to master the underlying principle of isolation during a whole–body activity. Particular attention was paid to isolating body parts and moving them in different directions while, at the same time, stabilizing them. To achieve this, Roberts drew on his dance training at Ohio State University and incorporated visualization exercises that imaged bones, muscles, and joints. So, for example, movement was initiated by placing awareness on the bones and skeleton. Other visualizations focus on muscle tone and shape: Are the muscles tense or relaxed? Are the muscles close to the bones or do they create a cushion to rest upon?

As already emphasized, Cunningham Technique demands copious amounts and constant use of strength, in particular when slow, directed, and expansive movements in space need to be stabilized, slowed down, or stopped by muscular strength. Support here comes from well–developed muscles in the back, ankle joints, feet, and legs.

How the center is perceived is important to Roberts, although he assumes that each student must discover and experience the exact location and sensation for her- or himself. Drawing on his experience, Roberts sees this as something that changes over time, as the body develops. Now in his thirties, Roberts perceives his own center as being lower in the pelvic region, whereas before his perception was of it being more in the abdominal area. Students in Linz also perceived varying locations: For some, it was in the abdominal region close to the chest, others imagined and felt it around the navel. This has consequences for a dancer's movement organization. Linz students remarked: "The center can always shift a bit, depending on the movements being done, and the center used for arch can be different from the center used for curve or for leg–work. In Cunningham Technique, the center seems to shift a little when jumping, when it transfers from the belly to the chest area."

Roberts emphasizes that perceived body center(s) are not explicitly discussed or even trained in traditional teaching of Cunningham Technique. The focus of attention is on the whole body and logic of relationships and spatial disposition—for example, how the body carries itself forward or backward—as the relationship to other dancers also plays a constant role. Combinations are always activated and structured using a balanced body center. Roberts thus speaks explicitly about the body center in his classes when teaching lifts, i.e., both interacting bodies can control their positions to avoid going off–balance. He teaches dancers how to economically position the center for optimal use of strength. The body center is generally treated as the center of movement, and less as an imaginary zone.

Body weight and gravity, in Roberts's technique classes, are principally treated as forces to be resisted; while moving, one tries to use body weight (meaning the gravitational pull exerted on any natural object) as something to be countered. Body weight must be physically controlled; stabilization when falling or leaning must be learned. Momentum must be formed, in a manner similar to the Humphrey/Limón use of swing and oppositional 'fall and recovery'. But Cunningham Technique does work with body weight; it is a strengthening factor as the weight falls along a vertical axis (the spinal column) when aligning the body. Roberts understands body weight, similar to Zen philosophy, as force that impacts the earth and, with it, also the body; this strength, however, does not have an inevitable limiting effect on movement. Rather, it is about garnering this force, as an active element, for movement.

Roberts refers to energy differently for each exercise and movement phrase. The energy varies depending upon the movement being performed, and in accordance with the individual. Roberts encourages students to experiment with their own energies. This relates also to weight shifts, depending on where the shift takes place—and where the movement is headed.

Cunningham Technique pays special attention to space as a complex for kinetic design. In this aspect of training, Roberts sees a great opportunity for students to develop both better body awareness and sensitivity to the space. In the first two phases of Roberts's classes, students focus on their bodies 'in place'; in the following phase, they use the information to concentrate on filling movement with greater volume, giving them a sense of the surrounding space.[19] Linz students Petit, Swietlicka, and Herrlein emphasize that a relationship to the space is central to Cunningham Technique. This applies both to the kinesphere, wherein one learns about spatial correlations within the body space, as well as to a constant orientation in the room. Students find this concept (i.e., awareness of their kinetic and kinesthetic space) presents an opportunity to see

19 See Teaching: Principles and Methodology.

both the body and space as malleable, free space, because movement shapes emerge from the interplay between body and space. Muscle groups and configurations, and the joints' coordination potential are all recognized as malleable free space. A comment Roberts often makes is: "Feel both sides of your back as they support your verticality."

In Roberts's teaching, all movements address the space, almost with a sense of "spatial responsibility," as he emphasizes. Dancers can and should develop an awareness of where they are in the room and what they are currently doing, "for the sake of him- or herself, the choreography, and others in the space." Directive and formative awareness for the room, as well as for the spatiality of movement, enables a conscious perception of one's own body.

Cunningham Technique understands space as an open network, in which joints are given a flexible place for physical articulation. Putting that to use in the physical body means employing constant presence and agility in the limbs and joints.

Awareness of the environment also influences Roberts's teaching; for example, awareness of sunlight shining into the room. The student Katja Bablick described one exercise wherein she was asked to execute an upper body circle and, to help her, imagine sunlight streaming onto her chest. The visualization helped Bablick perform the biggest possible movement.

Combinations used in technique classes are oriented in all directions and use all available space; directions are often changed mid-movement. The preferred spatial level is the middle level. The lower level is used for pliés, whose movement radius both marks and delimits this level, while numerous jump combinations constitute the use of the upper level.

Roberts finds it essential for dancers in his class to be conscious of exterior rhythms, but also to be aware of how the inner rhythm works with the outer one. In his classes, he teaches students how to tap into both equally by placing great importance on rhythmic detail and investigating musicality, i.e., using music to design movement. Roberts wants to share his knowledge about the complexity of time, a feature of Cunningham's work, in order to highlight time's endless possibilities for shaping movement. He says:

/ "Merce used to say to Pat Richter, the piano accompanist for his class, that it did not matter to him what she decided to play, as long as the rhythm was clear. She loved that! She said it opened up a world of possibilities to her, that she could think melody, but that it was not tied to eight phrases of 4/4. I believe the same has to be true in the work of a dancer, that we are not predestined to function on counts of eight—we could also think of it as a phrase of five, and a phrase of three. How do we subdivide a musical structure, in regards to phrasing and breath, while still holding true to the described amount of time and space?" /

Students enjoyed the distinct differences between rhythmic structures in Roberts's class to those in other classes, even when counts of nine, ten, or twelve were unusual for some. New phrasings were very difficult for those dancers who were used to training in 3/4 or 4/4, as the movement

When asked about fundamental movement principles, Roberts's interesting answer was that he wanted to reflect further, with care and clear referencing to the philosophical dimensions implied by the question. Physically speaking, principles of isolation, centering of energy in

initially felt arhythmic and forced. Roberts helped by giving clear musical directions and counting aloud. Dancers gained confidence by counting quietly to themselves. Live music strongly supported the rhythmic development of the combinations. Katja Bablick pointed out how live music created a balanced atmosphere and energy in the room, and made the class flow. Roberts adjusted the tempo constantly and explained meter and rhythm in detail to both musicians and dancers. Structuring time is therefore an essential aspect of Roberts's teaching; he develops it cumulatively, yet organically and spontaneously.

There are no special instructions regarding the use of breath, nor are there specific exercises for breath–awareness. Each student should, instead, discover his or her own breath rhythm, and this can vary greatly. Therefore, Roberts does not use breath to phrase or rhythmically structure movement. He wants each dancer to work out phrasing with their own breath. As he adjusted class pace to the respective level of the students, depending upon the group, similar exercises were taught with different tempos. Roberts did consistently accelerate the tempo so students had to cope with unfamiliar circumstances, creating both a physical and mental challenge and possibly helping them break through self–imposed limits.

the body, as well as rhythmic coordination skills are certainly among these fundamental principles. The types of movement have already been described above. Roberts mentions steps, jumps, turns, extensions, and balance as components. These are used in the second phase of class, preceded by phase–one warm–up swings as well as leg–work with pliés, foot exercises, tendus, and jetés, which, similar to ballet training, are followed by ronds de jambe for balance and rotation, as well as Cunningham's characteristic 'bounces', i.e., soft seesaw (expanding and relaxing) movements with a curved chest performed in different directions (but always in standing). In the third phase, steps, jumps, turns, extension, and balance are practiced in combinations.

An incisive comment from Dorota Lecka cited the Cunningham Technique's principles (in reference to movement style and physicality), insofar as these could be placed in a character–building sense: "There is always a choice about how one feels and presents oneself to the outside world. This attitude can relate to body structure, to muscle tone, to a sense of drama that one can carry through a dance class, and to a certain parameter or objective you focus on. All this appears as a personal flavor of a movement."

THEORETICAL AND PRACTICAL INSIGHTS INTO *DANCEFORMS*

Henner Drewes

In addition to technique classes with Daniel Roberts, students in Linz also participated in a workshop with Henner Drewes, who familiarized them with the animation software *DanceForms*. It seemed logical to investigate the relationship between this computer visualization for dance and the students' reflections on Cunningham's dance technique. As with other analytical movement representation systems, *DanceForms* software can only handle selected aspects of movement—thus it utilizes a limited amount of movement information. The fact that Cunningham worked effectively with this software points to a clear correlation between the movement aspects the software offers and Cunningham's perception of movement. Cunningham was a member of the program's development team and made a substantial contribution to its design. This means that the presence of—as well as the absence of—certain movement possibilities and concepts gives us some indication of Cunningham's preferences.

The type of movement and image of the body found in *DanceForms* is based on the following scheme: The figure of a dancer, the model, has body parts that connect to each other via a network of joints, corresponding, in simplified form, to human anatomy. Every joint of the virtual model can perform all geometrically imaginable positions, even when these are anatomically impossible. For Cunningham, there was a utopian aspect to this virtual body; it can explore movement through segmentation and coordination as well as being able to overcome physical and movement limits—*to an extent*. There is a tree–like hierarchical system, whose roots are always in the pelvis (the 'root limb'). Movement by a body part near the root limb (i.e., near the pelvis) will affect the position of a body part further away from the 'trunk', even if the angle between these two body parts remains constant and the root limb does not change its position.

In order to represent human movement fully, the software would have to include dynamic, changing root limb(s)—meaning that any body part could take over the pelvis's role for the duration of contact with the floor. Without this ability, de facto connections between the body and floor are incorrect, and a realistic representation of locomotion and weight shifts is impossible.

The program requires that body shapes, or poses, be placed into 'keyframes'; only key images need to be created as they serve as cornerstones for the animation. Keyframes are superimposed over a timeline. The computer generates (interpolates) the images necessary to create a fluid movement sequence between keyframes. Such interpolation, however, can only be manifested directly, i.e., via the shortest possible movement path between keyframes.

Therefore, the program's movement solutions are a limited subset of the body's true capabilities.

Movement phrases (which might be created in a myriad of ways) can be developed further by copying and pasting, or repeating and re-combining. This makes provision for designing group choreographies as well as for choreographing typical Cunningham 'coordinated' combinations wherein the upper body is choreographed separately from the legs. This process reaches its limits in complex scenarios involving differentiated, 'coordinated' rhythms and the interplay of various body parts. If a position is pasted onto the timeline at an automatically interpolated interim frame rather than at an existing keyframe, a new keyframe is generated. With additional keyframes and repeated edits, the data quickly becomes indecipherable. Efficient processing of the material becomes increasingly difficult and, ultimately, impossible.

Despite the substantial limitations, Cunningham was able to work with the program successfully. What are the parallels between the software's scope and Cunningham's movement concepts? In fact, direct movement paths predominate in Cunningham's work: his movement coordinations and constructions reveal a relatively simple time structure for individual components, and movements by unrelated body parts generally begin and end at the same time. In contrast, there are no 'coordinated' sequences in which individual body parts are used successively, or in which more complex temporal structures follow. Almost without exception, weight shifts occur from a standing position. As the software cannot account for weight bearing, it is unable to model weight shifts realistically. However, representation of the arms, upper body, and working leg (available body parts that are not root limbs) is not restricted by the program's limitations. Had Cunningham needed to incorporate more floorwork, such as rolls and weight changes from one body part to another, then *DanceForms*, in its current format, would not have served him as well.

Sabine Huschka

TEACHING: PRINCIPLES AND METHODOLOGY

"What fascinates and inspires me so much about Daniel's class is the mix of clear structure and space for freedom."

Dorota Lecka, student

CONCEPTUAL BASIS

It is also possible to look at Cunningham Technique from a social and aesthetic perspective. Classes take place in a sensitive environment in which social interaction happens, an environment characterized by pedagogical instructions and different degrees of physical contact, as well as by clearly stated or subliminal behavioral, physical, and clothing codes.

For Daniel Roberts, there is no question that the physical, mental, and social aspects play a large role in Cunningham Technique; they implicitly promote a personal and mature relationship to the material. Students must have a certain level of maturity[20] to handle the movement principles, to embody these principles, and for these principles to emerge as dance. As mentioned, Roberts describes his aesthetic objective as follows: Education and training in Cunningham Technique are geared towards performance, i.e., ultimately at presenting the moving body. However, the aesthetic aim of the training is to understand movement as a physical–mental, spatial–temporal, and as an individual discovery and developmental process—and to avoid differentiating between a physical (exercise) movement and a dance movement. Dancers should be taught to transform movement into something in and of itself, to be able to perform with great confidence. Roberts considers this to reflect the debate that a student must have with him- or herself—a debate that demands personal responsibility and takes time. Therefore, one learning goal is maturity.

20 Simone Forti: *Handbook in Motion. An Account of an Ongoing Personal Discourse and its Manifestation in Dance.* New York: New York University Press, 1974, p. 34. Forti assesses Cunningham Technique as particularly mature, specifically because of its complexity and the concentration needed to fluidly coordinate movement.

From a social perspective, teaching Cunningham Technique means establishing a network of relationships between dancers who share a space and who need to be aware of spatial configurations. Although this may also apply to many other dance techniques, Roberts sees Cunningham Technique as unique in its awareness of the space–time relationship and movement design skills. A relationship between these two factors is established by working consciously and intensively, and gathering experience (i.e., in class)—and not by means of physical contact or through emotionally expressive moments.

As to the communicative structure of the class, the corrections Roberts makes—even those made by touch—provide students with feedback intended to enhance execution and further student reflection. Linz students found this to be quite positive, as corrections made 'hands–on' enabled them to better sense physical mechanisms and processes. Here, Roberts's teaching style differs from Merce Cunningham's: Cunningham's teaching, as with many other teachers at the Cunningham studio, was characterized by sparse commentary and few corrections.

Roberts mostly teaches in settings like Linz, where continuous and professional work is best achieved, and where he finds a basic amount of knowledge is coupled with the desire to understand (something that is particularly relevant considering the movement complexity). In Roberts's experience, youth or very young students find it rather difficult to keep up. Cunningham Technique is also unsuitable for children, according to Roberts, because it is simply not a technique for beginners. Roberts prefers working in institutional training contexts or with professional dancers. He admits to being able to work with such dancers in a more essential and less structural way than was the case in Linz. Regardless of the context, technique classes are always group classes. The speed and thoroughness with which fundamental principles are learned may differ depending upon students' skill level and willingness to learn, as well as upon how deeply dancers get involved with the material.

As mentioned, previous movement and dance experience are decidedly helpful when learning the Cunningham Technique. These provide a basis for appreciation, to varying degrees, of Cunningham movement—whereby, in Roberts's opinion, the technique in which a dancer has already trained, or that he or she is still learning, is of secondary importance. He finds it a problem when students want to learn Cunningham Technique on the spot, or if they attempt to jump between other techniques and a Cunningham class without an ability to differentiate between principles. Despite, or indeed precisely because of, the myriad of offers in the contemporary teaching and training sector, it is crucial that students understand the differences between various techniques, and be able to analyze (and differentiate) on a conceptual level.

One clear difference between Cunningham Technique and various Release Techniques (as well as other somatic work) lies in the fact that the former requires muscular control. As Roberts explains, a relevé balancé cannot be executed without consciously engaging muscles. Without strength, the body would simply fall over. Movement characteristics that define Cunningham Technique and Release Techniques are clearly different, therefore a dancer should be clear which direction he or she would like to take—although that does not necessarily mean pinning oneself down to a single technique.

Even if classes are not taken daily, results can be achieved in Cunningham Technique—as was the case during the two weeks in Linz—when two one-week sessions were held in different months. That said, exact results from Linz cannot be ascertained as too many factors involving individual students would have to be taken into account.

More significant is the approach to the work, which calls on students to develop self-confidence and social skills. Priorities here include a willingness to work in a disciplined fashion, to stay focused on the matter at hand, and, if there are difficulties with the material, to stick with it. Students must also learn, for example, how to prepare for class, how to perceive movement, how to observe and listen, how to know when to be ready to perform the movement combinations, etc.

It is important to note here that there are many methods at a Cunningham teacher's disposal, depending on the situation and context. Sometimes it is important to give lots of demonstrations or explanations, sometimes it is important to say little, and sometimes it is important to leave plenty of room for experimentation. Some students need to see a movement often, some need to hear a lot about it, some go home and understand the movement by reflecting on it, and for others it is important to see their fellow dancers make mistakes in order to better understand the logic behind the movement. In practice, it is crucial to learn by recognizing errors, and allowing oneself to make mistakes.

Roberts's teaching is therefore open-ended in terms of results, although he employs results-oriented structures. Roberts orients his teaching goals toward the institutional and situational context: Specific movement standards must be reached in professional training situations and at institutions of higher learning, while in other contexts, i.e., in Linz, students should be able to grasp the individual exercises and basic principles about coordination that underpin the technique. Regardless of the situation, the guiding principle remains the same, i.e., to activate each individual's skills.

PEDAGOGICAL METHODS

A lesson is structured into three phases that have been described above. Using whole-body swings, the first phase warms up the body, followed by traditional Cunningham bounces. Back twists are followed by intensive ballet-based leg- and foot-work (pliés, tendus, jetés, and ronds de jambe) for balance. There is no barre work in Cunningham Technique. Students stand center floor for the duration of class and thus, according to the student Arnulfo Pardo Ravagli, must find their own center for good placement.

After the first exercises are executed to well-defined rhythms, like the 'exercise on 6' and 'exercise on 8', comes the second phase with more exercises on place, which activates and assists the body to sense space. Accelerating combinations and adding larger movements, like développés, battements, rapid foot articulation, and jumps train strength, coordination, and stamina.

Using exercises learned thus far, phase three expands upon spatial volume by including jumps and combinations through the room (*triplets*) that are varied and accelerated with different tempos and rhythms. The final part of class includes fast and slow combinations, turn combinations, and big jumps through the space. All exercises happen in the middle and upper levels of the space (referencing Laban's spatial theory).

Every class is thus structured, although exercises vary slightly in rhythm, tempo, and spatial directions. Training takes place in intervals; phases of activity alternate with phases of recovery. Each exercise is only practiced once per class and is not repeated. Combinations found in the last section of phase three might be repeated in successive classes, depending on the students' skill level, and if needed. In Linz, Roberts presented students with new material each day so as to present them with the greatest possible spectrum of movement; the goal was not to execute a polished movement combination at the end of class, i.e., exercises were not result-oriented.

For Dorota Lecka, one effect of a technique class without exercise repetition was that she learned to perform movement immediately and straightforwardly, and did not concentrate on the right or wrong way to do it. Arnulfo Pardo Ravagli also pointed out a 'just do it' attitude towards the exercises. Lecka found this aspect to be particularly worthwhile because in class—and not only during rehearsals or performance—the focus was on 'doing' and not just trying out movement according to Roberts's verbal instructions. This means that a student is always performing in class, learning movement with passion and dedication, and working to attain a clear focus, clear start, and the clear knowledge necessary for performing.

Movement execution focuses on the embodiment of clear shapes, lines, and rhythms so as to give them kinesthetic life. Exercises run the gamut from easy to complicated, include no improvisation, and are learned by imitation (mimetic function). As Lecka says, "it is learning by doing." A lesson works though the entire body, including various muscle groups and coordination capabilities.

In general, class has a dynamic progression and requires a student's uninterrupted concentration. One exercise comes on the heels of the next without any clear–cut break during a (usually ninety–minute) class. This continuum demands a dancer be physically and mentally alert and ready to 'imbibe' movement and awareness, which, along with the accelerating tempo of the class, creates a strong sense of flow.

For Roberts, it is imperative that a student stay focused on the matter at hand and not 'lose the thread.' Roberts must do the same: use these skills and abilities as a teacher to deliver a class that is driven by ever–present energy and passion, and stay true to his own body of knowledge. The focus must remain on one's own physical body, using its capabilities to find new movement possibilities. These possibilities should also be realized, even on a proprioceptive (intuitive) level. This goes hand–in–hand with Roberts's basic pedagogic and professional fundamental belief that students must assume personal responsibility in the work of becoming a dancer. It is self–understood that professionals not only need to train every day, but that they otherwise stay focused on the matter at hand with their attention, energy, passion, and discipline. According to Roberts, a dancer must learn to navigate this highly competitive professional field—a terrifying but also wonderful field. Not only must a dancer learn to work for and on her– or himself, the dancer must also learn *how* to train and know what he or she desires from the training. Technique classes are thus, in the broadest sense, preparing dancers for professional life by fostering emotional and mental skills, the same ones that shape Roberts as a teacher.

"It feels as if you are completely naked. It is all about this pure form and nothing else. No decoration."

Andrea Maria Handler, student

All in all, Roberts views teaching as an artistic process, a constant confrontation with his own, and others', movements and bodies. For Roberts, teaching is a on–going process in which he receives fresh input every time he encounters the creative potential of movement; in this way, dance remains alive as a spontaneous, communicative, and physical encounter.

21 See Class Plan on DVD 1.

To prepare for teaching, Roberts plans a class that he will vary, if necessary, in certain situations and specific contexts. Classes are carefully planned; moreover, Roberts outlines the structure for students at the start of class.[21] His movement tasks are tied to the plan, but he is also willing to react spontaneously to situations that arise during the course of classes or workshops. As class progresses, the plan might be affected by Roberts' assessment of the students, by his sense of exercise progression and which movements or phrases could be interesting, or by seeing aspects that need a more differentiated or clearer focus on detail. Combinations may highlight excerpts from Cunningham's choreographies, or can be drawn from other contexts. Roberts generally develops the phrases in silence, although there are exceptions.

Self–assessment and feedback takes various forms, and Roberts has not set any particular method for doing so in stone, but talking to the musicians is one way, as are individual discussions with students—if they choose to approach him.

Briefly returning to the motor learning process, which is closely related to how rhythm is embodied: Movement is learned primarily by putting it into units of time, enabling the individual to embody it by use of his or her own rhythmic sensibilities. Movement, as said, is precisely counted; execution is supported by live music that has a clear and definable meter. Rhythms and exercises vary from class to class, a principle that Roberts has taken directly from Cunningham's teaching. Motor learning is expedited by mentally counting movement material so as to aid memorization, thus a personal kinesthetic structure and embodied musicality can develop. An intrinsic musicality, one that is independent of the time signature, is nurtured step–for–step—a characteristic Cunningham aesthetic. Roberts says that Cunningham dancers have a strong sense of musicality, as the entire repertoire was created independent of, and often prior to, the music.

Mistakes are allowed in the open environment of Roberts's class. His goal is not one of a successful performance, but to train the dancers' movement intelligence. Students in Linz welcomed and responded positively to the open environment, to the opportunity to dance without having to think about judgment (other than their own). The students Ochvat, Prokopová, and Jasinski saw Roberts's role as the 'transformer' of Cunningham's movement style. Ravagli stressed that Roberts's good energy galvanized the class and motivated everyone to dedicate themselves to the complexity and speed. Roberts demonstrates movement and uses his voice to energize the class, which, he admits, can sometimes be exhausting. Students felt that the discipline he demanded was useful for learning. Petit, Swietlicka, and Herrlein saw Roberts as a "constant orientation point for coordination, rhythm, and shape," and they described his as an "inductive teaching method."

A dominant means of communicating is mimetic function, i.e., learning by watching and imitating, in which the teacher demonstrates until students are able to execute the exercise or combination. As to verbalization, Roberts uses ballet terminology throughout class; he often teaches in places where ballet vocabulary is familiar and used daily. Many leg and foot exercises are clearly identified by ballet vocabulary. Roberts uses this to further expound upon particular aspects and aesthetics in Cunningham Technique. So, for example, the energy flow (as well as the centering of energy) is different than in ballet, and Roberts makes the differences clear using imagery (as mentioned above). Although various images are used to aid in movement execution, Roberts rarely uses imagery to explain a movements' mechanisms or aesthetic design. For the most part, communication takes place on a visual level as Roberts demonstrates exercises and combinations with precision, certainty, and perfect coordination. Rhythms and tempos are explained verbally.

"It is important to be attentive. If one manages to be attentive in class, learn things quickly, and coordinate them differently, you are well prepared for all tasks that you may encounter as a result of the artistic process."

Philine Herrlein, student

Sabine Huschka

CONCLUSION

In class, Roberts's objective is to teach and nurture the performance experience, and to impart a passion for spatial–temporal movement design. A constant engagement with the material and a 'readiness to learn more' characterizes not only Roberts as a teacher, but also what he demands from students. After all, Cunningham Technique, whether talking about the simple or the profound components, cannot be mastered. The only thing that can be mastered is an ever–open attitude towards change. Students are taught a paradox: The technique should teach them about movement, and, at the same time, about moving beyond the technique.

Two closing comments from the student Dorota Lecka explain this further:

╱ "What I find particularly exciting is experiencing dance in a totally different way. Even if the technique might initially feel stiff, strange, inorganic, or too rigid, after a while it becomes very organic, very clear, and the structural lines of the body become clearer from day–to–day. It makes you aware of each body part and joint. Dancers can do whatever they want after that because they have the freedom; their bodies are awake, ready, and well prepared for any kind of movement, even for Release movements."

"Students often get lost, lose direction, the rhythm, coordination, their perspective…then, most of the time, one more repetition of the exercise is required, or another 'attempt' is postponed for another day. What I find extremely interesting in this way of teaching is that students are constantly challenged. These challenges are linked to positive rather than negative encouragement. Even if one is not able to repeat the exercise, one can sense an atmosphere of 'new skills'. Even if everybody 'failed' because nobody could repeat and perform a certain exercise properly, Roberts's approach challenges students positively, encourages them, and makes them eager to tackle and overcome his or her own limitations." ╱

LITERATURE

Cage, John
Silence: Lectures and Writings
Middletown (CT): Wesleyan University Press, 1973

Carroll, Noel | Banes, Sally
"Cunningham and Duchamps"
In: Ballett Review, 2/1983, pp. 73–79

Charles, Daniel
"Au-delà de l'aléa: Jenseits der Aleatorik."
In: Barck, Karlheinzl | Gente, Peter (Ed.)
Aisthesis: Wahrnehmung heute oder Perspektiven einer anderen
Ästhetik. Leipzig: Reclam Verlag, 1991, pp. 322–331

Copeland, Roger
Merce Cunningham: The Modernizing of Modern Dance
New York/London: Routledge, 2004

Cunningham, Merce
in **The John Tusa Interview**
[Transcript] 2008
www.bbc.co.uk/radio3/johntusainterview/
cunningham_transcript.shtml (accessed on 08/25/2010)

Cunningham, Merce
Der Tänzer und der Tanz
Published by Jacqueline Lesschaeve
Frankfurt a. M.: Dieter Fricke Verlag, 1986

Cunningham, Merce
"The Function of a Technique for Dance"
In: Contact Quarterly. A Vehical for moving Ideas, 7/1982, pp. 7–9
(First published in: Sorell, Walter (Ed.): The Dance has many Faces.
Cleveland/New York: The World Publishing Company, 1951, pp.
250–255)

Cunningham, Merce
Changes: Notes on Choreography
Published byFrances Starr
New York: Something Else Press, 1968

Fiedeler, Frank
Die Monde des I Ging: Symbolschöpfung und Evolution
München: Eugen Diederichs Verlag, 1988

Forti, Simone
**Handbook in Motion: An Account of an ongoing personal
Discourse and its Manifestation in Dance**
New York: New York University Press, 1974

Foster, Susan Leigh
**Reading Dancing: Bodies and Subjects in
Contemporary American Dance**
Berkeley/Los Angeles: University of California Press, 1986

Gil, José
"The Dancer's Body"
In: Massumi, Brian (Ed.): A shock to thought: Expressions after
Deleuze & Guattari
London/New York: Routledge, 2002, pp. 117–148

Han, Byong-Chul
Abwesen
Berlin: Merve Verlag, 2007

Huschka, Sabine
**"Subjekt-Körper-Leere: Diamanten: Merce Cunningham
zum 90. Geburtstag"**
In: corpus, 12/2008, www.corpusweb.net (accessed on 08/25/2010)

Huschka, Sabine
**Merce Cunningham und der Moderne Tanz: Körperkonzepte,
Choreographie und Tanzästhetik**
Würzburg: Königshausen & Neumann, 2000

Katz, Vincent
Black Mountain College
Cambridge/MA: MIT Press, 2002

Anne Seymour
"Foreword"
in Anthony d'Offay: Dancers on a Plane: Cage–Cunningham–Johns
New York: A. A. Knopf in association with Anthony d'Offay Gallery,
1990, pp. 9–12.

d'Offay, Anthony
Freundschaften: Cage, Cunningham, Johns
Bonn: Edition Cantz, 1991

Vaughan, David
Merce Cunningham Fifty Years
New York: Aperture, 1997

Vaughan, David (Moderator)
**"Cunningham and his Dancers. Transcript of a Discussion with
Carolyn Brown, Douglas Dunn, Viola Farber, Steve Paxton,
Marianne Preger-Simon, Valda Setterfield, and Gus Solomon."**
In: Ballett Review, 3/1987
Republished in: Kostelanetz, Richard (Ed.): Merce Cunningham:
Dancing in Space and Time. Chicago: cappella books, 1992, pp. 101–123

LINKS

www.merce.org/mondayswithmerce.html
dlib.nyu.edu/merce/mwm/2008-01-12

DVDS

Elementary Level
Directed by Merce Cunningham and Elliot Caplan
Commentary by Merce Cunningham
Instructors: Susan Alexander, Ruth Barnes, Merce Cunningham, June
Finch, Susana Hayman–Chaffey, Chris Komar
Dancers: Allison Cutri, Jill Diamond, Nancy Langsner, Kate Troughton
Produced by Cunningham Dance Foundation, copyright 1985

Intermediate Level
Directed by Merce Cunningham and Elliot Caplan
Commentary by Merce Cunningham
Instructors: Merce Cunningham, Diane Frank, Catherine Kerr, Chris
Komar, Robert Kovich, Rob Remley
Dancers: Heidi Kreusch, David Kulick, Larissa McGoldrick, Dennis
O'Connor, Yukie Okutama, Carol Teitelbaum
Produced by Cunningham Dance Foundation, copyright 1987

GILL CLARKE
MINDING MOTION

INTER–UNIVERSITY CENTER FOR DANCE PILOT PROJECT TANZPLAN BERLIN

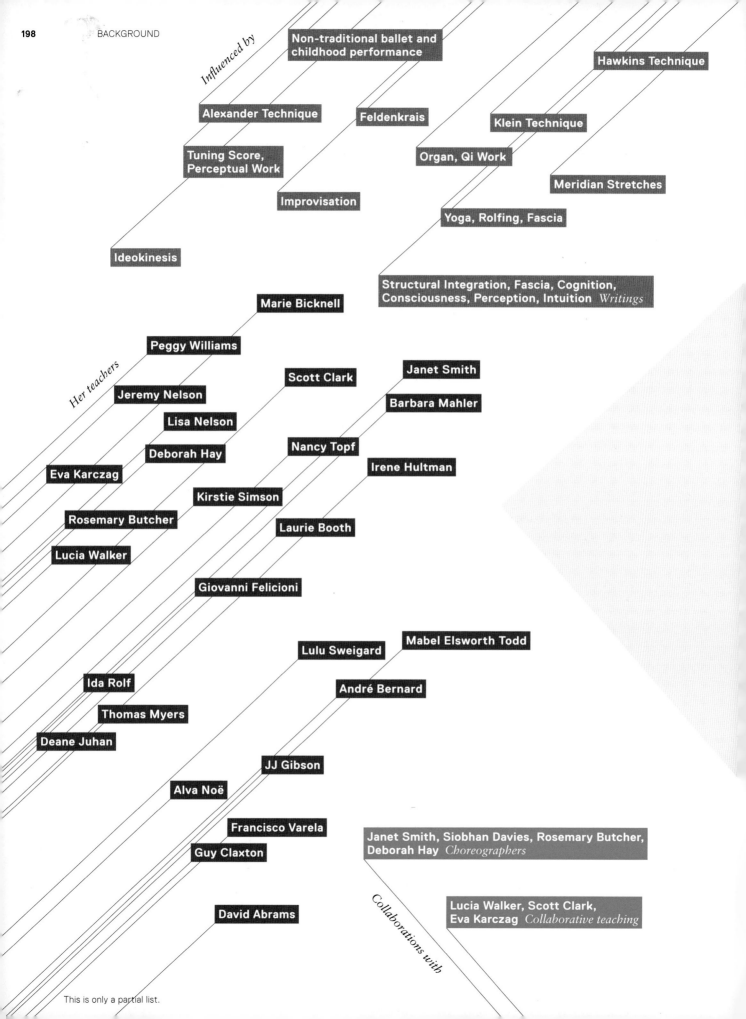

Influenced by

Non-traditional ballet and childhood performance

Hawkins Technique

Alexander Technique

Feldenkrais

Klein Technique

Tuning Score, Perceptual Work

Organ, Qi Work

Meridian Stretches

Improvisation

Yoga, Rolfing, Fascia

Ideokinesis

Structural Integration, Fascia, Cognition, Consciousness, Perception, Intuition *Writings*

Marie Bicknell

Peggy Williams

Her teachers

Scott Clark

Janet Smith

Jeremy Nelson

Barbara Mahler

Lisa Nelson

Deborah Hay

Nancy Topf

Eva Karczag

Irene Hultman

Kirstie Simson

Rosemary Butcher

Laurie Booth

Lucia Walker

Giovanni Felicioni

Lulu Sweigard

Mabel Elsworth Todd

Ida Rolf

André Bernard

Thomas Myers

Deane Juhan

JJ Gibson

Alva Noë

Francisco Varela

Janet Smith, Siobhan Davies, Rosemary Butcher, Deborah Hay *Choreographers*

Guy Claxton

Collaborations with

Lucia Walker, Scott Clark, Eva Karczag *Collaborative teaching*

David Abrams

This is only a partial list.

GILL CLARKE — MINDING MOTION

Research Team at the Inter–University Center for Dance—Pilot Project
Tanzplan Berlin (HZT): Gill Clarke, Prof. Dr. Franz Anton Cramer,
Prof. Gisela Müller

AUTHORS
Gill Clarke, Franz Anton Cramer, Gisela Müller

INTERVIEW
Edith Boxberger

STUDENTS AND GUESTS
of the bachelor's degree programm Contemporary Dance, Context, Choreography: Johanne Bro, Sara Canini,
Siriol Joyner, An Kaler, Nina Kurtela, Ivana Rončević, Julia Schwarzbach, Nils Ulber, and Ante Ursić

GILL CLARKE (*1954)
studied English and Education at York University before becoming an independent dance artist, performer, teacher,
advocate, and movement researcher—and recently received an MA in Social Sciences. She was a founder–member
of the Siobhan Davies Dance Company and has performed and collaborated with many other choreographers, including Rosemary Butcher, Rosemary Lee, and Janet Smith. She teaches masterclasses and workshops internationally
for students, independent artists, and professional companies. She was director of performance studies at LABAN,
London 2000–2006 (where she is now a consultant), received a fellowship from NESTA, a London Dance and
Performance Award, an MBE (Member of the Order of the British Empire), is a visiting professor at Ulster University,
and co-director of Independent Dance—an organization supporting professional dance artists in London.

Gill Clarke Interviewed by Edith Boxberger

MOVEMENT AND LEARNING CAN

HAPPEN EVERYWHERE

/ **What types of training have you done, and what influenced you?** My teaching has been influenced continuously by my own learning, my dancing and performing. I never went to a three–year professional training course. I studied ballet from five till I was eighteen, just some evenings a week as a hobby, a passion. I met contemporary dance partly through artists from London Contemporary Dance Theatre whose training was Graham–based. That technique was never very natural to me, but the introduction to contemporary dance was important. I then worked and studied with a choreographer named Janet Smith who had trained with Erik Hawkins. That technique was softer than Graham and I enjoyed its flow and connectivity.

And then the journey was never a straight line. I had always been interested in what I saw happening in improvised performance, thinking there is some interesting attention, some range of qualities here. In England in the 1980s, New Dance also emerged; sometimes the movement forms struck me as a bit general or undefined, but the range of textures and the sensory awareness of the work intrigued me.

I also did Cunningham open classes. I liked the challenge of it in terms of coordination—how one can have so many things going on at once—and the irregularity of rhythms. I loved it as a learning challenge, less as an aesthetic that sat inside or agreed with my body. But I was curious, and I was learning from different things. I never thought, 'I want to find the one thing that is right.' I was just working and learning.

All the time, teaching has been alongside of and a part of my learning; I haven't had to make a conscious decision what I will use in my teaching—just all the time tasting, digesting, and then something different emerges. Of course, in the planning of a class, one takes conscious decisions about the material one makes, or the principle one wants to work with. But there was never any dividing point between working this way or working that way; for me, it was a continuum.

By the late 1980s, things had begun to change a little. Before that, the world that was improvisational and sensory and the world of technique felt very far apart. As an audience member, I could move from one to the other, but it was quite hard to make a bridge between them as a dancer. For example, I did a few classes at a Dartington festival with Mary Fulkerson—later she was very influential in the new education that was emerging in

Amsterdam and Arnhem. Improvisational work, releasing work, and I was intrigued by that, but I could not make sense of it in my body in just two classes. I thought, 'The movement is simple, but yet I cannot let go of my muscle–holding to achieve it.'

/ **How did these different experiences develop into what you are doing now?** The great opportunities to try and bridge these two ways of thinking came for me when I started working with Siobhan Davies, a choreographer from London Contemporary Dance Theatre with a background in Graham and then in Cunningham. She got a scholarship to travel for a year in America, and she visited and worked with some of the release and body awareness artists there. She came back wanting to explore the sensing body as a choreographic resource. I started working with her. We had a visit from an Alexander teacher, and one of my fellow dancers was just starting a Feldenkrais training, so I was able to learn alongside him as his guinea pig.

Also as soon as my curiosity was stimulated by these experiences, I was reading a lot. I was reading about Alexander Technique, I was reading about Feldenkrais Technique, I was reading *The Thinking Body* by Mabel Todd, the writings of Ida Rolf. I was doing my own ideokinesis practice, imagining movement directions in the body, and I would go sometimes to New York and do classes at Movement Research—a center for exploratory dance. I was just really hungry and my experiences would lead me to questions and then take me to further reading.

I was introduced also to the work of Susan Klein and Barbara Mahler through a wonderful dancer, Jeremy Nelson, who danced for a long time with Stephen Petronio and is an official teacher of the Klein Technique. He was very thoughtful and clear in the technique, and also applied it to his own dynamic dancing. Jeremy was an inspiration to me, as were the Alexander and the Feldenkrais techniques.

/ **What were the things you learned and how did they affect your teaching?** I found an inspirational Alexander teacher who had studied with Alexander himself, who had extraordinary power and information in her hands. The Alexander work really helped me find a connected torso, head, neck, and back. And the spine became, in a way, an organizing principle in my making movement. I really enjoy the hands–on work that I do now, and I feel that is very influenced by what I learned through Alexander lessons—something about trying to notice what is going on in the tissues of a body through touch, rather than look at the shape and adjust it. Feldenkrais—which I also studied—works in a very different way; it works with complex coordinations, which felt like a great puzzle for the mind and body. It felt a great way of noticing one's habitual patterns and being able to find more choices. It works a lot through three–dimensionality and spiralling and connectivity, and also with noticing, perceiving the tiniest movement. If you can differentiate at that level, then you can expand that clarity through the body.

And then I got interested, through the Klein work and ideokinesis, in the power of the imagination and the visualization of our skeletal structure. For example, it was striking to me that from ten days of morning class with Jeremy Nelson, who was working very simply but very clear in his direction of the skeleton in space, I felt dramatic changes in how my body was organizing itself. I thought, 'How can this be possible?' I had assumed improvement came through physical practice. This was before brain research became so popular, but it was obvious when I started thinking about it, when I read about it, that our mind is the director of our intentioned movement. So what we have to influence to change our movement is how we are thinking, and to clarify the intention that we send through our body to direct our bony structure in space. And then we are more likely to access the deep, supporting muscle. That was a great stimulant to my own reading, and to the desire to understand, and to my teaching.

The initial phase of my class has become simpler and simpler because what I am interested in is not, like a Cunningham class, challenging the coordinating and memorizing brain, but having some form that each day we can take a different attention to. So one day I am taking my attention to the spine, and another day I might be thinking into the hip sockets. So by having a form that is familiar, although never the same, you are not distracted by wondering what comes next. I am really trying to be in the present moment of noticing, refining, tuning the awareness inside the body. And then later comes a complex sequence that is unfamiliar, as a vehicle through which to try and apply that information and attention.

Other influences have been the work of Lisa Nelson, of Eva Karczag, and Deborah Hay. All of these, in different ways, are working with perception and attention, and refining awareness of our movement—and these areas intrigue me. There are many, many people I have learnt from! I always continued teaching through the year. With Siobhan's company, we only worked for about six months in the year. In between I would perform and teach elsewhere, in different parts of Europe or with British Council outside Europe, and I would go and learn elsewhere.

/ **Are there new influences on your work?** More and more, my reading influences the teaching—trying to understand the work, the experiments, the research that is happening in cognitive science, for example. That might be about how the mind relates to the body, about perception, about attention. Also I have become concerned not to separate our dancing from the world and, in this context, have become interested in anthropology and social sciences. I am also interested in how our dancing evolves through social interactions; it is an oral tradition like folk music, and we don't often acknowledge that. We think of pure styles, but in fact, everything is hybrid in a way. We are all being influenced by the movement exchanges and conversations we have in the studio every day.

/ **You mentioned different worlds of training in the UK. How did these worlds develop? Did they inform each other?** Training in the UK developed very strongly in the late 1970s and 80s. The Graham work came a bit earlier, and then Cunningham took over, and still those techniques are taught now. Release Technique is also a strong strand. But that is a confusing term that needs clarifying: It is not Skinner Releasing technique developed by Joan Skinner, although that is also popular in the UK, but usually indicates a formal training influenced by somatic approaches in the sense that what becomes important is the sensing experience of the dancer, and not only the form and the line. So there is a lot of that work happening in the UK, which I would say is enriching the UK dancing. It is enabling audiences to enjoy dance as the playing out of the intelligence in the body, beyond the disciplined imprint of a technique or style.

I feel these two worlds that I once saw as so separate have now been bridged. There was a complexity of articulation offered through more technical approaches (although sometimes the muscular tension remained a little monochrome in its tone quality), and then the quality–shifts and individuality and textures that this other work has been exploring. Both have informed current work. So I think the bridge is an exciting place to be!

/ **How would you label what you are doing, and what are the aspects you stress in your work?** I tend to resist giving a label to what I do because I think the term Release Technique can be very misleading. 'Release' can be misunderstood as meaning 'relax'. What I teach is clearly grounded in refining awareness of the body in movement, in experiential anatomy, relation to gravity, integration. Yet how and what I teach is very influenced by the context I find myself in, by the people that I am teaching and what they have done before, and what they are wanting to be able to do as well as my reading of their bodies in movement.

Often I am teaching people who have trained in more formal techniques, and I can provide an opportunity for them to let some unnecessary muscular tension go, find more flow, become more aware, or give them a space for attention to their sensing and experience. So in that context I might also draw a little bit more on improvisation to open up choices. I am not saying one thing is right or another thing is wrong, but as dancers, we want to have choices available to us.

/ **How do you conceive the process of learning?**
I was aware, even as a child, there were some things I learned so much more through my dancing than I did at school, that some of the school education was about memorizing something and then repeating it, rather than about thinking or working something out. So I have been intrigued by how we learn, and have got interested in research and writing that explores the continuum between analytical and rational modes of thought, and thought that is more intuitive, indirect, or poetic. These verbal, scientific modes of processing information, as well as notions about objectivity and truth dominate in our society. So it feels to me our dancing–learning can open up this different state of attention and awareness to allow a different kind of learning to happen.

/ **What is most important for you in teaching your work?** More and more as a teacher, I am trying to create an environment that can facilitate learning. That is also about using different tools to encourage this state of openness, readiness. Using drawing or automatic writing or partner work, or making sound. So even if I am not dealing with improvisation, I am concerned with an improvisational mind. How can we be in a state of mind and body in readiness? To be open to new experience, to new sensation? The German word *stimmen* (to tune) feels useful in relation to how we work with our body, like tuning a stringed instrument.

What feels important to the learning, for me, is immersion over an intensive period because the information accumulates within the body. And it needs time for new information to first arrive in the body as sensation or awareness, and then to be applied and tested in practice, and then to allow another layer of information to come in, in relationship to this. To do really thorough partner work and swap over takes sometimes more than one hour—and then you want to put this into movement and practice. That is not to say that one then continually needs so long. Once the information has been embodied, then one can access it more quickly, more readily. But if it is only ever met superficially, then it is only going to be an idea in the head, not experiential knowledge thought through the body.

/ **How would you describe the relationship between teacher and student?** Working with dancers, I feel I am a co-researcher at one level. Of course that depends on the context that you are working in. Sometimes you are with fellow professionals, so you are just the

person that holds and frames the learning space. In this situation here, of course, it is very clear that I am the teacher. But I really feed off the dancers' questions, and their observations, and their curiosity. And I am constantly revisiting the information and learning myself. It is not as though I think I have found something finite and am trying to help other people find that as a truth. It is more like a question. It feels very important to me to continue to be a learner.

/ **Which skills do you need in teaching this work?**
It is quite a challenge, how to hold the energy in the room, or to sometimes let the structure become looser to allow individual exploration, which is really important even if I am not getting clear evidence of learning at every moment. But there are times when, as a group, you feel the energy disperses and one needs to re-harness it. I come with a sense of what I want to explore this day, but I have to be ready to change direction. Sometimes somebody's question might really lead somewhere interesting and be pertinent so you need to take a diversion. And sometimes there are so many questions that they would distract and un-focus the group's attention.

But then again, one has to trust the process. One day here, I allowed the partner work to take a little longer, we took one extra step with it, following a student question. I could predict this would take us to a deeper place, but would be harder to bring our energy back out from and into dancing. But the next day, I observed the embodiment and heard the sensory feedback from the dancers, and realized that the investment had been worthwhile in terms of the depth of learning.

Sometimes this kind of work can be perceived as lacking rigor, as more concerned with feeling good in ourselves, or about personal development rather than professional education. But there is a real progression, a clear developmental sense to the work, and a clear sense in which one piece of information builds on another. I might be working on spine and I might see something not clearly embodied in the relationship to the ground, but I have to know that we are not dealing with that now. In this moment I have to hold the attention on the spine and not clutter the information. There has to be a clarity to the journey, so that the body will be able to absorb, and if it is too 'noisy', too busy for the nervous system, it won't be taken in so well.

Thinking about the environment for learning has made me let go of more of the formality in terms of the time structures and phases of a class, and to believe that sometimes the learning is more effective if you leave space, some unstructured time, and opportunity for exploration. Of course it is important that you feel like you have achieved something in a session, and that can come through complex dancing, but also our job as teachers is to try and facilitate the learning, not only as evidenced in each day but over a longer time span. And sometimes one can allow students to stay with a little confusion and trust that over night—through sleeping and living and reflecting—something will begin to make sense rather than feel every class has to be a 'successful' unit gauged by having done a bit of everything and feeling satisfied like after a good meal.

/ **What does the term 'technique' mean for you?** Technique, in a way, is only some skills and tools that help somebody do what they want to do. We need to think about what we call technique as a means to an end. And the end, or the aim can be about the embodied understanding, which can then feed everything we do—making work and choreographing, but also performing. It is also really important to relate all of this inward attention out into space. Both through our seeing, but also through sensing the volume of our body. Making our body permeable, 'see-able'. Deborah Hay has a wonderful phrase: to invite being seen. So we make that information readable, otherwise it becomes more about personal development. Sometimes during the process of learning, our attention can go very inward, but our aim has to be to make the form and experience connect to a world.

/ **How do you prepare yourself before starting to teach?** I partly prepare by preparing my own mind and body; I could not walk in off the London street and be ready to teach. Because I am giving information or suggesting attention from my own embodying in the moment, it is like preparing oneself to perform or to improvise. I have to try and be in readiness. I have to access a connectedness of mind and body before I begin. And then, of course, I prepare in the sense of the theme of the day and the imagined sense of that progression, the stages, the language. But there might also be different alternatives, and which route we take will affect what we do the next day.

/ **When, would you say, a movement is accomplished?** Accomplishment, I would say, is when I see an intelligence at play in the body. When I see connection through a body and that a body has a sense of this whole system, this whole organism working in agreement. Working in relation to gravity, and to space. When it is open to be seen, when I feel that I see decisions being taken in the moment rather than a predetermined form being followed. In other words, when that concentration in the body can sit lightly enough for it to go in any direction at any moment and experience that moment—which, to me, is something about connectivity of the body, about how one part relates to another so I can move it this way as a whole, but at any moment be ready to redirect somewhere else.

/ **Where do you see the meaning and place for this work in the future?** As for the future, one of my ongoing questions now relates to teaching dance material, or even dancing dance material: What is the role of dancing in movement learning, and what is dancing? For example in this project, many of these dancers are more interested in making their own artistic work than dancing for other choreographers, so the way that they will use that embodied information is diverse. One aspect I have come to emphasize is the questioning of the information and the material, and the sensing of it as principles and puzzles to play with—and not as a movement vocabulary to replicate. Also, what has felt really important for me is that we take one day in the week that is a laboratory. I am there if I can be of use in any way, but the students spend time exploring, assimilating the information, or abstracting what is useful to them, applying it to what they are working on at the moment in their own dancing or their own practice, using my resource of books. So it is about reinforcing the notion that the work is only a means to an end, some tools for your curiosity and that end is what you are trying to do or investigate. It is not that I want to draw you to do what I am doing as a style or aesthetic. How to make that explicit in what I do, whilst retaining the rigor and particularity of my focus, feels an important question for me at the moment.

On a bigger scale I feel this work is vitally important because our society leads us more and more outside of the lived body; it leads us towards digital technology where what we need is a brain, where we don't act so much physically. And we no longer see wonderful metaphors in jointed, articulated machinery, we just press a button. And we are losing connection with our natural world. So for me, this work is vitally important in turning that intelligence back into our own system. And acknowledging it as a system, a system that is always in relationship, the internal to the external, to each other and the world, which feels to me an important tiny contribution in refinding a sustainable relationship with the world through acquaintance with ourselves. And in the twenty-first century, it feels like we have got to address individuality and complexity and systems and relationships rather than old notions of harmony and truth.

/ **What do you want to deliver to students?** What I want for students is to feed their curiosity as being the most important thing, in terms of their learning, in terms of being an artist, in terms of being in a learning situation and asking questions of it. And in terms of movement, I suppose, I would say something about tuning. Tuning the mind, the body, and the imagination as one thing, which is our instrument, our medium. And to go further with finding its possibilities, its information, its wisdom. And finally, that the learning goes on, that dancing is not isolated or separated from life. That the learning, and our movement, and our dancing in effect happens everywhere, at every moment.

Gill Clarke, Franz Anton Cramer, Gisela Müller

INTRODUCTION

When the Inter–University Center for Dance in Berlin (HZT)[1] was invited to conduct a research project on contemporary dance teaching methods, it was rather clear that Gill Clarke would be the person whose specific conversational approach to physical work should be at the center. She has taught within the Bachelor of Arts pilot project, she was involved in an extended research unit in preparation for HZT's set–up, and she has been an informal advisor to the BA program on several occasions.

The goal of the intended four–week research and analysis project was to reconsider certain aims of dance–artist education and the role of mindful movement practice and embodied learning within it. This was to be achieved through an in–depth investigation of Gill Clarke's teaching and the underlying assumptions, processes, questions, reflections. *Reflective practice* would be an important aspect, and theory and practice would not be seen as separate entities.

In preparing and discussing possible perspectives and directions to take in such an endeavour, in an email exchange with the HZT team, Gill Clarke wrote the following in response to the original proposition[2]:

/ "1. Although I'm not interested in making a pretence to teaching a fixed method which could be documented/represented, I think I left out my tacit assumption that the project would be grounded, as my own questioning is, in *my* practice. So rather than being an abstract research project into, for example, what is technique, this would actually be quite focused in and around, and out from, and into, our practice in the studio. That for me is not general or objective, but strongly, passionately value–laden, situated!!!

---

1 This project was launched in 2006 and aimed at developing new study programs in contemporary dance and choreography. Funded by Tanzplan Deutschland, an initiative of the German Cultural Foundation, and the Federal State of Berlin, one bachelor program and two master programs were successfully conducted in what was called the pilot phase, ending in March 2010. The programs have since continued on a regular basis.

2 'Before being able to establish or analyze a specific method of physical teaching, some basic questions need to be addressed. Such as: What is a technique? What is needed in order to facilitate learning? What can be learned, physically speaking? And what are the relevant bodies/agents, both physically and socially? In order to conduct this kind of research, dance and physical exploration would need to be observed from different an-

gles than just the aesthetic or 'dancerly' ones. The input/participation of e.g. a geographer (spatial/volume aspect), of an anthropologist (contextual setting), of social science would be necessary so as to enlarge the field of vision and exploration. [...] However, the investigation would always start from the concrete learning situation with students in a studio. This investigative process might then be the object of a video documentation

In fact that accumulation of experiences, dialogue, practice, experimentation, is what the approach is!

2. My immediate resistance to the notion of a 'method' was the notion of teaching as a 'thing' rather than a 'process'. So what does interest me is the teaching seen as a fluid and conversational process based on certain tenets and ideas around what might be valuable tools for, and attributes of a dance artist, but a process that aims to facilitate learning and enquiry, that is based on questioning, and evolves in constant adaptation to groups and individuals; to the histories written in their bodies, their curiosity, embodied understanding. Even as it has its own logical development of, for example, anatomical information, some of these assumptions for me might be around the integration of mental and physical, mindful body and embodied mind, the place for both perceptual and conceptual, intuitive and rational, relationship of internal and external environment.

2b. I would not claim to be able—or interested—to tackle 'contemporary physical learning practices' in general; but I can contribute to that debate certainly, and maybe with a strong desire to expand the frame so that 'physical' learning is not seen as separate from the artistic education, which is concerned with the creative and intellectual development as well, and sees dance within a wider social context.

3. Like other artists, I am of course modifying existing techniques/approaches—not claiming originality, but drawing from many perspectives; digesting; making my own shifting sense. All this in relation to ideas from outside dance as well as within / and not in relation to one codified technique or choreographer's methodology. However, the investigation would always start from the concrete learning situation with students in a studio.

demonstrating some basic approaches. […]
The overall aim of such a project would be
an in-depth investigation of contemporary
physical learning processes, possibilities and
fallacies, proposing a basis from which to
reconsider the question of technique, movement, and dance in an artistic and social
context. […].' (Draft 23rd November, 2008)

4. To contradict myself I suppose I would say my teaching is in a way a 'method'—in the sense it tries to be a rigorous, coherent, developmental approach (as well as deliberately chaotic or open sometimes!!!). But it is not wanting to be 'set', as in 'set content' or only one 'right' way to approach something, not least because it is aiming to open up available 'choices' in action/imagination."

While reading this chapter, it is important to keep in mind that the term *Minding Motion* is used as the title of a particular workshop offered in Berlin as part of the Tanzplan Research Project. It is retained here as convenient shorthand for Gill Clarke's pedagogical process within this context, but is not intended to imply a fixed system or closed method of teaching.

The term *body* is used in this chapter as shorthand for *body–mind*. It is not intended to imply a dualistic stance that, following Descartes, sees the body as separate from mind, and mind as the sole source of meaning–making.[3] The limitations in language reflect the powerful influence of this separation of body from selfhood. German fares better than English in having the term *Leib,* which implies a lived body, but as this is not in current and common usage, it has not been adopted here.

The research project on Minding Motion was realized during the summer term of 2009 in Berlin, using the Uferstudio space. The working periods were from May 4–8, June 1–12, and July 13–19, 2009.

The group was composed of students from the Berlin Inter–University Center for Dance's bachelor's course Contemporary Dance, Context, Choreography, along with external participants from the dance scene, comprising altogether a group of ten. The condition for participation was full commitment to all of the three research units. Ongoing feedback was received in

3 'On the one hand I have a clear and distinct idea of myself, in so far as I am simply a thinking, non-extended thing; on the other hand I have a distinct idea of body in so far as this is simply an extended, non-thinking thing. And accordingly it is certain that I am really distinct from my body, and can exist without it.' (Descartes, 1984, p. 54)

written form and also through dialogue. Material from these sessions is included here (noted as: Group comment). Whilst Gisela Müller was actively participating in the workshop sessions, Franz Anton Cramer was an outside observer during most of the afternoon sessions (held from 1–5 p.m.).

After the group had discussed the research questions as presented by Tanzplan, and then summed up the discussion in written form, the writing team approached the assignment in three phases: analysis of coherence between the questionnaire and Minding Motion practice; rough answers to questions; free conceptual writing around the major topics. Only in the last editing phase did the team arrange the material so as to make it fit smoothly to the outline of the research questions.

Audiovisual documentation has been realized by British filmmaker Becky Edmunds and Lucy Cash (additional camera work) as well as by Berlin–based video documenter Andrea Keiz, who was responsible for capturing and delivering the DVD material contained in this book.

Gill Clarke, Franz Anton Cramer, Gisela Müller

HISTORICAL CONTEXT

TIME, PLACE, AND SOCIO-POLITICAL CONTEXT

As explained with more detail in the interview with Gill Clarke by Edith Boxberger, the emergence of Minding Motion is closely linked to the experiences gained by Gill Clarke in various dance and movement contexts.

Especially since the 1960s, the process of diversification within modern and contemporary dance styles and the introduction of somatic research into individual performance practices has been an ongoing concern. Closely linked to what is conveniently called the Judson Dance Theater, a reconsideration of dance's essential elements and manifestations prevailed over and above specific technical or aesthetic goals. It was especially important to overcome the hierarchies between artistic and pedestrian movement so that everyday gestures and movement should and could become part of performance work. The gap between highly trained dancers and movement experts and physically less–abled audiences was considered obsolete for contemporary art practice. Therefore, appreciating physical and corporeal experience and the physical abilities of *any* body was seen as a needed artistic position in opposition to the elitist world of dance. Body experience should be accessible to anyone via research into non-specialised, organic, and individualized movement approaches. To achieve this, research was conducted to find a more functional understanding of the body's various subsystems (such as skeletal structure, muscular system, fluid systems), with the goal of finding a more integrative approach to sourcing movement material.

The body's cultural, social, and physical conditioning was to be explored, critiqued, and ultimately shaped, thereby assigning to dance and dance–related practices a more political role. The vision of what a dancer might or should be and do changed considerably.[1] What should be changed in relation to traditional dance teaching methods was to promote the idea of working *with* the body rather than *against* it. Generating new movement material should come from within, and the process of creating be rooted in the functionality of the body rather than on some aesthetic determination, as in ballet.

BACKGROUND: BIOGRAPHIES AND ENVIRONMENT

A pedagogical approach does not exist in isolation from a dance ecology; it is situated within it, and develops a complementary role within that aesthetic and educational landscape. So whilst the Minding Motion approach has developed as an integral part of Gill Clarke's artistic practice, driven by its questions and interests, it has also evolved in response to the strengths of existing practices. In relation to these other practices what might be aspects of movement that have received less attention?

On the micro-level, for example, her teaching is influenced by perceptions of what appears to be obstructing the free flow of movement through a particular dancer's body. Sometimes this is highly individual, but at other times there appear to be qualities of movement or choices in body organisation that are less available to an entire group of dancers—almost like blind spots in the dancers' mental map of the body.

Such observations accumulate through the process of teaching and are in dialogue with Gill Clarke's existing pedagogical aims. Over time they both influence the direction of the teaching and the emergence of certain characteristics, or primary tools.

An example can illustrate how Gill Clarke's own learning, combined with such observations, have led to particular emphases that have emerged within the Minding Motion process. The study of Alexander and Klein Techniques significantly altered Clarke's own movement organization through a newly experienced awareness of the connectivity of head, spine, and pelvis.[2] These approaches offered a new integrated strength through the directionality of the torso in space, a greater freedom of the torso from the legs, a long axis of support for limbs, and a new organizing system for whole body movement.

Some highly trained dancers retain a habit, (either through overdeveloped strength of abdominals, or conversely, through underdeveloped integration of upper to lower torso), that too easily defaults to a bending or shortening at the waist that can then serve as a perceived location for the articulation between legs and torso. As a result, the legs do not connect deeply through hip sockets and psoas, the back extensors do not support connection of the ribs through to the pelvis, the torso is restricted in its freedom of range of movement around the top of the thigh bones, and the head and neck can become dissociated from the back and pelvis.[3]

---

1 This wide and fundamental change within dance history cannot be recounted here in detail. For further information see for instance Jill Johnston: *Reinventing Dance in the 1960s. Everything was Possible.* Madison: University of Wisconsin Press, 2003.

2 We refer here to a term used in Alexander Technique: "the characteristic way the person uses himself [sic] in everything he does [...]. The term 'use' covers the total pattern that characterizes a person's response to stimuli." (Pierce–Jones, 1979, p. 46)

3 Support for this can be found in the various series of programs at Tanzquartier Wien (which includes "Inventur" 2004; „After the Act" 2005). Also in the exhibition "Move. Choreographing You" in the Hayward Gallery in London (2010–2011). Also see: Barbara Büscher / Franz Anton Cramer: „Beweglicher

From observations of such body 'use'[2], Gill Clarke's teaching began to pay more and more attention to the length and connectivity of the spine, and to a balance of front and back support of torso and pelvis. This is not advocating a specific, held posture of the torso or spine, but is, rather, about dynamic directionality into space, for example through skull and sit bones (ischia). Sequences of movement and partner–work explorations have been developed to support the sensing and reinforcement of these ideas. This focus can lead to a long torso being more characteristic than a significantly curved one in earlier phases of a class, and could be perceived as a stylistic feature.

It is therefore important within the more complex movement sequences and *puzzles* to inject curves and spiralling movements as contrast to this coordination, so as to reinforce that this focus of attention is not intended to promote an 'only' or 'right' way of moving, but to help balance out and open up the choices available to the body in organizing itself in response to intention and gravity.

Thus, although being an assimilation of many influences, Gill Clarke's physical practice has developed over time to include particular emphases, from which particular movement forms, tools, languaging, images, and partner–work explorations have originated that specifically facilitate experiential learning of principles and ideas that are central to her thinking.

The genealogy and interview give more precise information on the individuals who have been important in her process of learning and devising.

RELATION TO OTHER ART FORMS

As the development of physical practice in the framework of contemporary performance has become a field quite of its own (fully acknowledged in its historic dimension only recently[3]), the immediate connections to other fields of artistic practice (film, theatre, painting…) seem less relevant. On the contrary, whereas visual art throughout most of its evolution seems to have aimed at objectifying the body and its image, there now seems a tendency to introduce the more fleeting aspects of live presence, as can be exemplified by the work of Tino Sehgal[4], among others. In the context of this 'somatic shift', perceptual and exploratory aspects are introduced to film, exhibition, and presentation. But it should be kept in mind that since the early days of experimental somatic and choreographic practices, the collaboration with musicians, visual artists, and filmmakers has been key.[5]

Today seems to be a particularly important time, a transitional phase during which somatic practice converges and configures with performance practice. In order to use physical research as an artistic approach, the whole needs to be greater than the parts that build it. So while there is a long history of perceptual work within body–work, enmeshing concerns of 'new' compositional and choreographic ways with individualized body practice is still a relatively recent phenomenon. Minding Motion is closely linked to this integrative, non-exclusive idea of 'physical enablement'. This influence should be understood as more political than aesthetic.

RELEVANT THEORETICAL DISCOURSES

With dance as a performance practice no longer confined to narrative structures or expressionistic tableaux, the emergence of individualized approaches to body–work and physical shaping has led to new fields of research. This movement research has happened parallel to a differentiation of various art forms and artistic media in the post–World War II era, and one might consider these developments in dance as linked to those in other art forms, equally concerned with liberating themselves from certain constraints (economic, aesthetic, technical…). However, the emergence of Minding Motion is directly linked to the professional and pedagogical *parcours* of Gill Clarke, its founder and originator within the field of dance, as well as influenced by cultural shifts and her encounters with current thinking in disciplines within and beyond the arts. The reading list at the end of this chapter gives more information.

CURRENT PRACTICE

Minding Motion can be applied in various ways both by dance companies and independent dancers. Individual choreographers desiring to work with their dancers as creative collaborators rather then obedient interpreters have found its individual and exploratory approach relevant to their practice.

Zugang". In: Tanzplan Deutschland (Ed.): *Tanz und Archive. Perspektiven für ein kulturelles Erbe.* Tanzplan Deutschland Jahresheft 2009. Berlin: 2009, pp. 22–25.

4 Tino Sehgal is a visual artist based in London and Berlin. After an education in dance and artistic work as a choreographer and performer, his work of the last several years has explored the possibilities of live presence within the museum and exhibition landscape.

5 Refer to the performance series "Nine Evenings. Experiments in Art and Technology", 1966, and "Events" by Merce Cunningham in collaboration with John Cage and Robert Rauschenberg, as well as to Anna Halprin's performance work.

Companies dedicated to a specific style and aesthetics may draw on Minding Motion as an 'antidote' for dancers' fatigue after long periods of rehearsal and/or performing, as well as offering the dancers further resources to draw upon within the creative process.

The most widespread use made of Minding Motion is, however, as a resource for performance and choreography that fosters the imagination and embodied knowledge of dancers, and relishes difference and mindful attention. For a dancer, a better understanding of one's creative medium, (one's own body), enriches the generation of movement material, whether making one's own work or collaborating with a choreographer.

Minding Motion, like similar approaches, has been widely adopted by dance artists who are looking to develop and sustain their own movement practice both in and outside the studio, as it constitutes a way of organizing the body, of living in it and thinking through it, so that the learning can happen everywhere.

INDIVIDUAL APPROACH

Gill's approach could be considered hybrid in that it has been informed by her encounters with different approaches and artistic practices, each of which has been experienced through intensive immersion, and then assimilated alongside her ongoing creative, performative, and teaching practices. Hybrid, however, can imply a conscious piecing together of incongruous elements, whereas the teaching practice described here should be considered much more as an organic whole that has evolved intuitively, as spoken language does, through years of daily usage in the studio.

The movement language that a dancer's body speaks changes continuously, more by an unconscious process of response to each new experience and filtering this through subsequent actions than by consciously adopting new movement modalities.[6] In this way the body speaks a shifting movement language by filtering new experiences and experiments in action, more than through consciously imposing upon it new movement modalities or explicit knowledge.

RELATION TO OTHER DANCE AND MOVEMENT TECHNIQUES

Within the development of somatic dance practices, Gill perhaps sits on a cusp. She is just of a generation of dancers whose curiosity about somatic approaches to movement necessarily led them to original sources in various techniques outside of dance. For the current generation, however, much of this information has become embedded and integrated within dance practice and training, and informs dance performance. One can question what is lost or potentially homogenised through such syntheses, yet the incorporation of new information into current practice is a natural process and potentially frees dance practitioners to apply their energies and curiosity in new directions.

Minding Motion is not viewed as therapeutic in scope, even though its development has been informed by approaches to movement that have evolved and been researched within a therapeutic context. Movement practitioners who work therapeutically seek to help people towards optimum functioning. It is logical that dancers who specialise in developing optimum functionality as a creative and professional resource should appropriate relevant knowledge, research, and methodologies wherever they find them. Whilst there is an important pedagogical aspect to Minding Motion that offers tools to develop and sustain psychophysical readiness, its primary aim is to tune the body–mind as a resource for creative and performance practice.

6 See Noë, 2009; de Certeau, 1984.

Gill Clarke, Franz Anton Cramer, Gisela Müller

CONCEPT AND IDEOLOGY

IMAGING THE BODY

∕ "The body has acquired, through and for this explorative work, the status of a 'laboratory' of sorts. The body is considered a realm of possibilities that are being explored, combined, and (if possible) integrated into a movement form that claims to work with the individual body rather than against it." *group comment*∕

Minding Motion work is based upon the notion of the dancer as an investigative artist whose creative medium is their own moving, sensing, thinking 'self'. The work, therefore, does not aim to transmit notions of right and wrong ways to move or 'look', but rather to support a dancer's embodied understanding and awareness of their own movement. Through processes of attention and discrimination, it seeks to open up the choices available to the individual dancer in how they organize themselves—whether this be in response to their own conscious intention/direction, or in the movement they allow to arise spontaneously.

In this sense, there is a political element to the Minding Motion work because it aims to support the self-determination of dancers and dance-makers. It views dancers as experts in movement who bring their embodied knowledge and imagination to actively collaborate in the creative process, and who then act as agents in the communication of the work through performance. It also sees dance-makers as autonomous investigative artists/movement researchers who will devise their own ways of working and new movement forms.

The approach builds on a framework of embodied study of the dynamic, articulating skeleton, yet its focus is neither biomechanical nor aimed at an abstract knowledge of anatomy for its own sake. Instead, through the skeletal/anatomical/structural lens, a multidimensional view of volume, integration, and energy is introduced and emphasized. This perspective is reinforced by an appreciation of dancing as a play with gravity, through a process of continual, tiny adaptations and more conscious decision-making.

The skeletal structure is seen as deep support, yet the bones are also seen as spacers within the body system giving direction into space, with the limbs easefully articulating in generous arcs around oiled joints. Compression support through the skeletal structure to the ground is explored, but so too is tensegrity[7] and the support that comes from a multiplicity of directions, i.e., down through the ground and out into three-dimensional space. In this way, a balance of attention and an interconnectedness is emphasized between concepts that could appear to be in opposition: between groundedness and lightness (a sense of a downward force and a suspension in the field of gravity), between the settling of limbs deep through the hip and shoulder joints towards the central support of the spine and their clear reaching out into space.

The articulated skeleton provides a structured framework for Minding Motion's exploratory journey through the moving body. Yet whilst consideration of particular aspects of the skeleton might remain the explicit vehicle or entry point for visualizations and explorations, other layers of information are more subtly introduced. These include attention to a felt sense of volume or expansiveness in movement through internal support offered by organ and connective tissue tone, and to the three-dimensional sequencing supported by fascial layers that connect superficial and deeper layers to closer and more distant locations in the body.[8] This latter quality is often referred to within the work as a process of 'ungluing', of teasing apart layers that have become stuck together.

All individuals develop movement habits that become the unconscious default mode in patterning daily movement and dancing, otherwise no action would become automatic and there would not be enough brain capacity to keep developing new and more complex skills. Dancers often think, however, that what restricts their range of movement is a physical limitation and that this is what they must overcome. Yet it can be the mental image of the body that constrains movement choices. This could be, for example, through a misplaced image about where the hip sockets are located, or a pattern of use resulting from compensation following an injury that then becomes habitual, or from general poor use repeated over time until it comes to feel normal. If one can visualize an action differently and thereby direct a different intention through the body, then the body will, in its complexity, organize itself more effectively and produce the intended result more efficiently than if an effort is made to consciously control the detail of its activation.[9]

7 Tensegrity is composed of the two terms *tensile* and *integrity*. 'It refers to structures that maintain their integrity due primarily to a balance of continuous tensile forces through the structure.' (See Myers, 2001)

8 See Juhan, 2003.
9 This approach is based on ideokinesis, a key practice for somatic research.

10 'Whenever I quiet the persistent chatter of words within my head, I find this silent or wordless dance always already going on.' (Abrams, 1997, p. 53; see also Lefebvre, 2004)

There is no particular gender aspect in Minding Motion.

The relation to aspects of space is manifold and crucial in Gill Clarke's work. While in a general sense Minding Motion is about inhabiting space in relation to a shifting plumb line and multidirectionality, there are important particularities in how it animates what can be called the internal and the external space as a framework for movement realisation.

This movement exploration, even and especially in the hands–on work described in later chapters, places a real emphasis on the internal space without, however, letting this become isolated from the relationship to external space. Minding Motion retains an emphasis on the performance aspect—which is always hovering in the studio like a shadow—through attention to seeing and being seen. An important aspect of the work therefore is to establish a visual and perceptual relationship between the internal experiential space and the outward kinetic space.

The concept of volume supports a connecting of movement sensed from the inside to the outward shape that inhabits external space.

Addressing volume implies identifying the various connections and spaces between spine and skull, spine and shoulder girdle, spine and pelvis, spine and rib cage, between the bowl of the pelvis and the dome of the diaphragm, and also between the skull and the rib cage, the arches of the feet and the organisation of the pelvis, etc. These volumes and spaces are evoked, physically explored, and made conscious by various sensing methods such as hands–on work, partnering, visualization, and breath.

Whereas movement focused on line and shape is seen as activating external space, the movement flow created by the volumetric approach creates a different quality. This quality can be identified as 'sensed': The space that the movement inhabits expands through the individual patterns/reactions that emerge from the activation of inner volumes. Sensing and sensed–volume work together to give movement a certain truthfulness and freedom.

The attention to the expansion of inner volume enables dancers to extend their image of the body beyond the aspect of contour to the sensory realization of movement. This is enhanced or indeed, even made possible, by the foundation of such movement in visualized and embodied anatomical understanding. However, the forms of this movement will remain within a certain range governed by the reality of anatomical conditions—it is applied anatomy, so to speak.

Minding Motion embraces sonorous and musical elements such as timing, rhythm, breath, and voice/language. In that sense, musicality is always present, even though not often explicitly emphasized. Music is not used as an accompaniment, rather, the need to modulate timing or quality at any moment, in a way, excludes the use of music as it would inject too much of a fixed and regular structure. Gill Clarke's use of voice has therefore become the most important means to structure and modulate temporal and energetic/rhythmical delivery.

An enjoyment of rhythm and phrasing underlie Gill Clarke's own movement and movement–making, with dance seen as the animation of, or play with gravity, that arises from moving subtly in and out of balance.[10] These elements of timing and phrasing are manifested by the attention that is drawn to the breath in earlier phases of a class, through Gill's use of voice, and by her adoption and encouragement of irregular, syncopated, playful timing within the more complex sequences.

For this reason, musical accompaniment for these sequences is frequently asymmetrical in timing or polyphonic, either contemporary classical, experimental

genres, or traditional folk music from around the world—all of which offer many layers with which the movement can be in dialogue. Even though driven by an attention to the theme of the day, more complex movement material is usually devised whilst listening to a particular piece of music. This is not to nail down the timing but to provoke a particular rhythmic quality or provide a sound field from which the movement can emerge. The choice of music is one way of trying to ensure that the movement sequence is not a dry technical exercise to be accurately memorized and executed but rather a movement puzzle to be explored, and a dancing experience, with a particular quality, to engage with as a performer.

INTENT

There is no recognizable aesthetic fostered by Minding Motion. There are, however, certain visual and qualitative elements that can be considered helpful in identifying basic principles within the work analyzed here. Some of these qualities are easefulness, efficiency, and individuality. During feedback discussions with students, the question of aesthetics was considered at length. An interesting remark brought forth the idea of a hidden aesthetics, one that works by taking the side entrance, so to speak. Even in exploratory and experimental situations as employed by Minding Motion, there is still a concept of integrative movement that would seek to be embodied during the process of learning.

In general, Minding Motion is not about imposing an aesthetic of choreography and performance, but about feeding the embodied knowledge one has as a maker/performer so as to offer a range of possibilities in the quality and dynamics of a movement, rather than favoring a particular style or form. The question is: What can be produced with this knowledge, beyond specific aesthetic concerns? And what originates from within our own organism rather than from a visual image, an exterior perception? This would differ from teaching methods and technical set–ups that aim to realize and manifest certain styles (i.e., Vaganova, Cunningham, Forsythe). In other words, the choices arrive from the inside, from 'in–sight', and not from a form–driven focus replicating a specific style.

The element of flow marks a physical 'aim' or underlying concern within Minding Motion; the focus on un-gluing different layers of the body, so that movement can sequence through it, seeks to expand and inform greater choice. Therefore, rather then presenting fragmented visions of movement, the approach is concerned with integrating the different layers and aspects of the moving body in motion.

A recurring term for a special quality of movement in Minding Motion is *easefulness*. This designates a body organization that is more concerned with a particular way of generating movement rather than producing certain shapes.

Tools to better understand and incorporate this notion of easeful movement are anatomical visualisation and a heightened consciousness of the movement scope, i.e., the movement's dimension, its articulatory radius, its anatomical origin and support. For instance, the spine is experienced as a whole, as a part of the skeleton that essentially connects various parts of the body (hips, shoulder girdle,

ribs, pelvis, neck, head...). At the same time, it is flexible in itself, and can serve as an awareness tool to make clear both 'total' and 'particular' movement—as in the rolling up and over of the torso, going down on hands and knees, then moving slightly forward and backward. This general movement is initiated and supported by the spine, but also heightens awareness of the interconnectedness, the 'totality' of a movement and the effects on other parts and regions of the body. To give a clearer sensation of this wholeness, this movement is sometimes assisted by a partner. By exerting slight resistance to the forward movement, the repercussions of an effort made by the pelvis can be felt and sensed in the neck and the upper head. Central to this exploratory approach is the complexity of the movement phenomenon, always embedded, as it were, in a kinetic *parcours* defined less by a desired form, and more by the organic coordination and pathway of the movement.

This focus on easefulness and internally initiated movement is not primarily about 'loose bodies' or 'de-contracted bodies'. Easefulness needs to be explored, developed, and permitted. The focus therefore is on progressing through given forms or propositions (including certain dancerly moves, certain energetic impediments, certain distractions from the *parcours* as are generated by space, weight, impulses, etc.).

With Minding Motion, Gill proposes movement research that, among other things, also calls for an easeful efficiency of movement—without giving up control or consciousness of the movement itself. Even swinging should not be conceived of as something that generates eternal flow. Disruptive movement patterns, disruptions in the flow of movement, seem to occur all by and of themselves. The ideal way of moving easefully, then, might be identified not so much by exploring a certain way of generating or originating movement, rather it is about exploring ways to *not* obstruct the flow.

As has been explained in previous chapters, the Minding Motion approach concerns itself with a range of dance and movement practices, from visions of physical self–determination to the exploration of possibilities and individual scope of movement, to nonstandard performance making. However, this largely processual, nonconformist approach to practice is always closely linked to the notion of performance, to allowing the perceptual behaviour—moment by moment—to be visible/readable.

One of the key attributes of Gill Clarkes approach is how the body, as a system, is organizing and adapting itself in relation to gravity: an integration of the central

11 *Perceptual learning* as a progressive differentiation, perceivers becoming increasingly sensitive to distinctions within the stimulus information that were always there but previously undetected. (See Eric Clarke, 2005)

12 Feldenkrais, 1985, p. 20.

volumes of the body, whilst upright, around an imaginary plumb line, or midline; the simplicity with which the force of gravity falls through the structure of the body (the compression force), and the receiving of support and suspension back up and out from the ground through the voluminous spaces, extending through the body structures and into space (the tensile support); the readiness of these volumes and layers to constantly adjust to gravity in movement as the body flows between momentary balance and imbalance.

Closely allied to an adaptability to gravity is the degree to which the whole body is responsive to a movement that is initiated from one location within it. This is reliant upon the elasticity of the fascia to support a sliding sequencing of movement, or to facilitate a simple simultaneous agreement by the integrated system so it might be directed as a whole.

Within the Minding Motion work, this responsiveness is often referred to as *agreement*, and implies a readiness to allow movement to sequence through the body rather than pre-empting this by external shaping or holding of isolated parts. What might be obstructing this agreement is a habitual, muscular holding pattern around a joint, or a chronic imbalance between extensors and flexors, or a gluing and lack of elasticity in the connective tissue. The anatomical details underlying such elements do not constitute explicit content within the work so much as they emerge as indirect results of the close attention to breath, to experiencing and directing movement as it is in progress, and working through metaphor and imagination.

"It is never about right or wrong, it is more about exploring. And the interesting thing about it are the many options you have. This differentiates this training from other practices."

Ante Ursić, student

Another clear feedback indicator that principles of the approach have been embodied is the degree to which there is a free and generous range of articulation of limbs around their joints: a structural efficiency that minimizes unnecessary tension, aids connectivity, and thereby releases energy for expansion of movement into space.

This sense of efficiency can be misinterpreted as a desire to impose a certain neutral look on the moving body, or as reflecting a mechanical approach to movement. Rather, with Minding Motion, the emphasis is on minimizing the obstructions or unintended cluttering of movement including the unconscious, parasitic aspects, or so–called sensory noise burdening the nervous system. This un-cluttering is a process that usually works through a refining of attention,

a sharpening of perception and discrimination rather than through physical imitation.[11]

It is a process of paring away what is not needed. Yet, paradoxically this process can clear the way for an augmented range of possibilities and degree of control in directing or experiencing movement. "Most of the time we fail to achieve what we want by enacting more than we are aware of, rather than by missing what is essential."[12]

This, then, is a process not intending to 'neutralize' movement in the sense of erasing difference or individuality, but seeking rather to allow the individual to emerge from beneath the layers of unconscious muscular habit. In fact, a very clear indicator of progress in the work would be a shift from generalization in movement and towards a greater individual particularity, which emerges through close attention to one's own process in the present moment of moving.

If the movement sequence is not to be reproduced in order to make it look identical (as would be the traditional understanding in certain dance techniques), there are, however, certain elements that come into play in Minding Motion. For instance, the application of experiential content to the movement makes for its special quality that will become visible, for instance in the presence of the performer. The *Wiedererkennung*, the recognition, is less about formal aspects of a gesture or step, but about the inherent quality and concentration. In this way there would be a distinction, but often also an intertwining of 'neutral body' and 'personalized body', a body that adapts itself to a certain movement pattern/technique/quality, and a body that 'embodies itself' as it were—a body that has its own, personal shape.

Part of this personalization is the ability to relax those muscles that are not immediately in use. The physical tonus seems to be less defined by a constant activation of certain muscular groups, rather more by an articulation of using and resting. In this sense, there might even be a technical ideal: being clear, easeful and 'light' in doing integrated movements.

If the aim of movement exploration within an artistic education program is to generate movement that is not necessarily dance–like but somatically induced (as an infant's might be, or an animal's), then the intention of movement would not go towards shape (and form–related aesthetics) but towards the unfolding (i.e., realising the inherent potential of the body for movement).

This dialectical link between 'aesthetic' and 'inherent' creates new possibilities for the interaction and combination of the visual and perceptual. While unfolding the potential movement within a context of artistic strategies of composition and temporality, Gill Clarke's Minding Motion approach constitutes—or offers, suggests—an individualized means of finding form. The way in which the possibilities for interaction between construction and inhabiting of forms are combined, suggested, and enabled, is the core of the method.

Gill Clarke, Franz Anton Cramer, Gisela Müller

UNDERSTANDING THE BODY/MOVEMENT

PREREQUISITES

/ "Maybe any kind of previous experience with somatic practice and a sensibility for what it means to change patterns or habits is useful. But basically, there is no single definition of what might enhance the learning effect. On the contrary, it seems rather obvious that even beginners can enter this exploratory process (maybe they would be less able to integrate it in their own practice)." *group comment*/

Minding Motion can be practiced both by professional dancers, dance and movement students, and by amateurs. There are no particular physical skills required before embarking on this work. Nonetheless, Minding Motion will most often support dancers/performers in finding and re-

More than a physical disposition, participants should bring a mental disposition that will encourage immersion in an exploratory process through which one can discover and learn. This includes a willingness to sustain attention on one activity rather than shift restlessly from one to the next, and to allow time for digestion and incorporation of experience. The learning process is facilitated by the individual dancer focusing their energy on the present moment and developing mental stamina to sustain attention to the details of their movement. A readiness to switch/flip/swap between different phases of work and states of attention, and maybe even from performance to studying, is equally important. All of these elements add up to a disposition that understands learning as a state of playfulness (albeit serious in scope), and allows for an appreciation of process as well as result.

The balancing act in the teaching process is often made more delicate because of the varied backgrounds and experiences of the students. Some dancers will be well attuned to diving into the playful and nonjudgemental mindset necessary to learn through experience, and may find the questioning, or testing of alternatives less familiar territory; others will find it harder to open up their mental focus beyond the rational, analytical, or physical, and to experience their movement sensorially.[13]

fining their own practice and physical discipline. The work can also be a source for improvisation and for the generation of movement material that can be integrated into choreographic practice.

However, a recurrent element called *talking–through* complements personal sensing and discovery of movement qualities with a reflective approach. Differential qualities are suggested, never imposed. Each individual directs their

---

13 See Claxton, 1997 on the role of different modes of thought in learning.
14 Forsythe, 2003.
15 Comparison to spatial concepts can be found in: Concept and Ideology, *Imagining the Body*, keyword 'Space'.

16 For more detail, see Teaching: Principles and Methodology later in this chapter.
17 See also Pallasmaa, 2005.

own movement in response to the ongoing verbal input, the aim being to maximize the awareness upon which these movement choices are made. The use of language to facilitate rather than instruct movement reflects the differences in intention between 'technical' and 'sensed', or between 'training' and 'release work'. In this sense, Minding Motion is language–driven, but sense–led.

Other working methods that have influenced the development of Minding Motion can, of course, be fruitful as complementary experience, such as Alexander Technique or Ideokinesis.

The choice to work with, rather than against, the structure of the body is an inherent part of the Minding Motion learning process. In this sense it could be said to resource the dancer in preventing injury.

MOVEMENT CHARACTERISTICS
AND PHYSICALITY

⁄ "A major focus is on the spine and its large 'architectonic' function. Also, the point of entry is skeletal (as opposed, for instance, to BMC with its focus on fluid systems), that is to say the bone structure and its links to the muscular system are the focus. There seems to be an accumulative aspect of experience, a 'growing scope' of movement values and coordinations. While an important part of Minding Motion is sequential, the aspect of being in each movement with all of the care and attention developed in earlier phases of the process remains central. This has to do with the key terms and concepts of easefulness and low effort. *Krafteinsatz* (applying strength) is not aimed at." *group comment*⁄

Areas of the body, or aspects of body function are seen as differentiated anatomical units of exploration in Minding Motion sessions. However, the aim is not to consider these elements of the body as fragmented, rather to sense them as integrated. It is important to state that compared to, for example, William Forsythe's Improvisation Technologies[14] and the spatio-visual explicitness fostered in it, the Minding Motion approach is not effect–driven, nor is it segregative. It aims to develop an awareness of the dancer's physiological and anatomical structure that will be the basis of movement generation and understanding.

The body is always considered holistically, both in relation to its various regions and its layers and volumes. When certain elements are isolated in order to be studied in depth, they are always considered in relationship to the whole, never as an independent part. Thus the analytical separation of corporeal elements does not insist on immobility of the parts not concerned. However, on the level of the nervous system, the neuronal messages directing movement can be more effectively clarified when attention is focused for a while on one particular aspect of movement.

The different aspects of the work can be seen as helping the body chart a road map upon which to travel. Within this territory, various qualities and their origins (elasticity, swiftness, power, strength, eruption, force…) can be identified and described/visualized.

The work does not explicitly articulate an approach to building strength and muscle tone. Nevertheless, the practice encourages and nurtures a rebalancing of tonic muscle tone through its attention to efficiency in relation to gravity; it fosters an active dialogue between the ground and directing the oiled, articulating skeleton in space. In this way, attention is paid to balancing extensors and flexors, to re-enlivening an elasticity throughout the body. The muscular qualities prioritized in Minding Motion are sustaining rather then explosive, and strongly linked to gravity. A specific notion of strength can come from clarity of direction and connectedness through the body, rather than holding by small/isolated muscle groups. The notion is about working with the grain of the bony and fascial form and function of the body rather than forcing or countering it: to increase its range, its integrity, and to release it into expansion. An easeful interrelationship, for example, of the volumes of skull, rib cage, and pelvis will relieve excess and superficial muscular holding through the torso, and activate deep integration and support.

⁄ "It seems that there is a vision of 'multi-centeredness', of organising principles that can differ: They are more implicit centers, movement centres that are not made explicit. At the same time, the various notions of the 'domes' (skull, diaphragm, pelvis, feet arc) can serve, in specific sections or periods of the work, as such centres of attention, of dynamics, and of articulation, including breath. So the plumb line that can and does always shift and change according to the positioning of the body as a whole in space redefines and redistributes the 'centeredness' of the work. It is integral in deploying the inner volumes into the space[15] and in shaping the body in doing so. The points of attention that are called upon during the Minding Motion sessions articulate, as it were, the shifting centres, both spatially and internally." *group comment*[16]⁄

Different qualities of seeing are explored and utilized during various phases of the work. While doing sensing, partner–work tasks, and through initial elements of the 'shared familiar form' phase, closed eyes are an option that might aid the attention to other perceptual systems—in part through stemming the incessant flow of visual stimuli. The closing of eyes, by suppressing the habitual, sharply focused vision, can paradoxically expand both peripheral vision and perceptual attention.[17]

Progress in the discovery of movement potential is distinguished and gauged by paradigms other than the 'right' shape or the 'true' energy flow. The idea is to be non-normative, without implying that there is no rigor of intention or differentiation within achievement. This discernment of intention gives rise to certain visible criteria such as efficiency, easefulness, expansiveness etc., which, in contrast with the above–mentioned criteria ('right', 'true'), might also be inclusive terms—even though they imply that forceful, crisp/tight, or over–energized would be less desirable features of a movement execution.

It is clear from the findings presented thus far that gravity plays a crucial role within Gill Clarke's Minding Motion. In fact, gravity is a cognitive tool. Via the different aspects of volume, plumb line and relational forces, the element of gravity helps the dancer to define and understand organizational principles both with the skeletal system (relationship of limbs and torso to spine, three–dimensional connectivity) and the outward dynamics. While in other methods gravity is often seen as an oppositional force that needs to be overcome or given in to completely, Minding Motion embraces gravity so as to gather energy from it, instead of resisting it. Indeed, this ecological approach to the expending and harnessing of energy pervades Minding Motion.

As identified, basic movement principles in Minding Motion have developed from anatomical foundations, and any basic movement forms exist as vehicles for this experiential, anatomical exploration rather than as aesthetically valued forms in their own right. Inner and individual rhythm is emphasized and can come into conversation with outer rhythm in dancing the movement 'puzzles'.[18]

18 See the following chapter "Teaching: Principles and Methodology", Conceptual Basis.

Gill Clarke, Franz Anton Cramer, Gisela Müller

TEACHING: PRINCIPLES AND METHODOLOGY

CONCEPTUAL BASIS

The primary goal of the teaching is to facilitate an active process of mindful and embodied learning so as to support the individual dancer's enhanced awareness, discernment, and discrimination within their own consciously directed and spontaneous movement, and thereby to open up the possibilities available to them. Another aim is to help the student refine their perception and hone their attention to the extent that they can become their own proprioceptive feedback mechanism[19]—become their own teacher, as it were—so that their learning can become self–generating.

The core of the work, then, is immersion in the momentof perceptual experience while moving. The mindful body moving in space, alone or with others, is the laboratory within which observations arise and ideas and images are played out and tested, inside which the knowledge *of* movement rather than *about* movement is prioritized.

Yet around this core are layers of reflective and discursive activity intended to facilitate an experiential flow between internal and external attention, implicit and explicit knowledge, intuitive and rational states, perceptual and conceptual thought.

In more specific terms, the emphasis has shifted from one in which the work was seen as contributing to the training of a dancer to become one embracing a concern to contribute to an artistic education. In this sense technique is not conceived of as a defined movement content or vocabulary—it is not a thing to be transmitted, replicated, and performed with accomplishment as an end in itself, nor does it offer a fixed system to achieve this end. Rather, it is a process that continually evolves in relation to Gill Clarke's own research and practice. It adapts in conversation with any particular group of individuals in a specific context, guided by students' curiosity, their reflections upon their experience and Clarke's own observations of what might further facilitate learning.

The tenets that demand a flexible and nonlinear learning experience, however, exist in an enlivening tension with a belief in the benefit to physical learning of generating, sustaining, and directing a focused group energy in the studio. This state of concerted attention can create a powerful learning environment in and of itself.

This lively tension between freedom and structure extends to content and delivery. The work is founded on clear anatomical principles and offers a structured and developmental approach utilizing clear propositions, tasks, forms, images. Gill Clarke encourages this information to be experienced, explored, tasted and tested as a possibility, as one choice, rather than passively received as 'the right way' and replicated as a movement form.

The work requires teaching units of at least two or two-and-a-half hours, with a clear preference for three or more. In general, the more in-depth the experience, and the more opportunity for integration of reflection and practice, the better the dancers will understand and be able to apply insights and experiences to their own physical being/movement.

One might distinguish between a learning phase in the form of a course of study, (whether that be an introduction to this way of working, or a re-visiting to deepen embodied understanding), and the use of the work as a daily tuning in an ongoing professional practice.

During a learning phase, an intensive and immersive framework is required that provides time for ideas and images to be processed through deep sensory work and for embodied understanding to accumulate in layers from day to day. There needs to be an un-pressured atmosphere to encourage the body–mind to be open to notice and embrace unfamiliar sensations, which can lead to the allowing of new choices of pathway, direction, and patterning. On top of this, time is needed for the partner–work, individual exploration, and application to dancing, both through more familiar forms as well as through new and more complex movement puzzles, and, again, time for reflection.

Whereas some technical approaches might benefit from less intensive delivery several times a week over a long period of months, this work benefits, in a learning phase, from a daily practice of around three hours over a shorter period of several weeks, ideally followed by shorter opportunities for further application and practice so the embodied knowledge does not fade and can be further reinforced. Once sensed and embodied, however, and if one is in a relatively 'tuned' mode, applying the work through regular living and dancing practice, the information can then be accessed relatively quickly and easily. Periodic

---

19 This would include additionally interoception as well as exteroception; proprioception designating the feedback of muscles and joints as to movement and position, interoception of organs, exteroception of outside world.

20 See the DVD, for example.

opportunities to dive deeper again, to take time to retune the perceptual capacities, which might have been dulled through overwork or under use, are then beneficial to add depth and dimension to the embodiment.

Minding Motion approaches the work of dancing as a physical, mental, and perceptual activity. The physical beginning of the studio learning experience is enhanced and complemented by an invitation for students to offer their own reflections and self–observations. This opens a space for personal experience to be valued and shared, and for a dialogue between dancing and life experience. The work stirs up a curiosity in anatomical matters, and it opens up dimensions of physical learning otherwise often neglected: reading and watching/seeing.

Minding Motion establishes a reciprocal relation between teaching and doing, comparable to an apprenticeship. In order to make this reciprocity work, a fixed structure must be avoided. The interplay between imitation and exploration (or in other words, between forming and somatic experience) is a central issue in this conversational approach and applies not only to the physical and sensorial aspects. It also holds true for the development of an individual's work discipline and the constant application, re-investigation, and expansion of experiences gained. In this sense, an understanding of dialogical learning and working processes and contexts is enhanced, drawing to a large extent from the social skills of working together and an openness towards the experience of others.

"Gill's work is about readiness, a readiness in the body to be able to move and not to separate the warm–up session from the session where you can only do certain other material once you get to it. Such a separation did not take place and I find that rather exciting. Many techniques were used as a basis although the repertoire you work with afterwards is actually something different."

Julia Schwarzbach, student

The question of whether or not a method or technique is product–oriented needs some reflection as to what 'product–oriented' might signify. One understanding might be to enable a student to perform certain movements. Thus, doing a pirouette would be a product of training/teaching. In a more general sense, one might be skeptical about whether or not *any* physical practice can do without some kind of model or ideal–a *Formung* in German, something like an 'in-form-ing'—so that even an open–learning concept like Minding Motion would still have to confront the fact that a participant goes from one point to another with specific expectations or intentions. Might this *intentionality* be the product of the work?

However, it seems clear that Minding Motion is more concerned with the process a student/participant will experience; a particular physical process is offered, yet the aim is to enable a participant to guide themselves and ultimately to generate their own practice rather than reproducing something existing. Again, the very openness somehow contradicts the idea of a fixed learning outcome, even though this process–orientation can be considered to be a result that is sought, i.e., a product. The self–generating of physical understanding is more concerned with the *how* than with the *what*. In that sense, the movement content (in terms of movement form) is a vehicle for the learning, not as en end–product with its own value.

PEDAGOGICAL METHODS

Lesson structure: The class might begin with a group discussion, as such, an 'arriving activity', 'taking the temperature', garnering overnight reflections and folding them back into the accumulating group experience, hearing 'news reports' of how yesterday's work and theme might have filtered through subsequent activity, sharing and discussing questions that might have arisen, welcoming a wider contextual frame of reference and drawing from Gill Clarke's library of textual and visual materials when appropriate.

Another way to begin might be to pick up on the focused attention in the studio, of individuals engaged in their own 'arriving activities'. They are guided to notice what they are engrossed in, to continue in their current activity, or move on as they choose. A particular focus of attention might be suggested within the body, to draw memory back to the previous day's theme and might then shift to introduce the day's new topic. This provides another way in which to reinforce the accumulation of information in the perceiving body, with the knowledge that this will be a nonlinear process with a different route and timing for each person.

In a teaching encounter that is a course of learning rather than, for example, an open professional class, a rigorous, structured, developmental journey through the body is followed. A specific focus is given to each day's work, introducing one new element at a time so as to better hone attention and avoid too much neural 'noise'. The level of anatomical detail will be determined by the overall timeframe.

The 'theme of the day' will be most frequently introduced using anatomical pictures and metaphorical images, often accompanied by found photographs from magazines, or simple toys, made or found.[20] Specific attention is given at this stage (and in preparing the class), to clarity and simplicity of language, to the ordering of information and images so as to encourage the sustaining of an open perceptual state and not to encourage one that travels too far into processing complex abstract information before moving into first–hand experience. Anatomical jargon is kept to a minimum and the degree of detail is tailored to the prior experience as well as to the curiosity of individuals and groups, and might enter at a later stage in response to questions arising from the practice. So, again, the information supports and stimulates embodied exploration and discovery rather than determining or delimiting it; nor should it be memorized as abstract information.

A usual next step would be guided partner–work in which one partner is learning through touching and observing from the outside, and the other through sensing the touch, and observing from the inside. These roles are both seen as of equal value and always swapped. Pairs are encouraged to change partners every day (sometimes within one session) so as to enhance learning through experiencing the difference between one relationship and organism and another, both in the giving and receiving of touch.

This phase is an opportunity to take the anatomical information of the day and allow it to filter through sensed experience and imagination in order for it to become embodied. For the partner receiving the touch, the hands hone the attention to a particular location within the body, and the teacher's verbal guidance encourages breath as a tool to support the mind's eye, and the softening and opening of volume through the space between the two hands. The partner who is doing the touching sometimes begins with a quite practical (often termed 'archaeological') exploration of the bony landscape, and then experiments with the appropriate quality of touch that they imagine will support their partner's awareness without restricting freedom to move with the breath. It is important, too, that they are not overly busy with touch, which would clutter the receiving partner's nervous system and distract from clarity of perception. Both partners are encouraged by the teacher's verbal guidance to draw upon visualizations of the skeletal and metaphorical images previously introduced, whilst the touch provides another, tangible, common reference point, and harnesses additional sensory input. This phase often begins relatively stationary, the 'receiver' frequently choosing to close the eyes to aid internal attention. Often it will progress organically to the 'receiver' allowing the sensing to draw him or her into movement that can support the sensory observation and the enacting of new images or perceptions, without judging the movement that arises.

Once the theme of the day has been explored through partner work and/or individual movement exploration, the class usually enters a group phase with a progression of shared movement forms. These forms might be called movement 'propositions', and have become intentionally simpler over time, with the emphasis being placed upon filtering the newly sensed focus of attention into familiar movement. In this way, new layers of information can be added to what is already known rather than this new attention being distracted through the need to learn and memorize new movement sequences. In addition, the familiarity of form allows for a continuity of energy flow in the group, rather than the stop–start rhythm frequently associated with a technique class. Slight variations in *how* the forms are used or in their selection or ordering are made according to the particular day's focus, and the talking–through in the moment aims to guide and support students' attention in the unfolding of the new movement. The intention is, as with performance, therefore, not to repeat familiar movement automatically but to experience it afresh in its unfolding, and to practice and hone specificity of attention.

This is frequently followed by a brief, playful transition phase to help sustain this lens of attention through individual, full–bodied improvisation in space before moving on to exploring a set sequence, a movement puzzle, which has been developed specifically with the theme of the day in mind. Whilst the material must be initially learned and memorized, in part through imitation, nevertheless a verbal commentary highlights the 'how' of the sequencing through the body; what might be termed the 'transitions' frequently receive more detailed attention than points of arrival. The emphasis is therefore on getting inside the material, to investigate it as an emerging process, and to draw upon the particular awareness acquired through the previous phases of class. This becomes a conversational process, a dialogue between noticing what the new movement coordinations might contribute to individual awareness of the theme of the day, and, in turn, testing the embodied understanding of this theme through its application to unfamiliar pathways of movement. Whilst correct execution of external form is not the focus, nevertheless attention to detail in the material and precision of articulation and sequencing is emphasized in the learning as a means of refining visual and kinesthetic discrimination, of becoming more aware of one's own movement habits by the encounter with unfamiliar patterns or coordinations. This phase provides a frame also for practicing what it is, as an artist, to hone the matter/the material of movement, to sustain

21 In group discussion about this element of the work, in which Gill shared her own ongoing questioning of its value, she referred to Fuyibi Nakamura's discussion of the role of copying traditional works within contemporary Japanese calligraphic practice: 'Without even attempting to imitate, how can we ever encounter and recognise what cannot be imitated?' (Hallam and Ingold, 2007, p. 80)

a working and reworking process from an initial sketch towards a deeper perception and more detailed articulation.[21]

This process is sometimes referred to as 'trying on someone else's clothes', seeing how that feels, and then exploring how one could make them one's own. As in other elements and phases of Gill Clarke's work, there is a lively tension between facilitating the development of specificity and control in decision–making, and embracing freedom and difference of response. Depending on the teaching context a sequence may be developed, added to, changed over the course of several days, so that gradually more and

more emphasis is on the 'making it one's own', on individual choice and decision–making within the performance of the material—and less on a preoccupation with memorization. In another context, however, students might have an appetite for new and complex movement challenges and be well versed in the memorizing process, in which case a new puzzle may be developed for each session, based upon the day's theme but influenced by observations from the previous day's work.

The Minding Motion approach is neither concerned with frontality nor with a hierarchy of levels. Thus the teaching units will not determine a specific spatial geometry for directing the gaze, nor does it prefer floorwork to standing, or vice versa. Both are determined by the theme of the day (see the following section) and the specific focus in any given teaching context.

In preparation for teaching, the theme of the day is usually determined by the progression along the anatomical journey (like hip sockets or shoulder girdle or rib cage). The journey through the body supports a developmental curriculum and provides entry points and a specificity of focus, whilst attention is also filtered to more qualitative and performative aspects.

Yet the work is also informed by observation of any particular group of individuals in movement, and inside a specific teaching context. Through its conversational aspect, the work aims to be always aware of what the dancers bring to the learning in the form of knowledge and curiosity, and thus elements are adapted or created responding to specific needs (pedagogical, artistic, sensory).

Minding Motion involves a distinctive two–fold process: The physical component and the reflective approach. The underlying question being: How is it that I am learning? This aspect makes for one of the specificities in a Minding Motion experience. In combining book–based knowledge and perceptual knowledge, the field of investigation becomes more expansive than just training, and embraces the idea that the generation of knowledge actually happens on the level of embodiment as well as on the level of reflexive strategies.

As the learning experience is considered to be ongoing, even outside the studio, the notion of self–assessment and feedback would have to embrace a wide range of modes of practice and reflection essential to the Minding Motion practice. These thread through the work, furnishing a range of tools integral to nonlinear learning and to its reinforcement by coming at any given element from another angle, or visualizing it through a different sensory lens. Opportunities for discussion occur at one or several points in class, at varying degrees of distance from the personal, sensed experience.

Immediately following the often intense and intimate partner–work experiences, partners spontaneously share their perceptions from the giving and receiving of touch, their observations and imagery. On occasion, some garnering of these conversations is invited within the whole group but this requires a further degree of abstraction from experience, and frequently it is judged more beneficial to trust the learning process of this exchange and fold it into the next experience straight away.

At the end of a session, a timed automatic writing activity frequently takes place, a short period when everyone is engaged in trying to let their thoughts, images, and sensations flow as directly as possible through the pen onto paper, without judgement, pre-forming, pause, or need for linearity or cohesion. This is an attempt to harness a language as close as possible to the sensory experience of dancing, and potentially a very different language from that of a more analytical and distanced reflection.

This might be followed by a group discussion intended to harness initial observations that might feed future learning as well as inform the teacher in class planning, but this depends not only on the time available, but also on a judgement as to whether it would feel a rather abrupt transition from the experiential, or whether a reflective process is already happening and can be fruitfully gathered into the group learning.

Another process that sometimes enters the practice is drawing. In this activity, a witness watches a partner in the act of dancing (usually in playing with a shared sequence that has had time to sift down into the body from a memorizing brain), and immerses him- or herself in letting what is seen flow as directly as possible onto the paper. Often, initially at least, this is done with eyes on the dancing and not the paper, thus making no judgement about the emerging drawing.[22]

Another important element, the so-called *Friday laboratory* has been developed into a pedagogical structure through which to reinforce the aim of the Minding Motion process to support the varied and nonlinear trajectories of individual learning, and the different creative uses to which the dancers may wish to apply their learning. The Friday lab provides a means by which reflection, considered as an integral part of the learning process, is brought within the teaching frame rather than assumed to be something that goes on only outside the studio.

On this day, the responsibility (and freedom) for structuring the time and learning is passed over to each dancer. The studio becomes a laboratory; each person is involved in their own process of reflecting upon, and further investigation of, the previous four days' information—applying the ideas to their own movement language or creative practice, testing it, taking time to re-visit or explore something more deeply, reconnecting an element from one day with that from another, using each other or Gill Clarke or the resource bank of pictures, images, and books to further their learning. The latter part of the session, as important to learning as the previous individual work, entails each person sharing—verbally, through physical demonstration, and/or performance—what they have explored, and anything they have discovered. In this way the whole group becomes a learning organism, each individual both teacher and learner, and the perspectives on the information are multiplied.

If music is used, it serves more as an additional layer of external stimulus with which the movement can converse, and is rarely concerned with a tight rhythmic relationship. The important thing is to always allow for shifting and alteration of rhythm, so as to enhance readiness and responsiveness in dancing. Time, rhythm, and dynamics, then, are manipulated according to individual choices within exploratory processes that embrace spontaneous deci-

sion–making and do not seek repetition or conformity of timing or sheer motor learning. Music is not relied upon as a prop or to give the dancers energy; energy should, on the contrary, be internally and individually generated and calibrated through the sensory experience of the movement.

╱ "The teacher's role in communication is paramount, not only for the knowledge transmission, but also for enabling the various individualised processes of acquiring and embodying experiences that the teacher is organizing for the participants. In fact, the essential element is the individualization of movement patterns, movement possibilities, of scope and dynamics of movement and the related experiences. Therefore the teacher's role comes in as often as in classical 'control situations', but not to correct, rather to point out those moments, articulations, and connections that seem important in the processual understanding of each person. The teacher seems to be the one who proposes the general subject or focus, and at the same time looks after the continuous adaptation of this proposal to the individual's possibilities, capabilities, and physics." *group comment*╱

The pedagogical concern becomes one of setting up or creating an environment in which individual and group learning can take place, to offer a range of experiences, modes of investigation—lenses through which new information (often anatomical) can be explored, tested, and practiced, and new discoveries made and knowledge generated. Over time the emphasis has shifted to asking questions about students' experience whilst they are moving, and to stimulate curiosity and encourage further questions within the studio, as opposed to, as a teacher, offering definitive answers.

Minding Motion as envisioned and practiced by Gill Clarke is language–driven to a high degree. While this is nothing unusual in dance education, with its oral tradition and one–to–one transmission of knowledge, the use of language here seems to play a substantial role in relation to the more usual emphasis on physical demonstration. With an emphasis on integrating theory and practice, it is important in Minding Motion that a metaphorical language is adopted so as to introduce concepts through sensory practices, as well as imagery through the encounters with new concepts. This starts with the introduction of anatomical connections via explanations and functional analysis, and visualization using dynamic volumes and articulating three–dimensional objects. In this sense, the terms of 'bowl' for the pelvis, of 'dome' for the diaphragm, or 'wheeling' around heads of the femur become operating terms, as much visual as they are conceptual.

---

22 "I saw and recognised quite ordinary anatomical facts, but I also felt them physically—as if in a sense, my nervous system inhabited his body." (Berger, 2005, p. 8)
23 See Johnson, 2007.
24 See Susan Langer, 1953.

25 After a period of working, the three–dimensionality of a model skeleton can still be a very useful piece of evidence for answering specific questions. It is usually used only after the inner visualization is already somehow 'done'.

Secondly, issues of rhythm, breath, quality of movement, concentration, timing, and the like are suggested through a broad range of vocal shades and tonalities. The voice unfolds possibilities of atmosphere, modulation, connection, and flow in the individual and group research process.

The language used in these units is highly figurative, immensely suggestive and imagistic: Language encourages immediate visualization and a movement execution that should avoid the pitfalls of formal imitation. Rather than using musical accompaniment in order to punctuate the learning situation, it is the accompanying voice that conveys the focus of a task or theme of work, as though every action were contained in the tonality, the melody, the pitch, the cadence, etc.

"Gill often speaks in conditional tense, for example: 'What would happen if?' or, 'Could it be that?' or, for example, in relation to a particular body part we are working with, 'Could it be that the volume expands?' or, 'If we move the body part in this and that direction, then...' or, 'How does it behave it relation to gravity?' She offers that up, and in doing so, leaves quite a lot of room for us to discover things." *Julia Schwarzbach, student*

Indeed, specificity in the use of language and voice is a fundamental pedagogical and methodological tool in Minding Motion. As an instrument of knowledge delivery, Gill Clarke pays great attention to wording (avoiding 'naming' and quantifying in a directive way). The language avoids generalizations, and chooses phrasing and words that stay with the particular of the individual's experience, in the conjunctive mode. Participants are therefore addressed in an inciting rathcr then directive way, more suggesting than telling. This is done so as to avoid obedience or other habitual reflexes that are triggered by too precise or didactic instructions, by use of over–familiar movement terminology, or by too generic (anatomical) a language. The aim of language choice is to disturb the experiential process as little as possible, to avoid instructing, yet inviting a 'noticing' alongside the 'doing'.

The work with touch reflects an overall approach that aims to tune the dancer's awareness to their perceptual systems and perceptual processes, so as to balance this with the more habitual, conscious attention we give to the information–grasping actions that these systems initiate. In this sense, for example, in partner–work tasks, the person who is touching is intent upon touching and supporting the experience of their partner but is nevertheless encouraged to also notice what sensations they themselves receive through this exchange, and to be aware that they too are being touched and receiving sensory–motor information about their own, as well as their partner's, tone, relation to ground, and connectivity. The processes are two–way in terms of the flow of information; both partners are able to tune their attentions to the sense of touch, per se, as well as to the intended action.[23] In this sense, movement knowledge is always processual and led by experience.

Perceptual learning, imagination, and visualization are key elements of Minding Motion. Skeletal pictures, metaphoric images, and objects, 'toys', are used when introducing anatomical elements. These aid the subsequent visualization whilst moving.

A metaphorical image can be grasped simply and in its entirety; it can be taken into one's imagination, where it can rest lightly.[24] It then can influence the quality or patterning of the movement instantaneously. Thus, habits of psychophysical coordination can be bypassed, and alternative possibilities experienced. The three–dimensional objects or toys provide an alternative and frequently dynamic metaphor for movement and relationship, such as a bicycle pump for the action of the diaphragm.

A wide range of skeletal pictures are utilized, so as to show a series of perspectives on any region of the body, and to reinforce the idea that bodies/persons are not identical; no one image corresponds to the dimensions and proportions of any dancer's body. Instead these anatomical images, too, work like metaphors: flat reproductions that insist on their incompleteness, and require the learner to make an effort to use imagination to make sense of their information and translate it into a felt–sense within their own body. The simplicity and framing of the images on the page also enable them to be absorbed as mental pictures that can be conjured up whilst moving. For these reasons, a three–dimensional skeleton is used less frequently to introduce aspects of the body for study, since it proposes, in one glance, a plethora of information, unframed, and in a form that we generally accept without question.[25]

During this process, the aim is to stimulate and enlist the imagination in clarifying and enriching the possibility, the efficiency, and/or the intricate complexity of movement. The anatomical structure of the body offers a tangible focus, a starting point from which the imagination can take off, revealing and generating movement to which the body, with its engrained habits, might not otherwise have been open.

As for the skills required to be a teacher of Minding Motion, it is difficult to generalize since Gill Clarke's individual journey has determined the development of Mindful Motion over many years, and whilst it is a coherent methodology, it has not aimed at becoming a certified method or a fixed technique.

One could, perhaps, identify certain qualities that support the efficacy of the teaching. Alongside in-depth, embodied, and conceptual knowledge developed through somatic research and practice, extensive experience in performance, teaching, and observation, it seems that a good mastery and use of language are desirable, as well as an ability to verbalize the unfolding process of one's own movement in the moment. This allows the teacher to guide participants through their own process, whilst a good eye for the nuance of movement helps to identify what might be useful keys in unlocking obstructions to the free flow of movement through a body. Patience is an important ingredient as well, as it can be counterproductive to bombard a dancer with too much information all at once. In order to facilitate learning, it is sometimes best to step back and allow time for a dancer's own experience and discoveries to work as a more effective teacher.

As for the artistic process fostered by Minding Motion, it has been made clear throughout this chapter that there is no single stylistic goal. Rather there is an emphasis on the refinement of the dancer's own perception of, and attention to, their own movement as well as encouragement for the individual dancer/performer to assimilate and apply this knowledge in their own way, according to their artistic interests.

Gill Clarke, Franz Anton Cramer, Gisela Müller

CONCLUSION

Minding Motion work is grounded in a notion that the dancer is an autonomous, investigative artist whose medium is their own moving body. The work does not aim to transmit notions of right and wrong ways to move, rather it seeks to develop tools that foster attention and awareness, discernment and discrimination, readiness and adaptability—tools that expand possibilities for the dancer in how their body–mind organizes itself while moving—both when responding to conscious direction/intention and when spontaneously following image and sensation.

In order to reach unfamiliar places, or to gain deeper insight from those already charted, new experiences need to be enabled, encouraged, and valued. The core of the work, then, is immersion in the present moment of perceptual experience while moving. The mindful body moving in space, alone or with others, is the laboratory from which observations arise, and ideas and images are played out and tested—where understanding *of* movement rather than *about* movement is prioritized.

Yet around this core of practice are layers of reflective and discursive activity intended to facilitate the experiential flow between internal and external attention, implicit and explicit knowledge, intuitive and analytical states, perceptual and conceptual thought.

Gill Clarke's process has become more dialogical as she has become more concerned with contributing to an artistic education. In this sense, technique is not conceived of as a thing to be transmitted, replicated, and performed with accomplishment as an end in itself, nor as a fixed system to achieve this end, but as a process. This process is grounded in Gill Clarke's artistic practice yet adapted in conversation with any particular group of individuals and guided by their reflections and curiosity, as well as by Clarke's own observations as to what might facilitate further learning.

Language is essential in advocating and acknowledging dance as a practice in its own right. Experiences from within the world of dance need to be articulated and communicated through specificity of language as well as through movement, dancing, and sensing. The combined attention to physical and mental elements within an artistic practice could suggest a particular quality and contemporariness in movement exploration. Minding Motion does not promote a defined technical style or objective values of movement. Yet it does offer a specificity in the ways it speaks *of* and *to* the agency of moving bodies of dancers in the studio, and in how it can communicate about movement to social agents outside the world of dance.

LITERATURE

Abrams, David
The Spell of the Sensuous New York: Vintage Books, 1997

Berger, John
On Drawing Cork: Occasional Press, 2005

Bernard, André | Steinmüller, Wolfgang | Stricker, Ursula
Ideokinesis: A Creative approach to human movement and body alignment Berkeley (CA): North Atlantic Books, 2006

Büscher, Barbara | Cramer, Franz Anton
"Beweglicher Zugang" In: Tanzplan Deutschland (Ed.): Tanz und Archive. Perspektiven für ein kulturelles Erbe. Tanzplan Deutschland, Year Book 2009. Berlin 2009, pp. 22–25

Capra, Fritjof
The Web of Life London: Flamingo, 1997

Clarke, Eric F.
Ways of Listening, An Ecological Approach to the Perception of Musical Meaning Oxford: Oxford University Press, 2005

Clarke, Gill
"Mind is as in Motion"
In: Animated, Spring, 2007, http://www.communitydance.org.uk/FCD/Article.aspx?id=606&bpid=1 (accessed on 10/06/2010)

Clarke, Gill
"Making Space for the Tortoise – Educating Creative Individual Artists" In: Finding the Balance. Dance in Further and Higher Education in the Twenty First Century. Liverpool: John Moores University, 2002

Claxton, Guy
Hare Brain, Tortoise Mind: Why Intelligence Increases When You Think Less London: Fourth Estate, 1997

Csikszentmihalyi, Mihaly
Flow: The Psychology of Optimal Experience New York: Harper, 2008 (1st edition 1990)

De Certeau, Michel
The Practice of Everyday Life Berkeley (CA): University of California Press, 1984

Descartes, René
"Meditations on philosophy, (with objections and replies)." In: The Philosophical Writings of Descartes, vol. 2. Cambridge: Cambridge University Press, 1984

Doidge, Norman
The Brain that Changes Itself: Stories of Personal Triumph from the Frontiers of Brain Science New York/London: Penguin, 2007

Dowd, Irene
Taking Root To Fly. Articles on functional anatomy New York: published by the authors, 1995

Feldenkrais, Moshé
The Potent Self San Francisco: Harper and Row, 1985

Forsythe, William
Improvisation Technologies: A tool for the analytical dance eye Karlsruhe/Ostfildern: ZKM/Hatje Canz, 2003

Hallam, Elizabeth | Ingold, Tim (Eds.)
Creativity and Cultural Improvisation Oxford/New York: Berg, 2007

Hartley, Linda
The Wisdom of the Body Moving: An Introduction to Body-Mind Centring Berkeley (CA): North Atlantic Books, 1995

Johnston, Jill
Reinventing Dance in the 1960s. Everything was possible Madison: University of Wisconsin Press, 2003

Johnson, Mark
The Meaning of the Body Chicago: Chicago University Press, 2007

Juhan, Deane
Job's Body – A Handbook for Bodywork New York: Hill Press, 2003

Langer, Ellen J.
Mindfulness Cambridge (MA): Perseus, 1989

Langer, Susanne
Feeling and Form: A Theory of Art London: Routledge, 1953

Lefebvre, Henri
Rhythmanalysis London: Continuum, 2004

Matt, Pamela
A Kinesthetic Legacy: The Life and Works of Barbara Clark Tempe (AZ): CMT Press, 1993

Myers, Thomas
Anatomy Trains: Myofascial Meridians for manual and Movement Therapists Edinburgh: Churchill Livingstone, 2001

Noë, Alva
Out Of Our Heads New York: Hill and Wang, 2009

Noë, Alva
Action in Perception Cambridge (MA)/London: MIT Press, 2004

Pallasmaa, Juhani
The Eyes of the Skin. Architecture and the Senses Chichester: John Wiley and Sons, 2005

Pierce-Jones, Frank
A Study of the Alexander Technique: Body Awareness in Action New York: Schocken Books, 1979

Rolf, Ida
Rolfing and Physical Reality Rochester (VT): Healing Arts press, 1990

Rolf, Ida
Rolfing: Reestablishing the Natural Alignment and Structural Integration of the Human Body for Vitality and Wellbeing Rochester (VT): Healing Arts Press, 1989

Rolland, John
Inside Motion. An Ideokinetic Basis for Movement Education Urbana: Rolland String Research Associates, 1984

Sennett, Richard
The Craftsman Newhaven (CT): Yale University Press, 2008

Sweigard, Lulu
Human Movement Potential. Its Ideokinetic Facilitation Lanham (MD): University Press of America, 1974

Todd, Mabel E.
The Thinking Body London: Dance Books, 1st edition 1937

Varela, Francisco | Thompson, Evan | Rosch, Eleanor
The Embodied Mind: Cognitive Science and Human Experience Cambridge (MA): MIT Press, 1993

JENNIFER MULLER
MULLER TECHNIQUE

CENTRE FOR CONTEMPORARY DANCE UNIVERSITY FOR MUSIC AND DANCE COLOGNE

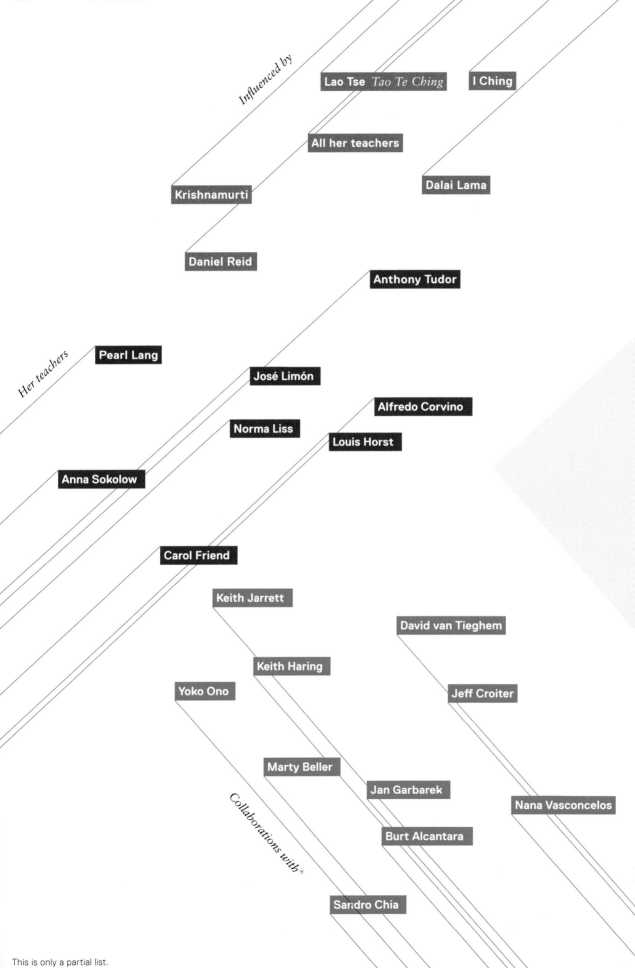

Influenced by

Lao Tse *Tao Te Ching*   **I Ching**

All her teachers

Dalai Lama

Krishnamurti

Daniel Reid

Anthony Tudor

Her teachers   **Pearl Lang**

José Limón

Alfredo Corvino

Norma Liss

Louis Horst

Anna Sokolow

Carol Friend

Keith Jarrett

David van Tieghem

Keith Haring

Yoko Ono   **Jeff Croiter**

Marty Beller

Jan Garbarek

Collaborations with *   **Nana Vasconcelos**

Burt Alcantara

Sandro Chia

This is only a partial list.

JENNIFER MULLER — MULLER TECHNIQUE

Research team at the Centre for Contemporary Dance, University for Music and Dance Cologne: Jennifer Muller, Prof. Vera Sander, Prof. Dr. Yvonne Hardt, Susanne Dickhaut, Dr. Martin Stern

AUTHORS
Yvonne Hardt, Vera Sander

INTERVIEW
Edith Boxberger

STUDENTS AND GUESTS
of the bachelor's and associate's degree (*Diplom*) program in dance: Anika Bendel, Jana Berg, Sarah Biernat, Sarah Bockers, Johanna Kasperowitsch, Annekatrin Kiesel, Jule Oeft, Jelena Pietjou, Hannah Platzer, Arthur Schopa, Valentina Schulte-Ladbeck, Kristin Schuster, Cornelia Trümper, Nora Vladiguerov, Katharina Vlasova, Kazue Ikeda (guest), and Jen Peters (assistant to/dancer of Jennifer Muller/The Works)

JENNIFER MULLER (*1944)
an influence in the dance world for over forty years, is known for her visionary approach and innovations in multidisciplinary dance/theater productions incorporating the spoken word, live and commissioned music, artist–inspired décor, and unusual production elements. She has created over one-hundred works including six full–evening productions. Artistic director of Jennifer Muller/The Works since 1974, she has toured with the company to forty countries on four continents. An internationally renowned teacher, she has developed a personalized technique and developed innovative programs in creative thinking. Her choreography has been commissioned by twenty-four international repertory companies including Alvin Ailey American Dance Theater, Nederlands Dans Theater, NDT3, Ballet du Nord, and Lyon Opera Ballet. Her work for theater includes The Public Theater, Second Stage, New York Stage and Film, and the Metropolitan Opera. Creating work since she was seven years old, she graduated from the Juilliard School, New York City. She danced with the Pearl Lang and José Limón Dance Companies, and was associate artistic director of the Louis Falco Dance Company.

* Partial List of invited Cooperations
Dance Nederlands Dans Theater, NDT3, Alvin Ailey American Dance Theater, Tanz-Forum Köln, Dansgroep Krisztina de Chatel, Ballet de l'Opéra de Lyon, Sächsische Staatsoper Dresden, Bat-Dor Dance Company, Les Ballet Jazz de Montréal, Ballet du Nord, Aterballeto (Italy), Ballet Stagium (Brazil), Ballet Contemporáneo (Argentina), Ohio Ballet, Williams/Henry Dance Theatre, Ballet of Annapolis, Hartford Ballet, Ballet Manhattan, White Wave Rising, BAPA **Theater/Film** New York City Opera, 2nd Stage Theater, The Public Theater, New York Stage and Film, LongHouse Reserve, Dodgers Productions, Fame Productions, The Juilliard Opera Center, Carson Productions, Da Capo, Verdehr Trio/Michigan State University

Jennifer Muller Interviewed by Edith Boxberger

SPACE FOR THE ENERGY TO TRAVEL

/ **Which teachers were important for you?**
I studied with some very strong and incredible people.
I started dancing when I was three-years-old in a creative
school for children; we did little choreographic
projects, always expressing oneself. It gave me the idea
that in order to dance, you had to create. I started formal
training at Juilliard School Preparatory Division in
New York, which was a Saturday school for children. On
Saturdays I studied with Alfredo Corvino, who later
was a ballet master for Pina. I did not realize until much
later what effect he had on me; the use of a plié, the
placement of the body, the musicality. I also studied there
with Pearl Lang. She had come out of Graham and
taught me an enormous amount: like, how to be professional—to the point where I haven't missed a day of
work in my entire life. She invited me to join her company when I was fifteen. Then I went to Juilliard School
proper. I studied with what then was the Graham
faculty: Mary Kingston, Bert Ross, Helen McGee. I also
studied with José Limón. After the first year, he invited
me into his company.

I studied with Antony Tudor before I went to
Juilliard proper, and for many years afterwards at the
Met Opera. He had a huge influence on me. He was
a unique classical ballet teacher and a very unique man.
He expected you to be aware of the finesse of what
you are doing. He did not teach technique as we think of
it now. He taught a general awareness—awareness of
music, awareness of light, awareness of phrasing. Another
strong influence was Louis Horst, the composer, who
was a collaborator and the right hand of Martha Graham.
He taught choreography based, to a great degree, on
musical form. I studied with him at Connecticut College's
American Dance Festival during all the years I was
at Juilliard, as well as creating extra projects for him.

/ **You continued Juilliard School while dancing
with Limón?** Yes. I had already been three years with
Pearl Lang's company when I entered Juilliard. I was
at the end of my first year when I joined José's company
in summer of 1963. The company was preparing a
tour to the Far East—a State Department tour for four-
and-a-half months. I was still in Juilliard, so during
the entire tour I would send in my homework on projects
I had been assigned.

Of all those very strong people, certainly Limón and
Tudor, Horst, Pearl Lang and Corvino—they were the
strongest influences on my formation. Each one gave me
something different. From Limón I learned about passion, about conviction, about putting yourself hundred
percent into whatever you were doing. From Tudor I
learned about phrasing, subtlety, and stage presence; from
Pearl Lang about professional perseverance and the
boldness of movement. From Horst, the craft of choreography and, from Corvino, the clarity of movement
and the use of the plié.

/ **In terms of technique, what did you learn from
those teachers?** The techniques then were slightly
different. Limón Technique those days was a much purer
Limón Technique than they teach now. Because I had
come out of a Graham and classical tradition, when I first
studied Limón I was surprised at the feeling of bending
off balance. After a while Limón's approach felt much
more like home, where I was supposed to be. Tudor got
very angry at one point because he wanted me to be a
classical dancer, but I knew early on I did not want to be a
classical dancer. I felt that classical dance was a historical form; I wanted to do work about what I was experiencing and observing about life now. I kept choreographing the whole time I was at Juilliard.

/ **So you were studying and dancing and
choreographing at the same time?** I had my own
trio when I was eighteen called *The Concert Trio*.
Each of us did our own work, and we performed around
the city. When I graduated from Juilliard I was still
with Limón, but I was creating my own work—it was just
an extension of the years before. I was Limón's assistant
at one point, helping him set pieces from the repertory for different companies. And I danced in the company.
Since the majority of the older company members
left after the Far East tour, Louis Falco, myself, and Sarah
Stackhouse moved into the principal roles for the rest
of the time I was with Limón. Overlapping this period,
Louis Falco started to choreograph his own work in
1967, and one year later I started to dance in his newly
formed company. I was in the Louis Falco Company
for seven years as Associate Artistic Director.

/ **How did you come to developing your own technique?** I started my technique from the influence of that first Asian tour, when I was eighteen. That tour was the first time I left New York. I got in the plane in NYC and out of the plane in Australia. Amazing! I was just inundated with the newness of everything. The next city we went to was Singapore. I will never forget the ride in from the airport to the city—the smells, the air, the look…everything. And we were a long time in Korea and Japan, in Thailand to Philippines, Hong Kong. It changed my life. I was so struck, I felt a closeness to it—which is weird—to the thinking, to the atmosphere. I was knocked over by the art, by the atmosphere, by the sensibility of it.

When I came back to New York, I started reading Eastern philosophy. And read, and read, and read. At that time I was also becoming a little bit dissatisfied with the techniques. I felt there was still too much tension in the techniques and still too much upright, vertical feel to the various techniques. So I started developing my technique out of the Eastern philosophy I'd been studying. It wasn't till much later that I came across approaches such as Tai Chi and Qi Gong. Now I do Qi Gong every morning, I feel it is like coming home. I had never studied Thai Chi or Qi Gong when I started developing my own technique yet I arrived at the same place, the same principles.

I remember very distinctly, at one point I was asked to teach a masterclass at the dance festival in Connecticut, and before my class there was a Tai Chi workshop. I looked in and the teacher was saying the same things that I had been teaching, and I was just shocked. I think because of reading *Tao Te Ching*, the *I Ching*, and various other books, I had arrived at the same understanding— cyclical nature, the polarity of nature from the *I Ching* the polarity between up and down, between large and small, the sense of naturalness, the sense of non-interference, the sense of organic life from the *Tao Te Ching*, from Lao Tse. Those books were my constant companions. I used them not just for the technique; I used them to evolve in my life.

/ **How did you integrate this knowledge into the techniques you had studied up till then?** I have never really gone back and done a comparison to things I learned. Doris Humphrey's fall and rebound—this formed a conceptual basis. But I felt that I wanted to take it a couple of steps further. A polarity technique goes deeper into the internal sense of changing the molecular energy in the body. The plié should be absolutely drained, and not drained just to the floor, but drained to be underneath the floor so that the power and the energy that you sourced has originated in two places:

under the floor, and in your abdomen. The Chinese word *Dan Tien* means the gate in your abdomen that is the source of your power, a source of energy. You also draw up energy out of the ground. That is the polarity, an energized 'up' and a 'down'—totally relaxed.

Only with an empty 'down' can you source new energy to come up. The up is extremely elongated, attenuated, and filled with energy, filled with electricity, with buoyancy. You fill it from inside the skin. You can trace the energy as it moves through the body. As I got more and more sophisticated in terms of what I was discovering, I started to understand all about the lines of energy in the body, what body parts related to each other, and how the energy was used. And that energy can then lead to different kinds of dynamics of energy.

The other discovery was the use of visualization, the use of imagination and how it relates to and affects your physicality. How listening relates to your physicality, how the creative mind relates to how you perceive your body. Filling and draining energy translates into sensation—it just feels different, it supports your dancing in a different way. Dancing from the inside out, not through muscle but through spirit and energy. Other techniques do not have the kind of deep internal change that I am talking about.

/ **What effect does this internal change have on the moving body?** It is an organic technique. There is much less cause for injury because you are not straining the body in any way. You replace tension with energy. Tension only blocks the energy from moving through your body, just like a rusted plumbing pipe will block water. So you think of yourself as an empty skin, a skin envelope that the energy inhabits. And that there is a lot of space, a lot of space for the energy to travel.

Along with the energy work is the placement work. Where are your hips? How do they relate to the small of your back? How do they relate to your ribs and your shoulder blades and your spine? The true strength is the back of your legs, the inside of your legs, your spine, and your abdomen. We emphasize placement: placing the body so the abdomen is absolutely perpendicular to the floor. If you stack everything over itself, you have no need to grip. The minute you grip, the minute you have tension, the minute you are dealing with musculature as your source of dancing—not spirit, not energy. And the more muscles you use, the more tight you are going to get. So, control of the body comes through awareness and placement.

Most dancers live in a middle ground. They don't really release the plié, and they don't really go past a kind of 'held energy' on the top. So they are never changing their energy, they are dancing in a similar energy all the time. Finding the vitality, the change in your body, that is what drove me—both the cause and the development of that concept, that sensation. It was only when I had my own company in 1974 that this approach became the technique that was taught to the company from day one. The change of energy in the body is the central concept of Muller Technique. Change of energy propels the body and is the source of all movement; it is both a concept and a sensation. One has to imagine as well as feel the change of energy. One has to be aware.

/ **What makes sense in training? What are you looking for?** When I first encounter a group, the first class usually is about energy because it is such a strange concept to most people. It still is. Hopefully by the end of a week, people are starting to understand the relaxation of the plié, and understanding that if they don't relax their plié, their plié will not be usable. That has to happen for the energy exchange to happen in the body. Then, sourcing from the ground an extraordinary energy, the 'up' energy allows you to extend your technique; it supports movement in a different way, for numerous turns, gives height to the jumps. It is this energy that allows you to balance. The softer the plié, the more usable the plié—and the more attenuated the 'up' can be to support more difficult movement and phrases.

The placement I use is slightly different. You have to place the pelvis right over the floor, open up the back of the leg to be able to get the curve in the small of the back, to feel the line of energy in the spine from the tailbone all the way up to the neck. With this placement you get a functional structure and that supports you, enables you to balance and extend movement.

The most difficult concept and sensation, as I said, is to have the plié be a usable, powerful plié. The floor is your power, the abdomen is your control, the spine and the back of your legs are your strength. If you can't discover that plié, the rest is not going to follow. It is not about positions; it is about the change in energy in the body. And that is very deep work. If you are not able to do that investigation, if you have not gone deep enough in understanding and sensation, then you are not going be able to teach that or use it to its fullest.

/ **What is important in conveying this work?** I encourage dancers to visualize, to make internal pictures. That's why we start with a short meditation; to encourage the process of making internal pictures of your body. Not an anatomical picture, but a highly personalized picture of your body. You begin to encourage an intimate sense of the body. Many dancers are not aware of their torso, they dance from their legs and arms. I believe everything comes from the inside of the torso, from the abdomen—the extremities are last. I start the energy exchange with placement, the strength of the spine, understanding shape work.

After you study the technique for a while there is this tremendous flow of strength and vitality that starts to happen in the body, creating both freedom and control—control through awareness. That is what one can begin to accomplish with a new group of people. The other element considered from the beginning is how to phrase. All steps are not even, and all steps are not just steps in a row; they have to become a line of movement. It influences the timing, the use of energy in certain shapes, how one arrives in certain shapes.

/ **What do you think is most important for your teaching?** My view of teaching is that you have the responsibility to create change. You have to use whatever you can until you can to make an impact. It is not just putting it out there and if people learn, they learn. The aim is that the student can end up becoming a dancer by dancing from the inside of his or her body, having power from the floor and energy on the top to sustain movement. As a teacher, you need the knowledge of what you are teaching. You need the knowledge of the principles and you need the passion to communicate it. You need to be egoless to communicate it. You have to know it so deeply and so well that you can convince, get inside people's minds and spirits to convince them to change. And you need to be supportive and non-critical doing so. For me, an essential part of allowing people to grow is for them to know that they have your compassion, and your approval.

/ **That means a certain relationship between teacher and student.** It is an atmosphere you put out. If you put out a supportive atmosphere, people are then willing to take some risks. If you only push, people close in and they don't want to do anything. People change if you push with a support underneath it. Because if I am trying to teach a technique that gets rid of all tension, it is tension not only in the body but in the mind and soul that's going to get in the way. That is why I use the music I do during class, why I sometimes make a lot of jokes. I sometimes keep it very light, I dance around a little bit. It is all very intentional—to keep the spirit light and the soul available.

/ **Do you have a concept for a class, and do you change it?** In the beginning, I did a different class every day. Then I realized a dancer cannot improve if they are trying to learn steps every day. What you need is to know the steps and then start working on the internal structures of your body, your body moulding. So we do one class per week, the same center, the same barre, same across the floor, and the following week we do a completely different class.

/ **The barre is essential in your class?** Absolutely, because it is one of the best systems of training for the legs—except we do it very differently. I studied modern techniques in which one did the entire class in the center of the room. I found improvement much slower than working with a barre. You can really work on your legs, on every single part of the leg. Barre work is logically developed to strengthen the legs. Why not, then, take that basic structure and approach it differently by adding the change of energy? One leg filling up, one leg draining down, so that there is a rain of energy—like rain drops coming down and out through your toes. So we work very strongly on a lot of principles of the technique during the time we are at barre.

/ **Where do you see the future for this technique?** I believe very deeply that the technique is the most positive approach that you can take for your body and for your dancing. It gives you a long life as a dancer, it gives you a range of dynamics in movement and a very deep knowledge of your body. Within one or two years, the body changes through the knowledge of how to sculpt the body, how to place the energy, and how to work with the energy. And there is an awareness that goes along with it, an awareness of what you are doing, of the potential of your body, of the drama and the spirit inside your body. Also, a lot of personal work goes along with it because we do a tremendous amount of visualization—a tremendous amount of spirit and heart–joining movement.

/ **Where is it taught? And where could, or should, it be taught in the future?** There are the direct descendants—some of my early alumni, the founding and senior members of the company—who have been teaching for many years now at different universities in the U.S., also in places in Europe and Japan, in Canada, and in South America. Some have opened schools. And there are people who do variations of the technique all over.

Some former members of the company were, for a long time, trying to get me to certify people who taught the technique. And my executive director also would like to see that happen so people would have to deeply study it and would then be accredited to teach it. I think it is less controllable than that. I went to set a piece on a repertory company a long time ago and the director told me, 'I am teaching Muller Technique.' He studied with me for a short time and wanted to teach what he knew of it, but it wasn't even close. Is that bad? I don't know. It retains something of it. I think it is almost impossible to control it.

/ **From your experience and knowledge, what would you like to tell young people who are learning to dance today?** Not to get stuck in a narrow band of the way they dance, the way they perform. Do the research, do the investigation. When I was growing up, I was very lucky to have distinctly different companies in existence; you immediately understood there were many ways to approach dance. Today it seems we are accepting only a small range of what is acceptable in terms of movement, or the way contemporary dance should look. The choreographers who are beginning to create have the idea there is only one or two acceptable ways. I find that extremely dangerous. They are not going to take on their own discovery, find something original. We are going to lose the new voices, the unique voices. When I was young I had so many different examples in front of me. I realized I had to find my own way, find out what I believed, what I wanted to say and how I wanted to say it—to find out what felt true and right to me.

Yvonne Hardt, Vera Sander

INTRODUCTION

The meditative sound of 'shima, shima' fills the space. In a studio at the Centre for Contemporary Dance in Cologne, the students are absorbed in the execution of a gentle, calm up–and–down movement. They are letting go as they bend over, then they return to an upright standing position—releasing and gathering energy. What for a modern dancer might, at first glance, appear to be a plié with an upper body curve—i.e., bending the knees and curving the upper body at the same time—is actually an exploration into a central tenet of Jennifer Muller's dance technique. This is about working with energy flow, with the play between polarities of 'energized' and 'drained', between moving up and down—which is why Muller calls this a 'polarity technique'.

The ramifications of working with energy, body tonus, and how imagination affects movement as compared to the other techniques will come up time and again. Jennifer Muller pioneered a dance technique based on the polarity between relaxation and an energized 'up' that retains the rudiments of ballet and historic modern dance (more so than the Release–based techniques that have since evolved) but fundamentally transforms it by incorporating and layering various movement and energy principles. The imagination, along with a working knowledge of 'body structure', are necessary to access Muller's energy–work. In summary: Use of energy, imagination, and knowledge of body structure are the three pillars of Muller's dance technique.

This deeply reflective and articulate New York dancer and choreographer taught her technique for seven days between 23 November and 3 December 2009; the two–hour courses were similar in length and format to her company class. During the workshop, Muller (assisted by Susanne Dickhaut) and fourteen third– and fourth–year students from the bachelor's program at the Centre for Contemporary Dance in Cologne explored core elements of the Jennifer Muller Technique. In addition Muller taught 'performance skills'

1 These recordings were transcribed in order to better analyze content in relation to language and lesson structure. We would like to especially thank Lisa Lucassen, Jana Berg, and Anika Bendel for their work.

for ninety minutes, a topic which she considers to be intimately linked to technique. This course targets principles of performance, presence, phrasing, and onstage skills. After a break, students and the research team returned for Muller's 'laboratory'—a two–hour teaching unit in which she presented and discussed theory, system, and the basic tenets behind her work.

The research team included dancer and choreographer Vera Sander, dance researcher Yvonne Hardt, and the sports studies scholar Martin Stern. To conduct a systematic evaluation, they used audio and audiovisual equipment to record the courses, laboratory meetings, and discussions.[1] Along with participating in class, the analysis of Muller's technique was based upon the transcription of these audio and video documents. This, the resulting written analysis by Yvonne Hardt and Vera Sander, closely follows the question catalog presented by Tanzplan Deutschland.

Jennifer Muller's short stay (due to commitments in New York) presented a challenge; participants could only begin to experience and realize changes in movement and body quality that are central to Muller's work in such a short time. While the students' movement execution did noticeably change over the course of the week, Muller— as seen on the DVDs—only saw a hint of those qualities she strives for. At the beginning of the workshop, some students were a bit reserved toward Muller's approach to energy. Thus, overcoming student barriers and helping students be open to all movements, energies, and shapes was an added goal. The process was supported by Muller's motivating teaching style, as well as by discussions and questions that helped guide students' reflection on her technique.

Yvonne Hardt, Vera Sander

HISTORICAL CONTEXT

TIME, PLACE, AND SOCIO-POLITICAL CONTEXT

In 1963 John Kennedy was assassinated; in Jennifer Muller's memory, this event is invariably linked with her first tour abroad with the José Limón Dance Company. Just eighteen-years-old, she toured through Asia for four-and-a-half months. This tour would become a point of departure for encountering and dealing with Asian philosophy and, at the same time, a source of inspiration that laid the groundwork for her own technique. Many of her contemporaries were also inspired by Eastern thought—it was fashionable at the time—but Muller's approach is decidedly different than those of, for instance, Merce Cunningham or Steve Paxton.[1] For Muller, coming to grips with Lao Tse's *Tao Te Ching*[2] and the *I Ching* helped her understand movement and technique as something that works with energy—for example, cyclical 'waxing and waning' as a central precept.

Muller Technique, as taught today with its exercises, shapes, and principles, was developed in a period of over ten years. It was first established when Muller founded her company in 1974 and it has been developing ever since. Originally Muller did not refer to her training as a technique, rather she considered it to be a specific approach to movement and principles that could use other techniques and transform dancers into relaxed, as well as energized, believable performers onstage. Only after her company, The Works, was established and Muller began instructing teachers did the term 'Muller Technique' come into use.

She developed the technique midst a diverse and vibrant dance scene in New York City; this included José Limón and Martha Graham as well as Merce Cunningham, Paul Taylor, Pearl Lang, and Alvin Ailey. It was a time when people could feel society's awakening (thanks to the Kennedy years), a time characterized by sit-ins, student uprisings, and the African American civil rights movement—and a time when New York was blossoming into one of the world's most important art capitals. Like other dancers, Muller was searching for classes that

offered more expressive potential than was found in ballet or established modern techniques. What was available did not, in her opinion, adequately prepare the body to become transparent in an energy–driven sense. According to Muller, this meant that dancers were neither taught nor encouraged to be believably 'human' when performing.

Muller's goal was to make dance more 'human'—meaning that she wanted a type of dance that was more credible, and independent from myths and heroic figures (as was the hallmark of Graham or Limón, for example). With some historical distance, one might say that Muller's technique takes the middle ground between the more radical postmodern work (like Trisha Brown and Yvonne Rainer's) and the established modern dance techniques of the time (i.e., Graham and Limón).

Development of the technique was also informed by Muller's experiences as a teacher and choreographer of established companies. Working with professionals who were trained in either ballet or modern dance, and who already had clear aesthetic forms of expression, Muller encountered the boundaries of the dancer's expressive potential. The confrontation with the abilities of working professionals helped her set a new goal; i.e., to direct these dancers towards finding new movement qualities and greater expressive potential.

BACKGROUND: BIOGRAPHIES AND ENVIRONMENT

Muller's biography reflects a large number and variety of influences, instructors, and sources of inspiration that informed her technique, its principles, and her teaching methods. In Yonkers—just outside of New York City—she began dancing at the age of three. While free creative work (taught by Norma Liss) was her initiation to the dance, Muller was soon admitted into the preparatory training course at New York's renowned Juilliard School. Here ballet was under the direction of Alfred Corvino (who would later become Pina Bausch's ballet master) and modern dance under the direction of Pearl Lang. Anthony Tudor was also a major influence on Muller. Her modern influences included José Limón as well as a number of teachers at Juilliard who taught Graham Technique.[3] Muller also names Anna Sokolow as a major inspiration, particularly in regards to Sokolow's classes in choreography.[4] At the American Dance Festival[5] held each summer in Connecticut,

---

1 Both are equally considered innovators of contemporary dance. Cunningham, a pioneer of postmodern dance, performed movement for movement's sake thereby detaching the dance from emotional associations as well as from organic or natural movement source material (see also the section in this book: Daniel Roberts — Cunningham Technique). Steve Paxton developed Contact Improvisation.

2 Lao Tse: *Tao te king. Das Buch des alten Meisters vom Sinn und Leben.* Translated by Richard Wilhelm. Cologne: Anaconda, 2006. Muller refers to this German translation, which was translated into English. Among the countless adaptations and new interpretations of the work, she feels this version is closest to the original.

3 See Edith Boxberger's interview with Jennifer Muller.
4 Anna Sokolow was a modern dancer, not well known outside the U.S., who is gaining in importance in dance history, especially in the context of her political engagement in the 1930s and 1940s; see Graff, Ellen: *Stepping Left: Dance and Politics in New York City 1928–1942.* Durham: Duke University Press,

Muller also took classes with Merce Cunningham although his training and choreographic style did not match her own interests.

Learning *and* working were closely intertwined for Muller from an early age. She was a dancer for the José Limón Dance Company while a student at Juilliard, and went on to work with Limón for nine years. Muller's time and work with Limón led to her current convictions about the benefits of apprenticeship under a master. Sub-

sequently, for seven years she worked in close cooperation with Louis Falco as principal dancer, choreographer, and associate artistic director for his company.

Despite these experiences, Muller would never describe herself as a Limón dancer because her background has too much variety. She views her working style as quite distinct from Limón's, and in opposition to (what she considers) Limón's unrealistic presentation/representation of emotionality. She continues to use some principles and impulses from ballet and modern dance, but takes them to a new place. Louis Horst, Martha Graham's accompanist and composer (whose demanding and critical teaching style Muller found provocative), also provided crucial stimuli in the development of Muller's choreographic oeuvre.[6]

RELATION TO OTHER ART FORMS

Music is one of the most important art forms for Muller; it informs her choreography and her teaching. Dance, however, is not dependent upon music, rather, music and dance meet on a higher structural level where Muller's extensive knowledge of music theory comes into play.[7] During her time at Julliard, she received a rigorous education in music. That said, classical music, (in which her knowledge of music theory is grounded), does not figure prominently in her own artistic and pedagogic work. Muller does not tailor movement to mimic music, nor does she prefer a particular style of music for teaching. Her artistic works are accompanied by music from avant garde genres, diverse sources of world music, and by live, contemporary composers. Muller's choreographic works include cooperations with the world–famous jazz pianist Keith Jarrett as well as with the experimental artist Yoko Ono, among others.

Muller sees an open relationship in respect to other art forms. What is happening in the world, in art, and society is fundamental to her creative work. For her, art is created because of a very human need to deal with the world and possibilities for expression. Muller seeks an on–going exchange of ideas and dialogue with other art forms in both her teaching and work with dancers rather than relying upon specific examples or specifying a singular direction.

In particular, photography and film have found a place in Muller's choreographies. 'Method acting'—the further development of Stanislavski's acting methods in the U.S.—is also employed because dance, for Muller, is about a believable embodiment of movement, emotions, and intentions.

1997; Warren, Larry: Anna Sokolow: *The Rebellious Spirit* (Choreography and Dance Studies Series). New York: Routledge, 1998.
5 About the importance of this summer festival at the time, see (among others) Anderson, Jack: The American Dance Festival. Durham: Duke University Press, 1987. Muller also speaks of the importance of this festival when she says that all the famous choreo-

graphers saved premieres of their works for the summer in Connecticut.
6 This source of choreographic inspiration is quite distinct from the dancers of so–called postmodern dance, which developed simultaneously; its choreographic methods were influenced in particular by Robert Dunn, Merce Cunningham's musical accompanist. Before Dunn began teaching choreography, Horst

was considered the most important teacher in this field. See Mansfield Doares, Janet: *Louis Horst: Musician in a Dancer's World*. Durham: Duke University Press, 1992.
7 See "Concept and Ideology", keyword 'Music'.

RELEVANT THEORETICAL DISCOURSES

For Muller, dance is a language—a means of communication. As such, she shares, with many modern dance artists of that time, a rather distanced position to the modernistic art discourse according to which form and material were seen as more relevant than the representational function of art.[8] For Muller, the body can do nothing else other than communicate.

In conversations, Muller repeatedly mentions the 'humanistic' concerns of her art. She finds dance a deeply human endeavor, and understands 'humanism' as the need for peaceful co-existence.[9] She points to her belief that all people are created equal; this was particularly poignant at the beginning of Muller's artistic career, at a time when African American citizens were marginalized. For her artistic work, this translates into the recognition and acceptance of differences, a need to make the working environment harmonious, and to present a dancer onstage who does not represent superhuman, historic characters (as she experienced in the works of Graham and Limón). She prefers to focus on the individual of today.[10]

In addition, Muller's understanding of 'humanism' is rooted in her reflections on the Asian philosophy of non-intervention—which she sees as the opposite of a Western tendency toward, and need for, control. Asian philosophy, first and foremost the writings of Lao Tse like the *Tao Te Ching* and *I Ching*, does not view the body as complete in and of itself, but as something that, through its energy, is permanently connected to the environment.

CURRENT PRACTICE

Muller Technique is taught daily in her studio, either by Jennifer herself or by long–standing members of her company, The Works. Technique classes prepare Muller's dancers for her choreographic work, which is distinguished by a high energy and virtuosity. When Muller or an authorized company member rehearses her repertoire for other companies, technique classes serve to help these dancers understand the fundamentals of the Muller Technique.

Dancers who have completed the Muller Technique teaching program have taken the method around the world, which has opened up a second career for many. In the meantime, the Muller Technique has inspired others to develop their own work or technique. A great number of her former dancers have taken teaching positions at American universities (in California, Florida, and Massachusetts, for example), and others teach regularly in Europe, Asia, and South America.

Muller also applies her ideas and theories outside of the dance field—for instance, at schools or when working on community projects. These projects are less about the technique itself than they are about the development of dance and creativity within a specific group.

INDIVIDUAL APPROACH

Muller's technique stemmed from a need to help dancers train with less tension, and from a desire that dancers be able to credibly embody human emotions and movement onstage. Beyond the objective of preparing the dancer for Muller's artistic work, the technique has a variety of applications.

While there is no specific information as to how teachers and choreographers are using the technique, the following aspects lend themselves to a broader application by individuals, to those practicing other techniques, and for performance situations:

1. Achieving an energized and clearly structured body;

2. Clarity in placement—especially a consciousness for hip placement;

3. The development of a supple, 'useful' plié;

4. Creating a 'sculpted body'—muscular shaping for a body that works without too much tension;

5. An efficient use of movement;

6. Strengthening the connection between body and mind, and preparing for performance;

7. Imparting fundamental social values, for example, acknowledging the individual and respecting others, thus enabling dancers to learn and grow in a supportive, motivating environment—which characterizes the general atmosphere in a Muller Technique class.

---

8   Under the influence of what was known as abstract expressionism in the U.S., the cultural theoretician and art critic Clement Greenberg identified abstraction and/or the self–referentiality of art to its own medium (for example, brush work) as the fundamental attribute of modern art. Accordingly, modern art was characterized by the absence of any clear mimetic function and was not interested in realistically depicting the world. Because a great part of modern dance cannot be easily explained within this theoretical framing, an extensive debate broke out about the modernism of modern dance in dance studies. (See for instance: Mark Franko: *Dancing Modernism/Performing Politics*. Bloomington: Indiana University Press, 1995; Sally Banes: *Terpsichore in Sneakers: Post-Modern Dance*. Middletown: Wesleyan University Press,1987) The 1960s can in no way be considered completely under the yoke of a modernistic artistic discourse as defined by Clement Greenberg and continued by Michael Fried, among others (Michael Fried: *Art and Objecthood: Essays and Reviews*. Chicago/London: University of Chicago Press, 1998.) For instance, Pop Art and some postmodern dance distanced themselves from this type of discourse (although differently than Muller has done). They were more interested

Potential applications for other, non-dance areas lie in creative thinking, non-verbal communication, consciousness, and mindfulness. The technique can support dancers and non-dancers alike in becoming conscious communicators and in using body language in daily life.

RELATION TO OTHER DANCE AND MOVEMENT TECHNIQUES

Muller's technique transforms movement and exercises that are clearly rooted in ballet and modern dance techniques learned during her education. Muller rejects neither the exercises related to these forms nor their respective movement languages; she believes that techniques like ballet, with its clear methodology, convey knowledge that remains relevant for contemporary training. But such techniques must be approached differently, she believes, and her energy–work transforms them fundamentally.

Her energy–work has a clear lineage to Asian movement practices based on energy, like Tai Chi and Qigong. She first came into contact with the latter in 1999. Finding parallels to her own work, she now considers Qigong to be complementary and has incorporated it into her own daily practice.

Consequently, Muller's work is difficult to categorize historically and/or to place amongst various movement techniques. Her life has been shaped by countless influences, and development of her technique occurred over a long time period. In the early phases, she played a pioneering role in body–work methods that are now commonly used; her work with relaxation and the flow of energy made groundbreaking contributions to the Release–based techniques of today.

in questioning the various representational functions of art. For a discussion on the various approaches to staging emotions and how they indicate a turning point in North American dance history, see Yvonne Hardt: "Reading Emotion. Lesarten des Emotionalen am Beispiel des Modernen Tanzes in den USA (1945–1965)." In: Margrit Bischof / Claudia Feest / Claudia Rosiny (Ed.): *e-motions. Jahrbuch der*

Gesellschaft für Tanzforschung. Vol. 16, Münster: Lit Verlag, 2006, pp. 139–155.
9 Muller does not use the terms *humanism* and *humanistic* in the philosophical context that has been evolving since the Renaissance. Rather, she is pointing out general qualities of humanity and the recognition of equality.

10 Since the 1970s, Muller has made contemporary people and contexts the main points of reference and topics for her works. She is not interested in the representation of archetypal, timeless, generalizable characters, but rather about the individual and how he or she lives in his or her ever–changing environment.

Yvonne Hardt, Vera Sander

CONCEPT AND IDEOLOGY

The conceptual basis of the Muller Technique rests on three fundamental principles: working with flows of energy, the power of imagination, and knowledge about the body's physical structure.

According to Muller, energy and matter form the essential elements of dance and movement, and they also inform all of life. Accordingly, every movement is initiated by a change in the flow of energy. Movement is cyclical, governed by a constant coming and going, by an up and down. This is why Muller describes her technique as being concerned with life forces. She localizes two energy sources: one is located within the center of the body, approximately two finger–widths below the navel; the other is outside the body, approximately two feet below the ground. Imagination is particularly important for locating these energy sources.

Shapes made by the body thus change because of the flow of energy. Muller states that while "an arm remains an arm," the sensation of the arm's weight and/or lightness changes with the change of energy. The body is subject to constant change as energy ebbs and flows endlessly, animating us to move. Muller's objective is to make the body transparent for the flow of energy, and overcoming tension is imperative for this process. Muller explains, "This energy needs space to move. Whenever you have tension in your body, you are going to stop the energy from moving."[11] Thus, in order to move, we must call upon the flow of energy as opposed to muscle power. Muller speaks of never allowing the flow of energy to die out, that the student must always be "sourcing the energy." Movement initiation comes from inside the body and is not formed or generated by anything exterior; accessing this energy is enabled by the imagination. Dancers visualize energy that, over an extended training period, can be experienced even more precisely; this sensed energy also includes physical vibrations. Muller explains it thusly: "…imagine energy as a warm spot that you can visualize. That is why visualization is so important, that you can visualize something that is in there that is like your motor. It is what makes you run."

The distinct importance of visualization and/or imagination can be considered the second key element of her technique. Visualization and imagination can train not only an awareness of the entire body, but also help discern the intention behind any given movement. Muller is fond of saying, "The strongest tool we have is our mind and our imagination." Such tools aid in fostering a body awareness that remains individual, and not necessarily anatomical.

Imagination also helps dancers position body parts in relation to one another; Muller's description of body structure utilizes positional relationships. This is the third key element in her technique. For Muller, this is not primarily about a medical and/or anatomical understanding of the body, even though the structure of the human body (i.e., the relationship between weight placement and the alignment of the legs and spine) is a core component. Weight should always be placed over the balls of the feet and the hips should be frontally aligned.

The interplay between freely flowing energy, proper body structure, and awareness of body and movement creates what Muller calls the "informed body." This is a body that, through training of constant awareness, only perceives, and does not attempt to dominate or control the energy—it is able, instead, to use the detailed knowledge and subtly channel it through the body. In relation to this, Muller notes that dancers must be 'intimately' familiar with all parts of their bodies and specific in the creation of individual movements. This is about both perception and detail: What are the eyelids doing at this moment? How is the energy flowing through the wrist? Muller uses this type of questioning in guiding her students towards a detailed awareness. Knowing what individual body parts are doing is important for the execution of every movement. The technique's goal is to achieve an awareness of both the intention and initiation of every movement using Muller's energy–based principles.

IMAGINING THE BODY

Referencing energy systems in the body, her understanding of the body is distinct and separate from the Western medical perspective. This approach disregards the classic mind–body dualism wherein the body is reduced to merely executing commands of the controlling mind—which would relegate the physical dimension to a subordinate and separate role from that of the reflective mind. At the same time, as she draws on a variety of descriptive metaphors, Muller's body imagery is in no way homogenous.

11 Unless otherwise indicated, all Jennifer Muller quotes are taken from transcripts of the Muller Labs from 23 November–1 December 2009.
12 In doing so, she broke with her influential mentor Antony Tudor.

13 The musician and composer Marty Beller has composed for international choreographers and dance companies, including Jennifer Muller/The Works, Sean Curran, Chet Walker/8and ah one, Julio Bocca/Ballet Argentino, RhythMEK, Heidi Latsky, Rebudal Dance, Alice Tierstein/Young Dancemakers,

Andrew Jannetti and Dancers, Bill Hastings, Kathy Wildberger, Kelli Wicke Davis, and Roger Williams University Dancewar. He was the drummer on the award–winning album *Washington Square Serenade for Steve Earle* (among others), and has toured with the Tony–Award–winning musician Stew. His

For example, the body is described as being surrounded by an 'envelope', or conversely understood as an envelope that can be filled with energy. Her body descriptions can also include technological metaphors; for instance, the energy source may be described as a motor, or the body's structure is compared to a series of tubes, or pipes, that might be clogged. Media influence has also made its way into her imagery, for example, when Muller asks students to imagine their hips as a frontally–directed television screen, or when she speaks about self–observation (when students appear to be judging themselves), she might say, "Turn off the camera." Muller isn't just fostering discourse about the body with her technique; she draws upon any number of impressions that help explain and assist visualization, any of which can, indeed, be contradictory. This is irrelevant as long as the images succeed in overcoming specific problems.

Overall, one can say the Muller Technique is founded upon a belief in thoroughly efficient movement execution, in clearing blockages, in achieving transparency, and in the 'usefulness' of individual movements. This approach ties into discourses about the economic and efficient use of the body. Terms like 'usefulness' stand in contrast to Muller's movement philosophy that assumes an organic basis and wishes to see energy flow freely, that does not wish to constrain the body, and in which visualization (as opposed to anatomical reality) plays a central role.

Muller is convinced that the body can be shaped through her teaching method, a process she calls 'body sculpting'. This does not happen simply by striving for an ideal body; physical changes are accomplished through work on increased attentiveness, alertness, and a more 'informed body'. For example, once dancers understand the principle of 'drop and out' in leg–work, a 'carving out' of the thigh musculature and flatness (or 'panels') on the inside of the leg is enabled. An outwardly rounded thigh, which indicates a strong musculature, is thus lengthened. Thus, depending on the dancer's body type and previous training, this technique can change the body's physical appearance.

Muller has no body–type preferences, she values her dancers' individual and unique corporeality. Dancers in her company have a variety of body types, reflecting the humanistic ideals in her work.

These humanistic ideals also provide insight into Muller's handling of gender issues. There is no difference between male and female in her training—based upon her belief in equality and respecting differences. Muller is, however, familiar with gender role stereotypes: One reason she mentions as her decision not to become a ballerina[12] was that she did not like the image of women in ballet at that time. She had no desire to be a floating, light, ephemeral being as this did not match her sentiments towards her own body, nor did it inspire her to move. In contrast, polarities are exciting for Muller because every person contains both yin and yang—principles of masculinity and femininity.

Muller's teaching also makes concepts about energy tangible through music. Her courses are dependent upon music, whereby one does not simply mirror the other; rather, music is used as a pedagogic, emotional, and energizing medium. This differentiated way of using music is primarily a result of Muller's studies at Juilliard, where she was a serious student of music composition, and secondly, as a result of her work with musicians and composers. She and Marty Beller[13] have a particularly intensive artistic working relationship.

Jennifer Muller selects music for her classes carefully. The choices are by all means eclectic, however most choices come from rock and pop (i.e., Joe Cocker, Boys II Men, Michael Jackson, etc.) and are usually pre-recorded (as opposed to a live accompanist).[14] She rarely uses classical or experimental music for teaching.

Music must support the qualities and goals of any given exercise. Knowledge about rhythm and the best rhythms for certain exercises is a key aspect in the teacher training that Muller offers her dancers. Not all exercises can be executed well in the same rhythm: 3/4-time is especially good for softer and warm–up movements; 4/4-time is for movements that are faster, more linear, and directed in design (as opposed to being curved or swinging). Music in 6/8-time is used to support two elements simultaneously, namely accentuation of the *drop* and rhythm for the breath. Since lessons are usually accompanied by CD, others teachers must spend time finding pop music with the appropriate rhythms.

Above and beyond this, music serves to energize and motivate students. Music is part of a strategy that creates a good working atmosphere and makes the hard work of training a little bit easier. Since grim determination and seriousness can sometimes close the mind to learning processes, music can help offset excessive concentration and bring fun and passion back into the studio. Pop music's recognition factor and emotional charge work particularly well for Muller. So, choice of music is yet another means with which a favorable class environment and learning atmosphere can be achieved.

drumming and percussion has been heard on television and film soundtracks, including The *Daily Show with Jon Stewart, March of the Penguins, Jon and Kate Plus 8, Confessions of a Dangerous Mind, Malcolm in the Middle, Sky High, Shallow Hal, Stuck On You, Higglytown Heroes, Roswell,* and many more.

14 In contrast, Muller training on the DVD is accompanied by Knuth Jerxsen's live percussion, a musical variation that she seldom uses. It was used here due to copyright issues.

Space has a meaning for Muller in an atmospheric sense. But the use of space in an abstract, geometric quantity, however, is not explicitly found in the conceptual foundations of the Muller Technique. Although Muller wants dancers to use spatial orientation precisely on stage (something she trains in 'performance skills' classes), spatial concepts are only marginally dealt with in technique class and attendant theory taught in the Muller laboratory. The form and energy of movement are emphasized in the technique and directly shape the space and its perception.[15] Use of energy and form will determine whether or not the space is properly filled, something that can only be achieved when the performer has self–confidence.

Thus classes are not characterized by changing spatial relationships, and incorporating various levels into the work takes a subordinate role. Since dance is a play of energy for Muller, floorwork is secondary. In her opinion, there are only limited possibilities to learn about 'sourcing energy' here. Dancers can certainly integrate floorwork into their choreographies, but, for Muller, floorwork has not demonstrated any explicit benefit or meaning for her technique. She is, of course, aware that other techniques make targeted use of the floor (she cites Pilates as an example), however, she feels that floorwork does not offer anything to help meet the objective of energetic transparency.

"A special characteristic in Jennifer Muller's work is definitely dealing consciously with energy and imagination... not just to dance, but to consciously be in the dance...the scope is quite large so that everyone can sense what it brings out for them. It's about lightness without any cramping and muscular tension." *Nora Vladiguerov, student*

INTENT

For Muller, energetic transparency is a key aspect and intimately related to the original intention behind the development of her technique. The technique evolved from a desire to help dancers train with less tension and to help them credibly embody human emotions and movements when performing (rather than presenting mythic beings and heroic figures onstage). Dance, for her, is a form of communication; a technique should enable dancers to have an exchange with the audience. Along with fostering physical abilities, the technique also hones performance skills. The dancing body should be able to communicate what the dancer wishes (consciously) to communicate. The dancer should, at all times, remain conscious of all body parts and be able to execute a movement without having to control it or by building up tension. The dancer should create and direct movement by and through the use of energy.

Mindfulness, alertness and clarity, awareness and subtle understanding of the entire body will lead to the previously described 'informed body', one that recognizes and implements the intention of a movement. An (in)formed dancer is able to dance any movement and choreography in a technically expert and emotionally believable way. A mental attitude that places particular emphasis on openness, mindfulness, joy, curiosity, and the experiential, instead of judging, is crucial.

Dancers can only achieve such openness when they are conscious of every body part without simultaneously needing to exercise control. This refers to understanding/knowing the difference between awareness and concentration—Muller finds that the latter blocks the body, just as the personal judging of one's own movement does. Thus another goal is to turn off the self–critique and not to attempt to view oneself from an external perspective, rather to put oneself fully into the whole body and honor the movement. This might be difficult if previous conditioning and self–identification processes stand in one's way. As Muller puts it: "I am limiting myself because I have a picture of myself. And therefore I cannot experience anything that does not fit in with the picture of myself. So my conditioning gets in the way of my experiencing. It gets in my way of trying to figure out and experiencing new things, and having things come to me."

Subsequently, another key element of the Muller Technique is the establishment of a working atmosphere free from constant judgment about movements and their execution—an atmosphere filled with a perceptive and lively awareness that does not judge. "Instant forgiveness" and "Turning off the camera" are mottos that Muller considers particularly important for onstage performance. Those who spend a long time railing at themselves and thinking about what might have been wrong will not be dancing in the present. Muller's technique demands exactly this focus on awareness and presence at every single moment. By letting go, one can overcome self–evaluation and conditioning, which can be manifested not only in the muscles, but also by freeing oneself of thoughts, values, and assessments.

15 See also "Understanding the Body/ Movement", keyword 'Space'.

Thus the technique's objective is to holistically form the dancer, and to teach principles that can be transferred to other dance styles. It includes being conscious of body part placement, as well as strengthening the connection between mind and body (as Muller finds in Eastern thought), and offers a basic attitude that dancers can bring into their work.

According to Muller, dancers and choreographers should create their art to communicate with the audience. This means that energy flows from the dancers to the audience, who should leave with 'memorable images'. Muller emphasizes that dancers must develop an awareness about the importance of memorable images in individual movements and their relationship to one another; this will produce clear phrasing in which not all movements are equally important. Ideally, a movement phrase has a clear high point and, potentially, additional high points—phrasing allows movement to remain in the audience's memory—high points are supported by movements that either prepare for or resolve them.

Muller contends that if there is a lack of clear phrasing, the movement sequence becomes too uniform and thus uninteresting for an audience. Since dance is a language, she compares the non-phrased movement sequence—in which all movements are equally weighted—to monotone speech. She humorously posits that the meaning gets lost and the viewer tires when choreographies are "as flat as Kansas"—where the landscape's unrelenting monotony can cause drivers to fall asleep at the wheel. Muller enjoys using this metaphor and repeats it often when she feels that dancers are not phrasing properly. Work on phrasing is an essential part of Muller's training, which is always preparing for performance. A developed consciousness for phrasing thus determines the quality of the dance as well.

How a movement is executed in terms of, and in relation to, energy–work will determine the movement quality. This is another core component of the Muller Technique. The body should be able to execute all movement qualities, from energized through relaxed, from floating to grounded. Muller's priority is that dancers be able to realize the oppositional poles of 'energized' and 'completely drained', and make these polarities clearly visible.

Furthermore, for Muller certain shapes have particular attributes and/or expressive qualities. Movement quality and emotional meaning are thus closely and specifically related to one another; movement qualities are the basis for communication through dance. As Muller emphasizes,

"Shapes really speak on a human level. And therefore carried into dance, they speak even more, because they communicate what that feeling is."

Quality—now in the context of evaluating movement—is defined by the movement's credibility and the awareness with which it is executed. Successful movement execution can be measured by how well it is communicated or to what measure the audience correctly read and understood the intended communication. For Muller, unfocused and less–engaged movements should only be performed when a dancer wishes to express these qualities. The dancer's physical stature is not as important for movement quality, as long as energy and body parts are placed and used with precision.

Choices made in how a movement sequence is phrased, as indicated above, play a large role in the movement quality and, according to Muller, its successful execution. She says, "I want to register the shape, register the next shape so that I almost have a string of pearls. Then I can decide my phrasing. Which shape is the important shape? Which shape is going to come out of it, and then which is going to serve." The dancer should thus listen to the phrase and mark points of interest; it is the dancer's task to make highpoints visible, and thus be constantly aware and preparing for them.

A soft, 'juicy', grounded plié is the building block for transitions between shapes. To achieve this, Muller draws on her flow–of–energy principle: The plié is always associated with a relaxation of the abdomen.[16] This ensures a safe arrival and contains the energy one needs to rise out of plié and continue moving.

Energy–work and movement intention are of central importance for a dancer's presence onstage, and Muller's training in 'performance skills' applies to both of these elements. An energetic and clear body is preferable to one that is indecisive and sluggish. Muller believes that a dancer can never simply be neutral onstage—communication is always occurring. When a dancer is 'neutral', unconcentrated, or tense, these properties are communicated to the audience. The tension, focus, and physicality that a dancer *should* have is determined by the intention chosen by the dancer. For Muller, dancers should be constantly seeking new inspiration for their intentions.

As presence and technical skill are intertwined, Muller trains for sustained awareness and consciousness of individual body parts. Above and beyond this, Muller has developed a number of exercises that she calls 'feeling–comfortable–in–your–own–skin exercises'. These are simple

16 See also "Understanding the Body/ Movement", keyword 'Center'.

exercises—sitting and walking through the space—that train physical awareness and aid in finding a movement's intention. What she terms 'emotional work' combines movement with attention to presence. For her, emotional work means initially understanding feelings as energy, as 'friends' and 'acquaintances' with whom one can work, but whom one can just as well let go of. Emotionality is thus not about overdramatic expression, rather a credible expenditure of energy with awareness, in relation to the movement's intention—as well as in relation to any single movement's meaning as seen in relation to other movements. Emotional expressiveness is thus affected, for example, by deciding which movements develop out of other movements and/or which movements support others, as well as awareness for a movement phrase's high points. We can therefore say that the Muller Technique combines a structural knowledge of movement and the body with imagination and emotional expression, allowing dancers to express a full range of emotions when performing.

Although the Muller Technique targets a specific aesthetic profile, the skills can be transferred to other contexts. In summary, the training attends to the holistic forming of the dancer as a performer, artist, and social being. It nurtures awareness of the body and individual parts as well as imparting knowledge about the body's structure, which leads to good placement and helps make the plié soft and useful. Dancers come to understand the interplay between these elements and how to consciously shape and use them. A dancer should have the ability to emotionally and visually interpret movements, and should further utilize the powers of imagination such that movement acquires meaning. This includes facilitating the dancer's ability to create a subtext for movements in certain contexts, even if the choreographer has not specified such. Finally, dancers should develop respect for one another in order to create a supportive and motivating working atmosphere. Beyond understanding dance as an art form, a dancer should gain social skills that can be applied to other aspects of his or her work and life. Along with discipline, (which dancers acquire automatically in their daily classes, and which Muller refers to as the 'deadline mentality'), dancers further benefit from Muller Technique experiences made in group process, working environment, and in the structuring of work processes. To that, the dancer acquires observation skills that range from the detailed to the analytical.

Yvonne Hardt, Vera Sander

UNDERSTANDING THE BODY/MOVEMENT

PREREQUISITES

Muller teaches primarily to professionals, seldom to beginners or children; i.e., dancers coming to her have previous training. Muller views every dance foundation as equal. Even though her exercises, in part, are based on a classical movement vocabulary, dancers do not need previous ballet training. She finds, also, there are many excellent contemporary training methods. Ideally dancers begin training at an early age—it is unusual for anyone, in her opinion, to start at twenty-one years or older and still become a professional dancer (although there seems to be exceptions for men).

Because Muller's is an intensive training program and her approach holistic, complementary training is not offered. She does encourage dancers to further their studies, and she practices Qigong on a daily basis. Ultimately, any practice that is geared towards supporting a flow of energy and transparency of energy, or that heightens awareness of body structure (as it applies to Muller's technique), can complement the training.

In terms of the 'ideal body', Muller is open and embraces differences. She points out that dancers in her company come in all shapes and sizes. What she does desire, however, is that dancers attain an ideally sculpted body. Rounded muscular forms that denote strength, especially in the upper thighs, should be transformed and lengthened.

A distinct mental attitude is as important as physical skills when learning the Muller Technique. This includes the willingness to engage in a philosophy that understands dance as a play between different flows of energy and sees the dance as a continual waxing and waning, not just a measurable, optimizable feat that is characterized by the expenditure of strength, muscle tension, and control. Becoming fully involved with this idea and the artistic vision behind it, to share this vision and to make it one's own—these are basic requirements that Muller contends are fundamental for working with her company. This attitude, paired with openness, is what Muller believes is the exact opposite to a dancer who simply wants to do his or her 'job'. For Muller, a dancer's engagement with her movement concepts is more important than any previous training.

In this comfortable environment—Muller often speaks of her 'family'—learning is not about looking for mistakes, rather about developing strategies to achieve more transparency, and focused on developing an awareness for movement that makes it more efficient and guards against injury. Muller understands her holistic approach to be one that trains life forces, and thus inherently protects the body.

MOVEMENT CHARACTERISTICS AND PHYSICALITY

In the Muller Technique, all body parts are trained sequentially. One exercise builds on the next, and there is progression from smaller movements and to bigger ones. Energy and the flow of energy initiate all movement, and generate movement material that can be described in terms of polarity, namely up or down. For the most part, the class takes place in standing (vertical alignment), and is characterized by abandoning and recovering vertical alignment.

While a third of the class material is reminiscent of ballet and/or directly derived from it, the exercises have been fundamentally changed by Muller's energy–work. Instead of creating a movement vocabulary for her technique, she draws on the established forms (and the intrinsic knowledge therein), using and transforming the exercises and the style.

Since the primary goal, as described above, is to train an articulate body (one that is transparent to energy), and to nurture body–part awareness, the first part of class employs simple movement and includes mental exercises: Meditative work encourages greater awareness of the body and directs the focus to various body parts. This is followed by demi-pliés and torso bends, as well as supportive arm movement, which assist in better sensing and easier execution of the ebb and flow of energy.

For the middle part of the training, Muller uses classical exercises (and their terminology) at the barre: plié, tendu, relevé, jeté, etc. The material, however, is transformed through her energy–work and by the way she combines it, for instance, with specific arm sequences that promote a clearer understanding of the flow of energy. Leg–work is an important part of the Muller Technique and is one of

---

17 See "Principles of Movement" in this section.

18 See also "Concept and Ideology", keyword 'Qualities', as well as this section, keyword 'Principles of Movement'.

the reasons why she trains at the barre. Here the plié—a 'soft' plié, or a 'useful' plié, as she calls it—is important.

This plié is basically drained of energy, encouraging a strong connection to the floor. The plié is the foundation for all movements: It allows landing, prepares the relevé and jumps, and makes phrasing possible.[17] A great deal of Muller's feedback to students is on the correct execution of this plié, and she uses many metaphors and struc-

on the plié and barre exercises serve this isolation task, as well as helping to elongate the musculature and hence endow all extremities with a lengthened appearance. This isolation, however, is not so much a basic movement principle as it is a physical and structural task that promotes an efficient flow of energy that will, in turn, enable integrated and holistic movement execution in which every body part is purposefully utilized.

tural directions to support it. (For example, Muller says that students should imagine a stream of hot lava flowing down through the legs.) For the 'useful' plié, it is particularly important that the heels remain well–anchored to the floor, that a 'crease' or 'break' is created between the hip and leg, and that the upper part of the thigh hangs relaxed.

Muller structures the body clearly, assigning individual body parts a supporting and basic energizing function while, at the same time, other body parts should hang and be relaxed (unless specifically choreographed otherwise). The back of the legs support; they extend and connect with the upright spine to create a line of energy. The weight is always on the balls of the feet. In contrast, the rib cage, the lower jaw, the front of the thighs, buttocks, and armpits should all hang. According to Muller, either tensing these areas, or pulling them up, blocks efficient and organic use of the body.

Hip placement plays a pivotal role in the structural and differentiated use of the body; the hips are positioned such that thigh muscles are not tense, and so that buttocks are relaxed and not 'tucked up'. Except for the deeper layers of the muscle, Muller contends the buttocks are generally of no use and should not be tensed. In order to achieve this, a dancer must be able to isolate those muscles, especially when considering the legs in relation to the torso. Work

Shapes and/or 'combination shapes' are a central component in the Muller Technique; these can only be realized by accessing lines of energy that connect various body parts. Muller believes that dance communicates with shapes— when shapes are realized with energetic precision.[18] Every exercise should be perceived as a holistic unit with a clear distribution of the flow of energy, which is why Muller begins with training whole body movements that are driven by the energy impulse. Every movement is initiated from the body's center. A stable, well–aligned structure and an understanding for Muller's energy–work must first be established before advanced exercises such as the combination shapes (whose execution directs various intensities of energy in different directions) as well as isolated body part movements (whereby one body part leads) can be added.

"The energy creates the form and the form somehow does not stand on its own. Perhaps that makes it lighter and not as forced to have to think about any given position and body alignment."

Jana Berg, student

Exercises that help train awareness of 'correspondence' between individual body parts—i.e., that make a structural similarity apparent between various body parts—guide students to understanding connections and relations within the body as well as assisting them in correct movement execution. For instance, during a relevé–passé exercise, students are asked to visualize a panel along the inside of the thigh to facilitate muscle flatness; the inside of the arm and palm are also rotated forwards for the same sensation of flatness. Upper body movements thus support movement of the lower body.

While Muller values good leg-work, the center[19] is particularly important for movement initiation. Here all movement begins, usually by releasing the center. Releasing commences by relaxing the abdomen, allowing it to move slightly forward—although Muller emphasizes that this is not about extending the abdomen outward. In the Muller Technique, curving the torso above the center (which can be executed in connection with releasing the center) differs from the classic modern curve, as here the center is not considered to be a lifting, stabilizing, or even contracting element. In contrast, when the body is energized and moving upwards the center is visualized as widening.

In order to facilitate hip alignment, Muller sometimes suggests students imagine the hips as a television screen. In order to facilitate the slight curve in the lower back, they should visualize an 'obi belt', which is a wide band encircling the lower back and the center. The energized center, when visualized thusly, is not achieved by using strength and tension.

An energized and stable center is required for playing with balance, for turns and tilts (whereby dancers can relinquish the center alignment of the hips for a short time before quickly finding it again). The center is not only the initiation point for all movement, it is also the driving force for all movements through the space. The movement of the hips and center are always clearly directed, which is initiated neither by (upward) thrusting nor by collapsing; this keeps the body in its axis and helps avoid any sudden imbalance. Balance is thus subtle, never powerful or forced, and achieved by targeted application of energy that flows throughout the entire body—all the way to the top of the head—and by hip placement. Muller describes this up–down polarity as a motor and support system available when executing off–balance and risky movements.

The use of strength is discouraged inasmuch as it has to do with contraction, control, and tension. For Muller, the objective is to employ strength efficiently and to overcome tension. By accessing the flow of energy and the body's structural alignment, stability can be achieved without activating high muscle tonus. A visible and high degree of muscular strength is used solely as a choreographic element that serves to increase tension.

Instead of strength, Muller commonly uses the term 'sourcing', i.e., constantly filling the movement with energy. This allows for longer, more stable, and more expressive suspension in balance or turns, and for maintaining and filling shapes for a longer time.

Fundamentally, energy can only flow in one direction: the relevé is driven by an upward flow of energy. The plié, in contrast, requires a complete draining of energy. When executing both up as well as down movements, it is paramount to use as little muscle strength as possible. During the relevé, there is no pushing upward and no opposing movement is visualized. This applies even more so to the plié, in which the body simply melts away. This melting goes hand–in–hand with sensing gravity.

Muller's technique is based on a play with and against gravity. Gravity is especially palpable and necessary for the plié. The Muller Technique plié is a grounded one that gives in to gravity, has a soft quality, and is accompanied by a release of the abdominal muscles. These qualities provide dancers the necessary connection to the floor, enabling them to better transition between what are sometimes risky moves.

One never collapses the body's structure; a measured release is called for. Muller speaks here of 'liquid weight', or the previously mentioned lava flows that 'melt' the legs, or warm energy that flows along the legs. 'Dropping' and 'dissolving' are two additional terms that suggest softness in reference to body weight.

Gravity is one of the few things that, according to Muller, can be felt directly in the body—as opposed to, for instance, flows of energy or the anatomical structure of the body, which she considers primarily accessible through visualization.

In the combination shapes, gravity will only be sensed in certain body parts (the legs, for example), while other parts (the arms, for instance) are energized. 'Sourcing of energy' is considered the counterpart to gravity. Energy is actively tapped by the dancer who then directs it, enabling

---

19 About localizing the body's center, see the introduction to Concept and Ideology.
20 See also the previous description of this exercise in this subsection.

21 See also the in–depth description about this in "Concept and Ideology", keyword 'Intent'.

22 For explanation of shapes, see also "Concept and Ideology", keyword 'quality', and in this section: 'Movement Characteristics and Physicality'.

a play with balance, relevé, and turns. Movements are never executed impulsively upwards or with extraordinary muscle strength. A measured exchange of energy, from energetic to drained, is the goal. Energy never 'bounces' the dancer away from the floor because dancers have gently released energy into the floor. Any type of bounce or collapse, or what Muller calls a 'forced drop', is thereby avoided.

Space is only indirectly referenced in the Muller Technique—through the 'up and down' or when speaking about the body's structural alignment along horizontal and vertical lines. A movement's initiation and characteristics are created by the flow of energy, and less by spatial visualization. In the third and final part of class, the entire space is used for across–the–floor combinations that happen on the diagonal or on straight lines.

The technique does, however, reference space using shapes. Straight, elongated movements that follow or create abstract spatial lines do not determine a spatial configuration; rather, the shapes themselves communicate, are energized, are directional, and configure space. Subdividing the body according to spatial levels can play a role here, inasmuch as the energy can be directed 'up and out' as well as 'down and out'.

The flow of energy should not end at the body's periphery: Clearly configured shapes, sourced with energy, will enter and fill the space. The extremities and the head, in particular, are places where energy passes through and out into the room, thus creating a continuum with the environment.

For the most part, individual exercises are executed facing forward, although dancers should always be aware of the body's three–dimensionality. Both the meditation and first exercises center floor (as well as those later at the barre) are done standing so that much attention can be paid to vertical alignment. The hips in particular remain over the legs, even when moving through space (except for certain turns and choreographic decisions). Muller Technique does not include work on the floor. Muller believes dance is an art of energy and, for her, floorwork limits the means by which generating and sensing energy is accessed and trained.

Other spatial notions are employed when talking about body sculpting; for example a flatness is desired, rather than roundness, of the thighs. Spatial visualization is thus also a principle with which dancers can experience the correspondences mentioned above. When rotated forward, the flatness of the arms correlates to the flatness of the thighs in relevé–passé.[20]

Rhythm, dynamics, and phrasing are significant reference points in the Muller Technique, much more so than a dimensional play with space. Muller considers rhythm important, both in relation to music and movement phrasing. Exercises and rhythms must match one another.

Ideally—as described the section about music—music in 3/4-time is used for softer and warm–up movements, 4/4-time is reserved for faster movements done across the floor.

The second aspect regarding her understanding of rhythm is the interplay between an individual's body rhythm and movement phrasing—which, in Muller's eyes, is the key to turning dance into language. Phrasing, which she compares to onomatopoetic structure of sentences, makes it possible to create movement that is memorable.[21] "If I do everything at the same dynamic and level, it is going to be very hard for the audience to remember what I am doing, because I am not dancing in sentences. And that means any kind of work, from Release to classical to anything else." Plié plays the key role in structuring a dancing 'sentence' as it prepares the high points.

Muller prefers a rhythmic and dynamic phrasing that is mindful of a movement's communicative value, as opposed to one that seems naturally created or based on breath rhythm. Breath facilitates the meditation and relaxation at the beginning of class as well as the energizing needed for the first waxing and waning exercises. Despite this, Muller finds that breath rhythm is not detailed enough for movement phrasing and she worries that breath flow might be inhibited if nailed down to phrasing. For Muller, what makes the technique organic is not relating breath and movement, but a conscious guiding of the flow of energy.

The basic movement principles in Muller's training include, as stated above, movement execution based on energy flow and structural alignment of the body—both of which rely on the use of imagination. Cyclic flow—the waxing and waning of energy—is the basis for every shape. This is about polarities. Visualizing a shape serves to generate and support movement. When combined with a structural description of the body that encourages the flow of energy, a basis for further movement is established.

Muller thus speaks of three support systems:

1. The polarity between energized and drained, up and down;

2. The floor as a place from which dancers can source energy;

3. The connection between the abdomen, spine, and the back of the legs.

The interplay between these three factors helps the dancer render shapes[22] with subtle awareness. The making of shapes is found in all aspects of her technique, from leg–work, steps, arm movements, and jumps. According to Muller, every shape communicates in that it conveys a message, a feeling, or an attitude. The dance is thus realized, understood, and designed by a series of moving shapes.

/ "For me, there's the shape and there's the transition into the shape. Doesn't mean that I can't…do movements that come into the next shape, but for me, the arrival in the shape, getting to the arrival in the shape, is the important point. And arrival doesn't mean that it's held or that it's controlled, or that it's hard—it's just that I recognize it as a shape. In my brain and in my sensation, I can recognize it as a shape. And I want to get to the shape so I can experience the shape. I'm not going to creep my way into the shape." /

Shapes are created in Muller Technique by energizing the entire body or certain body parts. Imagination, in turn, endows the shape with character, rendering it more intense and recognizable. Muller says that this is not about interpreting any given movement, rather that each shape has its own feeling. "So when I'm discovering the feeling of a shape, or when I am involved in the sensation of a shape, I can look at it and take into account the properties of the shape." This is, then, what Muller calls 'entering into' a shape, something that will have an emotional impact on the dancer.

Shapes are made even clearer by correspondences: dancers imagine connections between body parts in which anatomical principles are rather unimportant. This is about dancers' visualizations of corresponding body parts, for instance, the rounding of the arm can correspond to that of the back, or the line of the leg can correspond to the arm's line. These correspondences make the shapes clearer and thus, for Muller, allow the shapes to communicate more clearly.

This is supported by 'assumptions' and 'references'. Muller uses specific terms for these and has a humorous perspective of them: "We have different, very silly names for a lot of the shapes, because they're easy to remember. Evil eagle, somebody said, is like an evil bird. It's a reference. An assumption would be: two straight arms and a wrist flexed. That's the assumption of it." These images assist dancers in better remembering and internalizing shapes.

Muller believes that her methods can be transferred to all forms of dance, especially her work with energy and visualization. Even if one prefers doing floorwork or consciously wants to avoid energized shapes and phrasing, Muller's awareness and openness towards these elements can be helpful. Her personal movement choices and style should therefore not be considered a limit or defining element of her technique.

Yvonne Hardt, Vera Sander

TEACHING: PRINCIPLES AND METHODOLOGY

CONCEPTUAL BASIS

Muller's teaching concept is based upon several precepts. One is activating the dancer's powers of imagination, and another sensitizes dancers for perception, which she describes as residing between feeling and visualization/imagination. According to Muller, a person cannot directly sense the majority of things in or on the body (exceptions include touching the skin or the sensation of weight). Instead, these things (i.e., the flow of energy) are made real through the power of imagination. Thus students should imagine a movement—fully grasping it first in thought before attempting to physically perform it. This helps avoid pure imitation. For most students this presents a challenge as they must learn to inhibit the impulse to 'move first, think later'.

The powers of imagination guide the student in attaining Muller's second precept: namely, training dancers who can make themselves transparent for energy and their movements credible. Thus, along with a physical mastery, mental and social skills are crucial to her teaching.

Class begins with meditation in order to awaken the imagination and improve body awareness. Students observe the breath and the energy it creates, or call up images of individual body parts in order to clear their minds and let go of other thoughts.

This meditation reflects a clear principle: one thing builds upon the next in Muller's classes, every exercise prepares for something that will be explored more deeply in the next exercise and/or can be combined with other material. Class basically follows a progression from slow and simple to faster and more complex. Muller believes an instructor must know how individual exercises relate to each other and why they are being used, and, furthermore, the teacher has a responsibility to convey this information to students. Students should understand why exercises are being done in a certain order as well as connections between various exercises. Teaching potential and success in communicating principles is greater when classes can be

offered over a longer time period. Usually, Muller builds up her class systematically over a week, repeating the basics so students are able to focus on movement qualities and do not have to worry about recalling the order of exercises and combinations.

Muller's methodology is targeted to previously trained dancers whose perspectives she wants to broaden.[23] A dancer's background only indirectly influences the amount of time needed to learn the technique, as this will vary from person to person. Descriptions of isolated problems that dancers still have after dancing for years in her company imply, however, that learning the Muller Technique may never be fully accomplished.

Because Muller developed her methodology while working as a professional choreographer, she seldom instructs children and amateurs, and, if she does, adopts a different teaching approach. And because group dynamics and class atmosphere are essential for Muller, she only teaches technique classes to groups as she believes that the group atmosphere generates a kinetic force as well as providing moral support for the work of dancing.

Muller's pedagogic approach to the work is characterized by her determination to affect changes in her students and dancers. She differentiates between teachers who 'give' a class and those who 'teach', and means that the latter ensures students will experience change. Teachers should monitor students' development, and constantly motivate. Voice plays a key role in this process, for instance in determining whether an instruction comes across as 'strict' or 'harsh'. The latter should be avoided—and here Muller is consciously disassociating herself from what she experienced under her influential teacher Antony Tudor, who systematically tried to 'break' his students. Instead, Muller believes teachers should challenge and push for change but, at the same time, impart self-confidence to students, support students' development, and motivate them to remain interested in life and dance. She also believes that rivalry and jealousy result from a lack of self-confidence and are unproductive. She emphasizes the need for a supportive atmosphere, defined by respect for oneself and others. She is interested in training people who, in their own way, will be beneficial to the world—which is why she is not surprised by the fact that many of her dancers later change careers, moving into professions that deal with healing in the broadest sense of the word.

23 See "Understanding the Body/Movement", keyword 'Prerequisites'.
24 For details about the lesson structure and an explanation of individual exercises, see the Lesson Plans on DVD 1.
25 See also "Understanding the Body/Movement", Movement Characteristics and Physicality, keyword 'Movement Principles'.

PEDAGOGICAL METHODS

The two–hour classes follow a systematic lesson structure and are separated into three units: The first, which takes place in the middle of the room, involves meditation to rouse awareness of the body, and includes exercises in energizing as well as emptying the body of energy; the second unit is work at the barre; the third includes sequences across the floor. Each of these phases generally begins slowly and increases in both speed and complexity. The sections correlate to one another in that every exercise prepares for the next, or teaches elements from the longer phrase that is performed towards the end of class.

The class's beginning meditation allows students to arrive in the space and sensitize a consciousness for their bodies. It also aids in shifting the student's focus onto the power of imagination, an important dance tool.

The first physical exercise works with the simplest polarity, up and down, to harness the flows of energy. The second exercise adds arm movements to support this ebb and flow and/or to make it possible to sense different energy flows in simple combination shapes (in which, for instance, the energy in the legs flows downward and energy in the arms flows upward and outward). Both exercises are repeated several times at various tempos and thus pick up on the meditative quality found in the first exercise phase.

The lesson unit at the barre appears to be traditional barre work, but the emphasis is on movement quality and intention.

Starting with small tendus, pliés, and battements, small elements are added to each exercise; first turn–out and deep plié, then with the gesture leg and shifting weight. This unit continues with faster tempos for foot–work and higher leg–work.

In the third part of class, exercises allow the dancer to move out into the space. It begins, usually, with simple steps across the floor with pliés and relevés. Then longer movement sequences are introduced in which arm movements from the first part of class are combined with steps across the floor. As in the meditation section at the beginning of class, Muller might include constant repetition with slight modifications, additions, and accelerations in this phase as well. Here dancers also have the opportunity to work on phrasing the longer movement combinations.

Finally, small jumps prepare dancers for larger jumps that conclude class.[24]

During the course of the workshop in Cologne, Muller slightly adjusted the class's dynamic structure. Early in the week, because of an extensive introduction and explanation of the exercises (which students were only to visualize at this point), there were more quiet moments and thus a clear switching back–and–forth between explanation and movement. Muller's series of exercises progress from easy to complex and from slow to fast in each phase of class—progressing in this manner at the barre then again when working through space—thus during the easy and slow start to a new phase the dancer has time for rest and recovery—which is accomplished through movement and as part of an exercise.

Muller's teaching approach is also characterized by talking dancers through the exercises. She first demonstrates an exercise and calls on the dancers (as described above) to begin by visualizing the exercise, as she wants students to internalize the movement sequence using their active and creative mind before they move. In her descriptions of the movements, she is articulate and chooses her words carefully.

Exercises are selected and/or designed in pursuit of a clear objective, which is derived either from the company's choreographic work or students' needs. Muller's demonstrations of exercises always include verbal information about the quality and purpose of each exercise. This provides us with another example of Muller's principle of correspondence: indicating interconnectedness between exercises goes well beyond illustrating connections inside the body.[25] Lessons are carefully planned; Muller places particular importance on the rigor and interplay of exercises during her classes, and the teacher is the central point of reference for students throughout class. Muller sees herself as teacher. In her role as choreographer, she sees herself as an author and the person responsible for designing and ordering movement material in order to achieve a certain effect. Improvisation is not part of her class.

Nonetheless, she repeatedly invites her students to reflect on the material, thus breaking with the traditional structure of a technique class. After the students first attempted an exercise in Cologne, Muller often demonstrated several interpretations she had seen and prompted students to analyze by asking, "What's wrong with the body?" Usually she makes corrections only after posing

the question and establishing the link between the exercises and the relevant movement principle.

While dancers are performing the exercises, she helps individuals focus their attention on certain body parts by use of touch. She uses touch prudently, taking care to support and encourage the learning process and not to inhibit it. She also seeks to maintain a balance between giving individual corrections and observing the group as a whole. Although classes are not designed for dancers to give each other feedback (no hands–on partner work, however) a group feeling is created through the supportive, motivating atmosphere and by working towards a common goal. Muller believes that the group situation promotes good energy, which is why she prefers teaching group classes to private lessons.

Language and communication are core elements in Muller's definition of herself as a teacher and dancer. They are fundamental for her teaching, and also serve to foster cooperation and expression through the dance. In Muller's teacher training, increased awareness of how language is used, noises, communication strategies, and dealing with feedback all play an important role. The voice should provide motivation and energy, speech should have highs and lows, be soft and loud. The entire range of rhythmic speech is used over the course of a single class. Transcripts of the recordings of Muller's voice during class highlight the repetitive and, in part, meditative nature of her verbal input. At the beginning, her voice creates a luxurious, rhythmic blanket of sound:

/ "Close your eyes… watch your breathing…just watch your breathing coming into your nose…all the way down to your abdomen…recognize the breath coming all the way down into your abdomen… watching…getting a very clear idea of the passage of air in the body and recognize that the air inside your body is the same as the air outside your body, that you have a direct connection to outside…and allow what we talked about yesterday, the liquid weight of your body, to sink down past the floor…the more you can come inside, the more you can recognize and sense the different parts of your body…we have talked about the combination of imagination and sensation."[26] /

Muller speaks almost without pause in certain phases of class. She uses language to sensitize awareness of specific body parts, or to describe exercises at the outset. The language is descriptive, and is often interspersed by giving specific counts for a movement phrase or when she explains a tie–in to the previous exercise. Her metaphors, rhythmic repetition, explanations, and directions help create a working atmosphere that is open and motivating for everyone.

For a learning situation to be completely communicative and open, Muller expects dancers to behave respectfully towards each other so that 'free' space is created for

26 Transcript of class from 24 November 2009, p.
27 See: Concept and Ideology / Imagining the Body, keyword 'Music'.

28 'Creative Mind Work' is a teaching format that addresses and fosters imagination and creative thinking for dancers and non dancers.

29 For a description of this 'supportive atmosphere', see above, subsection: Conceptual Basis / Foundation, keyword 'Approach to Work'.

individuals, yet students must also recognize that group activity and class are the priorities. Dancers should not disrupt the group with their problems. Students arrive with their respective moods and concerns; these, however, cannot be discussed at the expense of others.

/ "You come in with yourself. If you are the person who is sad, that's who you are, but then you focus. We talked about emotion being an energy. So, you take that energy, and you use it to focus on the work you're doing… The most important thing is to bring yourself into the work… Because it is an energy, and you could say, 'Okay, at this moment, this is a new space. So I have a new focus. I'll let this go for the moment.' If you can't quite get to that point of letting go, then you can take that energy, even sadness, and you can still work in an incredible way. But you don't want to impose it on someone else so that they can't work." /

Muller believes that dealing with feelings is positive and constructive, but discussions about feelings are likely to be disruptive—especially when the concerns have nothing to do with the others and the overall atmosphere is affected.

Nonetheless, arguments between dancers or feelings of unease should be dealt with quickly. Communication is fundamental for creating openness and a safe working space, and is especially important to her. Communication is not only the cornerstone for a successful working environment, it is the foundation for the humanistic potential Muller sees in her work.

/ "Human values are very important to me… It shows up in the work, it shows up in the way that I conduct myself when I teach, it shows up in the way the company is when it goes out into lecture demonstrations. You know, this is a kind of atmosphere that is very passionate, but very respectful of other people. A very supportive atmosphere… And so that's for me one of the big motivating factors… I think we're put on the earth to serve and make the earth a better place, and to make everyone's life a better place. And dance happens to be the one thing that I know how to do, so that's my contribution." /

Thus communication for Muller goes above and beyond class and the meaning of her own work. Communication contributes to a good environment as well as to teaching values that are significant beyond technique. These working environments and values help make dancers into better human beings by sharpening social and communication skills.

Along with communication, rhythm also informs the motor learning process. In the Muller Technique, movement is generated with awareness for phrasing and is danced in time with the music. Music and rhythm both facilitate learning and structure the time spent in class; they have an energizing effect— especially when a 'beat' corresponds well to the movement. 3/4–rhythms, for instance, are better for slower sequences, and 4/4 for the faster sequences, especially when doing foot–work.[27]

In summary, The Muller Technique requires teaching skills on various levels. On one hand, the technique requires a physical and mental comprehension of basic principles that includes, among other things, good understanding about body placement and the meaning of phrasing and 'phrase work'. On the other hand, teachers must also know how to structure a class sensibly, as well as having a thorough knowledge of music and rhythm so as to support the exercises. A teacher should also either have or develop a skilled use the voice, and other means, to rouse students' imaginations. Muller's 'Creative Mind Work'[28] supports these processes.

Teachers are encouraged to constantly check that their teaching goals and class structures reflect the target group, and that exercises are adapted accordingly. Teachers should also be able to establish a supportive learning atmosphere.[29] If moods or dynamics block or inhibit the learning process, a teacher must analyze the situation and develop strategies for transforming it into a positive experience.

Since special skills are necessary for teaching the Muller Technique, Jennifer Muller has created her own teacher–training program, which is open to long–standing company members.

The artistic process, in the sense of invention and development of a student's own movement material, is only indirectly found in Muller's technique classes. However, themes dealing with humanity and credibility, and a passion to communicate, are carried over into Muller's artistic work. Because Muller always has an idea and/or an exact outline before starting a choreography, the teaching, from the beginning, is designed in such a way that it will foster understanding about the ideas and intentions behind the movement. Both the choreographer and performer are obliged, in her opinion, to know what they want to express before commencing on a choreographic journey. In class, Muller talks about her artistic works and teaches phrases from her repertoire. Although students do not experiment or create their own choreographic work, they are nonetheless given insights into artistic and creative processes. Additionally, they learn how to interpret and give life to choreographies as well as how to make their performances experiential and credible. Muller explains her artistic process as follows:

/ "I see the shape and I'll draw that, so when I'm referring back to it and working very fast on my feet, I will look at it, and think, 'Aha, aha, alright. Like that.' So it works like a vocabulary for me, as a reference. It doesn't mean that the shapes will be placed in the order that I drew them. It means that I think those shapes are appropriate for that piece, to communicate what I want to say… that was part of what I decided was my vocabulary for that piece. And therefore I had little drawings and little things like that, so I could refer back to the shapes in my mind." /

After establishing a vocabulary, Muller works out movement ideas with the dancers. With certain dancers in mind, she choreographs scenes tailored to them or with particular challenges. Scenes might be scrapped or material turn out differently than planned (i.e., what starts as serious may, for instance, become funny and ironic, like a cartoon). Muller allows the shapes to take on a life of their own and abandons her original intention if necessary. Despite cooperative work with her dancers and however much the original idea evolves during rehearsals, Muller views herself as the author; she is responsible for her works and decides on all details. Thus, Muller's teaching methods instill (indirectly) an understanding of the artistic process that puts the choreographer center stage.

The dancers, for their part, have the responsibility to perform with credible emotional intensity and intention. In this respect, Muller's artistic work and her technique are fundamentally interconnected. Since dancers often work with Muller for years, they have become part of an artistic team in which their identification with the technique, working methods, and the company are a central to practicing their art. Dancing, in Muller's company, is not a 'job' that is simply performed, rather it is a profession characterized by dedication and commitment over a longer period of time.

Much to her chagrin, Muller's main task these days is in chasing down funds for continued company financing. Her international teaching work, as well as training dancers to become teachers, are part of what she does to advance the company, both materially and as a means to provide dancers with additional qualifications.

The thoroughness found in the teacher–training program is evidence of how much importance Muller places on preparation and structure for teaching. A class is planned with great detail, and basic class structure is rarely changed, although she does prepare exercises anew to correspond with specific objectives. Usually a particular theme is worked on over the course of a week, and certain phrases and movement sequences are prepared to permit and support this focus. For new groups, class planning must be adjusted to needs, and it must progress as the students become more familiar with the material. This requires that the teacher not only work out the lesson structure, but also make decisions about tempos and/or appropriate music choices.

Dancers who are selected for Muller's teacher–training program learn about structuring classes and how to teach the basic principles, especially how to rouse the imagination using the voice and other means. Muller's fixed class structures are the product of many years of hard–earned knowledge. Because she is always passing her knowledge on to her (teaching) students, she is constantly reflecting upon the material. Dancers can and have impacted various aspects of her training.

Muller depends upon student feedback for self–assessment purposes. While she acknowledges, to herself, particular exercises and tasks that could be better prepared, she also asks students for their feedback and to talk about problem areas. Where do they have questions? Which aspects remain difficult? Where does one feel progress is being made? Muller usually incorporates the answers into the next lesson. She tries to analyze the blockages and consequently change her verbal instructions (rather than the training sequence) to provide new imagery, or she slows down the exercises. Follow–up work also includes considering how to transform these blockages into positive experiences.

Yvonne Hardt, Vera Sander

CONCLUSION

The topics of change, ebb and flow of energy, acceptance, and motivation characterize Jennifer Muller's approach and form the philosophical foundation of her dance technique. She combines the influence of Asian philosophy with the objective of training dancers who can credibly communicate onstage, because, for Muller, dance *is* communication. Along with increasing dancers' potential for movement, her technique also focuses on enhancing performance qualities (fostered through energy–work) with additional teaching formats like 'Creative Mind Work', 'Performance Skills', and 'Solo Phrasework'.[30] All of these practices are brought together in order to focus on the free flow of energy within the body, to create knowledge and meaning from the powers of imagination and visualization, and to train awareness about the technique's movement principles.

The Muller Technique refers to energy systems that are visualized as an 'inner motor for movement'. The technique, which is organic, mentally stimulating, and works with energy, increases the body's transparency for energy, creates movement flow, trains awareness for individual body parts (and their interplay), and imparts an understanding of the body's structure. The technique thus broadens previously acquired technical skills, promotes the power of expression, and aims to protect the body from injury through its holistic approach.

Jennifer Muller, and her technique as it emerged in the 1970s, is thus considered a pioneer in the field of relaxation–based training. However, more so than the Release–based techniques that have since come into existence, she retains the rudiments of ballet and traditional modern dance while fundamentally transforming both by applying various movement and energy principles.

30 'Solo Phrasework' is a teaching format directed toward soloists; it addresses dynamics, phrasing, intention, concentration of movement, structure, and focus.

Her working and movement principles can thus also be recognized in other techniques or transferred onto them. Elements that are applicable to other techniques include, for instance, her work with relaxation and movement efficiency, awareness of energy, the idea of achieving control through the knowledge of body structure, using the powers of imagination, and avoiding too much strength or muscle tension. The technique further assists in clearing blockages, achieving transparency in the body, and strengthening the connection between mind and body—all of which can be applied to other training and performance contexts.

Thus Muller's body of work is groundbreaking as it is less interested in drill than in humanistic values, and in the belief that a constructive and motivating learning atmosphere is crucial. Muller is interested in the people she teaches, and in encouraging them individually. Aspects of the technique that target communication skills and creative thinking are utilized by students in other areas of their lives. Moreover, Muller's teaching format is also used in schools and social projects, thereby helping to convey an understanding of art, creative thinking, dance, and non-verbal communication to youth, schoolchildren, and students.

Because of the guided nurturing of her dancers and the teacher–training program, the Muller Technique is being taught and developed around the world. The intimate relationship between artistic work and her dance company, teachers and her technique, are what make Muller's body of work so special. Her choreographies and her technique have been nurturing each other for more than forty years. Muller, whose works are characterized by cooperations with renowned artists from other disciplines, has developed a distinguished artistic signature. Her artistic vision, along with her pedagogic approach and the Muller Technique, has been influencing the dance world for decades.

LITERATURE / LINKS

For more information about Jennifer Muller and her artistic work, see her homepage: **www.jmtw.org.**

Transcriptions of the Muller Laboratory from 23 November–1 December 2009 (TML) and the transcriptions of individual technique lessons (TKT) are available as supplemental material at the library of the Centre for Contemporary Dance in Cologne (ZZT). Additionally, there is video documentation of the entire research project.

Anderson, Jack
The American Dance Festival
Durham: Duke University Press, 1987

Banes, Sally
Terpsichore in Sneakers: Post-Modern Dance
Middletown: Wesleyan University Press, 1987

Franko, Mark
Dancing Modernism / Performing Politics
Bloomington: Indiana University Press, 1995

Graff, Ellen
Stepping Left: Dance and Politics in New York City 1928–1942
Durham: Duke University Press, 1997

Hardt, Yvonne
"Reading Emotion: Lesarten des Emotionalen am Beispiel des Modernen Tanzes in den USA (1945–1965)"
In: Bischof, Margrit | Feest, Claudia | Rosiny, Claudia (Eds.)
 e-motions. Jahrbuch der Gesellschaft für Tanzforschung. Vol. 16,
Münster: Lit Verlag, 2006, pp. 139–155

Laotse
Tao Te King. Das Buch des alten Meisters vom Sinn und Leben
Translated by Richard Wilhelm
Cologne: Anaconda, 2006

Lewis, Daniel
The Illustrated Dance Technique of José Limón
Hightstown (NJ): Princeton Book Company, 1999

Mansfield Doares, Janet
Louis Horst: Musician in a Dancer's World
Durham: Duke University Press, 1992

Todd, Mabel E.
Der Körper denkt mit: Anatomie als Ausdruck dynamischer Kräfte
Bern: Hans Huber Verlag, 2001/2003 (The original was published in 1937, entitled The Thinking Body. A Study of the Balancing Forces of Dynamic Man. London: Dance Books, 1937)

Topaz, Muriel: **Undimmed Lustre: The Life of Anthony Tudor**
Lanham (MD): The Scarecrow Press, 2002

Warren, Larry
Anna Sokolow: The Rebellious Spirit
(Choreography and Dance Studies Series)
New York: Routledge, 1998

LANCE GRIES
RELEASE AND ALIGNMENT ORIENTED TECHNIQUES

FRANKFURT UNIVERSITY OF MUSIC AND PERFORMING ARTS

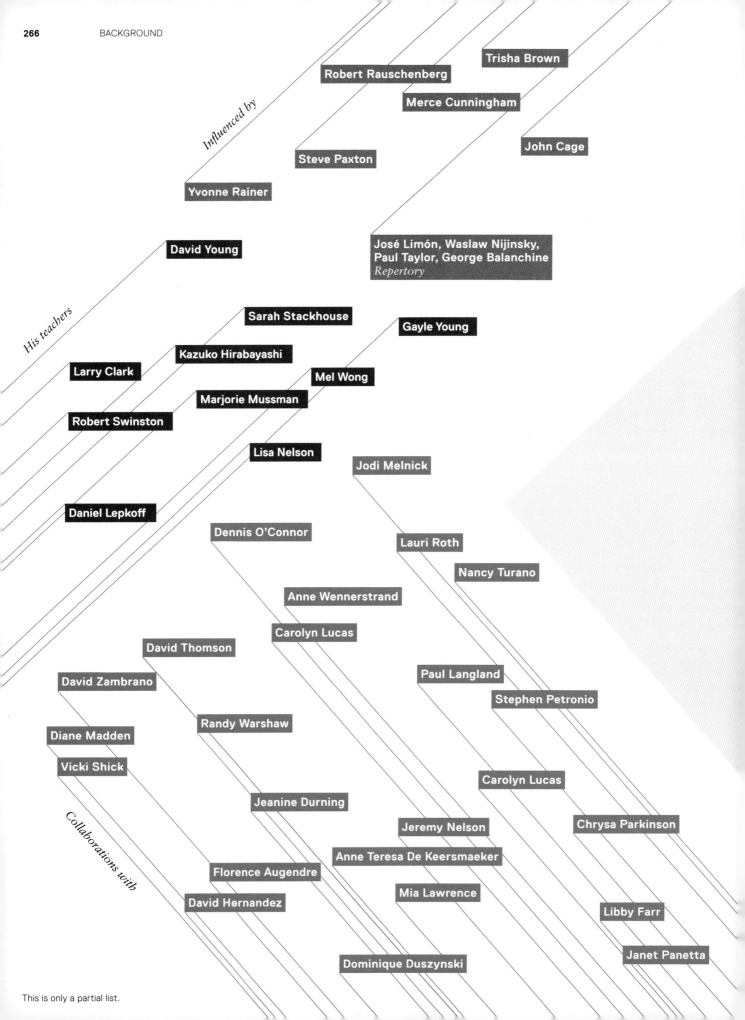

Influenced by

Trisha Brown

Robert Rauschenberg

Merce Cunningham

John Cage

Steve Paxton

Yvonne Rainer

David Young

José Limón, Waslaw Nijinsky, Paul Taylor, George Balanchine
Repertory

His teachers

Sarah Stackhouse

Gayle Young

Kazuko Hirabayashi

Larry Clark

Mel Wong

Marjorie Mussman

Robert Swinston

Lisa Nelson

Jodi Melnick

Daniel Lepkoff

Dennis O'Connor

Lauri Roth

Nancy Turano

Anne Wennerstrand

Carolyn Lucas

David Thomson

Paul Langland

David Zambrano

Stephen Petronio

Diane Madden

Randy Warshaw

Vicki Shick

Carolyn Lucas

Collaborations with

Jeanine Durning

Jeremy Nelson

Chrysa Parkinson

Anne Teresa De Keersmaeker

Florence Augendre

Mia Lawrence

David Hernandez

Libby Farr

Janet Panetta

Dominique Duszynski

This is only a partial list.

LANCE GRIES — RELEASE AND ALIGNMENT ORIENTED TECHNIQUES

Research Team at the Frankfurt University of Music and Performing Arts, in cooperation with the Institute for Applied Theatre Studies, Justus–Liebig–University Giessen: Lance Gries, Gabriele Wittmann, Sylvia Scheidl, Prof. Dr. Gerald Siegmund

AUTHORS
Gabriele Wittmann, Sylvia Scheidl, Gerald Siegmund

INTERVIEW
Edith Boxberger

STUDENTS
of the master's program in Contemporary Dance Pedagogy (MAztp), the bachelor's program in Dance (BAtanz), and the master's program in Choreography and Performance (MACuP): Erica Charalambous, Siri Clinckspoor, Hannah Dewor, Natalia Gomez, Berit Jentzsch, Jungyeon Kim, Kaya Kołodziejczyk, Anastasia Kostner, Ulla Mäkinen, Lili Mihajlović, Monica Muñoz, Katja Mustonen, Sylvia Scheidl, and Romain Thibaud-Rose

LANCE GRIES (*1963)
while pursuing an early love of music and an economics degree, began formal dance training at Indiana University and later completed his BFA in dance at SUNY Purchase College, New York. From 1985–1992 he was a member of the Trisha Brown Dance Company and was honored for his work there with a New York Dance and Performance Award ('Bessie'), and a Princess Grace Foundation Award. Since 1990 Lance Gries has created and presented solo and group choreographies in various venues in New York City, including The Kitchen and Danspace, and in cities throughout Europe. He has taught workshops and masterclasses throughout the world and became a 'founding teacher' of P.A.R.T.S. in Brussels in 1994, where he is still a visiting teacher. He has taught for many European dance companies and institutions including Rosas, UltimaVez, Lyon Opera Ballet, London Contemporary Dance, CND in Paris, Toulouse, and Lyon, France, the Frankfurt University of Music and Performing Arts, Tanzfabrik in Berlin, The Danish National School of Contemporary Dance in Copenhagen as well as Movement Research, Janet Panetta Studio, and Trisha Brown Studios in New York City.

Lance Gries Interviewed by Edith Boxberger

GUIDING THE BODY IN EXPERIENCE

/ **What techniques have you studied?
Which teachers have been important for you?**
Like many young men, I did not start dancing until quite
late. I was a swimmer, a diver, and above all, a musician.
I played piano, guitar, French horn, string bass, and I was
a vocal artist. I went to the university as a musician,
and was also studying business. Because I had some free
time in my schedule, I added a ballet class. Quickly I
discovered that my body was very adept, so the second
half of my first year at Indiana University I changed
my focus and became a full–time dance student.

/ **And you quit music?** Yes, I was very happy to find
an art form where there was a shared experience,
lots of community, and exchanging in a group—I
somehow knew I did not have the discipline to be a
musician, exercising mostly alone. At the end of
1982 I changed to State University of New York at
Purchase, a university for the arts about forty-five minutes outside New York, yet very connected to the
city. At that time, alongside Juilliard, it probably had
the most reputable dance department. This was a
very healthy time for American dance; young men were
getting into the university system and there was a
balance of men and women. The program was quite the
representation of American Modern Dance; we had
Cunningham, Graham, and Limón Technique. And we
had ballet every day with teachers mostly from American
Ballet Theatre, plus some improvisation, some composition, and music. Also we learned a broad repertoire
of both classical and modern works.

Probably the most influential teacher, not only for me
but also for quite a group of dancers at the time, was
Sarah Stackhouse, a Limón dancer. And I am very proud
to say my dance history teacher was Sally Banes. At
the time we did not have a lot of practical information
about the postmodern tradition or about Contact
Improvisation.

/ **What was so influential about Sarah
Stackhouse's teaching?** It was the quality of her
working and dancing, the depth of inhabitation in her
body, this real human, very human depth of her
quality, of her body and her dancing. Certainly the use
of technical language, the use of weight, the drop and
swing—qualities that are integral to the Limòn Technique, and which transferred in terms of qualities into my
later work when I started working with Trisha Brown.

/ **Do you see a connection between Sarah
Stackhouse's work and postmodern teachings?**
Yes, with the simplicity of presentation—again,
the human quality of presentation—and the use of
weight as opposed to Graham and Cunningham
Technique, where there is a different carriage, presentation in the body, a different sense of attack, and the
energy is used differently as well. In fact, a group of people who were communicating and dancing together,
and working with Sarah on different levels, eventually
ended up dancing in Trisha Brown's company.

/ **What happened inside the group of people you
worked with?** With a group of colleagues, we did
readings about the pioneers in American dance. We knew
the work of John Cage, the conceptual work of Robert
Rauschenberg, of the happening and performance
artists, and we did, in our own small way, try to make
explorations. There was an identification, for sure,
and that period of the 60's and 70's in America still hangs
on. Having worked the last years in Europe, I feel it is
being relived, at least the investigation, in places where I
teach—like P.A.R.T.S. It makes such a difference,
being involved with a group of people, privately and in
class, where you can be creative, be challenged, and
develop ideas.

In my last year at SUNY Purchase, one of my colleagues who worked in the Limón Company and also in
Trisha's Company, showed us some of Trisha's material and talked about how different it was, how it was organized, and what the principles were. So we got a
taste of this whole other kind of aesthetic and movement.

/ **When did you join Trisha Brown's company?**
I auditioned in 1985, some months before I finished
school, and I was the third male in the company.
Late '85 was our first full European tour, and it was also
the moment when Trisha was on her way to creating
a lot of really rich movement studies. Her focus was on
developing more vocabulary. I hadn't had a lot of
Contact Improvisation in college, so I was lucky that
when I joined the company that Steven Petronio,
Randy Warshaw, and Diane Madden—who had been
students of Steven Paxton and Lisa Smith at Hampshire
College—were still dancing with Trisha. I learned
a lot from them about applying Contact Improvisation
principles to partnering technique, as well as applying it to my own technique.

So we began to get a new generation of dancers doing this evolving style of movement—both in and around Trisha's company—who needed different training. I think this is when we really find people taking from the historical body of research already loosely defined as Release Technique and putting it into a more pedagogical form. I had an Alexander teacher, June Ekman, who tried very hard to transcribe some of those principles onto the dancer's body, giving the pelvis a lot more strength and the body a lot more depth and opposition. She tried to make her ideas useful and practical for the dancer, which is what I tried to do when I started teaching. I started teaching pretty early, on the first or second tour. We would go to one place to perform and they would ask for a master class, so I tried my best: I did a few basic exercises and some repertory. At that time, this was a big influence on how other choreographers and dancers started to research their own movement freedom.

/ **What do you mean by 'movement freedom'?**
That vocabulary can be anything. Trisha's identity as a movement researcher was her way of looking at movement, of exploring qualities and structure. So I was put into situations where I didn't really know what I was doing. But slowly I was able to create—first of all for myself, which I think is really important to say about this work in general—and my colleagues and I, we all worked on developing a very, very rigorous personal practice. We were working separately, but we would ex-change some ideas. We prepared privately and arrived at the rehearsal studio together, ready to do the work for the day. And so did Trisha. It is important to note that it was a period when people assumed the dis-cipline to create a personal practice. When a dancer assumes that responsibility—How can I prepare? What do I need to study? How do I solve this problem? How do I learn more about my leg joints? and so on—it becomes a very good way to teach oneself how to teach. You, the dancer, are creating the system, and you are articulating your thought processes.

/ **And what helped you on this way?** My Alexander teacher was extremely helpful for understanding basic functioning: How does the elbow joint feel and function? How can you think about it in relationship to the spine? So the anatomical functioning is from my Alexander teacher, re-interpreted by my experience and then re-interpreted again by exploring how I can best deliver it to a group. My teaching started from studying, receiving the practical information and the sensations into my body, and from direct experience through expert hands and guidance. From there, I took a lot of private time to digest the information and apply it to my body, to personal-ize and integrate it, and finally I applied it to my way of dancing the repertory. Then I found a way, a form, sim-ply by working with others in teaching situations, to give the information to a group of dancers in a class. It changed a lot when I decided I had to somehow share or transmit that kind of internal information to a group, as this type of information is often transmitted just between two people with the hands. One part of my class uses my way of interactive touching so people can experience specific sensations—at the spine or at the pelvis or in the legs—there are experiences for each part of the body. That is one part of transcribing a personal experience into a form that works in a larger group.

/ **So your teaching was intertwined with your dancing practice?** I danced with Trisha from 1985 to the beginning of the 1990s. By the end of that period we were doing some larger residencies. Maybe I was interested or maybe I was chosen, I don't know exactly, to lead two or three weeks of a workshop in a university when the company was rehearsing. So I was able to start thinking about creating three weeks of information that could really bring these technical ideas together in a much broader way and the nice thing, of course, apply them to the repertory. Because my teaching, or my emphasis, is different than that of others in the company, or the starting point is different, I never heard the word like 'Trisha Brown Technique'. Even two people who studied with the same teacher adapted the base information into a personal point of view that would then serve the repertory or one's own research.

/ **That means it is highly individualized work?**
As I went further and started to teach more in institu-tions and in Europe, I was continually starting over with new groups in different places. One is always con-fronted with groups of people in which some have a lot of experience and ideas, and others do not. So how could one best formulate an introductory experience about this kind of work on many levels? This is a ques-tion about trying to go beyond the personalization, about trying to find a way that certain principles of usage of the body can be experienced by as wide a range of people as possible, including non-dancers. I always work with the point of view that what I am offering is, like any kind of movement researcher of this period, some-thing that hopefully fits into a student's development—but for sure it is not the only story.

/ **How did the name 'Release Technique' come about?** At the end of the 1990s, two issues of the *Movement Research Performance Journal*—a journal published once or twice a year with news of the research that was happening—were devoted solely to the ques-tion of Release Technique. We had this big questioning: What is this? We were confronted with this classifi-cation out there, and what did it mean to the individual artists who actually worked with it. There was a compilation of quotations by some people about whom one could say their work fell into the Release category because of their history, of their lineage—but then that person would say, 'No, my work is not Release Technique.' So people had a different reaction to being part of a classification. I personally don't feel any conflict being inside the classification or not, but I think it is important that people understand how messy, how crazy the classification is, how difficult it is to pinpoint. And it is really important that people understand the difference between Trisha Brown repertory and a technique that allows you to do better at performing repertory.

When I am able to be with a group of students longer, then I do some kind of historical building, perhaps introducing some repertory, and I try to emphasize that before Release work became so associated with a style of movement, there were other options. There was simple pedestrian information and people who worked with images, people who did other kinds of crazy improvisation that fell into Release Technique. Overall, I believe there is something that is constant about this research that is beyond a style or quality of moving— something about coming back to the reality of the body and the functioning of the body and trying to understand it better, trying to make it more efficient, more elegant, more personal. Almost all of these people, like F.M. Alexander, are trying to get back to some holistic balance in the function of the body—to the anatomical base, the relationship between awareness and function.

/ **What do you like about training, and what not?**
When I am teaching, I get full of new thoughts and new ideas. It is hard to find a balance between just letting things be okay and trying to come up with new adventures. When I exchange ideas in a group and I understand that a person thinks differently, then, how am I going to help? An idea of Release is that the body is working in multi-directions and the thoughts and awareness are working in multi-directions so we cannot get too rigid in one idea—which has to do with also learning that every person has a different point of view. What is difficult about teaching is that I have a hard time turning my head off. Also, it is difficult to make a separation between teaching and research and making art. There is a categorization, still perceived and enforced, that teaching is only a pedagogical experience, sometimes a research experience, and rarely an artistic experience. Sometimes I even see it from the student's side: Are we researching now? Are we learning? For me, it is all–together.

/ **What is most important in teaching your work?**
Hopefully a teacher might sense, if working one–to–one, how the student can accept certain information. I can listen to how the other person is organised, and can say, 'Maybe you feel it this way.' I think I'm trying harder now because there is also a different generation of dancers; there is a resistance, they don't want to be told what to do. There is no didactic way of giving information, and I have to be able to accept that one person's entry point is different than another person's entry point. I am thinking more and more that information is not fixed. Information is not the truth. Information is here to be tasted and worked with.

/ **What does that mean for you as a teacher?**
I have to realize that some information that, for me, seems very precise and necessary is not necessarily the truth for someone else. I ask people to always consider the question: How are you building your support system? On an individual basis, the student is responsible for building knowledge in a way that works well for him or her.

I find that to be a real responsibility for the student. Hopefully the dialogue, what we research in class, and connecting it to what the student has researched or learned in the past, creates something. In terms of Release work specifically, I offer this very open idea: The initiation, or the key to a sensation of release, can start in many different places, and it is different for different people. In terms of the physical sensation of release, or in terms of the psychological sensation of release, I find there are different keys for each person. It is an individual's responsibility to find what those are. I am there to give lots of information and to be helpful in guiding each person towards that. I think it is a part of the work, in general, that there be a personal responsibility to developing a web of information that takes the student to the next level and supports the release experience.

/ **What has changed in your teaching over the years?** The way my teaching has changed is pretty much what I just articulated, which is a kind of trusting that the information I put into the room does not have to be the final information. And that the information is out there for all of us to work with in a mode of research, of personal responsibility. That modality really changed a lot in the last twenty years— along with the confidence that I now have to let go of my own information in a way.

∕ Is there, then, something like accomplishment in the work? Yesterday we discussed and worked with some Release principles in our bodies and then we did a small, somewhat open improvisation with those ideas. I could feel and see very clearly that people were operating in a very nice way: they were full and supported by the people around them, by the energy in the group, in the class, and by the information. I feel personal accomplishment in those moments when I sense that everybody is taking responsibility for their experience, and it is clear that their bodies and ways of being have changed. And, when somebody articulates an experience—and is articulating it in a way that is very profound for themselves—it is something that will inform their future research. That is particularly satisfying to me.

∕ What qualifications does a teacher need?
Number one, I want to see in the teacher's body, in their embodiment, what they are working on. And I want to see it alive. And secondly, that the others in the room are able to feel it in their bodies. If a student is not feeling what we are working on, then the student must say something so that I, as a teacher, can come and work with my hands. I want the student to have the physical sensation. Some things arrive slowly, but I think it is important to be able to transfer—and I use my hands a lot for guiding the body in experience. The philosophy or the kind of touch that a teacher is working with can vary a lot; this has a lot to do with the quality or the interior work of the techniques. In this work, a teacher cannot be too pushy, one has to be a little more—we use words like allowing, or granting permission—it is not, say, to push the pelvis one way and it is better. And a teacher has to be careful when touching that he or she is not just manipulating. I don't even like to use the word correcting or repairing; I am guiding towards another possibility. In my class, students do a lot of touching of other students, so they are also practicing the quality of transmitting information.

∕ Are there new influences on your work?
I am very interested in theoretical physics. There is a discussion between physics and Eastern philosophies—disciplines that look so opposite—and thinking about how our consciousness does or does not affect the material world. I hope that conversation gets more connected. We, as dancers, are dealing with those two things: how the consciousness or the inhabitation of the consciousness works in the body. Body–mind/mind–body, we are back to that. Today nobody could defend the idea of body–mind duality. We, as dancers, are not just training the muscle, we need a little bit more of this philosophical discussion.

∕ How and where do you see the future of this work? As a practice or as a group of ideas, Release is aimed at clarifying the body. I have felt that as my functioning body becomes more simple—or less confused—that I am more aware of other parts of myself. There is a level of working with the self, or with awareness, that means one is also very much learning how to work with oneself as a teacher, as a guide. And I am very excited to see that, hopefully, this work has the potential to be a bit of a connection to other disciplines, that we are getting closer to the research in Eastern philosophies, in metaphysics, in neurology, or in theoretical physics about consciousness. This work is moving in those directions; it is incorporating ideas. I work a lot with certain Buddhist ideas. It is fascinating, what is happening in the field of neurology, in studying consciousness.

For sure, this work will continue to be used for the stage because it continues to support the aesthetic that is on the stage. Flexibility is built into the work. In some ways I don't see the future of the work necessarily having its high point as a stage product. I see there is more potential for the research to be reaching out to these other disciplines—or bringing them to us! Twelve, fifteen years ago there was much more of a process of cleaning out, of breaking down or simplifying or taking away habits, especially for super–trained dancers. A lot of the process then was: We go back to zero. Today people are much more informed, and they are pretty free young people. They still have things to work on, but it is not about breaking down. They are open and rich and flexible in their brains, in their bodies.

∕ What do you want to deliver to them?
This is the challenge. Sometimes you wonder, 'what can I deliver to them?' Because students seemingly have so much richness already, and freedom—they are, as we say in English—so well adjusted. What this work and this tradition of work gives them is like: Hey, this is not the end of the story, there are more things to discover. In some ways I feel—and this is the reason I want to stop for a period—my work has been a lot about bringing people information from the past to make sure that they have all their information more or less up–to–date.

And when I look back at some of the people from twelve, fifteen years ago, I see that through teaching this kind of work they just turned out to be really good human beings. They are very good dancers, but they are also mothers and fathers, they are community people, they have a nice humanity. This is also an outcome: Living a good human life with other human beings.

Gabriele Wittmann, Sylvia Scheidl, Gerald Siegmund

INTRODUCTION

"'Release' is a bunch of research people."[1] This was Lance Gries's answer to the question: "How do you define Release Technique?" He is implying that no single person created this technique, rather there was a group of people who cooperatively—each with their own approach—researched similar questions and solutions about the body. This made Gries the best possible workshop leader for us. Gries does not claim to teach *the* technique; he comes directly out of the 1980's New York dance scene that can be seen as a direct line from the Judson Dance Theater—which was defined by an open, collective, and pioneering spirit. This group's approach takes the word 'research' seriously—even in lessons.

As such, Gries researched, along with participants during the workshop's four weeks, and allowed them to develop their own paths of discovery and movement phrases. He brought historical material and pointed out that there is not only his, but a variety of different approaches to Release Technique with different origins and interpretations available. He also pointed out that, among all the various approaches, his version is one that is strongly oriented toward the spatial orientation of the bones rather than imagery, thus on the skeleton and its inherent possibilities for movement, i.e., alignment. Hence our title, *Release and Alignment Oriented Techniques*.[2]

This workshop at the Frankfurt University of Music and Performing Arts, attended mostly by students of the master's program for contemporary dance teaching, had two primary goals: The first was to offer participants new gateways into various Release Techniques' research universe so that they would be able to internalize and apply the physical principles over time; the second was to cooperatively undertake an initial historical classification. For this, Gries drew a wide chronological arc: From the 1970s he drew upon early task–oriented improvisation exercises as used by Trisha Brown (following

---

1 Lance Gries in a conversation about definitions and the history of the Release Technique with Gabriele Wittmann, Frankfurt, 14 October 2009.
2 About definitions of 'release' and 'alignment' see also John Rolland, 'Alignment and Release. History and Methods. Jacques van Eijden interviews John Rolland,' Jeroen Fabius, *Talk. SNDO 1982–2006* (Amsterdam: International Theatre and Film Book, 2009), pp. 117–129, p. 119.

Anna Halprin), for example, as the improvisational framework for her choreography *Locus*. He next introduced complex and physically refined, multidirectional movements that aspired to several directions, as Trisha Brown had used for *Set and Reset* in the 1980s. Finally, Gries also used large dance sequences that moved through the space extensively—material he taught at P.A.R.T.S. in the 1990s. His current research interest is directed toward group energy work inspired in part by quantum physics, which he also worked into various exercises.

About the research team: Gabriele Wittmann observed the workshop from outside and—in selected sessions—also took part. In particular, she researched the historical relationships and understanding of body and movement. Dr. Gerald Sigmund was an outside observer who reflected upon method concepts and ideology. Sylvia Scheidl, a graduate of the teacher–training course at the HfMDK, participated in the workshop and described the methodology of the instruction. Dieter Heitkamp, director and professor of contemporary dance at the HfMDK, was responsible for the preparation of the research project and further resources, and Kurt Koegel, director of the master's program for teaching contemporary dance at the HfMDK, contributed in the selection of the workshop leader.

Some of the research questions and topics were discussed with all the students in the workshop. The research team discussed most of these in lengthier sessions twice weekly with Gries after class. At the same time, students of the master's program wrote essays for their Creative Scientific Writing class reflecting upon the workshop's impact on four various levels: physical, mental, emotional, and spiritual. They then wrote a final essay about their experiences. A battery of questions and answers arose over the weeks that turned out to be less akin to a common thread than to a woven fabric full of knots; this weaving, as a metaphor, reveals the approach taken by the research team.

Gabriele Wittmann

HISTORICAL CONTEXT

TIME, PLACE, AND SOCIO-POLITICAL CONTEXT

The early roots of various Release Techniques are found in the emergence of postmodern dance in the U.S. after the end of the Second World War, and mark a new beginning in art as well as in dance. In order to distance themselves from modern dance and to orient their bodies anew, dancers needed an open platform accessible to as many people as possible, and yet specific enough to serve their needs as performers. It was then subsequently necessary to re-examine the balance between general accessibility and the specific needs of professionals in various dance techniques. The greatest common denominator was a biologically[1] grounded understanding of the body and its possibilities for movement and experience—especially the anatomical construction of the skeleton, the bones, and joints. Somatic investigation of the bones and muscles proved to be groundbreaking for future experiments in the Judson Dance Theater.

Starting in the 1960s, the primary social concern was strengthening the individual: Individuals should have freedom, and take on responsibility for themselves and societal relationships. Concerns were proceeding along similar lines in the developing Release Technique: *Release* means 'letting go' in the sense of opening oneself to other possibilities—as well as being open about the ways to utilize these new possibilities. Central concepts are freedom, taking responsibility, and making choices. So this is not just about letting go *of*, but particularly letting go *for*, i.e., allowing energy that was blocked to flow so that it can be used in new ways. These new ways can serve a variety of purposes, but, essentially, the point is to understand how each body part connects with other body parts, and to work on clearly aligning the whole body, along with the intention and awareness, in time and space.[2]

Release Technique emerged as an amalgam of these developments in the collective environment that included a group of researchers, primarily from New York (in the 1970s and 80s) and in a few satellite locations in Europe.

BACKGROUND: BIOGRAPHIES AND ENVIRONMENT

No one person invented the term Release Technique—and there is no clear definition of it. "If, some day, the term 'Release Technique' were to be defined, it would contradict the work," says Gries, "it would be antithetical."[3] At the end of the 1990s, the magazine *Movement Research* devoted two consecutive issues in an attempt to historically classify Release Technique. They concluded that there are a variety of approaches and definitions that cannot be reduced to one common denominator. Some, like Joan Skinner, see themselves as pioneers or inventors of the method; others, who are at least as important for its development, had no desire to be tied down to the classification of the technique at all.[4]

The work of Mabel E. Todd, the founder of ideokinesis, is often viewed as the root and core to Release. Her work, which began early in the last century, uses visual and kinesthetic internal images of the body to investigate and change physical movement functions.[5] Assisted by anatomic visualizations and movement exercises, Todd investigated the impact that thought processes (imagination) and feelings leave on the structure of the body, and how patterns of movement are informed by such. She thus created a holistic, psychophysical theory about the interaction between anatomical and psychological threads of action and experience. Sections of her book, *The Thinking Body* had already been published in 1929 and influenced many dance teachers: Lulu Sweigard and Barbara Clark also contributed to the development of the ideokinetic school of thought, as did André Bernard, Irene Dowd, Erick Hawkins, and Pamela Matt.

Joan Skinner is understood by some to be one of Release Technique's creators. She did not, however, name her technique 'Release Technique', but 'Releasing Technique'— more precisely, Skinner Releasing Technique. Four things influenced her thinking: the teachings of her instructor Cora Belle Hunter (who worked in Mabel E. Todd's tradition and used internal images of the body, along with the examination of the skeleton); the Eastern philosophies of D. T. Suzuki from John Cage and Merce

---

1 Here *biologically* means many correlations of living processes in the body. For Mabel E. Todd, this included not only anatomical questions, but also, for example, the chemical balance of the lung's contents while breathing (p. 241), the effects of emotions (for instance, in trying to react to feelings

of uneasiness by controlling one's own limbs in space by overstretching of the neck or knee areas (p. 275)). See Mabel E. Todd, *The Thinking Body* (Princeton (NJ): Princeton Book Company, 1959).

2 Diane Torr, 'Release, Aikido, Drag King, Aikido, Release,' *Movement Research Performance Journal*, No. 19/1999, p. 5.
3 See the Editorial in Movement Research Performance Journal, No. 18/1999, pp. 2–3
4 Vgl. Editorial zu *Movement Research Performance Journal*, Nr. 18/1999, S. 2–3.

Cunningham (for instance, ignoring the ego and training perception for the idea that every thing in time and space has its own essence); F. M. Alexander's technique, which she learned and incorporated into the ballet barre; and, finally, her own research into kinesthetic questions, which she presented as exercises to students of the University of Illinois. They, in turn, created the term Releasing Technique.[6] She was interested in images researched by the psychologist C. G. Jung, and also used them as archetypal symbols. Nowadays, choreographers like New Yorker DD Dorvillier come from a Skinner–oriented education.

Another prominent representative of release work is Mary O'Donnell Fulkerson. She studied under Joan Skinner and connected Barbara Clark's anatomically–based Release images to a concept of the flow of force along energy lines through the body.[7] Fulkerson defined her goals as follows: alignment (the orientation of body parts to one another and in space); concentration; focus; being completely involved; exploring one's own constructional thought process; simplicity in the approach to everyday challenges; and active integration of mind and body.[8] She taught a class she called Anatomical Release Technique at Dartington College in England.

In the early 1970s, Steve Paxton along with Nancy Stark Smith, Lisa Nelson, and Daniel Lepkoff, began to develop Contact Improvisation. By the 1980s, this became a primary form for the practice and development of Release Technique. Several future dancers of the Trisha Brown Dance Company, and future colleagues of Lance Gries, such as Stephen Petronio, Randy Warshaw, and Diane Madden, connected with this group at Hampshire College and became part of that exploration. They learned to trust the structural integrity of the body and qualities of awareness. "They were researching the same questions, but they tried to solve them through the problem of sharing weight," says Lance Gries.[9] Mary Fulkerson simultaneously published her research in the magazine *Contact Quarterly*, which gave birth to a 'mutual growth'—a complimentary inspirational growth process for the release–oriented techniques. John Rolland, Pamela Matt, Nancy Topf, and Marsha Paludan further developed this school of thought.

Trisha Brown also contributed to the development of Release Technique—if only indirectly through her move-

ment vocabulary and its increasing impact. According to Gries, she was not interested in being limited by a specific dance technique and did not specify any expected training for her company—except for masterclasses for repertoire, composition classes, and/or demonstrations on tour. The dancers organized their own training. As the choreographic vocabulary became increasingly physically demanding, for instance in *Set and Reset*, the dancers investigated other training methods in order to be able to physically manage the material's demands. Several of them, like Lance Gries and Eva Karzag, received private lessons in Alexander Technique from June Ekman. In her early years, Ekman was with Anna Halprin and had danced in the Judson Dance Theater in performances by Yvonne Rainer, and later, worked with these dancers in reformulating and expanding exercises from Alexander Technique to meet dancers' current requirements.

Gries defines his work as having emerged from the New York research community of the 1980s, where he was particularly influenced by June Ekman from 1985–1991. Not extensively knowing the work of Joan Skinner, he doesn't see a connection with it, as he does not use as much imagining and imagery, rather he relies more on more purely physical exercises with a practical, anatomical focus.

The term 'Release Technique' was not yet widespread in Europe in the 1980s; in France, for example, where Trisha Brown had been invited to more regular guest performances than in Germany. Gries often taught

5 John Rolland defines ideokinesis as "the connection between idea and kinesthetic action or stimulation." Rolland 2009, p. 123.
6 Joan Skinner, 'Letter to the Editors', *Movement Research Performance Journal*, No. 19/1999, p. 3.

7 Claudia Fleischle–Braun, *Der Moderne Tanz. Geschichte und Vermittlungskonzepte.* Butzbach–Griedel, 2000, p. 141.
8 These are the goals of Release Technique as defined by Mary Fulkerson on her website. See www.releasedance.com on 14 January 2010.

9 From a conversation with Lance Gries by Gabriele Wittmann, Frankfurt, 14 October 2009.

'Trisha Brown Workshops', which were a mixture of Trisha Brown repertory, his own dance material, and the technical information that he was exploring. Staying true to her priorities as a maker of dance material, Trisha Brown herself never taught the developing Release and Alignment Oriented Technique, nor did she have a desire to form a technique that bore her name. As her name was well known in France, it was used when ensemble members like Gries taught technique classes, and thus the myth of a Trisha Brown Technique came into being.

Gries taught Release and Alignment starting in the 1990s at educational institutions around Europe, most notably at P.A.R.T.S. in Brussels, founded by Anne Teresa De Keersmaeker. In contrast to other release teachers like Mary Fulkerson, who cultivated a calm and introspective mode of research, he structured a teaching course using similar techniques that engaged a broad range of physicality, allowing students to develop a technical base from internal sensation and building it into high energy technical dancing. He developed courses in which the group collectively familiarized themselves with Alexander Technique (as reworked by June Ekman through hands–on[10] partner work), through their own explorations based on improvisational structures to be used alone, with partners, and in the group. The goals at the time were functional joint work, comparative anatomy, and training perception within large movement sequences that used the space expansively.

RELATION TO OTHER ART FORMS

Grand narratives were passé in American art by 1945 at the latest. Now the material itself was being explored. In painting, Abstract Impressionism emerged as the successor to European Dada and Surrealism. Jackson Pollock created energetic 'action paintings' with color that went well beyond any figurativeness or representation. Society's reality and reproducibility became a topic and material for art: Andy Warhol duplicated prints of Campbell soup cans and media spectacles of tragedies like car crashes. In music, John Cage abandoned melodies and chords and, like the Italian Futurists before him, explored the phenomenon of the experience of sound itself; noises edged into the music and the arrangements became *scores*, i.e., directions about how they were to be played were graphically similar to arrangements, and progression was often composed, or not composed, with the assistance of the Chinese *I Ching*. Interpreters became more important, could make decisions for themselves, and follow their own tempo. Listen-

ing, thus the very process of sensing, became central. The practice of meditation also made its way into the musical experience: inviting and permitting silence as well as everyday noise, and accepting it non-judgmentally. Improvisation—alone and in a group—became a building block of twentieth century classical music.

Dance also turned its back on the grand psychological narratives of modern dance, like those of Martha Graham. Anna Halprin, Merce Cunningham, and in the next generation, from 1960 onward, Yvonne Rainer, Trisha Brown, and Steve Paxton, explored the body's autonomy and its potential for movement. At this time, the issue was non-decorative movement that did not refer to anything; instead, movement was organized on a purely functional basis. Pop Art led the way: 'The Real' was a topic. For Release—oriented Techniques today, Lance Gries says, "I am inhabiting my arm. I can lift my arm. And to be clear: not *my* arm, but my *arm*." So this is no longer about the dancing 'self' that inhabits the body and senses, but about the physical reality of movement.

At this time the 'real' meant not just the body's physique, an object, or an action, but also those of everyday life. Art and life permeated one another. While Anna Halprin and dancers from the Judson Dance Theater like Trisha Brown brought everyday movements into dance—such as walking, standing, stacking bottles, frying pancakes, lying down, and sweeping the floor—visual artists brought Happenings to everyday locations like riversides or intersections. With the beginning of the Fluxus movement, intercommunication thrived between the American East and West Coasts, putting the focus on 'direct action' performances that took place in real life in reaction to societal and political events. The arts informed each other reciprocally; visual artists, theater people, dancer–choreographers, and music composers worked together on projects. Merce Cunningham and John Cage are a prominent example.

The everyday entered into all fields of art and life: in literature, Allen Ginsberg berated his country in the long prose poem *Howl*, using supermarket metaphors. In *On the Road*, Jack Kerouac recounted the collective vagabond life without a period or comma, one that Bob Dylan also celebrated in song. In dance, Yvonne Rainer gave away her *Trio A* to a variety of trained (and untrained) bodies, who then proceeded to pass it along. In *Satisfyin' Lover*, Steve Paxton had a group of laypeople execute pedestrian movement, like walking, before he increasingly focused on communicative encounters with physical parameters, like the actual weight of the body.

10 *Hands–on* Is widely used in American English to describe both physical touch as well as diagnostic and therapeutic tools in various body–work techniques.

11 Lance Gries in conversation with Gabriele Wittmann, Frankfurt, 14 October 2009.

Topics revolving around identity–politics came to the fore in the 1970s and 1980s. Soul became an important musical genre for artists in downtown New York (after the protest songs of Bob Dylan and Joan Baez). In dance, it was the black identity of Bill T. Jones, who was also active in the gay movement. For countless artists like Keith Hennessy in California, questions of gender and hetero/homo/bisexual orientation became a central focus of their work, from which—while taking into account the intellectual achievements of Karl Marx, Wilhelm Reich, Fritz Perls, and Michel Foucault—all other societal topics could be extrapolated. Women explored their own history and—as the musician–performer Meredith Monk already had done with *Education of a Girlchild*—brought it to the stage.

Artists worked in several fields simultaneously: after the Happenings that Robert Rauschenberg created with dancers, experimental artists from the minimalist scene, such as theater director Robert Wilson, composers like Phillip Glass, and choreographers like Lucinda Childs emerged. Laurie Anderson designed musical performances by playfully deconstructing words and sounds. Trisha Brown, in turn, used Anderson's music for her seminal piece, *Set and Reset,* which showcased dancing and dancers who were embodying Release Technique. Among them were some of the same dancers who earlier collaborated with Steve Paxton and would later become Lance Gries's dancing partners and influences. In his first year with Trisha's company, Lance lived in dance historian Sally Banes's SoHo loft for a time, sharing the space with a friend from Merce Cunningham's company, and it became a meeting point for colleagues. Lance says, "The story is much more tactile than historians often tend to make it. It is basically about people sharing lofts, people knowing certain people, and circles mingling within the small New York art scene."[11]

RELEVANT THEORETICAL DISCOURSES

As mentioned previously, the beginnings of various Release Techniques can be considered to start with Mabel E. Todd's research in her seminal work *The Thinking Body*, published in 1937. Dance as discourse and research—this improvisational, process–oriented approach by the release community can be traced back to the 1930s. The director of the dance department at the University of Wisconsin, Margaret H'Doubler, who was greatly influenced by Todd, did not define improvisation as a means to a finished dance product, but rather as a scientific research process in John Dewey's sense. Anna Halprin adopted this approach, which was then shared by Yvonne Rainer and the Judson Dance Theatre. The Contact Improvisation scene also took up this line of thinking.

What became important was, on one hand, the developing somatic approaches, and, on the other, Asian approaches that were making inroads into parts of the

American art scene. Artist and composer John Cage disseminated D. T. Suzuki's ideas, a Japanese philosopher who had lectured about Zen Buddhism at Columbia University in New York from 1952–57. Suzuki's influence reached the humanist movement at California's Esalen Institute through his student, the philosopher Alan Watts, and through the music teacher Charlotte Selver. Here, body practice techniques were taught and researched that, in turn, sprung from dancing, therapeutic, and philosophical contexts like those espoused by Fritz Perls, Moshé Feldenkrais, Ida Rolf, Anna Halprin, Alexander Lowen, and Rollo May. Ideas and the body practices taken from meditation techniques spread, particularly on the U.S. West Coast and in New York. D. T. Suzuki's writings were just as popular as were, later, Robert M. Pirsig's work *Zen and the Art of Motorcycle Maintenance*, Ram Dass's *Grist for the Mill*, and the Chinese *I Ching*, and—somewhat later—the convergence of Western science and spiritual Eastern traditions of thought in *The Tao of Physics*.

Dance historian Sally Banes became a central figure of theoretical discourse and analysis for postmodern dance as it developed from 1960 onward. Dance students training in universities in and around New York received their education in dance theory and dance writing from her—like Lance Gries, for example. Within the New York dance scene from the 1980s to the 2000s, theoretical discourse took place in the *Movement Research Performance Journal*, which had been founded by artists. The periodical *Contact Quarterly* was also an important forum for discussion and debate.

CURRENT PRACTICE

Release Techniques are currently used in many artistic and educational processes, especially by those dance artists who come from the postmodern tradition in the U.S. These artists are connected to the Judson Dance Theater, later with Trisha Brown or Steve Paxton, and the Contact Improvisation scene. Most major dance festivals in Europe offer workshops based on Release Techniques.

In Brussels, choreographers like Anne Teresa De Keersmaeker invite release teachers like Lance Gries to P.A.R.T.S. in order to teach students body awareness, clarify their alignment in space, strengthen them physically, and to acquaint them with the practices and movement vocabulary of American Post Modernism. The curriculum includes courses in contemporary training methods developed on the basis of various Release Techniques.

INDIVIDUAL APPROACH

Many companies have started using Release and Alignment Oriented Techniques rather than, or along with, traditional ballet training because, with continuous practice, they can train presence as well. What choreographers like about the method is that it enables dancers to use parts of their bodies in nimble, versatile, and differentiated ways. This can be especially advantageous when the choreographers are not relying on a predetermined movement vocabulary, but rather allowing the dancers to offer material. Gries personally also uses the technique to introduce movement to actors–in–training.

RELATION TO OTHER DANCE AND MOVEMENT TECHNIQUES

Release work has been incorporated into many techniques in the meantime, not only contemporary, but also ballet. According to Andrea Tallis, who danced with Forsythe, this influence is especially widespread in France.[12] Conversely, there have also been many influences on release work. Some name Susan Klein in this context, but she and others deny this.[13] Body–Mind Centering followed its own development alongside Release Technique, but it stands to reason that some Release practitioners incorporated BMC principles. The greatest influence, however, came from the Alexander Technique. Developed by F. M. Alexander around the turn of the twentieth century, it specifically contributed to such principles as letting go of blocking behaviors, imagining an upright posture while being as relaxed as possible, and following as efficient a movement sequence as possible with as little effort as necessary. The, at times, meditative pace of a Release class mirrors an Alexander session; slowing down the process involved in perception enables participants to sense microscopic differences in similar postures and movements. The postmodern dancers in New York in the 1980s adapted the material to the times: for Gries, for example, the primary 'solution' to tension in the body is not located in the head and neck region as it is for F. M. Alexander, but instead can start anywhere within the body (or even the mind)— depending upon where a dancer notices the blockage most distinctly.

Many principles overlap with other body–awareness practices. The idea of 'receiving, not manipulating', for example, is also found in Moshé Feldenkrais's work, where it represents one's own inner observations. In Release Technique it additionally refers to a hands–on approach, the way one touches another person's body in partner work.

Buddhism, Asian martial arts, and body–awareness techniques that made their way into American society as of the 1960s were also important influences. Meditation and Release Techniques share several key terms: *permission*, allowing oneself and others to sense something, to express oneself, etc.; *letting go*, releasing predetermined notions and behavior patterns in the muscles, as well as relinquishing thoughts and expectations; *staying present*, the attempt to remain in the here–and–now instead of dwelling on thoughts and patterns formed by the past; *precision*, training exactitude in perception and action, including the organization of the body in time and space; *gentleness*, the general mode of a considerate and nonjudgmental attitude toward oneself and to other beings that becomes a supporting, multidirectional kinesphere surrounding the bones and body. In both meditation and Release Technique, a person assumes that a technical exercise trains both body and mind. In Buddhism, the pause before the action is called the *right intention*, in Alexander Technique it is known as *inhibition*—to interrupt patterns that habitually block action by using a moment of attentiveness before moving. In terms of improvisation within the Release Technique, this can mean, for example, dancers using attentive sensing can notice when they fall into a 'habit' or 'style' of movement or reaction, and they can gently move out of the pattern and back into the here–and–now.

"It's become clear to me how quickly our awareness veers away from the here–and–now." *Natalia Gomez, student*

12 Conversation between Gabriele Wittmann and Andrea Tallis, Frankfurt, 13 October 2009.
13 See Susan Klein in *Movement Research Performance Journal*, No. 18/1999, p. 5.

Gerald Siegmund

CONCEPT AND IDEOLOGY

IMAGINING THE BODY

In Lance Gries's Release and alignment work, the body is in constant contact and communication with its environment. It is a multidimensional body that exists in relation to others in the space; this body is open and ready to move in any direction, able to react to things in the moment. It is a body prepared and available for any situation.

This readiness is due to active release work, which does not begin with the muscles but with the skeleton—and in particular by focusing on the joints. For Gries, therefore, the body is primarily an anatomical body that he metaphorically elevates as little as possible. In class, in a matter-of-fact and clear way, he describes the bones' relationship to one another in order to illustrate their connection; for example, how the bones between the ankles and hips align and create support from floor. Accessing and using the most direct line of connection possible conserves energy and leads to clearer articulation. The joints are not perceived as rigid blocks but as moving parts in and of themselves; they create volume in the body that then contributes to the movement's directionality. "Moving away from the joints" and "using the three-dimensional space in the joints" makes it possible for Gries to speak about the body as a network of lines connected to one another that are not oriented around a fixed center.

The body is naturally suspended by the spine in space, connecting it with up and down, with the earth and with what might be considered the immaterial spiritual sphere. To understand the spine as Gries does, as the body's 'living support', means it cannot be conceived of as a solid line, but rather as having manifold directionality.

The body is therefore a volume made up of movable and dynamic parts on a central scaffolding. The body can access all of its connections, from and to its furthest points, thus enhancing the continuity of movement. The goal is to find an alignment from which movement can flow in any and all directions. This helps avoid

14 The term *neutral* here means a physical and spiritual attitude that precludes manipulation—that thus wants nothing, doesn't wish to change others, but is solely a palpable counterpart.

blockages resulting from overextended joints or overused muscles. Overextension forces the body into a certain position. In contrast, a body that is on a 'middle' path, one that is neither overstretched nor over-relaxed, encounters other bodies with a much greater openness and allows for decisions in the moment. "It's not about doing something right, it's about having options and making choices," says Gries about the goal. The body is therefore a place of potentialities, and with such potential it radiates great alertness. The body does not represent anything; it does not elevate itself, does not, for example, thrust the breast forward, but opens itself up and is at ease for an encounter.

Two terms heard time and again during class, terms that are essential for the specific active passivity and passive activity of this body are *support*—meaning a neutral directional activation—and *receive*—a neutral receptive awareness.[14] Support does not just mean supporting a partner; the term has further, multilayered implications that conceive of the body as fundamentally open and connected with its environment and the dancer's imagination. Support can be of a physical nature, thus connecting the anatomy and one's conceptual imagery in assisting the bones to carry weight easily. The concept also has an intellectual dimension, as a student might be asked which book she or he had been read recently that provided food for thought.

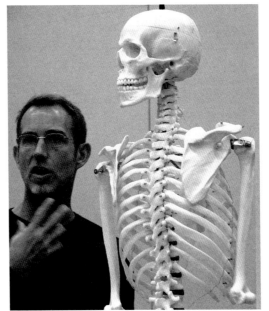

Support can also imply an energetic dimension, the field of energy exchange that one creates with one's environment, or perceives. "When I touch somebody, I give *permission* to do something," Gries says, whereby he is indicating that support is an invitation to dialogue.

The concept includes a complimentary term: *receive*. This is not about, for example, one partner supporting the other so that he or she can hold a certain position, nor is it about lifting the other's weight. *Receiving* always contains a *yielding*, a giving in and abandoning oneself. Essentially, the idea means that both partners enter an exchange through touch that connects them to their environment.

According to this, the body's multidimensionality has a direct impact on general questions of human existence. How the body is placed in space has an effect on one's behavior in society. Questions of gender do not play a role here.

Being able to accept and give: this accentuates the fundamental connectedness of the body with the space. The space is always being actively perceived. In doing so, the eyes and sense of sight do not play the central role. Sensing the space behind one's back and integrating it into the action means to feel it, to receive it through proprioception and kinesthetic sensibilities. The space is the body's partner in that it supports the body (i.e., as though surrounded by and suspended in spherical modules), and in which the direction of movement continues. This is not about controlling the space. Allowing something to happen means ignoring oneself and one's own interests in order to be available to a larger, societal body. Participants should be able to gain an inner distance to their own importance and emotionality. Watching the sequence of exercises in Gries's class, one can read a type of developmental pattern tracing human development from infant to upright–standing

adult. The exercises begin laying on one's back, continue crawling on all fours, on to the body standing upright— but with its lines of energy leading back down to the floor.

Music does not play a role in this movement research process. As such, exercises are not counted. Music can however be used in order to lead the group to another form of energy, to allow students to react to something external with their own internal rhythm. In this case, the music acts as an additional partner. On the other hand, a live musician—a percussionist would be preferred—can support the work on more complex movement phrases that are based on quick and direct directional alignments.

INTENT

Release and Alignment Oriented Technique as taught by Gries does not have a predetermined aesthetic; it provides the students with tools for self–development. The work promotes the notion that the parenthetical, the everyday, effortlessness, lightness, and the alleged simplicity of movement is an art. The resulting aesthetic is an anti-aesthetic when measured against the classic definitions such as a 'beautiful appearance' or the 'sensual presentation of an idea'.

The idea of dance conveyed here does not present an image of the body as a product that can be worked towards or achieved—nor is it a predefined idea that the body must express. The dance is understood as a fundamental tool with which one can work on perception and change the consciousness of the body. Such a body can, as described above, act differently in society and is open to other experiences.

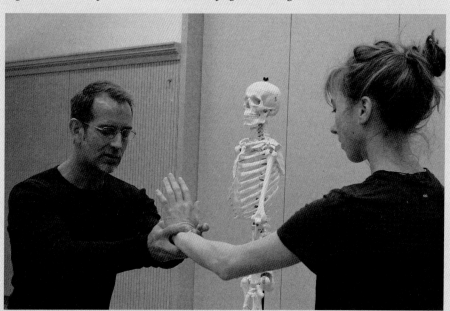

The approach to art is thus based on the fundamental permeability of art and life. Art is no longer primarily understood as a finished work that conveys timeless values or archetypal conflicts. This art, rather, provides a disposition or a field of perception with which the audience can interact, especially because the art is not categorically separated from its life context. The goal is also to perceive the everyday as beautiful, and to shape it. This tendency was evident in the 1960s and 1970s, in the Judson Dance Theater experiments and the work of the improvisation collective Grand Union, who considered performances to be more a presentation of research results than a dance performance. This is why events often took place in non-theatrical spaces like gymnasiums or even—like many of Trisha Brown's pieces in the 1970s—in parks or public places where they attracted passersby as audience. From the 1980s onward, in pieces like *Set and Reset*, Trisha Brown began staging her works and returning them to the theater space, and her dancers, influenced by Release Techniques, influenced her work. The effects can today be found in the aesthetics of numerous dance artists, among them Anne Teresa De Keersmaeker and Thomas Hauert.

The relevance of release and alignment work, independent of performance practices, is in training perception, proprioception, and injury prevention. In this sense, alignment and release work can be used as a basis for other techniques.

The special quality/attribute conveyed here is an alertness of the body that results from dancers making decisions in the here–and–now. In doing so, they deal with weight by directly challenging gravity, putting themselves on the line. A movement sequence is successful when it uses as little muscle strength as possible to coordinate individual body parts. This actually makes the clear transfer of energy from one point in the body to the next visible. The body becomes transparent. This movement quality does not depend upon the physique of the person being trained because the communicated ideal is purely anatomical–physiological. Any and every body can realize these concepts; the challenge is to execute movement to the utmost.

This process takes place in relation to the individual's current state. Presence does not result from muscular exaggeration or exertion; it is more dependent upon making clear decisions in the moment, meaning, of course, that in every decision made, possibilities not chosen remain present as potential. Presence results from interaction with the situation and other performers.

"It's not about being hard on myself, but instead allowing myself to be both this *and* that. To sense what's heading my way. To feel what it's doing to me. And then to externalize it."
Siri Clinckspoor, student

Gabriele Wittmann, Sylvia Scheidl

UNDERSTANDING THE BODY/MOVEMENT

PREREQUISITES

A high degree of differentiated organization and articulation within the body is especially relevant for the technique. The fewer bad training habits participants bring with them, the better. Dancers who, until now, have only been trained in one style of movement will have difficulties—for example, if they habitually tilt their hips forward they will have difficulty doing otherwise. Conversely, according to Gries, street dancers[15] have some of the best prerequisites because, in contrast to professionally trained dancers or athletes, they are usually unspoiled, easygoing, and jointed in their movements.

Every type of functional movement is supportive: for example, the everyday activity of picking up a fallen object, or movements in natural surroundings like climbing, diving, and swimming. However these should not be performed as competitive sport, but remain utilitarian. Only then can the body's natural intelligence and reflexes be exercised, and confidence strengthened.

There is little or no danger of injury in Release Technique; to the contrary, it helps to prevent injuries.[16]

MOVEMENT CHARACTERISTICS AND PHYSICALITY

All body parts are felt to be actively motorized, even if they are not actually actively moving. For example, if one moves one's hands, one additionally imagines the back of the head and the back of the heels. This leads to integration of the entire body although only a simple movement is seen. One is also always aware of the spine and the empty spaces between the vertebrae as well as the entire multidirectionally–aligned body in space.

Not only the center of the body, any body part can become trigger movement that will then be answered by another body part. For instance, Gries calls the basic phrase of *Set and Reset* by Trisha Brown a 'study in functionality'.

The phrase begins with a fall from the vertical into walking: step to left, while the fingers of the right hand pull backwards, swing in small arcs upward to the shoulder with a gradually bent elbow and shoot (*toss*) past the shoulder and forward into the horizontal, such that the outstretched arm is now parallel to the floor. While this is happening, the step to the right has started, whereby the arm shortly acts as a *space hold*, i.e., remaining held in the space horizontally. Weight is brought back to the left foot through the heel, which turns the body ninety degrees from the continuing momentum. The right foot, now free, takes a small step forward and lands in front of the left foot, the right arm moves downward and brought into line with the right leg (*line up*). This leaves the body leaning slightly forward, where it suspends for a moment. Then the right leg is suddenly bent, thus breaking this line (*break the line*), freeing the left leg for a light swing forward and both arms for a slight swing to the right; as a result, the left knee again turns to the side along the left rear diagonal. Both arms pull back with a light swing, one after the other, to this diagonal across the front of the torso.

This is about the functionality of falling, swinging, and breaking, and about the reorganization of body parts in space. The goal in doing so—at least in my experience—is always to engage the entire body even when the initiation of a movement comes from an isolated body part or, at times, only applies to individual parts. Coordination develops through the internal route that a movement takes through the body. The synchronization of body parts helps because it is intuitive: the knee and elbow, for example, are imagined as having a coordinated connection in all of the sequences described above. The same holds true for the hands and heels. Someone turning their wrists, for example, will attempt to sense what the ankles are doing at the same time, making new paths in coordination possible.

Bones are another central aspect of the work. The instruction to 'activate the bones' is more than a metaphor, it also physically animates the bones and their energy. In very concrete terms, this means the physical, chemical composition: calcium crystals in the bones are stored by the body differently in space depending upon how they bear weight and load. These constantly regenerating crystals are induced, by use of imagery, to align themselves directly and evenly against the force of gravity such that future movements can be completed as effortlessly as possible. This clarity is also transported into an aesthetic dimension; the dancer does not perform several tasks at once, rather she or he moves directly and clearly with gravity, even if a number movements must happen simultaneously.

---

15 *Street dancer* is not referring to a specific style like hip–hop, for example; instead the term is used as an umbrella term for all emergent subcultural dancing forms beyond the studios and on the streets and in clubs where the improvisational and social character prevails and the bodies, en passant and without blocking fixation on technique, inform one another.
16 See also: Teaching: Principles and Methodology/Pedagogical Methods.

"Being able to think about the leg as 'leading away from the body' was revolutionary information—and so was the idea that this is possible for many additional physical connections. I first had to feel it differently and relearn. That is why my relationship to the floor changed daily."

Monica Muñoz, student

The intended expenditure of **strength** is relaxed, but 'not dead', as Gries puts it—thus not completely passive. Like Buddhism's *middle way,* it is a continuous flow of light tone, just as much or as little as is needed to keep all body parts active and in contact with one another. The bones should rest on top of one another and provide stability without unnecessary effort. Which type of tension in the body is desirable? Gries handed out several strands of spaghetti to the students, either raw or cooked to varying degrees of al dente. Participants feel the tension. If a strand is too soft, then there is a tension deficit: if you place the

torso and legs and balance out the back muscles, especially in the groin area. The psoas muscles should be neither slack nor overly taut, rather they should be lengthened with a gentle tonus. The diaphragm extends as a dome of muscle below the rib cage and its tendons connect deep into the lumbar region of the spine. If the diaphragm is full and fluid in its breathing movement, it offers significant support for the upright body. One can then rely on the body's natural breath rhythm, which will intelligently adjust itself to the movement's needs without consciously controlling the diaphragm.

Spatially there is no assumed hierarchy to up and down, and no concrete motor **center** in the sense of a defined center of the body, as is the case in some concepts of modern dance. Instead, there is a temporary, imaginary, and energetic center that can be assigned to changing places in the body and from which energy flows can be observed. This is because the body is fundamentally understood as 'suspended' in space, like a jumping cat in flight. Any body part can potentially become the center, depending on how forces are acting. "We are a psychophysical system of energies, an energy system within larger energy systems in

strand upright on a table it immediately collapses into a heap. If it is too hard, then there is excess tension: if you stand it vertically on the table and let go, it falls to the side in one piece. The desired tension is thus not too little and not too much, so the body can accept the movement and direct it further.

Training is not aimed at strengthening musculature, quite the opposite: unnecessary activity, especially of the outer musculature, should be avoided. Instead, inner musculature is strengthened particularly in the spinal region. Only the diaphragm and the psoas group are specially mentioned. The psoas muscles, as hip flexors, integrate the

the universe," says Gries. The following exercise is helpful to 'tune' the diaphragm's tonus, for example, and thus to transfer energies from above and below: a dancer lies on her side with her partner. The partner gently puts his hand on her lower rib cage and rocks her whole body with a light, calming rhythm. Her diaphragm and breathing gradually relax. Energies from her legs and arms, from head and hips, can now make their way to the opposite ends of her body and can flow more freely; her organs find more space, and the torso becomes more voluminous. This is how Gries understands the diaphragm as a potential and tangible center: center is where two energies permeate one another, integrate, and move through each other. This experiential center, however, can shift depending upon the touch; the center can be the diaphragm or elsewhere in the body.

The spine is not imagined as the center, but as a core structure. Ribs and pelvis hang from it and interior mus-

cles are connected to it. They, in turn, impact exterior muscles. Everything else depends upon this core structure, which is why work on the spine is central to the training. A student works with selected body layers and experiences them as the central connection—central not in the sense of 'middle' or 'center', but rather as the meaningful center in an investigated context.

Working with *balance–center* or *off–center* will depend upon the pedagogical context and/or the dance artist's preference. Some choreographers, like Trisha Brown, prefer dancers who can fall well. In larger movement phrases, as frequently performed in late–1980s postmodern dance, both on– and off–center can play a role.

Body weight is always well distributed—each body part carries its own weight. This is practiced best when lying supine and gradually surrendering one's weight into the floor. Over time, the spine, for instance, sinks ever closer to the floor, away from the front side of the torso. This easing of tension must be maintained and then transferred into a movement sequence leading to standing: the spine is thought of as being released downward, which, in an upright position, is 'towards the back'. Gries, quoting

his teacher June Ekman, says, "Release happens from the front to the back."

Gries does not often use the word *gravity*. This is not about going down toward the floor, but rather about *levity*,[17] moving up from the floor. Gries relates that his teacher June Ekman often used to say, "The body wants to organize away from the floor." This means that the body uses the floor as a source of power to keep the spine erect and to fire the imagination—and thus also reality—enabling the body to organize itself up and away from the ground.

This principle applies to every weight shift: energy is drawn from the floor and then used to reconstruct, reorganize, the body. This happens, for instance, in the Bus Stop exercise: the entire upper body leans sideways against a wall, as if waiting at a bus stop. When the bus arrives, participants no longer jump unorganized into the upright position, but instead attempt to reorganize their anatomical structure. One first imagines the heels sinking down into the ground. Once this interior image is established and anchored in the body, the next step is to actualize it: release the heels toward the ground. From this release and contact with the floor comes the upward energy flow that straightens the body by using the imagined ankle–knee–hip–lumbar spine–twelfth thoracic vertebra–third cervical vertebra connection. Gries does not use the term 'weight shift' in class, however, as he emphasizes the continual reorganization of the body and not the shifting.

Energy is an important field of work; it is expended as efficiently as possible, and preferably not as overly active but as responsive energy. This means that the energy used is predominantly energy that does not first need to be produced, but rather it should be garnered as power. This training in continual and definitive *non-doing* has many variations. One principle is the *drop*, as in "drop the heels into the floor." One hears this often. The heels should not be actively pressed into the floor, but continuously released down into the floor. In this way, no energy is wasted. In fact, releasing blockages and strenuous movement patterns actually returns freestanding energy that the body then has at its disposal.

In Gries's work, energy is not just related to individual bodies; it also applies to groups of bodies. Energy can also be drawn from contact with other bodies. As a result, in

17 The term *levity* is used in release contexts to mean *lightness*, i.e., the opposite of *gravity*.
18 Sally Banes defines postmodern dance as an artistic era that began in 1962 and ended in 1989: After the initial experimental breakthroughs of the 1960s came the analytical postmodern dance of the 1970s,

followed by that of the 1980s, in which the question of content again received attention. See Sally Banes: *Greenwich Village 1963*. Durham (NC): Duke University Press, 1993 and *Terpsichore in Sneakers*. Middletown (CN): Wesleyan University Press, 1987.

19 About this, see also the analysis of *Set and Reset* by Trisha Brown earlier in this section.

an improvisation context, not everyone has to work hard alone but instead can, through *responsiveness*—a trained ability to quickly respond to the environment—draw ideas, imaginations, movements, motivation, energy from the environment, and from the bodies that coincidentally happen to be present in the here–and–now.

When a group works with energy, individuals determine and inhabit their personal energy level. In an improvisation exercise everyone stands in a circle and holds hands. Each dancer then slightly turns the back of their hands alternately inward and outward at their own pace, in relation to personal changes of state inwards or outwards. This shifts the presence of the energy in the process: When turning the hands inward, the presence also moves inward, whereby the sensing of oneself now emphasizes inner closure and rest—analogous to other curves of the body, like the eyeballs for instance, which should sink into imagined round sockets in the back of the head. In turning outward, the presence then moves outward and the body tosses the collected energy out and passes it into the space or to neighboring bodies. This continues as long as the stream of energy lasts. When this energy begins to wane, the body turns 'inwards'.

Dealing with the space is analogous to what has already been said about dealing with energy: as the body is imagined as a continuation of energy directions in space—with lines of energy that sink into the floor, that move 'up, out of, and forward' from the head, and from various anchor points for horizontals—the space is also understood as an energetic principle that permeates us. If the space is constricted, the energy moves inward; if it is opened and widened, there is an exchange and giving of energy outward.

Directionality can change depending upon the research function or style of the dancer. Trisha Brown in the 1970s, for example, had already internalized a continuous, rapid play with changing directions through a long improvisational phase and was able to harness this in preparing pieces like *Locus* (1975). For Gries, these spatial dimensions go out far beyond the body's skin boundary: it is about exchanges of energies—alone, in pairs, in a group—and about use of collected energies for the purpose of clear attentiveness and devotion. In doing so, the focus in space can be architectural points, as in *Locus*, or a reconceptualized energetic space, infinitely dimensional with the potential to expand or contract.

The rhythm is determined by the dancer's chosen presence in each case. As is the case in some graphic scores of contemporary music that no longer have any predetermined pulse, each dancer can perform the score or improvisation exercise as they see fit—depending upon which research interest they have currently chosen. Thus an improvising group may not necessarily have a common rhythm, instead, each dancer acts in their own time. Changes then occur, for example, through the shifting

presence—here meant as a steering of the consciousness of the energy inward (being conscious of oneself) and outward again (being conscious of others).

Breathing provides neither rhythm nor beat, but flows freely and unhindered. It is there to support the movement. Dancing happens "on top of the breath," surfing it, so to say, whereby the dance composes its own voice and is not perforce dependent on the breath. Additionally, the use of music—since modern, and this holds even more true for postmodern dance—is not mandatory. Many hours of training are dedicated to sensing and utilization of inner-body organization, often in resting positions on the floor during which music would be more of a hindrance. Only in training larger movement phrases—as, for instance, in the sometimes very physically demanding postmodern[18] dance of the 1980s and 90s—is music used. But in this case, phrasing is not necessarily executed analogous to the music; instead, the energetic impression of the music is used.

Since the Release Technique is by nature open and varied, there are no fundamental movement principles. More so the converse applies: the technique is adapted to the style and movement vocabulary of the respective dancer and choreographer. Despite this, there are a few key ideas that are experimented with repeatedly.

Research in the 1960s was more focused on fundamental pedestrian movements like laying down, sitting, standing, walking, and hopping, and thus it is these movements, or those derived from them, that are found (at the latest) in task–oriented improvisations. Stability/instability has been an area of interest in modern, later also in contemporary dance, since Doris Humphrey. Trisha Brown was interested in specific variations during the middle phase of her creative work in the 1980s, for example in *Set and Reset*, in which, along with falling principles, appear *tossing* (throwing individual body parts into space), *dropping* (letting individual body parts fall), *breaking* (allowing a shape to explode outwards with its energy), and *organizing* (bringing individual body parts into stable organization, aligned on top of one another). In those years, execution always focused on what is 'real': with Gries tossing does not lead to a fully executed and perfected swing, nor does a breaking arm hold back its energy. It is necessary to really and truly hit the middle: execute simply and clearly the real energy expenditure of a tossing motion originating from the joint.[19]

Breathing can also be used in a variety of ways: Gries says, "Let your breathing do what it does, don't interfere. Give the diaphragm its independence." Breathing is a distinct movement of the diaphragm, an independent voice beneath the dancing phrase. As the body is somehow always working in suspensions between directions in space, jumping becomes lighter and more like a momentary escape from gravity—the body stretched through space like a cat in flight. Turns are also not necessarily made more complicated and technically accomplished, rather the movement is made interesting by the quick, newly found alignment in space, or when exploring principles of rotation. With Gries, this happens through exercises and variations felt quasi 'microscopically', like the diaphragm's minimal sway while lying down, through the partner's rocking hand movements, or in a contralateral pulling through the entire body carried out when standing by a partner gently and continuously pulling on an arm positioned diagonally across the body.

Specifically designated training or movement forms run counter to Release Technique; it defines itself for the most part *ex negativo,* i.e., from what a body releases. *Rest* is thus a movement that often appears in training. Laying on the floor in a *Constructive Rest Position (CRP)*— a stable position in which the body must expend very little effort—the body can feel into specific regions or themes and can direct attention to these, similar to a guided meditation. This enables awareness of anatomical connections between individual body parts above and beyond the immediate situation.

The only principles of Release Technique are based on figurative perceptions inspired by the range of somatic studies that picture the alignment of the bones and joints in space. Essential, for instance from Alexander Technique, is the principle of *up, forward and out*: the spine is imagined upward, and this line continues in an arc above the head heading out into the space, from inside to outside, and further downward and forward—into the future.

"Lean myself back into my spine. Trust that the things will come to me and that I don't have to search for anything— that's what it's about."
Siri Clinckspoor, student

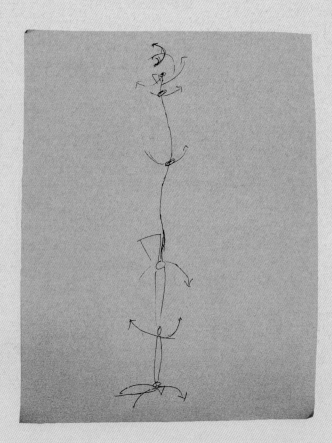

Sketch: Lance Gries

Sylvia Scheidl

TEACHING: PRINCIPLES
AND METHODOLOGY

CONCEPTUAL BASIS

Lance Gries's teaching offers participants comprehensive personal development that addresses them holistically and allows them to enter into their own research process. The goal is to put participants in a place where they can autonomously research where corporeal or energy system is blocked, where it is lacking and how to get it flowing again. Above and beyond this, Gries adds, "How much of our full 'self' is actively creating movement can be discovered and articulated so that you can express yourself with more and more differentiation." The aim is to achieve the greatest possible differentiation in a variety of dimensions, including the physical body, the body–mind[20] system, and society's system of communication—both in everyday life, as well as performing on stage.

At the physical level, it is especially important to align the bones such that they support the body's weight and leave muscles free for movement. Thus joints have the freedom for a high degree of mobility, empowering the body to move and to access multidirectionality.[21]

The research team observed that, on the body–mind level, Gries particularly encourages participants to become more aware of their mental attitudes and physical patterns so that, in the next phase, they can decide what they wish to change.

This also has an effect on the communicative and social levels: in Frankfurt it became apparent, during the course of the research, that decisions were eventually made more quickly and clearly, both when dealing with the space and with other people, for instance, during an improvisation exercise.

The target group is broadly conceived: according to Gries, all dancers—regardless of their contemporary or ballet backgrounds—can strengthen their work through the anatomically–grounded Release Technique approach. The research team's experiences show that beyond this, the work can also benefit amateurs: they learn to express themselves with greater differentiation and movement creativity is stimulated.

Gries does occasionally teach individual lessons in which he works hands–on to approach specific problems with alignment or movement and that work is often done on a table, standing, sitting, and moving. But as observed during the workshops in Frankfurt, he attaches strong importance to group work because of his own history and development.[22] Additional social aspects and dimensions of learning from each another have an effect on the group. In the dialogue of touch within hands–on work, for example, students learn a lot from their role as supporter because they learn sensibility for themselves and others. They also learn from the decisions others make during improvisations; they communicate with their surroundings and everything that is happening.

According to Gries, a student needs three to four weeks of daily training to understand the essential anatomic–functional concepts, and an additional three weeks for the important building–blocks of energy research.[23] His teaching insight: some people accept the holistic experience and change quickly, others in contrast build up a holistic understanding from many details over a longer period of time. Both groups must be taken into account.

Pupils' specific previous dancing knowledge may not necessarily be more or less advantageous, depending on the group, and according to Gries, can even interfere in the case of learned bad habits.[24] However, the research team was able to observe that dancers who may not have learned any special dance technique but who had a background in other body–awareness techniques did learn more easily. They could, for example, more quickly understand and implement the directive 'touch without manipulating'. Experience in other practices that require self–observation, such as meditation practice, are also beneficial.

Gries's approach to the work is characterized by postmodern ideals: each individual is responsible for their own process. Each person puts together what is important for themselves. And people are different, which is why each one needs different stimuli in order to come to an understanding. At the workshop in Frankfurt, we observed that some students were initially confused about the many approaches to the various materials, approaches that ran the gamut from creative tasks to technical exercises. For Gries this is not a contradiction: he does not make a distinction between training, rehearsal, improvisation, creating, and performance. The body should always be completely present and the performers always conscious of what they are doing. Some of the participants were able to access this concept only after the second or third week, partly due

---

20 Body–mind is a common term in dance since Bonnie Bainbridge Cohen's work, at the latest, and means—as with F. M. Alexander—the interplay of mental and physical processes. The concept assumes the terms are inseparably linked with one another and/or represent a communicative unity. See

also the remarks in the essay by Irene Sieben in this book.
21 About the *directions* of the body parts, see: Understanding the Body/Movement, keywords 'Movement Characteristics and Physicality'.

22 See the description of the developments in Brussels in the section Historic Context/Background: Biographies and Environment.
23 See also: Pedagogical Methods/Lesson Structure.

to the fact that establishing one's own research questions and recognizing relationships first becomes accessible after lengthier practical experience.

"The profound experience and arrival in one's own body architecture made an easy–going, ready access and flow of movement possible for me."

Berit Jentzsch, student

The training can either serve a particular physical goal, like the acquisition of physical skills to enable the interpretation of a range of dance vocabularies, or it can make a student open and unbiased for personal research. Those who invited Gries to Frankfurt had overlapping objectives. For example, the dance and dance–pedagogy professors wanted their students to acquire physical skills, and specifically, the anatomical orientation that Gries taught for a long time at P.A.R.T.S.: instead of 'release', they wanted more alignment—i.e., a clear orientation of the bones and the flow of movement in the space. These were to be practiced with the aid of movement phrases from Trisha Brown's *Set and Reset*. The research team's theoretical faction wanted Gries to teach the historic development of postmodern dance and the role that Release Technique played therein. The third component was Gries's own interest: merely re-dancing a repertoire no longer interests him, instead he is more interested in what Release Technique can bring about for the individual's support system and creativity, namely the productive use of energetic principles.

A variety of goals thus required a variety of approaches that Gries wove together. Fortunately this weaving fits into his teaching concept, which can be understood as loosely bound modules that he defines as open and unbiased; he is more interested in processes than in rehearsal.

PEDAGOGICAL METHODS

Gries does not use a linear lesson structure. He accesses his universe of individual, intertwined training modules from a variety of perspectives. Despite this, several characteristics repeat and can be observed in the exercise sequences.

Often modules are arranged such that students are directed through various spatial levels, from the floor to standing. The training day starts with body–work in

specific skeletal alignments. A Constructive Rest Position[25] allows body weight, especially the spine, to be released into the floor. Hands–on research with a partner, standing, or individual movement exploration provide students with alignments that can be applied later. Roll–over, weight displacement, and pliés are linked together in a fluid warm up. This is when the body establishes support from the ground up, from the ankle along the knee into the hip, because skeletal alignment remains in focus. Torso and head are oriented multidirectionally, with a free–swinging shoulder girdle, along with the arms as separate appendages.

Later in the day, Gries changes over to improvisation or to work with specific movement material. This material is not only rehearsed, but also used to practice anatomic–functional and energetic concepts. The Bus Stop[26] exercise described above is brought to bear here too, for example, the hand is the last body part that still has contact with the wall. When the hand finally releases, the shoulder girdle and arms can swing free from the chest and above the soles of the feet. The ability to allow the shoulders to float detached from the torso is, in turn, essential for the differentiated demands of the dancing material, such as in performing the *Set and Reset* phrase precisely.

Endurance is neither a training tool nor goal; it is more about feeling out currently available energy and its best possible use. In partner and group exercises, participants explore their motivations to move, what they are imagining in the process, and how they perceive themselves and their surroundings. For instance, one exercise is about sensing the space's architectural details, following inspiration's inner path in the process, and not to question oneself when doing. "Just do what is there to do" is the instruction—and to continue on to the next inspiration without attaching any ideas.

A class can vary. There is no repetition with Gries, except when rehearsing a choreography; an exercise is always slightly changed from the previous day.

His work emphasizes interval work: the day usually begins with quiet phases that foster releasing and sensing, which from time to time go over into more dynamic phases. The change between phases of greater activity and quieter phases is essential. Release training methods especially take advantage of thought's influence on movement. Thus in a slow process, dancers internalize their newly organized muscle–balances in order to later be able to reliably draw upon them for faster, more space–encompassing, and more demanding movements. Thus rest in body–work is crucial for extended perceptional phases.

24 See: Understanding the Body / Movement; Movement Characteristics and Physicality.
25 The Constructive Rest Position is as follows: the body is resting on its back on the floor, and the knees are bent and leaning against one another.

26 See also the description of this exercise in: Understanding the Body / Movement; Movement Characteristics and Physicality.

It is also important to slowly bring movement into these newly sensed connections; the freshly developed, delicate interplay between the skeleton's support, the freedom of the joints, and harmonious muscle activity should not be endangered.

In order not to be seduced by the outside world's demands for 'more' or 'bigger', Gries instructs, "Don't dance out of your range. Respect your range." One should not move beyond personal limits of integrated body organization, since this can lead to lopsided stresses and to an increased risk of injury over time.

Unidirectional attention on a body region, for instance, or overly intense concentration on an exercise is not beneficial. "You should distribute your abundance." And as detailed as Gries can be in his information, parts must be studied by going back to the whole. Students react to his recurrent instruction "globalize your sensation," by sensing throughout their entire bodies, and perceiving each part as being equally important and thereby integrated into the consciousness and the movement.

Repetition of a short hold in the movement allows participants to practice non-doing, namely to do nothing out of habit, to mindfully pause and come to a new solution either through kinesthetic memory or a mental instruction bringing new information.

Gries often says, "Don't prepare." Dancers should not prepare—not save their presence for dancing correctly or execute the warm–up with reduced attentiveness. Dancers should live in the dance in each and every moment, without thinking that they must do something else beforehand, for instance take up a tensed stance, hold their breath or become stiffer. This internal freezing up interrupts the energy flow.

Gries eschews imitation as a learning path for the most part; to a greater degree, he allows participants to feel out differences through improvisation and body–work. To accomplish this, he alternates between complex and simple exercises. A quiet, internally oriented exercise can be followed by an outwardly oriented group improvisation. A complex series of movements can conversely be interrupted with meticulous detail work. While the specific movement specifications may be simple in their outward form, their interconnectedness is complex.

One example: students practice getting up from a stool. The concentration on this simple activity enables them to identify when and how individual body parts edge forward in every phase of standing up, and when they are under too much tension. They practice releasing excess tension

and returning to a multidirectional alignment. They learn that the entire body must change at every moment, and that they cannot hold on to anything.

Along with an exemplary embodiment of Release principles, workshop leaders also require the skills and abilities that include risk–taking and decision–making in situ. If improvisations come to a standstill, Gries steps into the dancing. He adapts his plans constantly—starting from a change in word choice for anatomical details on down to the choice of the next work topic.

Regular discussion rounds between all participants are key elements. The teacher must therefore be aware of social processes and deal with conflicts in the group, which requires a sensibility for when intervention is necessary. What the Frankfurt research team found more important, however, was the leader's trust and patience in leaving participants alone, even in frustrating learning phases, and not interrupting the autonomous learning process—except when asked for assistance.

Gries explains the skills required of him as follows: that he, with his own body–mind, is able to sense small changes in participants' anatomy, energy, and cognizance; then the ability to induce small changes in anatomy, energy, and cognizance with his own hands and/or instructions; and finally, the artistic temperament to trust the unknown and to follow it, even in unproductive lines of research. And, when teaching, to recognize what is artistic, and pursue it.

Rhythm and motor learning are not determined through music, rather by use of the teacher's voice, which is always present. Gries's calm voice promotes easygoing concentration, an affirmative attitude toward the working process, and patient inner–sensing. Participants experience a high degree of freedom to pursue embodiment[27] of technical skills—as wild or gentle, complex or simple, as appropriate to themselves and their individual bodies. There is a very narrow dividing line between a pace that supports movement research and one that, because it is overly self–reflective, is too slow and inhibits opening. That is why a slow phase for re-organizational processes is followed by time 'just to move'. Seldom–used live music, or often recorded music brings participants to a high physical energy level that supports quick and light movement over a large radius. Musical qualities that suggest lightness encourage the muscles to work with less tension.

Conceived by Gries as a holistic body–mind development, his Release Technique offers differentiated tools for self–observation and self–determined changes that

27 *Embodiment* means the incorporation of thoughts, ideas, and knowledge of a sensory–physical and holistic experience and has been used in American body–awareness methods for the past several decades.

28 See: Understanding the Body/Movement; Movement Characteristics and Physicality.

can often yield an artistic process. Students are constantly challenged to shape the freedom offered, to identify their personal problem–solving strategies, interests, and habits, and to apply these in their dancing. This is to strengthen their "use of self," as F. M. Alexander put it, and to increase decision–making powers in order to develop a high level of awareness—both important soft skills in artistic processes. Even the Constructive Rest Position, here a microcosmic landscape, is an artistic research field for thinking and perceiving.

Gries brings students face–to–face with elements from his artistic biography as a springboard for deeper involvement. *Task orientation*, a radical early postmodern practice, targets searching for tasks from pedestrian movement and freeing oneself from self–reflection and self–evaluation when doing so. It is about discovering things anew, in a condition of not knowing, and gaining freedom for new movement. This is a practice that, over the years, has led to increasingly complex movement compositions. One example of this is the *line up* that Trisha Brown often used—a planned or spontaneous 'lining up in the space', as in aligning one's lower arm with that of another dancer. While doing, participants find and invent what they can line up, exchange ideas about this in small groups, and decide upon a collective strategy for the next round of improvisations.

Preparation for teaching is also modular, not linear. In order to introduce a new group to the work, Gries selects several topics for research material, usually simple, basic physical principles. Then, depending upon the interest, needs, and level of the group, he connects these during instruction step–by–step with the other modular building blocks from his Release and Alignment universe. These include: multidimensional consciousness;[28] non-fixation as a concept for integration and integrity and as undertone for vitality in the here–and–now; a balanced condition as optimal (and in the meantime, as Gries puts it, also refusing constant optimism); deconstruction and reintegration as two movements belonging together as a whole; autonomy and cooperation in the collective; sensitivity towards the process as opposed to being product–oriented (in Gries's words, "release versus fixation"); easygoing self–observation in the sense of Buddhist non-attachment. Lightness as an approach to work is a choice; freedom to change grows along with the increasing consciousness of the individual body parts and connection to the whole.

Self–assessment and feedback mostly takes place during class. Gries brings students into discussion rounds between exercises and training modules. They start with descriptions of and reflections upon what has been experienced; this can lead to a discussion about how participants experience their physicality in interaction with their expressed emotions, for example, or which decision–making strategies they can recognize in an open improvisation. This can also continue after class, with some students, for example when someone wishes to contribute personal observations. An appointment before or after a class for personal coaching, wherein Gries attempts to clarify specific questions, can follow.

When he leaves the space, Gries stops thinking about the class. He says he "needs time to not think." His process of reflection is integrated into the attentive, perceptive attitude he takes with him into the rest of his day. He does not make notes directly after class, instead occasionally takes time for personal research and documentation and, in doing so, creates a three–dimensional model of words and drawings.

Since there are various impressions and thus many definitions of Release Technique, the instructor plays a large role in the selection and communication of content. In Gries's way of teaching, speech, touch, and movement examples interact in a variety of ways. As a detail–oriented thinker, he frames things close to the body's anatomic reality, whereby observed relationship structures in the body–mind often also lead to observations about one's own everyday conduct that can be mutually shared and discussed. He leads the group with his calm, never–ending flow of words. In body–work sessions, he circles among the pairs, assisting in guided touch, and from this, he generates his next instruction. If presenting dance material, his facile movement demonstrations provide a good example for those participants who prefer learning through emulation.

Gries offers his personal perceptions, experiences, and imagery as points of reference. Using this information, students can deduce their own imagery and key words for anatomical concepts. Personal embodiment happens in the process. According to Gries, dancers are responsible for their own physical, mental, social, and creative development, and should fundamentally be independent of teachers in their ongoing personal research practice.

Gries often chooses metaphors using space and light to trigger kinesthetic reactions in the dancers. With his 'golden ball of light'[29] metaphor, he is inviting us into an imagined spherical space for movement. Inside this space, the body is in a balanced place and can move almost equally well in all directions. This means that the legs are liberated from the task of having to carry the body, and that the body can move in circles and spirals through space. "Feel the support of the space around your bones" further implies spherical surroundings. This has a supportive effect because the body's interior spaces are also imagined as spherical. The correspondence between interior and exterior space assists participants in actively opening their bodies, to feel welcomed by, and supported in, space.

Gries's instructions subtly influence the students' psychophysical body images. Here are a few examples: "Bring all of yourself to standing" animates whole–body presence; "Don't stand under, stand on top of your bones" changes the energetic alignment. With the metaphor "receive yourself," participants should welcome and perceive themselves, returning to an already centered and embodied self, as starting point for dancing. 'Centering the bones' calls for every bone to have its correct, released position in relation to its environment. To affirm one's current condition is something Gries calls "being in the center of your own experience." And from that, he explains, arises the grace of a performer.

"The decisive point is that we are able to develop an idea of acceptance and integrity that allows us to realize that idea. The result isn't important, but rather the respective action that we decided to take to get there." *Anastasia Kostner, student*

29 This figure of speech can sound somewhat esoteric, however here it is related to a very real process and references a spherically shaped organization of the body's energy, which is thereby well distributed and the transfer of which is transparent, similar to rays of light.

Gabriele Wittmann

CONCLUSION

The workshop with Lance Gries provided, on the one hand, an overview of the wide range of influences Release and Alignment Oriented Technique draws from various dance 'research scenes'. Gries has taken part in its development for several decades; he danced in his Frankfurt workshop, physically reproducing exceptional movement qualities from various eras and, through authentic improvisations, made them available to students. On the other hand, his unique approach showed participants how anatomically and functionally aligned inner–sensing work on the floor, in standing, moving, with or without hands–on by a partner, can lead to a greater consciousness of physical and mental awareness. Participants experienced this not only in the context of physical and mental alignment in space, which for some became definitively clearer, but also in other areas. For instance, the work also noticeably improved the propensity for decision–making during improvisations, something that the participants experienced firsthand. Gries's methodical modular teaching methods additionally made clear how diverse aspects of the dancing world are strongly connected: warm up, training, improvisation, rehearsal, performance—all of these are part of a 'research attitude' for Gries that encompasses the whole personality. The combination of all of these things enabled participants to grow and explore varied and personal research directions.

What does the future hold? Gries hopes that the term Release Technique will remain open and not be subsumed by special definitions. The quality of exchange and evolution are essential for the community of dancers influenced by Release Technique—including the exchange across the Atlantic. What was once a new technique in many dance communities as early as the 1980s, has long since been integrated and is an essential element in contemporary training in institutions as well as in the independent scene. Conversely, some of the forerunners of this research are no longer interested in a purely movement–oriented aesthetic—some even fundamentally question the idea of dance for a Western stage.

Gries has a much broader view of the future: he hopes that younger sciences, like neuroscience, will succeed in explaining the types of communication torrents that rush through the body. "That would be the ultimate legacy, if aspects of Release Technique would move on into our understanding of consciousness, spirituality, health." With this, Release Technique research would then find itself in a pioneering context where it has, time and again in the past, furthered aesthetic, artistic, and everyday development from a pedestrian vantage point.

"It is body training focused on economy that gives you the chance to organize yourself as efficiently as possible. After that you can do with it what you will. You can dance ballet, flamenco, or hip–hop, you can become a dramatic actor—you can apply the tools taught universally." *Sylvia Scheidl, research team*

ESSENTIAL LITERATURE

Dorvillier, DD | Harrell, Trajal | Michelson, Sarah (Ed.)
Movement Research Performance Journal Issues Nos. 18, 1/1999
and 19, 9/1999. New York: Movement Research Inc, 1999

Rolland, John
**"Alignment and Release: History and Methods: Jacques
van Eijden interviews John Rolland"**
In: Fabius, Jeroen: Talk. SNDO 1982–2006
Amsterdam: International Theatre and Film Books, 2009, pp. 117–129

ADDITIONAL LITERATURE

Alexander, F. M
Der Gebrauch des Selbst Basel/Freiburg: Karger Verlag, 2001

Bainbridge Cohen, Bonnie
**Sensing: Feeling and Action: The Experiential Anatomy
of Body-Mind Centering** Northampton (MA): Contact Editions, 1993

Banes, Sally
Reinventing Dance in the 1960s
Madison (WI): University of Wisconsin Press, 2003

Banes, Sally
Writing Dancing in the Age of Postmodernism
Middletown (CN): Wesleyan University Press, 1994

Banes, Sally
Democracy's Body: Judson Dance Theater, 1962–1964
Durham (NC): Duke University Press, 1993

Banes, Sally
Greenwich Village 1963 Durham (NC): Duke University Press, 1993

Banes, Sally
Terpsichore in Sneakers
Middletown (CN): Wesleyan University Press, 1987

Bernard, André | Stricker, Uwe | Steinmüller, Wolfgang
**Applied Ideokinesis: A Creative Approach to Human Movement
and Body Alignment** Berkeley (CA): North Atlantic Books, 2006

Bernard, André | Stricker, Uwe | Steinmüller, Wolfgang
Ideokinese: Ein kreativer Weg zu Bewegung und Körperhaltung
Bern: Verlag Hans Huber, 2003.

Brown, Trisha | Brunel, Lise | Delahaye, Guy | Mangolte, Babette (Ed.)
Trisha Brown: L'atelier des Chorégraphes
Paris: Editions Bouge, 1987

Burt, Ramsay **Judson Dance Theatre: Performative Traces**
New York: Routledge, 2006

Chödrön, Pema
Start Where You Are: A Guide to Compassionate Living
Boston (MA): Shambhala Publications, 2001

Chödrön, Pema
The Wisdom of No Escape and the Path of Loving Kindness
Boston (MA): Shambhala Publications, 1991

Clark, Barbara
Body Proportion Needs Depth – Front to Back
Champaign (IL): By the Author, 1975

Clark, Barbara
Let's Enjoy Sitting–Standing–Walking
Port Washington (NY): By the Author, 1963

Dowd, Irene
Taking Root to Fly: Seven Articles on Functional Anatomy
New York: Irene Dowd and Contact Collaborations, 1981

Fulkerson, Mary
**Release: From Body to Spirit, Seven Zones of Comprehension
Coming From the Practice of Dance** E-book
Hampshire, UK: Dance Books Ltd., 2004

Fulkerson, Mary
"Release Work. History from the View of Mary Fulkerson."
In: Movement Research Performance Journal, No. 16/1999, pp. 4–5

Fulkerson, Mary
The Language of the Axis Dartington, UK: Theatre Papers, 1975

Goldberg, Roselee
Performance Art: From Futurism to the Present
London: Thames and Hudson, 1988

Greene, Brian
**The Elegant Universe: Superstrings, Hidden Dimensions, and the
Quest for the Ultimate Theory** New York: First Vintage Books, 1999

Gries, Lance
"The Spirit Has Legs"
In: Movement Research Performance Journal, Nr. 19/1999, pp. 12–13

Hawkins, Eric
The Body is a Clear Place and Other Statements on Dance
Princeton (NJ): Princeton Book Company, 1992

Kornfield, Jack
**After the Ecstasy the Laundry: How the Heart
Grows Wise on the Spiritual Path** New York: Bantam Books, 2001

Matt, Pamela
**A Kinesthetic Legacy: The Life and Works of
Barbara Clark** Tempe (AZ): CMT Press, 1993

Olsen, Andrea | Caryn McHose, Caryn
Bodystories: Lebanon (NH): University Press of New England, 2004

Ricard, Matthieu | Thuan, Trinh Xuan
**Quantum and the Lotus: A Journey to the Frontiers Where
Science and Buddhism Meet** New York: Three Rivers Press, 2004

Skinner, Joan
"Skinner Releasing Technique."
In: Allison, Nancy: The Illustrated Encyclopaedia of Body-Mind Disci-
plines, New York: Rosen Publishing Group, 1999, pp. 265–267

Skinner, Joan | Davis, Bridget | Davidson, Robert | Wheeler, Kris |
Metcalf, Sally **"Skinner Releasing Technique. Imagery and its
Application to Movement Training"** In: Contact Quarterly, fall 1979

Skura, Stephanie
"Releasing Dance. An interview with Joan Skinner"
In: Contact Quarterly, Herbst 1990, pp. 11–18

Teicher, Hendel
Trisha Brown: Dance and Art in Dialogue, 1961 – 2001
Cambridge (MA): Cambridge University Press, 2002

Todd, Mabel E.
The Thinking Body Princeton (NJ): Princeton Book Company, 1959

Varela, Francisco J.
Ethical Know-How. Action, Wisdom, and Cognition
Stanford (CA): Stanford University Press, 1999

Varela, Francisco J. | Thompson, Evan T. | Rosch, Eleanor
The Embodied Mind: Cognitive Science and Human Experience
Cambridge (MA): MIT Press, 1993

Wood, Catherine
The Mind is a Muscle: Yvonne Rainer
Cambridge (MA): MIT Press, 2007

Zukav, Gary
The Dancing Wu Li Masters New York: Bantam Books, 1980

LINKS

ww.ideokinesis.com
www.releasedance.com
www.skinnerreleasing.com
www.trishabrowncompany.org

WHO'S WHO

Steven De Belder studied philosophy and theater studies in Antwerp and Ghent. Between 1999 and 2003 he worked as research assistant at the Department of Theatre Studies in Antwerp. He started working at P.A.R.T.S. in 2003 and is currently coordinator of the Research Cycle and coordinator of the Départs network. He was member and president ad interim of the Flemish Dance Council (2001–2003) and is on the board of directors of several Flemish dance companies.

Christiane Berger, PhD, studied philosophy and theater studies in Tübingen, Giessen, and Berlin and completed her doctorate in theater studies at the FU Berlin. Her dissertation, *Körper denken in Bewegung*, was published by transcript publishing house in 2006. She researches theory and practice of professional and formal dance in the 20th and 21st centuries, as well as the role of the audience in contemporary dance. She has worked on numerous theater and dance productions as a choreographer, dramaturg, and production assistant. Since October 2008, she has been teaching for the master's program in choreography at the Inter–University Center for Dance (HZT) in Berlin.

José Biondi, Prof., trained at the Escuela de Aspirantes del Ballet Clasico Nacional in Madrid, (Spain). He was a member of the Ballet Contemporain de Bruxelles (Belgium) and of the S.O.A.P. Dance Theatre Frankfurt (where, for five years, he was assistant and director of training with the company under Rui Horta). From 1998–2000 he was rehearsal director for the Carte Blanche Danseteater Bergen in Norway. In October 2000 he was appointed professor of modern dance at the University for Music and Drama Hanover; as of September 2004 he became professor of contemporary dance at the Palucca Schule Dresden and director of the Teacher Training (Tanzpädagogik) program. From September 2006 to August 2009 he was prorector for academic affairs (Lehre und Studium) and since September 2009 he has been director of the master's program for choreography. He also works as a freelance choreographer and guest teacher for various international workshops and dance companies.

Edith Boxberger is a dance journalist, author, and translator. Following a two-year editorial traineeship with a newspaper, she studied sociology and social psychology in Munich before working as a teacher at the university and in the area of adult education. After studying at the Drama Department of New York University, she began, first in Munich and later in Frankfurt, to write about dance for various newspapers—including a many years for the *Frankfurter Allgemeine Zeitung*—and specialist magazines. She has lived in Hamburg since 1995 and also works as a translator (*Postmoderne Ethik* and *Die Krise der Politik* by Zygmunt Bauman, among others). In 2006 she began working for the Berlin office of Tanzplan Deutschland and for the project K3 at Tanzplan Hamburg.

Rose Breuss, Prof., studied at the University for Music and Performing Arts Vienna, at the Theaterschool Amsterdam, at Temple University Philadelphia, and at the Labanotation Institute at the University of Surrey. She has won several awards for her choreographic work (Max Brand Award for experimental music, the Theodor Körner Prize for Science and Art, and the Federal Chancellery Award (Prämie des Bundeskanzleramtes) for her choreography *Drift*). In addition to teaching assignments at the Vienna State Opera Ballet School and the University of Salzburg's Department of Music and Dance, she is director of the Institute of Dance Arts at the Anton Bruckner Privatuniversität in Linz.

Jacalyn Carley received her Bachelor of Dance Education at George Washington University, USA. Her teachers in the United States included Wigman students Maida Withers and Brigitta Herrmann. She danced professionally with Group Motion (Berlin) in Philadelphia, and in 1978 she cofounded tanzfabrik berlin. There she taught, choreographed, and co-directed from 1978–1997; during that time her works toured extensively throughout Europe and the United States. She also directed and organized the symposium *Dance in Berlin*, 1981. In 1998 she turned to writing. Her fiction works include *Was sagt das linke Knie zum Rechten*, and *Almas Tanz* (Eichborn). She co-authored, in 2010, Royston Maldoom's autobiography *Tanz um Dein Leben* (Fischer), and wrote *Royston Maldoom—Community Dance Handbook* (Henschel). She teaches for a U.S. study abroad program and lectures on German dance history at U.S. universities.

Gill Clarke studied English and Education at York University before becoming an independent dance artist, performer, teacher, advocate, and movement researcher—and recently received an MA in Social Sciences. She was a founder–member of the Siobhan Davies Dance Company and has performed and collaborated with many other choreographers, including Rosemary Butcher, Rosemary Lee, and Janet Smith. She teaches masterclasses and workshops internationally for students, independent artists, and professional companies. She was director of performance studies at LABAN London 2000–2006 (where she is now a consultant), received a fellowship from NESTA, a London Dance and Performance Award, an MBE (Member of the Order of the British Empire), is a visiting professor at Ulster University, and co-director of Independent Dance—an organization supporting professional dance artists in London.

Franz Anton Cramer, PhD, Fellow of the Collège international de philosophie in Paris, is a dance scholar and publicist. He studied Hispanic languages and literature, art history, and theater studies at the FU Berlin, receiving his doctorate in 1998. From 2003–2004 he was managing director of the Tanzarchiv Leipzig, and from 2004–2006 Research Fellow at the Centre national de la danse, France. In 2006 he contributed to the development of the *Contemporary Dance, Context, Choreography* pilot study program as part of the Cooperative Dance Education Centre Berlin, where he was guest professor until 2010. He is the project coordinator of Kulturerbe Tanz (Cultural Dance Heritage) for Tanzplan Deutschland and has written numerous publications, lectures, and workshops on aspects of contemporary dance, archiving, cultural policy, and the history of movement cultures.

Alan Danielson creates and teaches contemporary dance in the Humphrey/Limón tradition. His company, Dance by Alan Danielson, is based in New York City and has performed throughout the United States, South America, Europe, and Asia. His choreography has been commissioned by Danspace Project (NYC), Gala Arte (Mexico), Institut del Teatre (Spain), and F.E.D.E Danza Laboratorio (Italy) among others. Danielson is the school director of the Limón Institute in New York City. He is an internationally acclaimed master teacher of dance, music, and the methodology for teaching Contemporary Limón Technique. He has taught professional classes in New York City since 1984 and has been on faculty at New York University, Florida State University, and the Alvin Ailey School. Danielson was a professional musician before he began dancing, and worked as a conductor and music director in a variety of venues—from orchestra to rock band. He holds a Bachelor of Music in Choral Conducting and an MFA in dance from Florida State University.

Scott deLahunta has worked as writer, researcher, and organizer on a range of international projects bringing performing arts with a focus on choreography into conjunction with other disciplines and practices. He is currently Senior Research Fellow at Coventry University/R-Research Director Wayne McGregor | Random Dance, and program and research coordinator for Motion Bank/The Forsythe Company. He serves on the editorial boards of *Performance Research*, *Dance Theatre Journal* and the *International Journal of Performance and Digital Media*.

Susanne Dickhaut is a freelance dancer, holds a graduate degree in sports studies, and is lecturer for the Pilates Method at the Centre for Contemporary Dance at the University for Music and Dance, Cologne. As a dancer, performer, and choreographer she has participated in numerous independent dance theater productions and multimedia events. Since 2001 she regularly assists Jennifer Muller in Europe. Parallel to her artistic activities, Dickhaut has specialized in working as a Pilates instructor. Her international Pilates and dance teaching includes work with professional dancers and non-dancers of all ages, in classes, in personal training sessions and in workshops as well as lectures and further education e.g., at the University of Wuppertal, the Deutschen Bundesverband Tanz, and the German Sport University Cologne.

Ingo Diehl studied dance in Hanover and New York. He received his second degree in dance education in Cologne in 2003. Since 1988 he has been working as a dancer, choreographer, dance teacher, and choreographic assistant at Dance Forum Cologne, Tanztheater Bremen, Icelandic Ballet in Reykjavik, and at various festivals. He gives practice–related lectures and teaches at various colleges and universities, and has published diverse articles. Ingo Diehl is responsible for all educational issues and projects at Tanzplan Deutschland; he has initiated and (since 2005) overseen institutional exchanges to further dance and dance education in Germany. He was artistic director of the 1st Dance Education Biennale / Tanzplan Deutschland, (co-organized with Bettina Masuch in 2008), and developed the research project and concept for *Dance Techniques 2010—Tanzplan Germany*, of which he is senior editor (together with Dr. Friederike Lampert). He is a founding member of the Federal Association of Dance in Schools, the initiator of the Dance Education Conference, and since 2009 has been a member of the committee of experts for art, music, and design at the ACQUIN accreditation institute.

Anouk van Dijk is choreographer, dancer, teacher, and artistic director of her own company anoukvandijk dc. Her choreographies are characterized by a virtuosic, unpredictable dance vocabulary and deal thematically with people who manage to stand their ground despite the uncertainties and opposing forces of today's world. Since 1989 she has created more than forty choreographies that have been presented around the world. Not only does her company produce new work, she also initiates co-productions with theaters, festivals, dance academies, and other dance companies both nationally and internationally. In 2009 Anouk van Dijk renewed her collaboration with playwright / director Falk Richter, associate director at the Schaubühne Berlin. In their recent work, she has also resumed dancing. During her career Anouk van Dijk has developed her own movement system: Countertechnique. She uses this technique in her own choreographies and teaches the technique to students and professional dancers around the world.

Henner Drewes, PhD, studied dance and notation at the Jerusalem Academy for Music and Dance, at Kibbutzim College of Education in Tel Aviv, and at the Folkwang University in Essen. His most influential teachers include Amos Hetz (Jerusalem), Tirza Sapir (Tel Aviv), and Christine Eckerle (Essen). In 2002 he completed his doctorate at Leipzig University. Drewes has taught movement notation and movement since 1994, and since 2003 he has taught at the Kibbutzim College of Education in Tel Aviv, at the University for Music and Dance, Cologne, and at the Anton Bruckner University in Linz. He is a member of and dancer in the RikudNetto Dance Group (Tel Aviv) under the artistic direction of Tirza Sapir. In 2006 he was awarded the North Rhine–Westphalia Dance Studies Prize for his project 'From Notation to Computer–Generated 3D Animation'. Since October 2008 he has been working as a research assistant on the 'Visualizing (the Derra de Moroda) Dance Archives' project under Prof. Dr. Claudia Jeschke's direction at the Department of Art, Music, and Dance Studies at the University of Salzburg.

Wiebke Dröge is a choreographer, dancer, teacher, and project consultant. Trained in sports studies, contemporary dance, improvisation techniques, and theater education, she was a research assistant and director of the Dance Department at the J. W. Goethe University Frankfurt from 2001–2006. In 2005 she founded the www.ohnepunkt.info label, which consolidates her company, outreach, and text work. She stages productions and cooperates with artists working in various genres. Her ongoing artistic focus is a preoccupation with the topic 'beginning'. Since 2004 she has been developing workshop formats, texts, and performance series on this topic, including work at the Künstlerhaus Mousonturm in Frankfurt. In 2007 Dröge pursued her 'beginning' research in an exchange with work–trends researchers dealing with creative work. She is a guest teacher at universities and art colleges, and since 2006 has been developing and coaching Tanzlabor_21 / A Project by Tanzplan Deutschland in the context of the Dance–in–Schools initiative. Since 2008 she has realized projects for the Crespo Foundation.

Claudia Fleischle–Braun, PhD, was a research assistant and gymnastics and dance teacher at the Institute for Sports Sciences at the University of Stuttgart from 1978–2006. In 1999 she completed her doctorate on the history and teaching concepts of modern dance. She is particularly interested in the development of contemporary dance and how it is taught in the context of dance education, and the dance medicine aspects of functional movement and training design. Since 2005 she has been a member of the board of the Gesellschaft für Tanzforschung (Dance Research Society) and campaigned in various functions and committees for more, and better established dance in the education system.

Lance Gries, while pursuing an early love of music and an economics degree, began formal dance training at Indiana University and later completed his BFA in dance at SUNY Purchase College, New York. From 1985–1992 he was a member of the Trisha Brown Dance Company and was honored for his work there with a New York Dance and Performance Award ('Bessie'), and a Princess Grace Foundation Award. Since 1990 Lance Gries has created and presented solo and group choreographies in various venues in New York City, including The Kitchen and Danspace, and in cities throughout Europe. He has taught workshops and masterclasses throughout the world and became a 'founding teacher' of P.A.R.T.S. in Brussels in 1994, where he is still a visiting teacher. He has taught for many European dance companies and institutions including Rosas, UltimaVez, Lyon Opera Ballet, London Contemporary Dance, CND in Paris, Toulouse, and Lyon, France, the Frankfurt University of Music and Performing Arts, Tanzfabrik in Berlin, The Danish National School of Contemporary Dance in Copenhagen as well as Movement Research, Janet Panetta Studio, and Trisha Brown Studios in New York City.

Nik Haffner studied at the Dance Department of the Frankfurt University of Music and the Performing Arts and the Australian Ballet School in Melbourne and was a dancer with William Forsythe at Frankfurt Ballet from 1994–2000. During this time he was involved with the develoment and publishing of the CD-Rom *Improvisation Technologies*. He now works as a freelance dancer and choreographer on stage, film, and installation projects, and as a guest teacher at training institutions such as P.A.R.T.S. in Brussels and LABAN London. He is a member of the board of directors of the Inter–University Center for Dance— a pilot project of Tanzplan Berlin.

Yvonne Hardt, PhD, is a dancer, choreographer, and dance scholar. While training in modern and contemporary release–based dance techniques, she studied history and theater studies in Berlin and Montreal, and in the Körper–Inszenierungen postgraduate program at the FU Berlin, earning her doctorate for work on the political dimensions of free dance (Ausdruckstanz). She then worked as a research assistant at the Institute for Theater Studies and contributed to establishing the MA in dance. In May 2009 she was appointed professor for applied dance studies at the University for Music and Dance, Cologne. Prior to this she was assistant professor at the Department of Theater, Dance, and Performance Studies of the University of California, Berkeley. In addition to her research activities, since 1997 she has constantly been creating her own choreographies with her dance company, BodyAttacksWord, the most recent being *Jellyfish and Exuberant Love* (2006) and *TR_C_NG* (2007).

Wibke Hartewig, PhD, studied theater, film and television, general and comparative literature, and art history in Bochum and London. Her dissertation entitled *Kinästhetische Konfrontation. Lesarten der Bewegungstexte William Forsythes* (epodium) discussed the scope of movement analysis methods for dance studies using Forsythe's work as an example. While studying for her doctorate, she was an associate lecturer in contemporary dance and movement analysis at Ruhr University Bochum, worked as a dancer and choreographer for tanztheater macasju in Bochum, and then as a dramatic advisor for various (dance) theater productions in Berlin. After several years working as an editor for Henschel, she now works as a freelance dance expert, editor, and author focusing on the performing arts.

Anthony B. Heric, a freelance translator, graduated from Harvey Mudd College in Claremont, CA, with a Bachelor of Science in Engineering. He went on to work for the Jet Propulsion Laboratories in Pasadena, CA. Despite the excitement of QA / QC, he threw away a career with NASA to live in Europe. After permanently settling in Berlin with his husband, Dirk Ludigs, he started working as a translator in 2002. He has co-translated, among other works, the exhibition catalog *Albert Einstein—Chief Engineer of the Universe* (for the Max Planck Institute for the History of Science), *The World of Food* (Gräfe & Unzer), and Professor Udo Benzenhöfer's *Euthanasia in Germany Before and During the Third Reich* (Klemm + Oelschläger). His translations have also appeared in numerous magazines and newspapers. When not working, he enjoys yoga and the vibrant cultural landscape that Berlin offers.

David Hernandez studied studio music, jazz, opera, and dance in Miami. He worked as an apprentice for a time with the Trisha Brown Company. He moved to Europe with Meg Stuart to help her start Damaged Goods in Belgium, working as a performer, collaborator, training the company, and assistant to Stuart. Hernandez left the company to return to building his own body of work in Brussels. He has created several pieces including the solos Love letters, the quartet the essence of its going (1998), and the sextet Blueprint (2002). He frequently works as choreographer, dancer, composer, lecturer, and dramaturg and collaborates with Brice Leroux (France), Labor Gras (Berlin), Anouk Van Dijk (Amsterdam), and Rosas (Brussels). He developed the improvisation project CrashLanding (1996–1999) in collaboration with Meg Stuart and Christine De Smet, which crashed down in places like Leuven, Vienna, Paris, Lisbon, and Moscow in major festivals and houses, and did improvisations for several other festivals with many wonderful artists including Katie Duck, Steve Paxton, and Vera Mantero. He has also created several multimedia projects and happenings such as Filter, Innersections, and Performance Hotel in visual arts spaces and theaters. He developed and directed The Performance Education Program (PEP) in Leuven in residence at the Klapstuk Festival. He teaches regularly in Belgium and internationally and has been a core professor at P.A.R.T.S., teaching technique, composition and improvisation, rhythm and dance, and repertory projects.

Reinhild Hoffmann was one of the generation of pioneers of German dance theater. She trained with Kurt Jooss at the Folkwang University Essen. In 1978 she founded her own ensemble at the Theater Bremen. The pieces she developed in Bremen (1978–1986) and at the Schauspielhaus Bochum (1986–1995) were shown at many international guest performances and received numerous awards. She has been working as a freelance choreographer, dancer, and director since 1995. The focus of her work has shifted to directing musical theater. Norbert Servos's monograph on Hoffmann entitled Solange man unterwegs ist—die Tänzerin und Choreographin Reinhild Hoffmann was published in 2008.

Sabine Huschka, PhD, has been a part–time professor for dance studies at the Institute for Theater Studies at the FU Berlin since 2010, when she finished her postdoctoral research project Tanz und Wissen, Eine kulturhistorische Studie der Episteme choreographierter Körper (sponsored by the German Research Foundation (DFG)). She was previously a substitute assistant professor for dance studies at the Institute for Theater Studies at the University of Bern (2009) as well as substitute professor for theater studies at the Institute for German Studies II at the University of Hamburg. She studied German language and literature with a focus on theater and media, linguistics, and art history at the University of Hamburg. Her teaching and research focus is on the transmission of physical, representational, and movement knowledge in performing arts (theater and dance in the 18th and 20th centuries), culture theory, and theater theory access to the history of professional dance (dance and knowledge), as well other questions about aesthetics in professional dance and performance. In addition to her research activities, she has worked as a dramaturg at Theater am Turm in Frankfurt and for William Forsythe's Frankfurt Ballet. Her work is informed by her training in integrative dance education and her experiences in bodywork and improvisation. Publications include Wissenskultur Tanz. Historische und zeitgenössische Vermittlungsakte zwischen Praktiken und Diskursen (ed.; transcript publishing), Moderner Tanz. Konzepte—Stile—Utopien (Rowohlt), and Merce Cunningham und der Moderne Tanz (Königshausen & Neumann).

Pirkko Husemann, PhD, is dance curator at Hebbel am Ufer in Berlin. She graduated in theater, film, and media studies at Johann Wolfgang Goethe University Frankfurt am Main and wrote her dissertation Choreography as Critical Practice on Xavier Le Roy's and Thomas Lehmen's modes of work (transcript publishing). Together with Sabine Gehm and Katharina von Wilcke, Husemann curated the Tanzkongress Deutschland 2006 in Berlin's House of World Cultures, which resulted in the publication of Knowledge in Motion. Perspectives of artistic and scientific research in dance (transcript publishing, in German and English).

Ann Hutchinson Guest is an internationally recognized expert on dance notation. Her specialty is Labanotation, about which she has written definitive textbooks. Her study of dance notation systems of the past and present produced a history on the subject. In 1940 she was a cofounder of the Dance Notation Bureau in New York City, and in 1967 founded the Language of Dance Centre (LODC) in London, England. Guest's study of old systems made possible the revival of several ballets such as 'Pas de Six' from La Vivandière, and L'Après-midi d'un Faune from Vaslav Nijinsky's own notation score. She has received two honorary doctorates and many lifetime achievement awards for her contributions to dance education, including the 1997 Outstanding Contribution to Dance Research award from the Congress on Research in Dance (CORD).

Claudia Jeschke, PhD, studied theater and German studies in Munich, and received her doctorate in 1979. From 1980–1990 she was research assistant at the Institute for Theater Studies at the University of Munich before being appointed professor at the Institute for Theater Studies in Leipzig in 1994, where she also qualified as professor. In 2000 she was appointed professor of dance at the University for Music and Dance, Cologne. Since 2004 she has occupied the Chair of Dance Studies at the University of Salzburg and been a guest professor at European and American universities. Jeschke also works as dramaturg, choreographer, exhibition organizer, and author of television programs about dance. She is the author of numerous scientific publications in which she, as a trained dancer, highlighted the movement–analytical and practice–oriented aspects of dance history. The connection of history, theory, and practice is also documented in numerous reconstructions of dance phenomena of the 18th, 19th, and 20th centuries.

Irmela Kästner earned a psychology degree as well as an MA at LABAN London. She lives in Hamburg and works as an author, curator, and journalist. Her articles on dance and performance are published regularly in the specialist and daily press. She has also contributed to various books, both nationally and internationally, such as 'Zufall oder Streben nach kosmischer Ordnung? Das I Ging in der zeitgenössischen Choreografie', published in Tanz, Bewegung & Spiritualität, ed.: Fischer, Hecht (Henschel), 'Contradiction as a strategy for a future in motion' in P.A.R.T.S.—Documenting 10 Years of Contemporary Dance Education, published by P.A.R.T.S. She has also authored film and television projects in cooperation with the German Dance Film Institute Bremen. In 2007 her book Meg Stuart—Anne Teresa de Keersmaeker (together with photographer Tina Ruisinger) was published by K. Kieser Publishing House. In 1993 she was one of the cofounders of the Tanzinitiative Hamburg. As artistic director, she curates festivals, laboratories, productions, and also develops concepts and performance formats for dance in public spaces.

Andrea Keiz studied biology, trained to be a teacher of dance improvisation, and since the year 2000 has worked in Berlin in the area of the video documentation of contemporary dance. She has worked on several video / performance projects with various partners, teaches perception and video / dance, and has produced a diverse range of documentations for festivals and training projects in Germany and beyond.

Antje Klinge, PhD, is professor for sport pedagogy and methods in the Sports' Sciences Department at the Ruhr University in Bochum. Her research focuses on learning and education in the media of the body, movement, sport, and dance. She qualified as a professor of sports education with a research project on the topic of Körperwissen—eine vernachlässigte Dimension. She is a founding member and current board member of the Federal Association of Dance in Schools and a board member of Tanzplan Deutschland.

Friederike Lampert, PhD, studied ballet at the University of Music and the Performing Arts in Frankfurt and applied theater studies at the Justus Liebig University in Giessen. Afterwards she worked for ten years as a professional dancer and choreographer. From 2002–2006 she worked as research assistant at the Department of Performance Studies at the University of Hamburg and taught dance theory and practice there. Her doctorate was on the topic of *Improvisation im künstlerischen Tanz* and in 2006 she was awarded the North Rhine–Westphalia Dance Studies Prize for this work. She organizes dance conferences and is the artistic director of the K3 Jugendklub at the K3 Zentrum für Choreographie/Tanzplan Hamburg at Kampnagel. From 2008–2010 she was a research assistant at Tanzplan Deutschland and senior editor (together with Ingo Diehl) of the publication *Dance Techniques 2010—Tanzplan Germany*. In September 2010 she took on the position of an associate researcher with Jiří Kylián at the Rotterdam Dancy Academy (Codarts). Aside from diverse professional articles, she has also published the following books: *Choreographieren reflektieren. Choreographie–Tagung an der Hochschule für Musik und Tanz Köln* (Lit Publishing) and *Tanzimprovisation. Geschichte, Theorie, Verfahren, Vermittlung* (transcript publishing).

Mia Lawrence, originally from New York, currently works as the coordinator of the First Cycle at P.A.R.T.S., Brussels, where she switches between teaching yoga, contemporary, and creative work. She spent eight years touring internationally as a member of the Stephen Petronio Company. In 1997 she began creating her own work and teaching workshops in festival and schools in the United States and Europe. In 1998 she received the prestigious New York Dance and Performance Awards ('Bessie') for her first evening–length solo *Kriyas*. She relocated to Munich in 2002 where she continued creating pieces with the support of the Kulturreferat and other institutions. She received the Förderpreis Tanz in 2005 from the city of Munich for her artistic achievement. She continues to create pieces utilizing movement, text, and sound.

Anna Markard was born in Germany in 1931, eldest daughter of Kurt and Aino Jooss, and grew up in England after her family emigrated there in 1933. She studied at the Sigurd Leeder School of Dance, the Folkwang School Essen, and with Nora Kiss in Paris. She was a dancer at the Düsseldorf Opera House but soon followed her educational interests, becoming an assistant at the Folkwang School before teaching modern European dance in the United States, and from 1960 taught at the Folkwang School. Together with her father, she redeveloped some of his most important ballets for the stage and has been responsible for many productions of the Jooss repertoire all over the world. She set up the Jooss Archive and was working on the publication of partitures from Jooss's works in Labanotation. Markard lived in Amsterdam and was married to the painter Hermann Markard; she died in 2010.

Gisela Müller, Prof., studied dance in Paris, Amsterdam (SNDO), and New York. She has been a member of various dance companies and in 1992 founded the Move Company, for which she has also choreographed numerous pieces and received scholarships in Germany and abroad. She has taught at various training and educational institutions and studios in Germany and beyond since 1988, and has been a board member and principal for the Tanzfabrik Berlin since 2004. From 2006–2009 she was a guest professor at the Cooperative Dance Education Centre/Berlin, responsible for the Bachelor of Arts program in contemporary dance, context, and choreography.

Jennifer Muller, an influence in the dance world for over forty years, is known for her visionary approach and innovations in multidisciplinary dance/theater productions incorporating the spoken word, live and commissioned music, artist–inspired décor, and unusual production elements. She has created over one hundred works including six full–evening productions. Artistic director of Jennifer Muller/The Works since 1974, she has toured with the company to forty countries on four continents. An internationally renowned teacher, she has developed a personalized technique and developed innovative programs in creative thinking. Her choreography has been commissioned by twenty-four international repertory companies including Alvin Ailey American Dance Theater, Nederlands Dans Theater, NDT3, Ballet du Nord, and Lyon Opera Ballet. Her work for theater includes The Public Theater, Second Stage, New York Stage and Film, and the Metropolitan Opera. Creating work since she was seven years old, she graduated from the Juilliard School, New York City. She danced with the Pearl Lang and José Limón Dance Companies, and was associate artistic director of the Louis Falco Dance Company.

Janet Panetta studied ballet with Margaret Craske, Antony Tudor, and Alfredo Corvino at the Metropolitan Opera Ballet School. At fourteen she became Margaret Craske's teaching assistant, which served as on–the–job training for her lifelong career in dance education. She joined the American Ballet Theatre in 1968, and later began her foray into modern dance as a member of Paul Sanasardo's company. She went on to work with Robert Kovich, Neil Greenberg, Susan Salinger, Peter Healey, and numerous other modern companies, while continuing to teach. In the 1980s she began working internationally. She has been a guest teacher at P.A.R.T.S. and Tanztheater Wuppertal Pina Bausch. In addition, she teaches at Impulstanz in Vienna each summer, and maintains the Panetta Movement Center in New York, where she serves as artistic director of International Dance Dialogues, a program that hosts many European artists' workshops and lectures.

Chrysa Parkinson is a performer and teacher living in Brussels. She teaches regularly at P.A.R.T.S. and works as a mentor/coordinator for the Second–Cycle students. She also teaches regularly at La Raffinnerie and Danscentrum Jette in Brussels, Panetta Movement Center in New York, and at Impulstanz in Vienna. In 2010/11 she is touring and performing with Jonathan Burrows, Mette Ingvartsen, and Rosas/Anne Teresa De Keersmaeker. She is a member of ZOO/Thomas Hauert, and has also worked with Jonathan Burrows, Deborah Hay, John Jasperse, Meg Stuart, and David Zambrano. She was a member of Tere O'Connor Dance for many years in New York where she also performed with Irene Hultman and Jennifer Monson, among other artists. During that time she taught at Movement Research and at NYU. She was awarded a Bessie for sustained achievement as a performer in 1996. In 2008 Chrysa Parkinson worked as a teacher researching performance practices in Montpellier with 6M1L and Ex.e.r.c.e. Based on her work in Montpellier, she created an illustrated DVD essay called Self-Interview on Practice.

Barbara Passow trained under Hans Züllig as a dancer at the Folkwang University of the Arts Essen from 1968–1972, also completing a one-year dance education program specializing in dance for children and amateurs. In 1979 she was awarded a scholarship by the state of North Rhine–Westphalia that enabled her to travel to New York for a year where she studied Limón Technique intensively. She worked as a dancer at the Cullberg Ballet under Birgit Cullberg in Stockholm from 1972–1984, at the Tanztheater Wuppertal under Pina Bausch, and at the Folkwang Tanz Studio under Susanne Linke. Since 1986 she has taught modern dance at various universities and dance companies (Bremen Theater, among others) and workshops for professional and non-professional dancers, as well as working as a dancer and choreographer with Michael Diekamp. Since 1995 she has taught at the Palucca Schule Dresden—Hochschule für Tanz.

Jerry Remkes recieved his masters in Arts and Arts Administration at the University of Groningen. After graduation he was a cultural policy manager for the city governments of Eindhoven and Amersfoort and the managing director for theater company Het Oranjehotel. Since 2001 he has been working for anoukvandijk dc, first exclusively as managing director and from 2003 also as dramaturg for Anouk van Dijk's performances.

Daniel Roberts grew up in Pittsburgh, Pennsylvania, and started playing the piano at the age of seven. He was piano accompanist at various ballet schools. He studied ballet and modern jazz at the CLO Academy in Pittsburgh then took a Bachelor of Fine Arts in Dance at the Ohio State University, with a specialization in performance and Labanotation. Roberts received a scholarship to the Merce Cunningham Studio in New York and apprenticed with the Merce Cunningham Dance Company (MCDC). He joined the company in 2000 and danced in a vast amount of repertory, including films about Cunningham (for example, in *Merce Cunningham: A Lifetime of Dance* in the reconstruction of *Totem Ancestor*). He left the MCDC in 2005 and taught Cunningham Technique at the Danish National School of Contemporary Dance in Copenhagen. He is currently rehearsal director for Danish Dance Theater. Daniel Roberts has taught the Cunningham Technique at The Place (London Contemporary Dance School), at the Royal Academy of Dance in London, at the National University of Arts in Korea and at various companies, dance schools and festivals in Europe, Russia, the U.S., and Asia.

Theo Van Rompay has a Masters in Sociology (K.U. Leuven, 1978). He cofounded the arts center STUK in Leuven, Belgium, where he was director from 1978–1986. Afterwards he worked for Kaaitheater in Brussels (1986–1987) and for the Dutch theater company Maatschappij Discordia, based in Amsterdam (1988). In 1989 he became director of Beursschouwburg (Brussels) and in 1991 program director of the international arts center deSingel (Antwerp). In 1994 Anne Teresa De Keersmaeker asked him to assist in setting up a new dance school. Since then he has been deputy director of Performing Arts Research and Training Studios (P.A.R.T.S.), a school for contemporary dance that opened in September 1995. He was cofounder (1982) and editor (1982–1991) of the performing arts magazine *Etcetera*. He was co-founder of the Vlaams Theater Circuit (1980) and later of the Flemish Theatre Institute V.T.I. (1988). He was a member of the V.T.I. board for twenty years, and from 2006–2008 served as president. In 2008 he was appointed by the minister of Culture to be a member of the Advisory Board for the Arts of the Flemish Community.

Salva Sanchis is a choreographer and dancer based in Brussels who graduated with the first generation of P.A.R.T.S. in 1998. He has been choreographing his own work since then and presenting it across Europe. He co-choreographed with Anne Teresa De Keersmaeker the pieces *Desh* and *A Love Supreme*, and has been a guest choreographer for Rosas. He is also a guest teacher of dance technique and improvisation as well as research coordinator for the Second Cycle of P.A.R.T.S., and teaches dance technique in several other schools and companies in Belgium and abroad.

Vera Sander, Prof., studied at the London Contemporary Dance School and the Theaterschool Amsterdam. Before developing her first choreographies as a soloist at the Cologne Danceforum, she danced with the Dansgroep Krisztina de Chatel, with Itzik Galili, and as a soloist at the Saxon State Opera Dresden, among others. She has worked as a choreographer, dancer, and teacher of contemporary dance since 1996. In addition to the invitations she receives to be guest choreographer throughout Germany and abroad, she is artistic director of the VeraSanderArtConnects dance ensemble. The artist has been recognized with several awards for her work, including the Cologne Dance Theatre Prize, the Choreography Prize Hanover, and the German Video Dance Prize. Vera Sander is director of the Centre for Contemporary Dance and professor for contemporary dance at the University for Music and Dance, Cologne.

Sylvia Scheidl is a graduate of the Master of Arts program in contemporary dance pedagogy at the University of Music and the Performing Arts in Frankfurt. Her work focuses on movement research and body consciousness. She practices methods of body–mind integration such as the Alexander Technique, Body–Mind Centering, and ideokinesis, and investigates ways of using these in contemporary dance techniques. Supported by the Crespo Foundation, she led a model project at a children's daycare center in Frankfurt in which she enabled teachers and children to access communication and movement through contact improvisation. She works as a freelance artist in her hometown of Vienna.

Katharine Sehnert trained to be a dancer, choreographer, and dance educator from 1955–1963 with Mary Wigman in Berlin. In 1962 she cofounded Motion. From 1970–1974 she danced with the Folkwang Tanzstudio in Essen and assisted Pina Bausch. From 1974–1981 she taught in Frankfurt and in 1976 founded Mobile Frankfurt, which won a prize at the International Choreographer Competition in Bagnolet in 1978. She created productions at the Theater am Turm and held advanced teacher–training courses. Since 1982 she has worked as a dancer, choreographer, and educator in Cologne, which is where she also founded TANZRAUM as a creative center, and the Kontinuum group. She was the first winner of the Cologne Dance Theatre Prize in 1994. In 1992 she initiated the *MultiArt—Künstler zu Gast im TANZRAUM* series with regular interdisciplinary performances. She has been a freelancer since 2004, working on guest performances and regular seminars, and provided coaching for the *A Mary Wigman Evening* reenactment project by and with Fabian Barba at the K3 Kampnagel Hamburg. In 2009 she was awarded the City of Cologne Theater Prize for her life's work.

Irene Sieben counts Mary Wigman and Manja Chmièl among her most important dance teachers. She danced in the first independent ensembles of the 1960s (Gruppe Neuer Tanz Berlin and Motion), studied somatic learning methods, and has been a Feldenkrais teacher since 1990. In 1981 she cofounded Tanz Tangente Berlin. She has taught applied anatomy and the Feldenkrais method at the Universität der Künste Berlin, Faculty of Music, and has worked as a dance and movement research journalist since 1970. She has been a correspondent for *Tanzdrama*, *ballettanz*, *Tanz–Journal*, *jetzt Tanz* and is author of *Das große Feldenkrais Buch* (Hugendubel, with A. Peters), and co-author of *Gesundheit, Lernen, Kreativität* (Huber) and *Wissen in Bewegung* (transcript publishing). Sieben also coached Fabian Barba for his reconstructions of *A Mary Wigman Evening* at K3–Center for Choreography / Tanzplan Hamburg and at the fabrik Potsdam.

Gerald Siegmund, PhD, is professor of dance and director of the Choreography and Performance program at the Justus Liebig University Giessen. He studied theater, English, and Romance studies at the Frankfurt am Main University. His research focuses on developments in contemporary dance and in postdramatic theater in the transition to performance and the visual arts. Books he has published include *William Forsythe—Denken in Bewegung* (Henschel) and *Abwesenheit. Eine performative Ästhetik des Tanzes—William Forsythe, Jérôme Bel, Xavier Le Roy, Meg Stuart* (transcript publishing).

Martin Stern, PhD, studied sport science, chemistry, educational science, and philosophy at the Free University Berlin. From 2001–2007 he was a lecturer at the Institute for Sport Studies at the Humboldt University Berlin (Physical Education and Philosophy of Sports) as well as a Research Fellow at the 'Cultures of the Performative' interdisciplinary research center at the Free University of Berlin. Currently he is a guest professor of education science of sports at the Johannes Gutenberg University Mainz. His main research topics are sociological and anthropological dimensions of modern sport cultures, educational dimensions of sports, ethnographic approaches to new performance cultures and contemporary dance, and theories of the social body and gender. Publications include: *Stil-Kulturen. Performative Konstellationen von Technik, Spiel und Risiko in neuen Sportpraktiken* (transcript publishing).

Patricia Stöckemann, PhD, is a dance author, dance journalist, dramaturg, was editor of *tanzdrama* magazine (1987–2003) and of *tanzjournal* (2003/04) and is a board member and program director for the Mary Wigman Gesellschaft. She has also taught dance history and theory at various academies, colleges, and universities, lectured throughout Germany and abroad, and curated dance exhibitions. Her research and publications focus on (modern) dance in Germany and she has published *Etwas ganz Neues muß nun entstehen—Kurt Jooss und das Tanztheater* (K. Kieser Publishing), among other works. Since the 2004/2005 season she has been dramaturg at the Tanztheater Bremen at the Theater Bremen, and since 2007 director of dramaturgy and member of the directorship of the nordwest / Tanztheater Bremen & Tanzcompagnie Oldenburg.

Yoann Trellu is a multidisciplinary video artist from France who moved to Berlin in 2003. He is active mainly in the fields of dance/theater production, software development, DVD production, and visual arts. For ten years he worked with numerous musicians and performers in France, Germany, and the United States. Main dance collaborations include Motion-Lab, Wire Monkey Dance (USA), Howard Katz, Post Theater, and Ten Pen Chi (Berlin).

Maren Witte, PhD, is a dance scholar and dramaturg. She studied literature and cultural studies in Freiburg, Berlin, and Berkeley (USA), where she also trained in various dance techniques such as Release Technique, Contact Improvisation und Tango Argentino. She completed her doctorate at the Institute for Theater Studies at the Free University Berlin with a work on perception and the effect of movement in the theater of Robert Wilson. Afterwards she worked at the University of Hamburg, contributing to a sociological study about tango and salsa. Currently she is a freelance dramaturg and dance researcher in Berlin specializing in dance and performance outreach methods. In 2008 and 2009 she developed an artistic research project on the topic of *Grace—Über Anmut und Gnade* with residencies and performances at the fabrik Potsdam, Tanzfabrik Berlin, Dock 11 Studios, and Schloss Bröllin. Since 2009 Maren Witte's *TanzScout* project has been introducing non-expert audiences from outside Berlin to the city's dance and performance scene.

Gabriele Wittmann teaches dance criticism, dance history, and creative scientific writing at the University of Music and the Performing Arts in Frankfurt. She studied music and American studies in Paris and Hamburg, and since 1993 has worked as an independent critic for print media, radio (ARD), and television (ZDF/3sat). She has also written many specialist articles for *ballettanz*, *Tanzjournal*, and the *Gesellschaft für Tanzforschung Yearbooks*, among others. Since 1996 she has taught advanced journalism training courses in Hamburg, Hannover, Remscheid, and Bremen, and researched the possibilities of the transfer between movement, language, and text in a series of workshops. Her publications include, 'Vom Umgang mit Emotionen in der Tanzkritik' in the *Jahrbuch der Gesellschaft für Tanzforschung* in 2006 (Lit Publishing) and, together with colleagues from related disciplines, *Anna Halprin. Tanz—Prozesse—Gestalten* (K. Kieser Publishing).

Nina Wollny completed an intensive ballet education during her teens and continued her studies in the Netherlands at the Rotterdam Dance Academy, where she switched to modern and contemporary dance. After graduation she joined Anouk van Dijk's company and since then has been one of the featured dancers in almost all of van Dijk's creations. Currently she is one of the performers of *Trust* and *Protect me*, two of Anouk van Dijk latest collaborations with Falk Richter at the Schaubühne Berlin. Since 2006 she has been van Dijk's artistic assistant. Wollny is considered to be the embodiment of the Countertechnique and is an enthusiastic teacher of it. Together with Anouk van Dijk, she is continuously developing the Countertechnique.

Nick Woods is a freelance journalist, interpreter, and translator living and working in Berlin. A graduate in French and history from Manchester University, he went on to study journalism and became an award-winning political correspondent. He was on the verge of accepting an offer to become a lobby correspondent at Westminster but instead opted for change and accepted an offer by the German embassy in London to come to Berlin and learn German at the Goethe Institut in 2003, a stay that sparked his interest in the city. After returning to the UK to take a simultaneous interpreting course (French/English), he returned to Berlin in 2004 and worked for two years as a foreign language assistant, at the same time improving his German and building up his freelance career. Apart from a one-year stay in Paris, he has been in Berlin ever since. In addition to the day job, he studies oriental dance, ballet, and Ashtanga Vinyasa Yoga.

CREDITS

DANCE TECHNIQUES 2010 — TANZPLAN GERMANY

Director of the Research Project
Ingo Diehl

Researcher
Dr. Friederike Lampert

German Language Editor
Dr. Wibke Hartewig

English Language Editor
Jacalyn Carley

German Translation
Nadine Püschel, Franz Anton Cramer, Gisela Müller

English Translation
Anthony B. Heric, Nickolas Woods

Graphic Design / Typesetting
Nicole Schwarz

Photographs
Andrea Keiz, Katja Mustonen

Program Management at Henschel Verlag
Susanne Van Volxem

Production Management at Henschel Verlag
Thomas Flach

Finances at Tanzplan Deutschland
Frank Ottersbach

Further Research
Dr. Christiane Berger

Transcriptions
Lisa Lucassen

DVD PRODUCTION

Camera / Editing
Andrea Keiz

Authoring
Yoann Trellu

DVD Consultants
Prof. Nik Haffner, Scott deLahunta

Technical Revision
OK-Medien Service

Duplication
OK-Medien Service

Legal Advice
Prof. Dr. Rupert Vogel

Clearing of Rights
Katja Tewes

Usability Test
Quidam Production

CONSULTANTS
Edith Boxberger, Dr. Pirkko Husemann,
Prof. Dr. Claudia Jeschke, Prof. Dr. Antje Klinge

EXPERTS
Gill Clarke, Alan Danielson, Anouk van Dijk,
Lance Gries, Jennifer Muller, Barbara Passow,
Daniel Roberts

AUTHORS
Edith Boxberger, Gill Clarke, Prof. Dr. Franz Anton
Cramer, Anouk van Dijk, Dr. Henner Drewes,
Wiebke Dröge, Dr. Claudia Fleischle–Braun,
Prof. Dr. Yvonne Hardt, Dr. Wibke Hartewig,
Dr. Sabine Huschka, Irmela Kästner,
Prof. Gisela Müller, Prof. Vera Sander, Sylvia Scheidl,
Irene Sieben, Prof. Dr. Gerald Siegmund,
Dr. Patricia Stöckemann, Dr. Maren Witte,
Gabriele Wittmann

INTERVIEWEES
Steven de Belder, David Hernandez, Ann Hutchinson
Guest, Reinhild Hoffmann, Mia Lawrence,
Anna Markard, Janet Panetta, Chrysa Parkinson,
Theo Van Rompay, Salva Sanchis,
Katharine Sehnert, students and teachers at various
research projects

OTHER PROJECT PARTICIPANTS
Prof. José Biondi, Prof. Rose Breuss, Lucy Cash,
Susanne Dickhaut, Becky Edmunds, Philipp Fricke,
Reinhild Hoffmann, Kazue Ikeda, Yichun Liu, Anna
Markard, Jen Peters, Johannes Randolf, Jerry
Remkes, Dr. Martin Stern, Nina Wollny

MUSICAL ACCOMPANIMENT / IMPROVISATION ON THE DVDS
Robert Coleridge, David Eibl, Christian Einheller,
Michael Gambacurta, Markus Größwang,
Knuth Jerxsen, Maria Langbauer, Friedemann Stolte,
Greg Smith, Christoph Schacherl

ACCOMPANISTS IN SITU
Jens Baermann, James Keane, Antje Ladstätter

UNIVERSITIES
Palucca Schule Dresden—Hochschule für Tanz

Rotterdam Dance Academy, Codarts—
University for the Arts

LABAN, London

IDA—Institute of Dance Arts, Anton Bruckner Privatuniversität Linz

Inter–University Center for Dance—Pilot Project
Tanzplan Berlin (HZT)

Centre for Contemporary Dance, University for
Music and Dance Cologne

Frankfurt University of Music and Performing Arts

Justus–Liebig–University Giessen

P.A.R.T.S. (Performing Arts Research and Training
Studios), Brussels

STUDENTS

Dresden
Anna Fingerhuth, Cindy Hammer, Maria Nitsche,
Dagmar Ottmann, Camilla Schmidt, Eila Schwedland,
Zongwei Xu

Rotterdam
Valeria D'Amico, Matt Bade, Sven Bahat,
Yorrith de Bakker, Joris Bergmans, Antonio Borriello,
Alex Deijmann, Patscharaporn Distakul, Sonia Egner,
Sabine Groendijk, Fem Has, Audie Jansen,
Sandra Klimek, Eline Koeman, Asja Lorencic,
Lisa Meijer, Catia Oliveira Nicolau, Xanthe Opstal,
Vincent Plas, Christopher Renfurm, Federica Rizzo,
Chanel Selleslach, Ewa Sikorska, Naima Sommacal,
Cosimo Walter Spalluto, Karl Staaf, Roisin Verheul,
Thijs Vlak, Zoe Wijnsnouw

London
Yolanda Aladeshelu, Sarah Armstrong,
Anna Bergstrom, Fabian Brandt, Typhaine Delaup,
Charlie Dixon, Rachel Graham, Karin Floengard
Jonsson, Samuel Jordan, Sara Kemal,
Leonie Nadler, Aimee Parsons, Eleonora Pennacchini,
Marcella Piscitelli, Artemise Ploegaerts,
Caroline Roussy, Elisabeth Schilling

Linz
Katja Bablick, Juan Dante Murillo Bobadilla,
Andrea Maria Handler, Philine Herrlein,
Blazej Jasinski, Tamara Kronheim, Dorota Lecka, Petr
Ochvat, Amandine Petit, Anna Prokopová,
Arnulfo Pardo Ravagli, Aureliusz Rys,
Olga Swietlicka

Berlin
Johanne Bro, Sara Canini, Siriol Joyner, An Kaler,
Nina Kurtela, Ivana Rončević, Julia Schwarzbach,
Nils Ulber, Ante Ursić

Cologne
Anika Bendel, Jana Berg, Sarah Biernat,
Sarah Bockers, Johanna Kasperowitsch,
Annekatrin Kiesel, Jule Oeft, Jelena Pietjou,
Hannah Platzer, Arthur Schopa,
Valentina Schulte-Ladbeck, Kristin Schuster,
Cornelia Trümper, Nora Vladiguerov,
Katharina Vlasova

Frankfurt
Erica Charalambous, Siri Clinckspoor, Hannah Dewor,
Natalia Gomez, Berit Jentzsch, Jungyeon Kim,
Kaya Kołodziejczyk, Anastasia Kostner, Ulla Mäkinen,
Lili Mihajlović, Monica Muñoz, Katja Mustonen,
Romain Thibaud-Rose, Sylvia Scheidl

WITH SPECIAL THANKS TO THE DIRECTORS AND STAFF OF THE UNIVERSITIES

Prof. Jason Beechey, director of the
Palucca Schule Dresden—Hochschule für Tanz

Colin Bourne, head of undergraduate studies,
and Gill Clarke, consultant, LABAN, London

Prof. Rose Breuss, director of the Institute of Dance
Arts (IDA), Anton Bruckner Privatuniversität Linz

Prof. Dieter Heitkamp, director of the ZuKT—
Ausbildungsbereich Zeitgenössischer und Klassischer
Tanz (Department of Contemporary and Classical
Dance), and Prof. Kurt Koegel, professor of
Contemporary Dance Pedagogy, Frankfurt University
of Music and Performing Arts

Prof. Dr. Gerald Siegmund, Institute for Applied
Theatre Studies, Justus–Liebig–University Giessen

Eva-Maria Hoerster, managing director, and Sabine
Trautwein, administration, Inter–University Center
for Dance—Pilot Project Tanzplan Berlin (HZT)

Theo Van Rompay, deputy director, P.A.R.T.S.
(Performing Arts Research and Training Studios),
Brussels

Prof. Vera Sander, director of the Centre for
Contemporary Dance, University for Music and
Dance Cologne

Samuel Würsten, co-director, Codarts—
University for the Arts, Rotterdam

LIST OF ILLUSTRATIONS

Photographs, Andrea Keiz
pp. 28, 29, 40, 47, 49, 52, 55, 58, 59, 60, 61, 68, 73, 74, 79, 80, 90, 91, 97, 100, 106, 112, 119, 120, 166, 167, 176, 181, 183, 187, 188, 196, 197, 211, 213, 216, 219, 223, 230, 231, 241, 247, 251, 254, 257, 258, 264, 265, 275, 283, 287

Photographs, Katja Mustonen
pp. 279, 280, 284, 291

Graphics, Yoann Trellu and Nicole Schwarz
p. 304

Sketch, Lance Gries
p. 286

Sketches, Maria Nitsche
pp. 48, 49

EXTRA MATERIAL ON THE DVDS

DVD 2 extra material—Alan Danielson
Foreign Relations (extract)
Choreography: Alan Danielson
Text: Alan Danielson, Reneé E. D'Aoust
Actors: Melinda Haas, Andy Monroe
Dancers: Jennifer Chin, Alan Danielson
Video: Mark Robison / Character Generators, Inc.
Premiere: 2006, Danspace Project, New York

Scarlatti Sonatas (extract)
Choreography: Alan Danielson
Music: Domenico Scarlatti
Pianist: Melinda Haas
Dancers: Geraldine Cardiel, Jennifer Chin, Sadie Gilbertson, and Pam Wagner
Video: Mark Robison / Character Generators, Inc.
Premiere: 2006, Danspace Project, New York
The creation of *Scarlatti Sonatas* was made possible, in part, with funds from the Danspace Project's 2006–2007 commissioning initiative with support from the Jerome Foundation.

DVD 2 extra material—Anouk van Dijk
TRUST (extracts)
A project by Anouk van Dijk and Falk Richter
A co-production by the Schaubühne am Lehniner Platz, Berlin, and anoukvandijk dc
Direction and choreography: Falk Richter and Anouk van Dijk
Text: Falk Richter
Original music: Malte Beckenbach
Dancers: Nina Wollny and Peter Cseri (duet 1)
Anouk van Dijk and Jack Gallagher (duet 2), together with Vincent Redetzki, Stefan Stern and Kay Bartholomäus Schulze
Video: Moritz Riesewieck
Premiere: 2009, Schaubühne am Lehniner Platz, Berlin
By kind permission of S. Fischer Verlag GmbH / Theater & Medien and by kind permission of Malte Beckenbach

DVD 2 extra material—Barbara Passow
Reconstruction of a sequence from
Dido and Aeneas, rehearsal
Premiere: 1984, Tanztheater Bremen
Choreography: Reinhild Hoffmann
Dancers: second year students, bachelor's program, LABAN, London
Music: Henry Purcell
Performers: Anne Sofie von Otter, Stephen Varcoe, Lynne Dawson, Nigel Rogers, and others
The English Concert & Choir
Conductor: Trevor Pinnock
Title: *Shake the cloud from off your brow – Banish sorrow, banish care*
By kind permission of The English Concert and by kind permission of Universal Music Classics & Jazz – a division of Universal Music GmbH

DVDS 1+2 extra material—Gill Clarke
Musical extract in the training from Gill Clarke:
Nyama Kumambure by David Gweshe;
Album: Mhuri Yekwanehoreka / Mhumhi Records
By kind permission of David Gweshe and Joel Laviolette, Mhumhi Records

Illustrations taken from: Hale, Robert Beverly / Coyle, Terence: *Albinus on Anatomy*. Dover: Dover Publications, 1989, ISBN: 978-0-486-25836-2
With special thanks to Dover Publications

Excerpt from a documentary on Gill Clarke's work by Becky Edmunds
Camera / interview: Becky Edmunds, Lucy Cash

DVD 2 extra material—Jennifer Muller
Island (extract)
Choreography: Jennifer Muller
Assistant to the choreographer: John Brooks
Original music: Marty Beller
Dancers: Gabriel Contreras, Elizabeth Disharoon, Courtney D. Jones, Rosie Lani Fiedelman, Gen Hashimoto, Anne Kochanski, Tracy R. Kofford, Pascal Rekoert, and Yumiko Yoshikawa
Costume design: Sonja Nuttall
Lighting design: Jeff Croiter
Wigs: Martin Duff, Elaine Mitchell
Projections: Paul Vershbow
Video: Video D / Dennis Diamond
Premiere: 2005, The Joyce Theater, New York City
By kind permisson of Marty Beller

The Spotted Owl (extract)
Choreography & text: Jennifer Muller
Assistant to the choreographer: John Brooks
Original music: Marty Beller
Dancers: Michael Jahoda, Leda Meredith, Maria Naidu, Marcelo Pereira, Amy Prensky, Ricardo Sarcos, Tomoko Sato, Terri Shipman, Leonardo Smith, and Yasushi Tanaka
Music played by: Marty Beller / percussion; Andrew Demos / bamboo flute, woodwind instruments, and percussion; and Tim Givens / cello
Costume design / décor design: Karen Small
Lighting design: Kristabelle Munson
Video: Video D / Dennis Diamond
Premiere: 1995, The Joyce Theater, New York City
By kind permisson of Marty Beller

TANZPLAN DEUTSCHLAND

Project Director
Madeline Ritter

Managing Director
Frank Ottersbach

Director Educational Program
Ingo Diehl

Communication / Marketing
Barbara Schindler

Project Assistant and Researcher
Marguerite Joly

Project Assistant
Katja Tewes

HOW TO USE THE DVDS

Main Menu
The DVDs can be played on a computer or DVD player. Select either a German or English language menu. Further information is found in the main menu under "User Manual DVD". All those who were involved in producing the DVD are listed under "Credits".

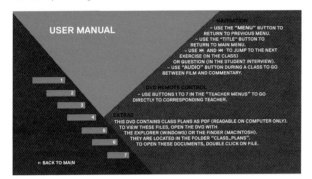

Menu Research Projects
Click on a teacher's name to access videos made at the various institutions participating in the project. The classes, and the teachers' commentaries, are spread out both DVDs. Background material—such as interviews with students, class plans, excerpts from choreographies, special exercise sequences, photos, or supplementary information—is available on both DVDs and accessed through the additional menu items. DVD's can be differentiated through color and labeling.

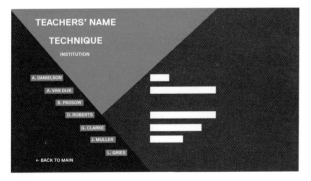

Class Plans
The class plans can only be viewed on a computer, and, if required, printed. As described under "User Manual DVD", the German and English class plans can be found in a separate folder in the Finder (Mac) or in the Explorer (Windows).

> DANCE_TECHNIQUES_DVD   > AUDIO_TS   A-Danielson.pdf
                                        > CLASS_PLANS   A-Van-Dijk.pdf
                                        > STUNDENVERLAUFSPLAENE   B-Passow.pdf
                                        > VIDEO_TS   D-Roberts.pdf
                                                                    G-Clarke.pdf
                                                                     J-Muller.pdf
                                                                     L-Gries.pdf